On Old English

BRUCE MITCHELL

On Old English

Selected Papers

Basil Blackwell

Copyright © Bruce Mitchell 1988

First published 1988

Basil Blackwell Ltd
108 Cowley Road, Oxford, OX4 1JF, UK

Basil Blackwell Inc.
432 Park Avenue South, Suite 1503
New York, NY 10016, USA

All rights reserved. Except for the quotation of short passages for the purposes of criticism and review, no part of this publication may be reproduced, stored in a retrieval system, or transmitted, in any form or by any means, electronic, mechanical, photocopying, recording or otherwise, without the prior permission of the publisher.

Except in the United States of America, this book is sold subject to the condition that it shall not, by way of trade or otherwise, be lent, re-sold, hired out, or otherwise circulated without the publisher's prior consent in any form of binding or cover other than that in which it is published and without a similar condition including this condition being imposed on the subsequent purchaser.

British Library Cataloguing in Publication Data

Mitchell, Bruce, *1920–*
On Old English: selected papers.
1. Anglo-Saxon literature – History and criticism
I. Title
829'.09   PR173
ISBN 0–631–15872–3

Library of Congress Cataloging in Publication Data

Mitchell, Bruce, 1920–
On Old English.

Bibliography: p.
Includes index.
1. English philology – Old English, ca. 450–1100.
1. Title.
PE109.M58   1988   829'.09   87-35532
ISBN 0–631–15872–3

Typeset in 10 on 12 pt. Ehrhardt
by Joshua Associates Limited, Oxford
Printed in Great Britain by
T. J. Press Ltd, Padstow, Cornwall

IN MEMORIAM
HENRICI SWEET
ET
KENNETHI SISAM
HOMINUM ADMIRATIONE DIGNORUM
QUIBUSCUM ET DOCTRINAM
ET VITAE VICISSITUDINES
CONSOCIO

Contents

Foreword	ix
Acknowledgements	xi
Abbreviations and symbols	xii
Bibliographical note	xiii

Part I *Beowulf*

1	'Until the dragon comes...': some thoughts on *Beowulf*	3
2	Two syntactical notes on *Beowulf*	16
3	An introduction to *Beowulf*	24
4	*Beowulf*, lines 3074–3075: the damnation of Beowulf?	30
5	1987: Postscript on *Beowulf*	41
6	Reviews	
	(a) *Twelve* Beowulf *Papers 1940–1960. With Additional Comments* by Adrien Bonjour	55
	(b) *An Anthology of* Beowulf *Criticism* ed. Lewis E. Nicholson	57
	(c) *The Structure of* Beowulf by Kenneth Sisam	58
	(d) *A Reading of* Beowulf by Edward B. Irving Jr	60

Part II Cædmon

7	Bede's *habere* = Old English *magan*?	65
8	*Swa* in Cædmon's *Hymn*, line 3	69
9	Postscript on Bede's *mihi cantare habes*	73
10	Bede's account of the poet Cædmon: two notes	82
11	Cædmon's *Hymn*, line 1: what is the subject of *scylun* or its variants?	88

Part III *The Wanderer*, *The Seafarer*, and Other Poems

12	Some syntactical problems in *The Wanderer*	99
13	An Old English syntactical reverie: *The Wanderer*, lines 22 and 34–36	118
14	More musings on Old English syntax	126

15 The narrator of *The Wife's Lament*: some syntactical problems reconsidered	134
16 The *fuglas scyne* of *The Phoenix*, line 591	146
17 Linguistic facts and the interpretation of Old English poetry	152
18 The dangers of disguise: Old English texts in modern punctuation	172
19 The syntax of *The Seafarer*, lines 50–52	203
20 Reviews	
(a) *The Wanderer* ed. R. F. Leslie	207
(b) *Sweet's Anglo-Saxon Reader in Prose and Verse* (15th edn) revised throughout by Dorothy Whitelock	208
(c) *Old English Poetry. Fifteen Essays* ed. Robert P. Creed	210
(d) *The Guest-Hall of Eden. Four Essays on the Design of Old English Poetry* by Alvin A. Lee	212
(e) *The Interpretation of Old English Poems* by Stanley B. Greenfield	214

Part IV Old English Language

21 Syntax and word-order in the *Peterborough Chronicle* 1122–1154	221
22 Paul Bacquet, *La Structure de la Phrase Verbale à l'Époque Alfrédienne*	243
23 The subject–noun object–verb pattern in the *Peterborough Chronicle*: a reply	253
24 Old English *oð þæt* adverb?	256
25 Old English *man* 'one': two notes	264
26 The origin of Old English conjunctions: some problems	269
27 Some lexicographical problems posed by Old English grammar words	296
28 Reviews	
(a) *A Descriptive Syntax of the Ormulum* by Robert A. Palmatier	305
(b) *A Descriptive Syntax of the Old English Charters* by Charles Carlton	309
(c) *An Analysis of Syntactic Patterns of Old English* by Faith F. Gardner	313
(d) *Imperative Constructions in Old English* by Celia M. Millward	315
(e) *The Language of the* Parker Chronicle, *Volume II: Word-Formation and Syntax* by C. Sprockel	317
(f) *Les Propositions Relative en Vieil-Anglais* by Georges Bourcier	319
(g) *Old English Syntax. A Handbook* by John McLaughlin	320

Part V Conclusion

29 1947–1987 Forty years on	325
The published writings of Bruce Mitchell	345
Index	353

Foreword

This book has no Introduction because many of the things traditionally said in an Introduction will be found in my Conclusion (pp. 325–44), where I give what is confessedly a highly personal account of Old English studies today. Three things need to be said in this Foreword.

I begin by admitting a passionate commitment to Old English studies in general and to Old English syntax in particular. This commitment may at times seem to some readers to result in excessive enthusiasm and even in belligerence. Indeed, at the conclusion of one of my recent lectures, a friend in the audience half jocularly accused me of being an angry young man. Perhaps, with little time left, I am becoming an angry old man of whom it may be asked, as it was of Jonah, 'Doest thou well to be angry?' But I do not think 'angry' is the right word. I have always tried to say what I thought needed saying. I have always tried to stimulate discussion by question and suggestion rather than to stifle it by dogmatism. My best apologia is probably that given by Mr Midshipman Easy when he was ordered to explain why he had called the purser's steward a cheat:

> 'If you please, Captain Wilson, that was all zeal.'
> 'Zeal, Mr Easy? I think it but a bad excuse. But pray, then, why did you kick the man down the hatchway? – you must have known that that was contrary to the rules of the service.'
> 'Yes, sir,' replied Jack, demurely; 'but that was all zeal, too.'

I must leave it to my readers to decide whether Captain Wilson's reply fits my case too:

> 'Then allow me to say,' replied Captain Wilson, biting his lips, 'that I think that your zeal has in this instance been very much misplaced, and I trust you will not show so much again.'

The second point concerns the method of selecting or rather of excluding papers. I have omitted from the publications listed at the end of this volume occasional addresses, those papers and reviews concerned with Middle English and Modern English, some reviews and short notices, introductions to volumes or recordings of translations of Old English poems, and, of the papers on Old English topics, those of a highly technical nature and/or those whose content has been absorbed into my *Old English Syntax*. I should like to mention one other exception: despite a continuing belief in their value, I have not reproduced my Appendices III, IV, and V to Kevin Crossley-Holland's translation of *Beowulf* (London and New York, 1968). These I have reserved in the hope of using them in an undergraduate edition of the poem.

Third, it is my very pleasant duty to express gratitude to John Davey, my publisher, for suggesting the publication of this volume and for overcoming the reservations I expressed at the end of item 6a. I also thank Hazel Coleman, the copy-editor, Sue Ashton, who read the proofs, Susan Irvine, who checked the Index, and Jennifer Speake, who edited and typed it. To their names must be added *in petto* those of the traditionally but unjustly anonymous friends at Blackwells, Joshua Associates, and T. J. Press, who have combined to produce this handsome volume. I acknowledge some early debts of gratitude on p. 327 below. A full list of those who have contributed in one way or another to the papers presented here would include most of the names mentioned in the Foreword to my *Old English Syntax* (Oxford: Clarendon Press, 1985). The book is dedicated to two Oxford men who have long compelled my admiration. I end with a heartfelt 'Thank you' to my wife Mollie, who typed and proof-read in their original form all the items reproduced here except 18 and 19, which were submitted in manuscript, and has now had to live through their exhumation.

Bruce Mitchell

Alphege, Archbishop of Canterbury
1988

Acknowledgements

The author and publishers are grateful to the following for permission to reproduce material already printed elsewhere: John Benjamins B.V., Amsterdam, The Netherlands, and Professor E. F. Konrad Koerner, Ottawa, Canada, for item 25; Cambridge University Press, Cambridge, England, and *Anglo-Saxon England*, for item 17; The Folio Society Limited, London, for item 3; *Leeds Studies in English* and Dr Joyce Hill, University of Leeds, for item 11; Dr John Stanley Martin, University of Melbourne, Australia, for item 10; *Medium Ævum* and A. V. C. Schmidt, Esq., Balliol College, Oxford, for items 28a, 28b, and 28f; The Modern Language Society of Helsinki, *Neuphilologische Mitteilungen*, and Dr Leena Kahlas-Tarkka, for items 7, 9, 12, 13, 14, 15, 21, 22, and 23; Mouton de Gruyter, Berlin, for item 26; *Neophilologus* and Professor Dr W. F. Koopman for items 1 and 2; *Notes and Queries* for items 8 and 24; Oxford University Press, *The Review of English Studies*, and R. E. Alton, Esq., for items 6a, 6b, 6c, 6d, 18, 19, 20a, 20b, 20c, 20d, 20e, 28c, 28e, and 28g; Verlag Friedrich Pustet, Regensburg, and Professor Dr Alfred Bammesberger, Eichstätt, Federal German Republic, for item 27; Shubun International Co., Ltd, Tokyo, Japan, and *Poetica* (Tokyo), for item 4; Swets and Zeitlinger bv, Lisse, The Netherlands, and *English Studies*, for item 28d; University of Toronto Press, Toronto, Canada, for item 16.

Abbreviations and Symbols

No list is given here because the abbreviations and symbols used are either explained in the item concerned or are so well known that they do not require explanation. The exception is *BPOEL*, which is Stanley B. Greenfield and Fred C. Robinson, *A Bibliography of Publications on Old English Literature to the End of 1972* (Toronto, 1980).

Bibliographical Note

Each item contains its own bibliography. One comment is, however, necessary here: Bruce Mitchell and Fred. C. Robinson, *A Guide to Old English Revised with Prose and Verse Texts and Glossary* (4th edn, Oxford: Basil Blackwell) appeared in 1986 and was reprinted in 1987 and again in 1988. I have not changed the references to earlier editions because the section numbers in what is now Part One remain unaltered.

Part I
Beowulf

I
'Until the Dragon Comes...': Some Thoughts on *Beowulf*

I

In a recent article on the harm done to him by 'a three year stretch in the Honours School of Eng. Lit.' Mr Osbert Lancaster has assured us that he still unhesitatingly rejects 'the idea that *Beowulf* can conceivably be regarded as a source of pleasure by anyone above the cultural level of a retarded ceorl'.[1] Since it is unfortunately impossible to check this statement by discussing it with an advanced *æðeling* or a sophisticated *gesiþ*, those who do find something worthwhile in the poem will have to content themselves with an egotistical reflection on the high standard achieved by retarded ceorls in the good old days.

That there are more retarded ceorls about today than some twenty years ago and that *Beowulf* is now viewed rather more as a poem and rather less as a museum for the antiquarian, a sourcebook for the historian, or a gymnasium for the philologist, is due in large measure to Professor Tolkien's famous British Academy Lecture of 1936 '*Beowulf*: The Monsters and the Critics'.[2] In the light of this, we have learnt to discount much of the earlier criticism of the plan of the poem. Because we now see that the dragons which flew over Northumbria in 793 and the monsters about which the *Beowulf* poet writes were (in some senses at any rate) enemies just as real to the Anglo-Saxons as were the Danes, we have come to realize that, when Ker and Chambers characterized the story as trivial, they forgot that by the same lights *Moby-Dick* is only a whale story and the then yet-to-be-written *The Old Man and the Sea* a yarn about a fish. By careful consideration of the structure and theme, we have come to recognize the strange and almost impossible contradiction in Ker's conclusion that 'the thing itself is cheap; the moral and spirit of it can only be matched among the noblest authors.'[3] For now we see that the basic point about Beowulf is, not

Reprinted from *Neophilologus* 47 (1963), 126–38.

[1] *The Times*, London, 19 Oct. 1961.
[2] References are to the 1958 reprint (hereafter cited as Tolkien). This withered nosegay of an article is my personal *Festschrift* in honour of its author, to whom I owe much.
[3] W. P. Ker *The Dark Ages* (London, 1904), p. 253.

that he kills three monsters and is himself killed by the third, but that he three times stands face to face with death – moments of such significance for any man that to speak of 'triviality' should be impossible – and inevitably succumbs in the end.

All this does not mean that we must look askance at Mr Sisam when he writes 'I am not among the whole-hearted admirers of the construction of the poem.'[4] There are certainly weaknesses. Some of these are the result of the form in which the poet inherited the story, two recently discussed examples being the reburying of the gold (ll. 3163 ff.)[5] and the role of the 'last survivor' (ll. 2231 ff.).[6] Others, such as Hrothgar's homily (ll. 1724–68) and Beowulf's recapitulation to King Hygelac of his adventures in Denmark (ll. 2069–151), are perhaps more directly attributable to the poet, though the former may be (in part or whole) an interpolation.[7] However, our attitude to the problem whether or not the overall structure is adequate depends largely on what we think the poem is about.

That there are 'defects of detail' cannot, of course, be denied and is indeed admitted by Professor Tolkien. But a good many of them have become apparent only as a result of that 'tendency to treat the poem as if it were written for modern scholars' against which Sisam has warned us.[8] The poem is not intended to have the consistency of James Joyce's *Ulysses*: if we are troubled by the conflicting accounts of Beowulf's youth, we must take comfort in the fact that the poet draws on different traditions to suit his particular purpose in different parts of the poem. Hence it follows that attempts to 'prove' from one line something about another must be made with great caution, if at all. Kemp Malone, for example, argues that in ll. 646–51 we cannot think of Grendel planning a fight (*hilde*), because he is sure of finding no opposition (ll. 600 ff.) since the hall has stood empty for twelve winters (ll. 138 ff. and 411 ff.).[9] Yet, since Grendel knew the hall to be inhabited again (ll. 712–13), there is no reason why, having planned an attack (*hilde*), he should not have sat all day in his lair, gloating in anticipation of the prey he hoped to win. Again, Hrothgar tells us in ll. 1331–3 that he does not know whither Grendel's mother has

---

[4] K. Sisam *RES* 9 (1958), 137 (hereafter cited as Sisam).
[5] Sisam, pp. 129 ff. and 139–40, and G. V. Smithers *The Making of Beowulf* (University of Durham Inaugural Lecture 1961, hereafter cited as Smithers), pp. 16–19.
[6] Smithers, p. 11.
[7] See C. L. Wrenn *Beowulf* (London, 1953), pp. 65 ff. [1987. I would now stress the importance of the fact that each of Beowulf's three fights is described three times, first by the poet (ll. 702 ff., 1251 ff., and 2200 ff.) and then twice in a speech by a character. The fights against Grendel and his mother are retold by Beowulf himself (ll. 957 ff. and 2069a ff. and ll. 1651 ff. and 2115 ff. respectively), that against the dragon by Wiglaf (ll. 2860 ff.) and by the messenger (ll. 2896a ff.).]
[8] Sisam, p. 129, n. 1.
[9] *MÆ* 2 (1933), 61–2.

escaped. In l. 1345 he embarks on the famous description of the haunted mere.[9a] But even Shakespeare is not without sins of this kind!

In the favourable climate produced by Professor Tolkien's lecture, numerous writers have aided us in our 'revaluation' of *Beowulf*. A few names only can be mentioned from a list which might be extended almost indefinitely. Mrs Chadwick's suggestion that, far from being commonplace, the theme of the struggle of a hero against three monsters is an old and significant one which finds its first literary expression in *Beowulf*[10] is of great importance, though it cannot yet be taken as proven.[11] In the inaugural lecture already cited, Professor Smithers has made some suggestions about the poet's handling of the material he inherited: these certainly demand investigation. From Bonjour and others, we have learnt that the digressions are generally not without point,[11a] while Brodeur and others have helped us to appreciate the use made by the poet of anticipation, irony, contrast, and variation, and to realize how great his poetic gifts were. Such comments as those of Bonjour on *Beowulf* ll. 3021–7 – 'the beasts of battle' theme[12] – and of Crowne on *Beowulf* ll. 562–70a – 'the hero on the beach' theme[13] – have illuminated the poet's careful craftsmanship in matters of detail by analysing his use of well-known formulae. (The possibility that the poet, in his genius, originated these collocations for himself must, I think, be dismissed – albeit regretfully.) To Klaeber's complaint of 'lack of steady advance' we have learnt to reply that the fights against Grendel and the dragon – the latter displaying, as Sisam has pointed out,[14] a careful treatment of those details in which an Anglo-Saxon audience could be expected to take a critical interest – show that the poet could tell a story when he wished. Indeed we can even urge the difference between his handling of the Finnesburh story and the treatment it receives in the Fragment as proof, not of narrative deficiency on the part of the poet, but of some deeper aim or aims: for, as Dr Johnson observed, men more often require to be reminded than to be informed.

All these things make it difficult for me to accept Professor Smithers' conclusion that 'English literature begins with a masterpiece, which had no comparable Germanic antecedents in the same literary kind or form.'[15] I prefer to think

---

[9a] [1987. I now accept MS *hwæþer* 'whether' in l. 1331, so removing the last-mentioned inconsistency.]

[10] N. K. Chadwick *The Anglo-Saxons: Studies... presented to Bruce Dickins* ed. P. Clemoes (London, 1959), pp. 171–203.

[11] See *RES* 12 (1961), 283–4.

[11a] [1987. For me, the great exception is the much-disputed passage ll. 1925–62. Not one of the numerous explanations is satisfactory. I accept the suggestion by Sisam (*Studies in the History of Old English Literature* (Oxford, 1953), p. 41 fn.) that a lacuna has occurred without a break in the alliteration.]

[12] A. Bonjour *PMLA* 72 (1957), 563–73.

[13] D. K. Crowne *NM* 61 (1960), 362–72.

[14] Sisam, p. 129 and *passim*.   [15] Smithers, pp. 23–4.

that, like the author of *Sir Gawain and the Green Knight*, the *Beowulf* poet had his *Patience*, his *Purity*, and his *Pearl* – now, alas, all lost.[16]

II

What then is the poet at? Doubtless he aims to entertain an audience in the hall – *healgamen . . . æfter medobence mænan*. This view has recently been denied by P. F. Baum,[17] who claims that the tense, crowded style and the convoluted method of narration – the very antithesis of the minstrel's art – are most unsuited for oral recitation. He sees the author as a serious and gifted poet who composed a quasi-heroic to please himself and a 'fit audience, though few'. Recalling Shelley's statement that *Prometheus Unbound* was designed for five or six persons, Baum continues 'It may seem odd to picture such an ivory-towered poet in the eighth century, but *Beowulf* is unique in every sense.' But this is not necessarily a conclusive argument. An audience who could not read would be skilled in recalling details of past narratives and, as the Anglo-Saxon love of riddle suggests, in picking up hints and implications. Even in our own time, those who listen to the long-running 'soap operas' which are a prominent feature of modern wireless programmes need long memories and the ability to carry many threads in their minds. How else could they make sense of a story whose preliminary abstracts include the following:

> Pat's girl friend Myra is back. Rodney left her and a baby is due quite soon. Pat took her home to his mother but can't find anyone to take her as a lodger. Mrs Morris has been wonderful but they may regret their generosity. Richard is still working at Margaret Cunningham's – not a satisfactory arrangement. Johnnie Harvill and Vicky are getting very ambitious in the shop. Mother seems worried . . . ?[18]

But, whether by design or not, the poem is certainly didactic as well. No would-be Beowulf could have come to any harm by reading it, for it gives us, in personified form, the ideal of Germanic heroic life. (Mrs Goldsmith's objections to this view are scarcely conclusive: see below.) We learn how to command a platoon (the preparations for the journey and the guard on the carefully anchored ship and on the arms left outside the hall) and the duties of high officials (the careful investigation of Beowulf's antecedents by the coastguard and the formalities observed by Wulfgar); the etiquette of the hall and how to fight a dragon; the code of the *comitatus* and the responsibilities and privileges of king and retainer. To argue whether the poet intended it for the

[16] For Professor Tolkien's comments on the similarities between *Beowulf* and *Sir Gawain and the Green Knight*, see *ES* 6 (1953), 16–18.
[17] *PQ* 39 (1960), 389–99.
[18] See further Sisam, p. 129, n. 1.

education of a young prince or (as Storms has suggested)[19] 'to impart wisdom and moderation to young and old pretenders' is beside the point: let us be content with the realization that we have (to quote Sisam again) 'a mirror of noble conduct, in which contrasted examples of good and bad conduct are often shown'.[20]

That *Beowulf* is also an elegy on the constant Old English theme *lif is læne*[21] cannot be denied. But there is, of course, more to it than that. It is now generally agreed that *Beowulf* gives us a view of man, of his life, and of his place in the universe: it is with the question 'What view?' that the most recent critics have concerned themselves – with vastly differing results.

The final interpretation we place upon the poem depends in great measure on our attitude to that vexed question 'the nature of the monsters'. T. M. Gang takes Professor Tolkien to task for overlooking the fact that 'the dragon is altogether a different sort of creature from the Grendel-tribe'[22] and, after claiming that 'if these criticisms are just, then Professor Tolkien's account of the structure of the poem loses some force, since it is based on the view that the two parts of the poem are basically akin, representing two aspects of the same struggle ...', concludes that 'the events of the first part of the poem do not influence those in the second; there is no cumulative effect. The poem may be a balance; it is certainly not a unity.'[23]

Two questions arise here. First, are Gang's criticisms about the nature of the monsters justified? The answer, in the light of recent work, must be 'Not necessarily.' After all, given the right audience, a Christian Anglo-Saxon poet could assume that the dragon would be identified with the devil: in Mrs Goldsmith's words, 'only if we refuse to admit that the *Beowulf* dragon is a Christian's dragon can we be confused into thinking that he is not God's enemy, as much as, and more than, Grendel is.'[24] Whether we wish to make this admission is a problem which must be discussed later.

The second question is this. Even if these criticisms are true, does it follow that the poem 'is not a unity'? In my opinion the answer is 'No': indeed it can be argued that the natures of the Grendel tribe and of the dragon are not identical, were not meant to be, and (we may even suggest) could not be without destroying the point of the poem as Professor Tolkien sees it. Here it should be noted that their identity is not insisted on by Professor Tolkien. The passage from which Gang extracts one sentence reads:

> If the dragon is the right end for Beowulf, and I agree with the author that it is, then Grendel is an eminently suitable beginning. They are creatures,

[19] G. Storms *E. Studies* 40 (1959), 3–13.
[20] Sisam, p. 138.
[21] Tolkien, p. 18.
[22] *RES* 3 (1952), 6.
[23] *RES* 3 (1952), 8–9.
[24] M. E. Goldsmith *MÆ* 29 (1960), 93: see also D. Whitelock *The Audience of* Beowulf (Oxford, 1951), pp. 10–11, and M. B. McNamee *JEGP* 59 (1960), 190–207.

feond mancynnes, of a similar order and kindred significance. Triumph over the lesser and more nearly human is cancelled by defeat before the older and more elemental. And the conquest of the ogres comes at the right moment: ... The placing of the dragon is inevitable: a man can but die upon his death-day.[25]

To say that things are 'of a similar order and kindred significance' is not to identify them. Indeed, far from identifying Grendel and his dam with the dragon, Professor Tolkien has pointed out some very significant differences. And what would be the point of identifying them? If they are the same, the poet is telling us that Beowulf, with God's help,[26] overcame two spiritual foes of God in his youth only to perish at the hands of another in his old age. We can scarcely assume that God's strength was inadequate to defeat the dragon. We are then left to think that God has deserted Beowulf because Beowulf has fallen off from the high standards of his youth, and that therefore the poem contains some criticism of him.

I fail to find in *Beowulf* anything which proves absolutely, and so forces me to believe, that the poet means to imply that God has deserted Beowulf. Nor can I say that the poem as a whole reads to me like a criticism of Beowulf: indeed, the reverse is true, for, as pointed out above, I would agree that Beowulf is being presented to us as a model. However, the view that Beowulf is being criticized has been advanced by both Professor Tolkien[27] and by Mrs Goldsmith.[28] Both interpret Wiglaf's famous observation

Beowulf l. 3077   Oft sceall eorl monig   anes willan
                  wræc adreogan,   swa us geworden is

as referring to Beowulf. This is certainly a possible explanation, but not the only one. After all, it is scarcely surprising that Wiglaf and his comrades failed to convince Beowulf that the best policy was 'to let the dragon be' (ll. 3079–83) – young or old, Beowulf was no man to risk a white feather – and the *anes* could well be the thief who first plundered the dragon's hoard (cf. ll. 2406–9). But this is not vital: the theories that Beowulf is being criticized do not stand or fall on this point alone.

Professor Tolkien's theory is that the last word of the poem *lofgeornost* implies that Beowulf is 'too eager for *lof*'. 'He is saved from defeat', says Professor Tolkien, 'and the essential object, the destruction of the dragon, only achieved by the loyalty of a subordinate. Beowulf's chivalry would otherwise have ended in his own useless death, with the dragon still at large.'[29] Professor

[25] Tolkien, p. 34.
[26] This is specifically stated in the case of Grendel's dam (e.g. ll. 15546–6). For Grendel it seems a reasonable assumption from ll. 811b, 786b, and the like.
[27] *ES* 6 (1953), 13–18.   [28] *MÆ* 29 (1960), 81–101.
[29] *ES* 6 (1953), 14–15.

Tolkien detects the same fault in Byrhtnoth at Maldon. It is in essence a failure to grow with one's responsibilities: Beowulf and Byrhtnoth were, according to this view, platoon commanders in outlook, but army commanders in responsibility. This youthful, over-bold Beowulf would still be worthy of the flood of tears, the splendid tomb, the treasures, the elaborate funeral rites, and the noble dirge, lavished upon him by the Geats,[29a] and is an altogether different person from the gold-hungry Beowulf Mrs Goldsmith presents to us in an article which seems to me an example of misplaced ingenuity and special pleading.[30] But he does not seem to me the Beowulf presented by the poet. For the dragon is, to our poet, a different kind of monster from Grendel and his dam.[31] Very simply, it is the instrument of Beowulf's death, as Professor Tolkien's last words suggest – 'until the dragon comes'. That it is pictured as an undiscriminating, elemental force need not therefore surprise us.[32] Since *lif is læne*, death is no reproach or, as the poet has it in

Beowulf l. 2890   Deað bið sella
           eorla gehwylcum   þonne edwitlif!

And that death will come on one's death-day is inevitable, for neither *wyrd* (ll. 572–3) nor *Waldendes hyldo* (ll. 2291–3)[33] can do anything for the man who is *fæge*.

[29a] [1987. The same could be said of the Beowulf portrayed by G. N. Garmonsway (1965, *BPOEL* item 2926), J. Leyerle (1965, *BPOEL* item 2928), and N. F. Blake (*MÆ* 35 (1966), 236–40), all of whom argue in various ways that Beowulf is, in Blake's phrase (p. 239), 'too much a hero'.]

[30] *MÆ* 29 (1960), 81–101. One has only to consider the character of Beowulf in the poem as a whole to realize what a caricature this portrait is: (1) Beowulf is regarded as a good, generous king (e.g. ll. 2311, 2382–4, 2390, 2417, 3002–7 etc.). (2) It was a king's duty to win gold (ll. 2535–7). (3) It was not his fault that the hoard was plundered. What else could a king do but fight in the circumstances? (4) Is it Beowulf's greed for gold that causes Nægling to break? (5) Why does Beowulf's death imply that God had deserted him? Would he otherwise have lived for ever? (6) If one does not wish to accept Professor Tolkien's explanation of them as 'a heathen and unchristian fear' (Tolkien, end of Appendix (b)), ll. 2329–32 need only be an expression of Christian modesty: 'he supposed that he had offended God . . .' (see Goldsmith, *MÆ* 29 (1960), p. 95). (7) Do Beowulf's last boast (ll. 2511 ff.) and his last speech (ll. 2794 ff.) read like a miser's? Does Wiglaf's speech (ll. 2634 ff.) sound like condemnation?

[31] Professor Smithers' observation (Smithers, p. 12) that 'the dragon, as the ghost of a human being . . . , clearly belongs to the same order of being as Grendel and his mother', does not invalidate this interpretation of *Beowulf*. For, as Professor Smithers himself tells us on the same page, 'there are no other examples known to me of the splitting of the mound-dweller and the dragon; we must therefore reckon with the possibility of a misunderstanding by our poet.'

[32] See further Sisam's discussion on this point (Sisam, pp. 133–4). Since we have not, in my view, to do with an allegory, we need not expect to find every detail of the dragon significant in its relation to 'Death'.

[33] Mrs Goldsmith (*MÆ* 29 (1960), pp. 94–5) seems to draw false conclusions from this passage. That sinners live and saints die is a fact of everyday experience which does not prove that God is with the former and against the latter.

What the poet wishes us to make of that death is again a matter for individual interpretation. Is the dragon a symbol of Death? Are we to take Beowulf's victory over the dragon as implying that in death man is both defeated and victorious?[34] The concept of some sort of victory over death is not restricted to the Christian doctrine that 'Death is swallowed up in Victory.' The pagan Horace boasts

> Odes iii. 30   non omnis moriar multaque pars mei
> vitabit Libitinam,

and in 1 Maccabees 6. 42–7, Eleazar gives his life to 'deliver his people and get him a perpetual name'. *Beowulf* expresses a similar notion in terms not specifically Christian or pagan in such passages as

> *Beowulf* l. 1534   Swa sceal man don,
> þonne he æt guðe   gegan þenceð
> longsumne lof;   na ymb his lif cearað.

This, of course, raises the fundamental question about *Beowulf*: how Christian a poem is it?

III

Our answer to this question depends both on the meaning we give to *lofgeornost* and on the overall impression we derive from the poem.

Lofgeornost is the poet's last word on Beowulf. Professor Tolkien's view of it commands respect, but not necessarily acceptance: some will feel that in the whole context of the poem a final whip-lash of criticism would be out of place and that *lofgeornost* could be a word of praise. If so, the question arises 'For which *lof* was Beowulf eager – the pagan *lof* or the Christian version seen in *The Seafarer*, ll. 72–80?' Both seem to be possible. In view of the great stress laid on etiquette and politeness throughout the poem, it can scarcely be claimed that 'mildness' and 'gentleness' are impossible epithets for a pagan king and that therefore a pagan interpretation of *lofgeornost* would be inconsistent with the rest of the epitaph. On the other hand, Professor Tolkien has not, I think, succeeded in demolishing the possibility that the poet is referring to Christian *lof*.

What impression does *Beowulf* leave on us? It does not seem to me a depressing poem. It does not deal only with 'old, unhappy, far-off things, / And battles long ago': it also extols generosity, loyalty, bravery, and other virtues. Beowulf's comment

[34] Such a view is not necessarily invalidated by the fact that Beowulf needed Wiglaf's help. It was Beowulf who got the dragon in a position where Wiglaf's thrust could be effective. It was Beowulf who dealt the final blow (Sisam, pp. 138–9). With Nægling intact, he may well have killed the dragon unaided. But, if Cordelia had not said 'Nothing, my lord, . . .'.

Beowulf l. 572   Wyrd oft nereð
                unfægne eorl,   þonne his ellen deah!

may well be a pagan gnomic utterance: 'Courage is best whatever the circumstances. If doomed, you must die: so fight bravely and win *lof.* If undoomed, you may perish before your time by being a coward, but bravery may save you and will win you *lof*.' Such a belief would keep a warrior going in an age when that must have required some courage. The poet expresses the same point in Christian terms when he writes

Beowulf l. 2291   Swa mæg unfæge   eaðe gedigan
                    wean ond wræcsið   se ðe Waldendes
                    hyldo gehealdeþ!

We see the truth of this when, in his fight with Grendel's dam, Beowulf is helped by his valour, his corslet, and his God.

Another reason why it is not a depressing poem is because it affirms that life is worth living. There is joy in ships and armour, in jewels and precious things, in warriors marching, in horse-races and beer, in being a well-governed people. It is true that these joys make the dark threats more ominous and stress the poignant irony of the hall doomed before it is built, of brides whose marriages are to end in disaster, and of peoples feasting peacefully with bloody war imminent: it is indeed that 'Joy, whose hand is ever at his lips / Bidding adieu'. But the emphasis of *Beowulf* is on the successful achievements of the individual rather than on the total weakness of mankind in general: the disaster which follows the death of a brave man without a successor is no reason for despair but merely part of the machinery of life. As it was with the Geats after the death of Beowulf, so it was with the Jews after the death of Eleazar, surnamed Savaran:

> Then Judas and his host drew near, and entered into battle, and there were slain of the king's army six hundred men. Eleazar also, surnamed Savaran, perceiving that one of the beasts, armed with royal harness, was higher than all the rest, and supposing that the king was upon him, put himself in jeopardy, to the end he might deliver his people, and get him a perpetual name: wherefore he ran upon him courageously through the midst of the battle, slaying on the right hand and on the left, so that they were divided from him on both sides. Which done, he crept under the elephant, and thrust him under, and slew him: whereupon the elephant fell down upon him, and there he died. Howbeit the rest of the Jews seeing the strength of the king, and the violence of his forces, turned away from them. (1 Maccabees 6. 42–7)

Like Bede's sparrow, Scyld is typical of us all, going through this transitory life from the unknown to the unknown. The poem starts with denial of the mead-benches and with a leaderless people: it ends with a leaderless people soon to be deprived of their mead-benches. It begins and ends with a funeral. But 'such is life'. And we are left, not with despair, but with a vision of the conflict of good and evil, of the dependence of man on man, and of the glory of individual achievement.

IV

One of the great difficulties in the way of a Christian interpretation of *Beowulf* is the poet's failure to mention any of the great dogmas of Christianity – the Incarnation, the Crucifixion, the Resurrection, the salvation of mankind by Christ – or the name of Christ himself. It can scarcely be claimed that the poem is overwhelmingly Christian in tone. In searching for a scriptural passage on which *Beowulf* might be a meditation, one thinks more readily of The Wisdom of Solomon 3. 1–9, and Ecclesiasticus 44. 1–15 than of Revelation 19. 6–10, and Revelation 7. 13–17. But this difficulty is not insuperable: indeed, it must be overcome unless we are to advance the ridiculous notion that the author of the poem was a recent convert to Judaism. In Appendix (b) to his Academy Lecture, Professor Tolkien has already shown good reasons why a Christian poet might have felt that Christ the Redeemer would be out of place in the pagan world he was portraying and we can see from *The Wanderer* and *The Seafarer* how a situation expressed in pagan terms could easily have led to Christian moralizing.[34a]

But in the final analysis we are unlikely to reach any agreement about the question 'How Christian is *Beowulf*?' because we are left without an adequate frame of reference. We do not know when, where, by whom, or for whom, the poem was written. We face the same difficulty with *The Wanderer* and *The Seafarer*. If the text from Hebrews 11. 13–16

> These all died in faith ... and confessed that they were strangers and pilgrims on the earth. ... But now they desire a better country, that is, an heavenly: wherefore God is not ashamed to be called their God: for he hath prepared for them a city

preceded these poems in the Exeter Book, Professor Smithers' view that the poems are allegories would presumably be right beyond peradventure. The same would be true if it could be demonstrated that they were written in a monastery for monks as a meditation on 2 Corinthians 5. 6 'whilst we are at home in the body, we are absent from the Lord' or on 1 Peter 2. 11 'Dearly beloved, I beseech you as strangers and pilgrims, abstain from fleshly lusts.' If this is what Professor Smithers means when he writes 'It can no longer be valid

---

[34a] [1987. This point is now better expressed in a passage on p. 253 of *A Guide to Old English* (4th edn), credit for which must go to Fred C. Robinson.]

to urge, against the type of overall interpretation offered here, that allegorical meanings are always made explicit in OE poetry',[35] we must agree and acknowledge the debt of gratitude we owe him for revealing to us the undoubted possibility that *The Wanderer* and *The Seafarer* may be meditations on the theme which receives clear expression in *Christ B* ll. 850–66 and is perhaps treated in *Exodus*.[36] But the establishment of a new possibility is not a reason for dismissing all others, and there can be no certainty because we do not know enough about the conventions in which the poems were written. So it is with many OE poems: their structure is not clear (or appealing) to us and we cannot agree on their meaning.

Beowulf suffers under these disadvantages and is therefore open to many plausible interpretations. Assuming that the poem is a unity and not a stringing-together of old pagan poems on a thread of Christian moralizing, we can perhaps distinguish three types, though these of course may shade into one another. Firstly, we could explain the poem as the work of the representative of a recently converted pagan heroic society who has assimilated the Old Testament to paganism rather than paganism to the New Testament. Secondly, it could be claimed that the poem is 'humanistic', glorifying 'man's unconquerable mind'. Gang perhaps occupies a half-way house between these two views when he writes: 'Perhaps it would not be excessively rash to suggest that *Beowulf*, so far from being a Christianized epic, is an attempt at a sort of secular Saints' life: the sort of poem that would meet Alcuin's strictures on the heroic poetry without altogether sacrificing the heroic stories to instruction.'[37]

The third type of interpretation is the specifically Christian one. Thus Klaeber wrote: 'We might even feel inclined to recognize features of the Christian Savior in the destroyer of hellish fiends, the warrior brave and gentle, blameless in thought and deed, the king that dies for his people.'[38] Mrs Goldsmith, too, after attacking those who believe 'that the feeling of the poem is essentially pagan or at the best only half-heartedly Christian',[39] comes out boldly with her title 'The Christian Theme of *Beowulf*'. Father McNamee, S.J., claiming that to an Anglo-Saxon audience with the taste for obscure allegory and riddles all that was necessary was a clue sufficient to suggest the identification, asserts that *Beowulf* is 'an allegory of salvation'. The clue which identifies Beowulf and the Christian Saviour is (according to Father McNamee) the fact that Grendel and his dam are repeatedly described as inmates of Hell, powers of darkness, and so on. Thus the poet expresses the Christian message through the Anglo-Saxon myth.[40] Like Professor Smithers' interpretations of *The Wanderer* and *The Seafarer*, this theory is by no means impossible. But the objection that allegory is usually made explicit can still be urged and it must be

---

[35] *MÆ* 28 (1959), 7.
[36] See *Neophilologus* 44 (1960), 122–7.
[37] *RES* 3 (1952), 11.
[38] *Beowulf*, 3rd edn, p. li.
[39] *MÆ* 29 (1960), 81.
[40] *JEGP* 59 (1960), 190–207.

said that the almost total absence of real Christian feeling makes it difficult to read the poem in this way.

The difficulty of reconciling a Christian interpretation of the poem with this absence of real Christian feeling is, of course, brilliantly met by Professor Tolkien, who sees *Beowulf* as the work of a Christian poet deliberately portraying ancient pre-Christian days and emphasizing the nobility of the pagan Germanic world. According to this explanation, we have to do with the Christian interpretation of pagan myths expressed in a very special way, namely, through the evocation of the pagan world at its best: hence the world of *Beowulf* remains pagan, though viewed by a Christian poet.

Once the necessary basic assumptions are granted, each type of theory is tenable (intellectually, if not emotionally). Each has its attractions. But in the end each reader will have to adopt the interpretation which appeals to him as an individual. *Beowulf* is not the only English poem for which more than one plausible explanation exists. *The Wanderer* and *The Seafarer* have already been mentioned. *The Owl and the Nightingale* may be read, with Peterson,[41] as an exercise in Christian dialectic in which the reader is supposed to see the triumph of the logical owl and his orthodox religious views over the nightingale, a showy debater out to win a specious victory by sophistry. It has also been explained as a conflict between gravity and gaiety or between asceticism and pleasure, between philosophy and art or between religious poetry and love poetry. But some modern readers at any rate may feel that these explanations overlook the sheer fun of it all and the brilliance with which the owl and the nightingale are made to talk as birds would – if they could. A similar variety of interpretations – many of which seem to neglect some important aspect of the poem – exists for *Sir Gawain and the Green Knight*: it would be out of place to recapitulate them here.

This sort of difficulty clearly arises from our ignorance of the conventions in which the poems are written. We do not know who wrote them or by whom, where, and when, they were first heard. What the author took for granted in his audience we can never determine with any accuracy. We are just as much out of our depth as a learned man of 1850 would be if he were suddenly and without any explanation put in front of a television set or transported to a cinema.

Even more modern works of literature sometimes suffer in the same way. The poetry of Blake, Joyce's *Finnegan's Wake*, and Yeats's Byzantium poems, are perhaps special cases. But failure to understand that Shakespeare's historical plays were shaped by the Elizabethan world picture or that the idea of the disruption of the proper order of things runs through his tragedies has been in the past a source of mistaken interpretations and theories. So too Milton's *Paradise Lost* has been misjudged because it was not clearly understood that Satan's arguments were based on a denial of the idea of hierarchy. Instances

[41] D. L. Peterson *JEGP* 55 (1956), 13–26.

could be multiplied from literature of all periods. One last one must suffice. If we had inherited no clear understanding of the conventions of Greek drama, what would we make of the scene in Aeschylus' *Agamemnon* where the Chorus, after hearing Agamemnon cry from within that he is being murdered, debates with unhurried calm the various courses of action open to its members? I do not know. But I feel sure of one thing – we should not lack ingenious theories to explain the inaction which continues until Clytemnestra is revealed standing over the dead bodies of Agamemnon and Cassandra.

This, then, is our difficulty with *Beowulf*. Through bad luck which leaves us in ignorance about its author and audience or through some fault of structure or presentation, it lacks a clear frame of reference and so, some would claim, fails to achieve that universality which would enable it to transmit its message across the centuries. But can we (even when we know the conventions in which he is writing) demand of a poet that he gives us a crystal-clear message readily understood by all on first reading? It is related that Nelson's second-in-command at Trafalgar, after seeing the famous signal, was heard to mutter 'I do wish Nelson would stop signalling. We all know very well what we are about.' And perhaps we all do in our own way, despite the confusion caused by those critics who frantically signal to us that they are right and the others wrong. Certainly, many see *Beowulf* as a great and strongly moral poem, positive rather than negative in tone, which speaks to us over the centuries, affirming that man who rose from the primaeval slime is capable of greatness and stressing the glory of achievement rather than the tragic waste and pity of it all. Perhaps in this atomic age, when the monsters and dragons seem closer to us and the powers of darkness seem to be in the ascendant, we can derive some comfort and encouragement if we hearken to the voice of this great English poet of the Dark Ages.

'Before being a dirge', wrote a young French pupil of mine, '*Beowulf* is a song of joy, of confidence in life, in the heroism displayed by man.' An eighth-century English poet who could speak thus to a twentieth-century Frenchman can scarcely be said to have failed: in *Beowulf* the young man of today clearly

> beheld the emblem of a mind
> That feeds upon infinity, that broods
> Over the dark abyss....

2
Two Syntactical Notes on *Beowulf*

I

The *þæt* clause in *Beowulf* l. 1141 has long been a source of difficulty. The manuscript has

Beowulf l. 1138   he to gyrnwræce
                  swiðor þohte   þonne to sælade,
                  gif he torngemot   þurhteon mihte,
                  ƥ he Eotena bearn   inne gemunde

and the editors naturally expand ƥ to *þæt*. C. L. Wrenn's note on l. 1141 reads:

þæt hē... gemunde. Transl.: 'in as much as he was inwardly (*inne*) thinking of the children of the Jutes [Finn's men].' He was, that is, thinking of his revenge. *Inne* has been emended by Trautmann to *īrne* 'with his iron (sword),' which Klaeber accepts. This gives an easier sense, and palæographically is very credible, since *n* and *r* are often confused.[1]

E. V. K. Dobbie also retains the manuscript *inne*, but accepts a different explanation:

No emendation is necessary in this line if *þæt... inne* is taken as the equivalent of a relative, following E. A. Kock, The English Relative Pronouns (Lund, 1897), p. 35. Cf. *þæt... on*, Daniel 418, Christ 326f., *þæt... ymb*, Riddle 23, 11, and probably also *þæt... þurh*, Judith 48f. This interpretation is adopted by Chambers and von Schaubert, also by Malone, JEGPh. XXV, 158, who translates, 'in which he would be mindful of the children of the Euts'.[2]

We must, I think, reject Wrenn's 'in as much as'; the evidence for a causal use of *þæt* in Old English poetry is very slender. If we exclude the solitary example of the formula *ðy... þæt* (*Waldere* i. 19–22) and examples like

Reprinted from *Neophilologus* 52 (1968), 292–9.

[1] *Beowulf with the Finnesburg Fragment* (London, 1953), p. 207.
[2] Anglo-Saxon Poetic Records iv. 179, part of note to l. 1141.

Andreas l. 257   Bið ðe meorð wið god,
                 þæt ðu us on lade   liðe weorðe,

where, while the translation 'because' is convenient, the *þæt* can reasonably be said to introduce a noun clause,[3] there are seven sentences which deserve our consideration.

Two of these occur in *The Dream of the Rood*, viz.

Dream of Rood l. 33   Geseah ic þa frean mancynnes
                  efstan elne mycle   þæt he me wolde on gestigan

and

Dream of Rood l. 103   Hider eft fundaþ
           on þysne middangeard   mancynn secan
           on domdæge   dryhten sylfa,
           ælmihtig god,   ond his englas mid,
           þæt he þonne wile deman,   se ah domes geweald,
           anra gehwylcum   swa he him ærur her
           on þyssum lænum   life geearnaþ.

In both of these the *þæt* clause would readily be interpreted as a clause of purpose if it were not for the presence of the verb *willan*. *þa* in *The Dream of the Rood* ll. 41 and 68 suggests that *þæt* in l. 34 might be a scribal error for *þa*, but this solution is impossible in l. 107, where *wile* would require *þonne* and not *þa*.[4] The construction occurs also in the prose, e.g. Matthew 22. 11 *Ða eode se cyning in, þæt he wolde geseon...* (Latin: *intravit autem rex ut videret...*) and John 12. 20... *Hæðene, þe foron þæt hig woldon hig gebiddan...* (Latin: *...qui ascenderant ut adorarent...*). The Latin equivalents suggest that the *þæt* clauses are final rather than causal and it would seem that we have here an idiomatic use of the verb *willan* rather than examples of *þæt* meaning 'because'.

Three examples come from the *Paris Psalter*. In *Paris Psalter* 57. 4, *nele*, the verb in the *þæt* clause, represents a Latin future tense in an adjective clause. The *þæt* clause is perhaps therefore better taken as consecutive than as final or causal. In

Paris Psalter 61. 12   Miht is drihtnes   ofer middangeard
                    and him þæs to worlde   wuldor stande
                   and mildheortness,   þæt he manna gehwam
                   æfter his agenum   earnungum demeð,
                   efne swa he wyrceð   on worldlife,

---

[3] This is, I think, another terminological problem. See *OED* s.v. *that*, conj. II. 2.
[4] See *Neophilologus* 49 (1965), 46–7.

þæt represents the *quia* of

> ... et tibi, Domine, misericordia: quia tu
> reddes singulis secundum opera eorum.

But the OE *þæt* clause can be explained as a noun clause on *þæs* equivalent to that introduced by *quia*;[5] compare the third example – *Paris Psalter* 143. 4, where the *þæt* clause represents a Latin noun clause introduced by *quoniam*.[6]

This leaves us with two examples from *Elene* where Miss Gradon glosses *þæt* as 'because'.[7] The first is *Elene* ll. 56–61, where *ðæt* can be taken as introducing a result clause and can be translated 'so that, in such a way that' whether we take *he* (l. 59) as singular or, with Miss Gradon, as plural. The second is *Elene* ll. 172–80 where, with Krapp's *ASPR* punctuation, *ðæt* introduces a noun clause on *lærde wæron*. If, however, we accept Miss Gradon's attractive punctuation of the passage, we can (even if we translate *þæt* as 'because') explain it as introducing a noun clause like the one in *Andreas* ll. 275–6 quoted above; compare also *Elene* ll. 939–42 and *The Winter's Tale* IV. iv. 476

> For thee (fond boy)
> If I may ever know thou dost but sigh
> That thou no more shalt never see this knacke. . . .

After all this, it is more than interesting that Miss Gradon, in her footnote, translates ll. 173 ff.: '. . . their spirits rejoiced *that* they might make known to the emperor the grace of the gospel [my italics]'. None of these examples – even those in which the translation 'because' can reasonably be admitted – offers any support to Wrenn's 'in as much as' for *þæt* in *Beowulf* l. 1141.

Can *þæt* in *Beowulf* l. 1141 be a relative pronoun? Dobbie's phrase 'the equivalent of a relative' is peculiar: either *þæt* is a relative pronoun or it is not. While its number and gender present no problem, its case at first glance seems suspicious: one might perhaps expect the dative *þæm* rather than the accusative *þæt* if *inne* is to be taken as a preposition. The four examples cited by Dobbie are not really parallel, for in all of them the accusative is the natural case, whether we take *on*, *ymb*, and *þurh*, as prepositions following the relative they govern[8] (the less usual position for prepositions governing the declined relative)[9] or as separable prefixes; compare *on* in

---

[5] See E. P. V. Nunn *An Introduction to the Study of Ecclesiastical Latin* (Eton, 1951), p. 63.

[6] Nunn, p. 63.

[7] P. O. E. Gradon *Cynewulf's Elene* (London, 1958), Glossary, s.v. *þæt*.

[8] The accusative after *locian on* (*Daniel* l. 418) is well-attested and need not surprise us after *wlatian on* (*Christ* l. 327). It is the more common case after *ymb* (*Riddle* 23. 11) and *þurh* (*Judith* l. 49).

[9] See Bruce Mitchell *Anglia* 81 (1963), 302.

Maxims i. 133   þæt is rice god,
           sylf soðcyning,   sawla nergend,
           se us eal forgeaf   þæt we on lifgaþ....¹⁰

However, the distinction 'accusative of motion/dative of rest' after prepositions was not always observed in Old English;¹¹ compare Ælfric *Homilies* (ed. Thorpe) ii. 452. 3 ... *se ne mæg nan fyr of heofenum asendan, seðe on heofenum sylf cuman ne mot* with Bede *Ecclesiastical History* (ed. Miller) 458. 17 ... *he com up on Frysana land*, and note the different usages after *on* in *Rule of St Benedict* (ed. Schröer) 12. 3 *þu gesawe gehwæde mot on þines broðor eage and ne gesawe þone mæstam [sic] cyp on þinum agenum eagan* and in

Juliana l. 304   Pilatus ær
           on rode aheng   rodera waldend,
           meotud meahtigne   minum larum.
           Swylce ic Egias   eac gelærde
           þæt he unsnytrum   Andreas het
           ahon haligne   on heanne beam....

In view of these examples (which can be multiplied), we can perhaps take *þæt* as an accusative on *inne* expressing 'place where' as opposed to 'place whither'.

But this assumes that *inne* can be used as a preposition. Can it? Bosworth-Toller notes only two possible examples – *Orosius* (ed. Sweet) 268. 29 *Æfter an þunor toslog hiora Capitoliam, þæt hus þe hiora godas inne wæron* ... and *Blickling Homilies* (ed. Morris) 145. 34 ... *ure Drihten Hælend Crist* ... *wæs ingangende on þære halgan Marian hus on þæt þe heo hie inne rest.*¹² In both of these we have the indeclinable relative *þe* (no clue here about the case *inne* would govern if it were a preposition) followed by *inne* (the natural position for prepositions governing the indeclinable relative).¹³

But it is, of course, by no means certain that *inne* in these two prose examples is a preposition, for in them too it may be a separable prefix; we could translate literally 'the house which their gods in-were' and 'the house which she

---

¹⁰ Dobbie's first three examples lend themselves readily to explanation as separable prefixes – the combination '*on/ymb* + verb' can be translated respectively 'which we see', 'which the wise man beheld', and 'which I discuss'. That from *Judith* – 'a net which the wicked man could penetrate ("through-see") with his eyes' – may be less convincing in the language of today (hence perhaps Dobbie's 'probably'). But that is no reason for rejecting it. Whether *inne* in *Beowulf* l. 1141 can be so explained is discussed below.

¹¹ See my *Guide to Old English* (Oxford, 1965), p. 116.

¹² Bosworth-Toller Supplement, s.v. *inne* B. The second example is quoted in a truncated and distorted form. But this does not, I think, affect the issue – *on þæt* belongs grammatically to the principal clause, as the B.-T. citation *on þ hus þe* suggests.

¹³ See Bruce Mitchell *RES* 15 (1964), 137–8.

in-rested' – the Old English equivalents of modern 'where their gods were' and 'where she rested'. And the fact that in *Beowulf* l. 1141 *inne* follows rather than precedes *þæt* suggests that it is a separable prefix rather than a preposition.[14] Yet it is hard to see how *inne* in *Beowulf* l. 1141 can reasonably be explained as a separable prefix.[15] Attempts to take it as an adverb have not so far prospered, but another solution based on this possibility is suggested below.[16]

However, it must (I suppose) be conceded that *þæt... inne* in *Beowulf* l. 1141 could be a relative combination. We should expect *þæt* (or *þæm*) rather than *þe* after *torngemot* unqualified by a demonstrative (though *þe* is not impossible),[17] but on the other hand a preposition tends to precede any form of the declined relative which it governs.[18] It could, perhaps, be argued that this was an early example of *þæt* (MS *þ*) used as a relative pronoun without regard for case. But if so, it should be recognized that we have here a crux not unlike that which confronts those who take MS *þ* in *Beowulf* l. 15 as a relative.[19] In this connexion, Fr. Klaeber's observation that E. A. Kock 'would connect *inne* with *þæt* (= *þe*), "in which"'[20] is interesting: Klaeber's bracketed '(= *þe*)' presumably reflects his uneasiness about Kock's interpretation.[21]

It is perhaps worth pointing out that it is certainly possible to take *þæt* as a relative[21a] and to translate '... a hostile encounter in which he might bear in mind the sons of the Jutes' or, as Kemp Malone has it, 'in which he would be mindful of the children of the Euts'.[22] But we can say 'certainly' only because

---

[14] See Mitchell *Anglia*, p. 302.

[15] I do not propose to pursue this problem here. The main difficulty lies, I think, in the two accusatives *þæt* and *bearn*. Verbs like *læran*, which regularly take two accusatives, can hardly be brought to our aid.

[16] See, e.g. the Bosworth-Toller Supplement, s.v. *inne* A. I. (I) (c) (an explanation not mentioned by Dobbie), and the first sentence of Klaeber's note on *Beowulf* l. 1141 (where the example cited in the Bosworth-Toller Supplement s.v. *ge-munan* VII might be relevant. But there *gemunan* does not govern two accusatives).

[17] See Mitchell *Anglia*, pp. 311–12.   [18] See Mitchell *Anglia*, p. 302.

[19] See Mitchell *Anglia*, pp. 314–15.

[20] In his note to *Beowulf*, l. 1141.

[21] E. A. Kock *The English Relative Pronouns* (Lund, 1897), p. 35.

[21a] [1987. The word 'certainly' was too strong and was inconsistent with the opening sentences of the paragraphs to which fn. 21 and fn. 27 refer. A further – and probably conclusive – argument against *þæt... inne* 'in which' in *Beowulf* l. 1141 emerges from the unpublished 1986 Oxford D.Phil. thesis 'The Verb and Particle Collocation in Old English Poetry: A Descriptive Analysis on the Basis of Syntax, Metrical Segmentation and Stress' by Denise Cavanaugh. On pp. 307–8 Dr Cavanaugh shows that *inne* always carries stress in the poetry and combines in post-position only with *þær* and *her*. This of course underlines the acceptability but not the inevitability of Sievers's emendation of *þæt* to *þær* (fn. 27 below). Whether it is conclusive against *þe... inne* 'in which' in the two prose examples quoted above (*Orosius* 268. 29 and *Blickling Homilies* 145. 34) depends on how closely the stress of Old English poetry represented that of the spoken language. This seems to me an unsolvable riddle.]

[22] *JEGP* 25 (1926), 158.

gif (l. 1140) introduces a noun clause 'whether...'. For unambiguous examples of the preterite subjunctive expressing the future-in-the-past are found in adjective clauses in the poetry only when they are in dependent speech, e.g. *Beowulf* ll. 3069–73 and

> *Daniel* l. 448
> Gebead þa se bræsna   Babilone weard
> swiðmod sinum leodum,   þæt se wære his aldre scyldig,
> se ðæs onsoce   þætte soð wære
> mære mihta waldend....[23]

Thus F. C. Robinson is on firm ground when he points out the possibility of retaining the MS *þone* in *Beowulf* ll. 67–70 and of translating 'It came into his mind that he would command people to build a palace, a great meadhall, which the sons of men should hear of forever.'[24] Again, R. F. Leslie rightly sees

> *Wanderer* l. 25   ... sohte sele dreorig   sinces bryttan,
> hwær ic feor oþþe neah   findan meahte
> þone þe in meoduhealle   min mine wisse,...

as a possible example when he glosses *wisse* as '3 sg. pret. subj.'.[25] Yet, since it is ambiguous in form, it could be taken as an indicative and translated 'felt, had felt' rather than 'would feel, might feel', though this is perhaps less likely.[26]

While the doubts about the case of *þæt* and about the function of *inne* do not demolish the possibility that *þæt* in *Beowulf* l. 1141 is a relative, they do suggest that Dobbie accepted the solution a little too easily when he made it the basis for his remark that 'no emendation is necessary in this line'. Which of the proposed emendations is best cannot be argued here.[27] I should like instead to glance at a possibility which has not, as far as I know, yet been suggested – that

---

[23] The preterite subjunctive can, of course, occur in adjective clauses which are not in dependent speech, with reference to actions or situations which are presented as unreal or impossible; see Mitchell *Anglia*, pp. 319–22. It can refer to the future-in-the-past in certain kinds of wishes, in noun clauses, and in some kinds of adverb clauses, e.g. final, even when they are not in dependent speech. It is, of course, the mood of unreality, which in Old English is timeless. See further my *Guide to Old English* (Oxford, 1965), *passim*. A full examination of the prose, however, may well reveal other uses.

[24] *Tennessee Studies in Literature* 11 (1966), 151–5. He does not, of course, insist that *gefrunon* must be subjunctive; see p. 159, n. 15 of his article.

[25] *The Wanderer* (Manchester, 1966), p. 98, s.v. *wāt*.

[26] Leslie glosses it as 'felt'; 'might feel' would, I think, reflect the subjunctive more accurately.

[27] If one is considered necessary, there is perhaps something to be said for Sievers's *þær* for *þæt* (MS þ), with the translation 'a hostile meeting in which he might bear in mind the sons of the Jutes'. We could still accept *gemunde* as subjunctive expressing the future-in-the-past (see above) and *þær... inne* can be paralleled in *Judith* ll. 44–5, *Rune Poem* l. 18, and in the two prose examples cited in the Bosworth-Toller Supplement s.v. *inne* A. I (I) (a ß) (ii). Cf. also *þar... on* in *Lord's Prayer* II. 41.

þæt introduces a final clause in which *inne* is an adverb referring back to *torngemot*. The mood of *gemunde* presents no difficulty and the use of *inne* referring back to a noun in a preceding clause or sentence can be paralleled from *Beowulf* itself, e.g. ll. 1281, 1570, 1866, 3059, and

> *Beowulf* l. 1799   reced hliuade
> geap ond goldfah;   gæst inne swæf....²⁸

Here, as in most of the examples, the use of *inne* is a local one referring to some physical object such as a house. But it refers to the 'inner man' in *Beowulf* l. 2113 *hreðer inne weoll* and it seems not unreasonable to postulate that it could refer to a battle. We could then translate *Beowulf* ll. 1138–41:

> He thought more about vengeance than about a sea-voyage, [wondering] whether he could bring about (*or* carry through to its conclusion) a hostile encounter, so that he might therein be mindful of the sons of the Jutes.²⁸ᵃ

II

In the course of his remarks on the Heathobard Episode in *Beowulf*, A. G. Brodeur observes of l. 2035:

> Hoops and Klaeber regard *dryhtbearn* as plural, and take the line as 'a loosely joined elliptic clause indicating the cause of the king's displeasure,' meaning 'the noble scions of the Danes [are] excellently entertained.' There are two objections to this....²⁹

These 'two objections' call for syntactical comment; I do not propose to discuss other problems.

'First,' says Brodeur, 'such elliptic clauses with the substantive verb omitted are rare.'³⁰ To say this is to admit that they occur, as they do – *Beowulf* l. 2297 *ne ðær ænig mon / on þære westenne* will serve as an example. This does not, of course, prove that we have one in *Beowulf* l. 2035. As G. P. Krapp implied in his note on *Genesis* l. 2809, there is no such rule in textual criticism or, I suppose, anywhere else; he speaks of 'Kock ... citing several other examples, which scarcely prove that this is one'.³¹ Brodeur, however, seems to be attempting to establish an equally bizarre rule, viz. that the rarity of examples is proof that this is not one.

---

²⁸ *Beowulf* l. 390 could perhaps be included. For further examples, see Bosworth-Toller and Supplement s.v. *inne* and the examples cited in fn. 27.

²⁸ᵃ [1987. But, as Dr Denise Cavanaugh has pointed out (private communication), *inne* could mean 'inwardly, within his heart', as in *Beowulf* l. 2113 above.]

²⁹ A. G. Brodeur *The Art of* Beowulf (Berkeley, Cal., 1959), p. 166.

³⁰ Brodeur, p. 166.

³¹ Anglo-Saxon Poetic Records i. 196.

'Secondly,' Brodeur continues, 'although the dative plural *duguðum* is, very occasionally, used with adverbial force, the genitive plural *duguða* is not so used anywhere else.'[32] Here again the principle invoked seems peculiar. It may be true that the genitive plural *duguða* is not used elsewhere with adverbial force, though the clause 'as far as we know at present' may be a very necessary qualification. But even if it is true, what does this prove in the face of examples of adverbial genitives such as *niða* in *Beowulf* ll. 845, 1439, and 2206? Such arguments from silence are notoriously dangerous. Are we really to conclude that anything unrecorded in extant Old English manuscripts never existed?

It seems to me, therefore, that – whether or not we agree with the interpretation proposed by Hoops and Klaeber for this passage – we must agree that Brodeur's objections have not dealt it a fatal blow.

---

[32] Brodeur, p. 166.

3
An Introduction to *Beowulf*

Beowulf is a poem of 3182 lines which survives only in the British Museum manuscript Cotton Vitellius A. xv (probably written about AD 1000) and in two late eighteenth-century transcripts. What evidence there is – linguistic, historical, literary and archaeological – has led most scholars to accept that it took its present form somewhere between about AD 680 and 800. But some still argue for a later date.[1] It could have been produced in Bede's Northumbria, in Offa's Mercia, in the East Anglia of the Sutton Hoo Ship-Burial, or even elsewhere in England.

It is, of course, an Old English poem, composed in the language spoken by the Anglo-Saxons, a Germanic people who inhabited much of England before the Norman Conquest, and in the alliterative measure which they inherited from their ancestors, a measure in which the alliterative unit was the line and the metrical unit the half-line:

Hröðgār maþelode,   helm Scyldinga
Hrothgar made a speech, helmet [protector] of the Scyldings.

Reprinted from *Beowulf*, translated by Kevin Crossley-Holland (London, 1973).'

[1] [1987. In recent years, enthusiasm for a later date has increased and scholars have argued for the ninth, tenth, and even the eleventh, century; see *The Dating of* Beowulf ed. Colin Chase (Toronto, 1981). This is not a question to be pursued here. But its nature seems to be neatly summed up in the title of the last essay in the book cited above: E. G. Stanley, 'The Date of *Beowulf*: Some Doubts and No Conclusions'. I must, however, make one point. In the course of his introductory survey, the editor wrote (p. 8): 'Nevertheless, some commentators reach an extreme limit of scepticism, as when Bruce Mitchell said in 1968 that "examination of the language can do little more than confirm the possibility that the poem was composed between c. 680 and 800 (or perhaps later)".' Yet he allowed the following platitudinous paragraph to appear in the course of an article called 'A Reconsideration of the Language of *Beowulf*' (p. 37): 'Our preliminary work with the linguistic forms of the poem has convinced us that the evidence of language should not be neglected in any inquiry into the date and localization of *Beowulf*. Although from our current understanding of the language of *Beowulf* we could not call any date in the Old English period impossible, on linguistic grounds, for the composition of the poem, we believe that further analysis of the language of *Beowulf*, of Cotton Vitellius A. xv, and of other Old English texts and manuscripts will provide useful information about the date and localization of both the poem and its manuscript.' I leave it to the reader to decide how much less worthy of rebuke these remarks are than mine. On the possible relevance of the alliteration of *g* and *ġ*, see initially *OEN* 16. 1 (1982), 75.]

The translator has had something to say in his Introduction about the power and range of *Beowulf*, its 'Englishness', and its many moods. It would be out of place when introducing a *translation* to offer detailed comments on the Old English poetic vocabulary, which included 'formulae' – set metrical compounds which could be varied according to the needs of alliteration, as one might say 'on the whale-road' or 'on the swan- road' when speaking of the sea – and 'kennings' – condensed metaphors in which (a) is compared to (b) without either (a) or the point of the comparison being made explicit, so that the ship out of control and driven by the storm is described thus: 'The sea-steed heeds not the bridle.' Much of this is inevitably lost in translation.

But many of these formulae clustered around a particular theme. Perhaps the most recurrent images in Old English poetry were associated with the idea of lord and retainers living in harmony within their hall, the lord a bold warrior and generous giver of treasure, the warriors loyal and ready to lay down their lives for him. But within the hall, there may be foes seeking the opportunity for vengeance; there may be cowards who will fail their lord in his need. Inside it the warriors will sleep each night with war-gear close at hand, for it may be the grim sound of battle which will waken them, not the joyous harp. Outside, in the cold and chill of lonely exile, are those who for some reason or other have no lord and must wander in hopeless misery, cut off from human joys.

Beowulf is full of these images. One sensitive American critic, E. B. Irving Jr, has noted a contrast between the first and second parts of the poem. In the first, the great hall Heorot stands unharmed and the poet, giving 'generous space to the high rituals of civilized life', makes 'most vivid to us ... precisely that busy, noisy, bright-colored world that Beowulf saves'. But in the second, the only public ritual is a funeral. Beowulf's hall has been burnt down by the dragon. 'What we have instead is the bleak and lonely setting of a windswept hill near the sea, where the main focus of all the action, an ancient grave-barrow with a curse on it, holds its dragon and its treasure far away in time and space from human society.' This contrast is reinforced by the fact that in the first half the canvas is crowded with numerous figures and incidents not directly related to the central story, whereas in the second half the only 'digressions' are concerned with the bloody conflicts between Swedes and Geats.

In his *Historia Ecclesiastica*, Bede gives a vivid account of how in 627 the Northumbrians, in council with their king Edwin, were debating the question 'Shall we become Christians?' In the course of this debate, one of the chiefs is made to describe human life in these terms (translated here from the Old English version):

O King, in comparison with that time which is unknown to us, the life we now lead on earth seems to me thus: as if you were sitting at a feast in the winter-time with your chiefs and your thanes. Inside the fire is burning and the hall is warm. Outside it is raining and snowing, and the storm rages. Then there comes a sparrow and flies quickly through the hall – in one door and out the other. While he is inside, he is unbuffeted by the storm of winter. But that is for no time at all, just the twinkling of an eye, for he passes straight from winter to winter. Similarly, a human life exists for a brief moment of time; what goes before it and what follows after it, we do not know.

In a sense, this comparison summarizes the theme of *Beowulf*, for the poem begins with a people who, having endured a dark winter of lordlessness, are to have built for them the great hall Heorot in which they will experience both joy and sorrow, and it ends with a people who in their turn have experienced joy, but whose hall has now been destroyed, whose leader lies dead, and who look forward with sorrow and fear to a dark winter of war, captivity and terror. So *Beowulf* could be described as a poetic exploration of the life of man in this world, of the blind forces of nature and the dark passions of men against 'our little systems [which] have their day and cease to be' – a contest seen in terms of the system symbolized by the Anglo-Saxon hall, the system within which the poet lived but of whose inevitable weaknesses he makes us aware through both the story and his own comments.

Such a theme, of course, lends itself very readily to allegorical interpretation. But I believe that many of the difficulties imposed on *Beowulf* by modern critics disappear if we look at it in the way I have suggested – superficially simple perhaps, but ultimately more just to the poet and more profound than many of the 'explanations' which have been wrung or twisted from the poem. That there have been so many interpretations is, I suppose, due to a combination of historical accident and critical ingenuity. *Beowulf* is unique in that it is the only lengthy Old English poem extant which treats of heroic rather than Christian material. So we have, as it were, no Old English touchstone to guide us. We do not know who wrote it or when, where and by whom it was first heard. We know little of the conventions within which it was composed and cannot be sure what the author took for granted in his audience. We cannot even be sure that it is the work of one man.

We must, of course, accept the text as we have it, assuming that (as Kenneth Sisam put it) it 'represents approximately the form given to the story by one man – original poet, or poet-editor, or accomplished reciter able to adapt and vary existing stories in verse'. But we must also see if it is possible to clarify this poet's aims. Few would deny that he had some idea of somehow entertaining somebody (whether he intended the poem for a monastic or a lay audience is disputed) or that, by accident or design, he instructed his audience by imparting an understanding of the responsibilities, privileges, and ideals of warriors and leaders from youth to old age. Moreover, like many other Old English poems, *Beowulf* is much concerned with the idea that life is transitory: in J. R. R. Tolkien's words 'it is an heroic-elegiac poem; and in a sense all its first 3136 lines are the prelude to a dirge.' But we have to ask ourselves a fundamental question: are we dealing with a poet concerned primarily with story-telling and entertainment or with a highly conscious artist who has composed a complex and carefully constructed poem full of subtle links, cross-references, and allusions? Do we agree with Kenneth Sisam that 'this kind of poetry depended on expression, not on silence, dark hints or subtle irony' and that the so-called 'digressions' – the mention of Sigemund and Heremod, the Finn Episode, the Heathobard–Danish conflict, the Swedish–Geatish wars – exist merely to add interest and variety to the entertainment? Or is the dragon which is mentioned in the Sigemund story deliberately placed there to remind us – in the moment of Beowulf's great triumph – that he is to die in combat with a dragon, just as we are reminded in ll. 81–5 that the newly built Heorot, towering in all its glorious magnificence, is to be destroyed by fire following an enemy invasion? And is this in turn meant to remind us that Beowulf's own hall is to be burned by the dragon's fiery breath? I think we are at liberty to believe in a somewhat more sophisticated poet than the mere teller of tales. But we must beware of making extravagant claims on his behalf or of insisting that others believe in him.

This, then, is one difficulty. Another concerns the poet's Christianity. It is certain that there were among the Anglo-Saxons men of deeply Christian education and conviction. Some of these men saw a stark contrast between the Christian warfare of the monastery – the life of the soldier of Christ – and earthly battle against temporal foes; some were ready to fight in defence of their country. But for other Anglo-Saxons, conversion seems to have been not a deep and lasting experience, but an easy shift for reasons of convenience from a not very vital paganism to what was perhaps a tenuously held belief in a formal Christianity which made little real impact on the heroic outlook. These variations, along with the Church's readiness to baptize what it could not suppress, mean that at times we meet a mixture of pagan and Christian concepts and attitudes, a mixture which often we shall not be able to disentangle. The absence from *Beowulf* of specific reference to the great dogmas of Christianity and of the name of Christ makes it difficult to claim that the poem is overtly Christian. How Christian is it? The impossibility of reaching a definitive answer can be demonstrated by considering the last word of the poem. The Geatish warriors pay their final tribute to Beowulf thus:

> of all kings on earth
> he was the kindest, the most gentle,
> the most just to his people, the most eager for fame.

The last phrase translates Old English *lofgeornost* 'most eager for *lof*'. When Christianized (as in the poem entitled *The Seafarer*) *lof* – fame on the lips of mortal men which pagan warriors had won by brave deeds against temporal foes – becomes fame among the angels and happiness in heaven won by good deeds and bravery against the devil. For which *lof* was Beowulf eager – the pagan or the Christian? How one answers this question is crucial to an interpretation of the poem. Yet how can it be answered with any certainty?[2] Whether the *Beowulf* poet was hot, cold or lukewarm to the new faith is (I fear) still a matter of opinion. This means that we cannot answer other vital questions. Are the monsters merely 'commonplaces', the proper matter of 'easy-going romances of chivalry, and of fairy tales'? Or are they 'Foes of God'? If the latter, are Grendel and his mother – descended as they are from Cain – of the same kind as the dragon? If so, why was Beowulf unable to defeat him too? (Here we see the genesis of theories that Beowulf is being criticized.) If not, is the dragon death? (As J. R. R. Tolkien has it, 'the placing of the dragon is inevitable: a man can but die upon his death-day'.)

It is no wonder that theories which purport to explain *Beowulf* are legion. Such is their bewildering variety that it is impossible even to catalogue them here. But a few can be mentioned. *Beowulf* is a wild folk-tale, not a properly conducted epic. It is a Christian reworking of a pagan poem. It is a soldering-together of three orally composed lays which were originally independent. It is a poem composed for recitation to warriors in their hall. An ivory-towered poet of the eighth century wrote it for a 'fit audience . . . though few'. It is a Christian allegory of Salvation written for a monastic audience. It is a Christian allegory of Man's fight against pride and greed – a fight which Beowulf loses. It is a Christian evaluation of the heroic code by which Beowulf lived and died – noble, but inadequate because the courage which it demanded of the leader made him too eager for glory and he thus became the instrument of his people's destruction. It symbolizes the as-yet-unended struggle between Heaven and Hell which is fought out on this earth in Man's thoughts and deeds. And so on.

None of these theories can be proved wrong. Each one may find sympathy somewhere in the audience to which this brief Introduction is addressed. I will nail my colours to some sort of a mast, but let me say this first: I believe that the poet meant us to admire Beowulf, not to condemn him. Who among us will escape condemnation if to die is to be condemned – a notion inextricably involved in some of these theories?

Whether the reader chooses to adopt one of the interpretations outlined above (and so unnecessarily to limit the poem by confining it in a Procrustean bed) or to find one for himself must be a matter of personal response. Personal response must decide, too, whether the final impression left by the poem is one of despair or of hope. Of course Beowulf's efforts were wasted in one sense: the Geats are no longer a great people. Similarly, since empires and civilizations

---

[2] [1987. On this point see now item 5 below.]

rise and fall, the efforts of all great men in a sense came to nothing. This is true of little men too. Yet there is no need for despair: 'The souls of the righteous are in the hand of God, and there shall no torment touch them.'

Today, in this nuclear age, with man's inhumanity to man daily more apparent on all levels and the powers of darkness in seeming ascendancy throughout the world, we may see *Beowulf* as a triumphant affirmation of the value of a good life: as the poet himself says, *Brūc ealles well* – Make good use of everything.

4
Beowulf, Lines 3074–3075: The Damnation of Beowulf?

In his article '*Beowulf*, Lines 3074–3075',[1] A. J. Bliss has made a very important contribution to our understanding of *Beowulf* ll. 3051–75, which he translates (p. 59):

> Moreover that mighty heritage, the gold of men of old, had been encircled with a spell, so that no man might touch that treasure-chamber, unless God Himself, the true King of victories (He is the protector of men) should grant it to whom He wished, to whatever man seemed fit to Him to open up the hoard.
> It was obvious that his course of action had been of no profit to the creature that had wrongfully kept the treasure hidden under the wall – the guardian had killed a man with few peers – when that feud was savagely avenged. It is a mystery in what circumstances a warrior famed for valour may reach the end of his allotted span, when a man can no longer dwell in the mead-hall with his kinsmen.
> When Beowulf went to meet the guardian of the barrow and his subtle enmity – *he* did not know in what circumstances his passing from the world was to come about – it happened to him just as the glorious chieftains who had put the treasure there had solemnly decreed it, that until doomsday the man who should plunder the place should be guilty of sin, confined in heathen precincts, held fast in hell's bonds, and cruelly tormented: in the past he had seen and understood the gold-bestowing favour of God much less clearly than he did now.

Here I begin by accepting his translation of *Beowulf* ll. 3051–73. But I do not accept his interpretation. The essential difference between us is this: Professor Bliss claims that in *Beowulf* ll. 3066–73 the poet says in so many words that

Reprinted from *Poetica* (Tokyo) 13 (1982), 15–26.

[1] J. R. R. Tolkien, *Scholar and Storyteller: Essays in Memoriam* ed. Mary Salu and Robert T. Farrell (Ithaca, NY, 1979), pp. 41–63. I acknowledge gratefully that I have profited from discussing this paper with Ivan Herbison, of St Edmund Hall, Oxford. But my main debt is to Professor Bliss himself. After a stimulating correspondence, we have reached agreement: we disagree.

Beowulf was damned. I do not agree. And so I argue that his explanation of *Beowulf* ll. 3074-5 – long ago described by Bugge as a *locus desperatus* – has not finally solved the problem they present.

Professor Bliss concludes his article with these words (p. 63):

> If Beowulf had paid heed to Hrothgar's warnings, he might have lived on to rule his people with honour; because he neglected them he discovered that the wages of arrogance is death, and the wages of avarice is damnation.

Leaving aside for the moment the fact that Beowulf had already ruled *fiftig wintra* (*Beowulf* ll. 2208b-9a) and, as Hrothgar warned him (*Beowulf* ll. 1761b-8), was bound to die eventually – and how better than fighting a dragon? – I do not want to believe that Beowulf was damned for avarice. But in order not to do so, I have to produce an alternative explanation of *Beowulf* ll. 3074-5, or an emendation, which will allow me to do so. It is not necessary for me to prove that Professor Bliss's explanation is impossible, although (as I hope to show) I have some doubts about its acceptability.

I start with a few general observations. First, it is my opinion that, if the poet meant what Professor Bliss says he meant, he deserves criticism for failing to make it clearer and for concealing vital clues. Professor Bliss requires us to believe that in

Beowulf l. 2747   Bio nu on ofoste,   þæt ic ærwelan,
goldæht ongite,   gearo sceawige
swegle searogimmas,   þæt ic ðy seft mæge
æfter maððumwelan   min alætan
lif ond leodscipe,   þone ic longe heold[2]

Beowulf displays what 'is plainly an improper attitude towards treasure, and unmistakably savours of avarice. Later, in his dying speech, Beowulf adopts a different attitude' (p. 58):

Beowulf l. 2794   Ic ðara frætwa   frean ealles ðanc,
wuldurcyninge,   wordum secge,
ecum dryhtne,   þe ic her on starie,
þæs ðe ic moste   minum leodum
ær swyltdæge   swylc gestrynan.

Professor Bliss truncates this quotation with a full stop after *starie* and writes 'This time Beowulf's attitude is irreproachable: he thanks God for bestowing the gold on him' (p. 59). Despite Professor Bliss's later comments on the two lines he does not quote here (p. 63), it can be argued that they cast doubt on the

[2] All quotations from Old English poetic texts are taken from the Anglo-Saxon Poetic Records.

alleged change in Beowulf's attitude, in that they express a sentiment similar to that in

Beowulf l. 2535   Ic mid elne sceall
                gold gegangan,   oðð́e guð nimeð,
                feorhbealu frecne,   frean eowerne!

This doubt is not assuaged by my failure to find any evidence in *Beowulf* ll. 2752–93 for such a dramatic reversal of attitude on the part of the dying Beowulf. He orders Wiglaf to get the treasure. He waits for it. He looks at it. He thanks God for it. He dies – and

Beowulf l. 2819   him of hreðre gewat
                sawol secean   soðfæstra dom,

which I still insist (see below) can be translated 'His soul departed from his body to journey to the doom of righteous men' or 'to the judgement of God upon the just'. Professor Bliss claims that 'the poet has given us an important clue to the part of the context we should look at. The collocation of *gear(w)e* and *sceawian* is paralleled in lines 2747–2751' (p. 58). I do not immediately see why what I should call a similarity (rather than a parallel) in wording is evidence for a dissimilarity in attitude. I am not even sure that such a similarity is evidence for anything. Some years ago, I drew attention to the dangers of using one passage from a poem in an attempt to *prove* something about another passage from the same poem.[3] I stand by these comments, despite T. F. Hoad's dismissal of them among 'the polemics, which seem less important',[4] and would extend them to verbal similarities and parallels. A glance at a KWIC concordance of *Beowulf* will show how frequently an identical or a similar collocation occurs two or three times in contexts where there is no parallel of meaning. I do not claim that members of an Anglo-Saxon audience were incapable of picking up hints and implications.[5] But I must confess that I find it a little difficult to understand how and why they would dismiss as insignificant the verbal parallels or similarities in *Beowulf* l. 246 *gearwe ne wisson* and *Beowulf* l. 878 *gearwe ne wiston*, in *Beowulf* l. 2062 *con him land geare* and *Beowulf* l. 2070 *þæt ðu geare cunne*, and in *Beowulf* l. 2339 *wisse he gearwe* and *Beowulf* l. 2725 *wisse he gearwe*, and yet immediately grasp the deep significance of that in *Beowulf* l. 2748 *gearo sceawige* and *Beowulf* l. 3074 *gearwor hæfde / ... gesceawod*. That reliance on verbal parallelism can be

[3] *ASE* 4 (1975), 23–4.
[4] *RES* 28 (1977), 193–4. I must however admit that the remarks on metre to which Professor Hoad objected did misrepresent Professor Bliss's position and take this opportunity of offering a public apology. Whether they did in fact completely 'miss the mark' is a question to which I hope to return. [1987. See now *OES* §2780, and item 17, fn. 7 below.]
[5] See *Neophilologus* 47 (1963), 128.

a dangerous game in formulaic poetry is further demonstrated in my discussion of *soðfæstra dom* below.

Second, I return to Professor Bliss's last sentence, which I have already quoted. According to Klaeber, 'Beowulf's fifty years' reign (2209) – which would leave him a nonagenarian at the time of the final battle – is meant only as a sort of poetic formula.'[6] None the less, he was no chicken – *Beowulf* l. 2421 *ðone gomelan*, *Beowulf* l. 2800 *frode feorhlege*, *Beowulf* l. 2817 *þam gomelan*, *Beowulf* l. 3095 *gomol*, and *Beowulf* l. 3136 *har hilderinc*. Professor Bliss's remarks in my opinion depend on the assumption that the Beowulf who thanked God in his youth forgot Him in his old age until the moment of death. This is only one of a series of assumptions which are accepted as facts by those who insist that Beowulf was damned and to which I have previously objected.[7] At the risk of becoming a bore, I have to repeat my objection to being continually jostled past one arbitrarily closed gate after another by a regular and sequential choice of that particular interpretation which suits the theory that Beowulf was damned. Beowulf was warned by Hrothgar against pride and greed and became proud and greedy; no mention of the fact that Beowulf was warned by Hrothgar that he must die – and did. The words of Wiglaf which can be accepted as criticizing Beowulf (*Beowulf* ll. 2642–6 and 3077–8) are frequently cited; no mention of the lines in which Wiglaf asserts that Beowulf will wait long in the keeping of the Almighty (*Beowulf* ll. 3107–9). Wiglaf's comment that the Geats could not dissuade Beowulf from fighting the dragon (*Beowulf* ll. 3079–83) are much used; no mention of what Beowulf's reputation would have been if he had been so dissuaded.[8] Beowulf attacked the dragon without adequate precautions and single-handed; no

---

[6] Fr. Klaeber *Beowulf and the Fight at Finnsburg*, 3rd edn with First and Second Supplements (Boston, 1950) (hereafter referred to as Klaeber *Beowulf*), p. xlv.

[7] See *Neophilologus* 47 (1963), 126–38 and *Beowulf*, translated by Kevin Crossley-Holland and introduced by Bruce Mitchell (London and New York, 1968), pp. 1–29.

[8] My sole point here is that the matter is not mentioned. Much could be said. It is true that in *Beowulf* ll. 862–3 the poet says that Hrothgar was not blamed although he did not fight against Grendel *ac þæt wæs god cyning*. John Leyerle (*MÆ* 34 (1965), 92 and 95) argues that 'Hroðgar's restraint in avoiding battle with Grendel was the prudent choice of a lesser evil. . . . Beowulf does not emulate the long-enduring restraint of Hroðgar. . . .' But these two lines read to me more like an apologetic afterthought than an enthusiastic encomium. (For the reasons given in *ASE* 4 (1975), 17–23, I resist the temptation to construe *wæs* as 'had been', although I should like to hear how various scops rendered the half-line.) Here again the danger of using one passage to *prove* something about another arises. Commenting on the apparent contradiction between *Beowulf* ll. 202–4 and *Beowulf* ll. 415–18 on the one hand and *Beowulf* 1992b–7a on the other (Beowulf was – and yet was not – encouraged to seek battle with Grendel), Kenneth Sisam (*The Structure of* Beowulf (Oxford, 1965), p. 46) writes: 'This illustrates a way of presentation which I have noted elsewhere: the poet exaggerates a mood or argument in order to make a strong impression, and at another place, for the same immediate purpose, says something inconsistent.' The poet's frequent concern with the effect of the moment is a feature of *Beowulf* which is in my opinion too often overlooked.

mention of the iron shield, of the sword which failed, of Wiglaf and the ten warriors who also failed.

Third, Professor Bliss tells us (pp. 49–50) that

> many readers of *Beowulf* find it difficult to accept the conclusion that Beowulf was damned, and to refute it it is customary to cite lines 2819–2820:
>
> > him of hreðre gewat
> > sawol secean   soðfæstra dom.
>
> Translations of *soðfæstra dom* vary, but Tolkien's interpretation may be taken as typical: 'the glory that belongs (in eternity) to the just, or the judgment of God upon the just.' Of course, if Beowulf was 'just' in this sense it is not possible that he can have been damned. In fact the standard translation of *soðfæstra dom* can hardly be defended. Tolkien himself notes that '*soðfæstra dom* could by itself have meant simply the "esteem of the true-judging", that *dom* which Beowulf as a young man had declared to be the prime motive of noble conduct'; it would be more accurate to say that this is what the phrase *must* mean. . . .
>
> There seems to be no reason at all why we should not translate lines 2819–2820 as follows: 'his spirit departed from his breast, hoping for the esteem of the true-judging.'

He supports this interpretation by a number of parallels (pp. 49–51). I agree that it is possible, though it seems to me somewhat strained: *secean* is given the sense 'hope for' rather than the more obvious 'seek'; *dom* is given the sense 'esteem' – for which no parallels are offered; and a translation is adopted which runs contrary to the expectation aroused by the syntax, for one would expect the infinitive to express the object of the journey. Be that as it may, the claims that *soðfæstra dom* 'must mean' 'the esteem of the true-judging' and 'that the standard translation . . . can hardly be defended' are demonstrably false. *Dom*, says Professor Bliss (p. 49), is a 'common word in Old English poetry, and it is very frequently preceded by a qualifying genitive; in every single instance the qualifying genitive specifies the author of the judgment, not its subject – the judger, not the judged.' I cannot see the logic of the argument that, because in all the examples known to Professor Bliss the genitive dependent on *dom* is subjective, it is impossible for *dom* to govern an objective genitive. Since the objective genitive is well established in OE, the implicit argument is the unacceptable 'because there are no parallel examples, this can not be one'. A more thorough examination of the contexts in which *soðfæst* and *dom* appear – with the aid of Bessinger and Smith's *Concordance to the Anglo-Saxon Poetic Records*, which was not available when Professor Bliss wrote – justifies my reluctance to accept his argument.

An objective genitive – referring to the judged, not the judger – occurs with *dom* in

Christ C l. 1232   Ðonne biðgæsta dom   fore gode sceaden
wera cneorissum,   swa hi geworhtun ær,
þær bið on eadgum   eðgesyne
þreo tacen somod,   þæs þe hi hyra þeodnes wel
wordum ond weorcum   willan heoldon.

That *soðfæst* can mean the opposite of 'sinful' is demonstrated by *Christ and Satan* ll. 608–58, *Soul and Body* i. 145–7, and

Phoenix l. 521   Hat bið monegum
egeslic æled,   þonne anra gehwylc,
soðfæst ge synnig,   sawel mid lice,
from moldgrafum   seceð meotudes dom,
forhtafæred.

I find the phrase *soðfæstra sawla* (or minor variants thereof) in *Exodus* l. 544, *Andreas* l. 228, *Christ A* l. 53, *Guthlac A* ll. 22, 567, and 790, and in

Daniel l. 393   And þec haligra   heortan cræftas,
soðfæstra gehwæs   sawle and gastas,
lofiað liffrean,   lean sellende
eallum eadmodum,   ece drihten!

More such evidence is available. But this is sufficient to justify us accepting, if we wish, 'the standard translation of *soðfæstra dom*'.[9]

But Professor Bliss's interpretation of *Beowulf* ll. 3074–5 does not collapse merely because I do not like the interpretation of *Beowulf* which its acceptance involves. So we must now ask whether we are bound to accept it to the exclusion of all other versions. My answer is 'No'.

I have to confess that I find his argument circular. He claims that the poet tells us that Beowulf 'incurred damnation' (p. 48); that

> we already know that Beowulf *did* become subject to the effects of the curse, so that the poet has no need to tell us that God did not intervene on his behalf; what we still need to know is *why* God did not intervene. We may therefore expect lines 3074–3075 to make some statement about

[9] Although *soðfæst* is used of both God, e.g. *Paris Psalter* 118. 137 *Drihten is soðfæst*, and of men, e.g. *Paris Psalter* 93. 18 *hi soðfæste sneome gehæftað*, it is likely that *soðfæst* in *Paris Psalter* 87. 13 *and min gebed morgena gehwylce / fore sylfne þe soðfæst became* is to be taken as accusative rather than nominative; cf. *Beowulf* l. 2704 *biter and beaduscearp* (dative with *wæll-seaxe*) and *Guthlac B* l. 1262 *soden sorgwælmum* (accusative with *þe*).

Whether or not to follow Charles Donahue (*Traditio* 21 (1965), 109–10) in seeing 'a deeply serious pun' in *soðfæstra dom* must be a matter of personal choice.

Beowulf's relationship to God, perhaps in general, or perhaps especially in connection with treasure (p. 52);

and that 'now at last we know why God did not intervene' (p. 59). I cannot see how 'we know' any of this unless we have already accepted Professor Bliss's interpretation of *Beowulf* ll. 3074–5 or some other interpretation which makes these two lines a syntactical unit completely independent of what goes before. If they mean something similar to *Beowulf* ll. 3054–7 – in other words, if they mean that God somehow showed favour to Beowulf and that Beowulf therefore escaped damnation, 'we know' none of these things. There is no contextual reason why *Beowulf* ll. 3074–5 should not carry such a meaning. Professor Bliss's chiastic pattern (pp. 51–2) would still be preserved, with the B elements – *Beowulf* ll. 3054b–7 and *Beowulf* ll. 3074–5 – parallel rather than antithetic. The statement that 'this is to misunderstand the nature of the parallelism' is true only if we accept his interpretation of the passage. If we do not, there is no reason why we should not 'expect lines 3074–3075 to make some statement about' God's intervention on behalf of Beowulf. Indeed, such an interpretation would give more point to *Beowulf* ll. 3058–62a, which could be taken as implying that Beowulf was God's instrument and as preparing us for a contrast between the fates of the dragon and of Beowulf.

But my major difficulty is with the last words in Professor Bliss's translation: 'than he did now'. 'A literal translation', he says (p. 57), 'must therefore run: "In the past he had not at all seen and understood the gold-bestowing favour of God more clearly [than he did now]."' Leaving aside as irrelevant for my purposes E. G. Stanley's claim that 'where a hoard is being discussed, *agend* must be its owner.... It must be the Dragon',[10] but accepting the possibility that there is here a comparison between Beowulf's differing attitudes at two different points in time, I find Professor Bliss's assignment of the temporal references hard to accept. His claim is that 'in the past' refers specifically to *Beowulf* ll. 2747–51 and 'now' to *Beowulf* ll. 2794–6. I doubt the former and do not think that 'now' can be right, for 'now' (i.e. by *Beowulf* ll. 3074–5) Beowulf is dead and, if we follow Professor Bliss, in Hell. So his literal translation should read: 'When he spoke lines 2747–51, he had not at all seen and understood the gold-bestowing favour of God more clearly [than he did when he spoke lines 2794–6].' I am very dubious about the attachment of such significance to two speeches out of the many made by Beowulf. I have already voiced my doubts about the value of the 'important clue' which, according to Professor Bliss, ensures that the hearers (or, if you wish, readers) of the poem will immediately associate *ær* with *Beowulf* ll. 2747–51. As for the association of *gearwor* with *Beowulf* ll. 2794–6, I find no similar examples in my collections. When the

[10] *Studies in Old English Literature in Honor of Arthur G. Brodeur* ed. Stanley B. Greenfield (Oregon, 1963) (hereafter cited as Stanley), p. 144.

second element of a comparison is left unexpressed, the reference is in my experience to the immediate context, as Professor Bliss implies (p. 56) when he translates

> *Beowulf* l. 913 He þær eallum wearð,
> mæg Higelaces,   manna cynne,
> freondum gefægra

'The kinsman of Hygelac became more pleasing to all mankind and to his friends [than he had been before]' and

> *Beowulf* l. 980 Ða wæs swigra secg,   sunu Eclafes,
> on gylpspræce   guðgeweorca,
> siþðan æþelingas   eorles cræfte
> ofer heanne hrof   hand sceawedon,
> feondes fingras

'Then the son of Ecglaf was more silent in boastful speech of deeds of battle [than he had been before]', i.e. before the action of the *siþðan* clause, which Professor Bliss does not quote.[11] I cannot agree with him when he extends the field of reference to 'the context, either immediate or remote' (p. 58). The most telling example I can think of in his favour would be *Beowulf* l. 980 above if we translated it 'Then the son of Ecglaf was more silent ... [than he had been when he *onband beadurune*] (*Beowulf* l. 501).' Many hearers (or readers) may well have made or may well make this connection. But the vital clue is in the immediate context, as Professor Bliss has shown – and Unferth speaks only once. Those who believe in the overwhelming decisiveness of the only syntactical parallels in extant OE poetry may care to note that in the other three places in which *gearwor* occurs with the second element of the comparison unexpressed – viz. *Andreas* l. 932, *Elene* l. 945, and *Juliana* l. 556 (all with *witan* 'to know') – the implication seems to me 'more clearly [than before]', which seems impossible in *Beowulf* ll. 3074-5. I would argue that, if the missing element in the comparison is temporal (but see below), it is the most recent temporal reference to Beowulf, viz. *Beowulf* l. 3066 *þa he biorges weard / sohte searoniðas*. This would produce the literal translation 'In the past he had not at all seen and understood the gold-bestowing favour of God more clearly [than he did when he went to meet the guardian of the barrow and his subtle enmity].' This would suggest that Beowulf had earned God's favour and was therefore not damned. This would be an unacceptable contradiction of *Beowulf* ll. 3066-73 as interpreted by Professor Bliss unless the

[11] Despite Professor Bliss (p. 56), I take *Beowulf* l. 3038 *syllicran wiht* as implying *þonne Beowulf*. The most certain 'absolute comparative' in my collections is *Dream of the Rood* l. 4 *syllicre treow*, where it seems desperate to suggest '[than any other]'. Here I suspect the influence of an untraced Latin phrase. [1987. See now *OES* §183 and p. 337 below.]

two passages are in some way syntactically linked. They can be if we put a colon after *strude*, as Professor Bliss does, but take *Beowulf* ll. 3074–5 as a noun clause with unexpressed *þæt* which is the subject of *wæs* in *Beowulf* l. 3066. We find noun clauses with anticipatory demonstrative *þæt* – respectively the object of *wiston* and subject of a verb used impersonally – but with unexpressed conjunction *þæt* in *Beowulf* ll. 798–803 and *Beowulf* ll. 2200–8a. We find a noun clause object of *wite* without anticipatory demonstrative *þæt* and with unexpressed conjunction *þæt* in *Vainglory* ll. 77–80. There seems to me no reason why *Beowulf* ll. 3074–5 should not be a noun clause subject of a verb used impersonally without either demonstrative or conjunction *þæt*.[12]

However, I must admit that, while I find Professor Bliss's interpretation of *Beowulf* ll. 3066–73 the most satisfying I have yet encountered and believe it to be basically right,[13] I am not really satisfied that either his interpretation of the manuscript reading of *Beowulf* ll. 3074–5 or my own has solved the problem; both of them remind me of A. E. Housman's comment that 'chance and the common course of nature will not bring it to pass that the readings of a manuscript are right wherever they are possible and impossible wherever they are wrong; that needs divine intervention.' So, although I started this investigation with no intention of emending, I find myself increasingly attracted by the emendation of *næs* or of *næs he* to *næfne*. I have already shown that we are not bound to accept Professor Bliss's objection that 'this is to misunderstand the nature of the parallelism' (p. 52). I would argue the contrary: that it provides a fitting climax to his own admirable translation of *Beowulf* ll. 3066–73, without the stimulus of which this article would never have been written.

I begin by offering my own translation of *Beowulf* ll. 3074–5 which, apart from the emendation, differs from Professor Bliss's 'literal translation' (p. 57) only in the missing element of the comparison: '... if he had not in the past seen and understood the gold-bestowing favour of God more clearly [than had the dragon]'.

If we read *næfne* for *næs*, we explain the absence of *-ne* as due to haplography. If we read *næfne* for *næs he*, we postulate an unexpressed subject in the conditional clause, citing

---

[12] See further my comments in *NM* 70 (1969), 178–82.

[13] I note here that there is in my opinion no reason why the *swa* clause in *Beowulf* ll. 3066–7a should not be used *apo koinou* with *Beowulf* 3062b–5 and with the *swa* clause which begins in *Beowulf* l. 3069. Professor Bliss decides for the latter (pp. 46–8). His reasoning is sound, but a decision is necessary only because of the limitations of modern punctuation, which reflects the movement of MnE written (rather than spoken) prose and not that of OE poetry and which produces MnE sentences at the expense of OE verse paragraphs. I have developed this point in *RES* 31 (1980), 385–413 (item 18 below).

Genesis B l. 618
>   Gif giet þurh cuscne siodo
> læst mina lara,   þonne gife ic him þæs leohtes genog
> þæs ic þe swa godes   gegired hæbbe

and comparing *Metrical Charm* 4. 6 *Ut, lytel spere, gif her inne sie!* and 4. 15 *Ut, lytel spere, gif her inne sy!* with *Metrical Charm* 4. 12 *Ut, lytel spere, gif hit her inne sy!* An apparent objection to my interpretation is the fact that the verb of the principal clause – *Beowulf* l. 3066 *wæs* – is indicative, whereas, since *næfne* introduces an unfulfilled condition in which the ambiguous *hæfde* is to be taken as preterite subjunctive, we should expect the subjunctive *wære* instead of the indicative *wæs*. This can be countered by reference to

> *Beowulf* l. 1655   Ic þæt unsofte   ealdre gedigde
>   wigge under wætere,   weorc geneþde
>   earfoðlice;   ætrihte wæs
>   guð getwæfed,   nymðe mec god scylde.

Here we have the indicative *wæs* under the same syntactical conditions in a similar situation – another significant 'verbal reminiscence'? In both sentences, the indicative *wæs* gives added vividness and dramatic point: Beowulf was finished, but God saved him; 'Thus it was' becomes 'Thus it would have been'. By taking the unexpressed element in the comparison as the dragon, we provide a contrast to

> *Beowulf* l. 3038   Ær hi þær gesegan   syllicran wiht,
>   wyrm on wonge   wiðerræhtes þær
>   laðne licgean;   wæs se legdraca
>   grimlic, gry[refah],   gledum beswæled

'... they saw there a more wondrous being than Beowulf...'[14] and give point to the mention of the dragon's lack of success in *Beowulf* ll. 3058–62a, so satisfying the expectation aroused by those lines.

This interpretation fits well with Professor Bliss's translation of *Beowulf* ll. 3051–73, but enables those who wish not to believe that Beowulf was damned because of avarice to continue not to believe so. This is my sole aim here: not to 'prove' that Professor Bliss must be wrong, merely to satisfy myself that he need not be right.

So I do not pursue the quite different problem raised by Professor Stanley, who cites Alcuin as authority for the view 'that *paganus* and *perditus* are cause and effect, that to be heathen is to be damned', beyond saying that it does not automatically follow that this was necessarily the view of all Anglo-Saxon Christians – whatever the depth of their theological knowledge and the intensity

[14] See fn. 11.

of their commitment – and of the *Beowulf* poet in particular. He, with others, may have shared what Professor Stanley calls 'our reluctance' 'to believe that Beowulf is damned'.[15] Professor Bliss, however, argues that 'Beowulf believes that he has done well, and that posterity will judge him as favourably as his own retainers do; but in fact he is heading for the damnation which he has incurred by *unwittingly* rendering himself liable to the curse' (pp. 50–1; my italics). Despite Professor Bliss's further explanation of the significance of the curse (p. 60) and his phrase 'the impurity of his motives' (p. 63) – who would escape condemnation on this ground? – I fear that this explanation reduces *Beowulf* for me to something approaching the status of an Old English analogue of the story of the Scottish preacher who reached the fiftieth head in his exposition of 'the infinite maircy and compassion of the Lord' by picturing the Lord in His infinite maircy and compassion gazing down at those who had sinned unwittingly and in ignorance as they writhed in the torments and agonies of Hell. 'And those ignorant sinners,' thundered the preacher, 'writhing in the torments and agonies of Hell, will look up to the Lord and will cry "Lord, we didna ken, we didna ken." And the Lord, in His infinite maircy and compassion, will look down upon those ignorant sinners writhing in the torments and agonies of Hell and will say "Well, ye ken the noo!"' I prefer to think and feel otherwise.

But I should like to end by saying that in my opinion Professor Bliss's contribution to the study of *Beowulf* ll. 3066–73 is a decisive one and by surmising that mine will not be the last words on *Beowulf* ll. 3074–5.

---

[15] Stanley, pp. 149–51. [1987. On this point see now item 5 below.]

5
1987: Postscript on *Beowulf*

Forty years have passed since I first became acquainted with *Beowulf*. It was in the height of an Australian summer and my first copy of Klaeber's great edition still bears the marks of that hot and sweaty encounter, Klaeber in his red cover and me in my black shorts. I remember my long wrestle with what I assumed to be the preposition *in* in l. 1300, a wrestle which did not end until I deigned to use the glossary; hence my insistence that undergraduates immediately master the conventions of their glossary and use it devotedly. I remember the difficulty I had in finding my way around Klaeber, a difficulty I still have; hence my advice to those who send me their work for criticism that they should bear in mind above most things the maxim 'Be kind to the reader.' I remember the confusion and near-despair which resulted from my too-early encounter with Chambers *Beowulf* (2nd edn); hence my reluctance to recommend pupils to read books which get them bogged down in controversies of secondary concern.

Forty years on, I see two things as vital to an understanding and appreciation of *Beowulf*. The first is the importance of the words *edhwyrft* (l. 1281) and *wyrp* (l. 1315) and of the phrase *Bruc ealles well!* (l. 2162) in a poem which begins with a leaderless people and a funeral and ends with a funeral and a leaderless people, and which concerns itself so much with the rise and fall, the life and death, of ordinary individuals, of kings, and of nations. The second is the folly of the idea that such a poem can have one 'meaning' – beyond, of course, the fact that it is a poem. Hence my decreasing patience with articles and books which argue (for instance) whether the mention of fire in connection with Heorot in ll. 81–5 and 781b–2a or the reference to a dragon in ll. 884a–97 was or was not meant to bring to the mind of the audience the burning of Beowulf's hall or the death of Beowulf in conflict with a dragon. For behind such arguments lies the conscious or unconscious assumption that the audience of *Beowulf* was homogeneous; that all its members reacted in the same way, had all heard – or not heard – the story before hearing the poem, had all heard – or not heard – the poem before; were all equally intelligent and equally knowledgeable about theology or the Church Fathers or scriptural exegesis or whatever; were all equally sensitive and capable – or insensitive and incapable – of making such connexions. A moment's comparison with any modern audience for (say) *Macbeth* at a Stratford (Warwickshire) performance should reveal the folly of this; it will embrace a wide spectrum from the reluctant schoolboy dragged into the bus as he tried to escape so that he could go fishing, to the producer from Stratford Ontario agog to see how the clever English interpreters of Shakespeare have improved his original this year. So I am prepared for a multiplicity of interpretations. What I cannot tolerate is the insistence that *this* is *the* meaning of *Beowulf*.

But each reader will have his own interpretation. Broadly speaking, my own view has not changed much over the last thirty years. I still see *Beowulf* 'as a triumphant affirmation of the value of a good life'. I still agree with the French pupil who wrote 'Before being a dirge, *Beowulf* is a song of joy, of confidence in life, in the heroism displayed by man.'[1] I still remain reluctant to believe that Beowulf was damned for the sin of pride or for the sin of avarice[2] or to believe that Beowulf earned admiration as the ideal Germanic hero and damnation as a pagan. I deliberately did not pursue this problem in item 4.[3] But I wish to do so now.

I wish to do so not from any desire to convert those who believe that *Beowulf* is a pessimistic poem to my own view that it is an optimistic one but from a feeling that I ought to explain why I continue to disagree with them and in particular why, while agreeing that some Anglo-Saxon readers or hearers may have shared them, I cannot share the views expressed by Ushigaki, for whom the poem is essentially pessimistic –

> Seen in this way, our poet seems to tell us finally: heroism is itself a fine thing in so far as it evokes our admiration and sympathy, whether it ends in success or failure or even death, but it is also essentially and fatally bad, rooted as it is in a ferocious and destructive impulse and, therefore, threatening to human life. Moreover, there is an undercurrent in the work, not expressed as such, but very strong and deep, which might also be called philosophical and religious. In our poet's fundamentally pessimistic view, which stands in marked contrast with Chaucer's essentially optimistic one, the world is full of strifes and evils, life is uncertain, human efforts are often vain, with good intentions ending in bạd results, and human knowledge is extremely limited and, to crown it all, death is nothing but a mystery: in a word, life in this world is a tiny spot of light flickering in the vast, unknown darkness[4] –

[1] See pp. 29 and 15 above.
[2] See p. 9 above and item 4, *passim*.
[3] See p. 39 above.
[4] Ushigaki 1985a, p. 19 (see below). The sudden death on 16 January 1986 of Professor Hiroto Ushigaki of Kagoshima University robbed us of a gifted *Beowulf* scholar. His publications include the following five sensitive and well-written essays which deserve to be better known than they appear to be:

or by Stanley, who sees Beowulf as damned because he is not a Christian:

> One thing, however, may be discerned clearly in *Beowulf*, that though a heathen may be virtuous, his life being without faith is, in the strictest sense of the words, without hope.[5]

I find myself more in sympathy with Robinson, who argues that the poet, with poignant ambiguity, leaves Beowulf's fate open:

> In *lofgeornost* they could only have seen that the hero lived and died in ignorance of Christian truth. He was gentle, kind, and self-sacrificing and had almost every other virtue. By any human standard of judgment he would seem deserving of a place in Heaven. But human standards are of no consequence in circumstances such as these. It is the judgment of another, more mysterious power that matters here.[6]

But it seems to me that, if we follow him and accept the possibility that Stanley is right in arguing that *lofgeornost* means 'most vainglorious' (a question which I discuss below), there is little room for real ambiguity about Beowulf's fate.

This problem is so vast that I must limit the discussion. I begin by admitting that my view is based on feeling. But feeling is not out of place when one is concerned with poetry. Indeed, when I contemplate the great variety of totally irreconcilable interpretations of *Beowulf* which have been produced by thinking, I am tempted to go further and to claim that feeling rather than thought should be paramount.

In the past I have spoken of the dangers of trying to prove something about one passage of *Beowulf* from another,[7] have expressed my objection to being continually jostled past one arbitrarily closed gate after another by a regular

'The Image of "God Cyning" in *Beowulf*: A Philological Study', *Studies in English Literature* (Tokyo), *English Number* (1982), 63–78 (hereafter cited as Ushigaki 1982);
'The Ideal of Kingship in *Beowulf*: Mainly with Words as Evidence', *Cultural Science Review of Kagoshima University* 19 (1983), 25–45 (hereafter cited as Ushigaki 1983);
'The Image of Beowulf as King and Hero: Some Interpretative and Critical Problems', *Studies in English Literature* (Tokyo), *English Number* (1985), 3–20 (hereafter cited as Ushigaki 1985a);
'On the Backslide of the Danes: *Beowulf*, ll. 175–88', *Cultural Science Review of Kagoshima University* 21 (1985), 41–59 (hereafter cited as Ushigaki 1985b);
'On the Moral Reflection of Beowulf: *Beowulf*, ll. 2327b–32', *Kagoshima Studies in English Language and Literature* 17 (1986), 1–15 (hereafter cited as Ushigaki 1986).

A fuller list of his writings will be found in *Poetica* (Tokyo), 25–6 (1987), 202–3. To them must be added a Review Article, Raymond P. Tripp, Jr *More About the Fight with the Dragon: Beowulf 2208b–3182, Commentary, Edition, and Translation* (Lanham, 1983) in *Poetica* (Tokyo), 25–6 (1987), 193–200.

[5] E. G. Stanley '*Hæthenra Hyht* in *Beowulf*', *Studies in Old English Literature in Honor of Arthur G. Brodeur* ed. Stanley B. Greenfield (Oregon, 1963) (hereafter cited as Stanley), p. 151.
[6] Fred C. Robinson Beowulf *and the Appositive Style* (Tennessee, 1985) (hereafter cited as Robinson), pp. 81–2.
[7] See p. 166 below.

and sequential choice of that particular interpretation which suits the theory that Beowulf was damned,[8] and have urged the desirability of agreeing to disagree instead of seeking to convert others to my own point of view.[9] A brief discussion of the contradiction – or apparent contradiction – between *Beowulf* ll. 86–98 and 170–88 will, I hope, demonstrate what I mean. The first passage tells how the *scop* sings a song in Heorot about the creation of the earth and the second tells how the Danes, afflicted by the attacks of Grendel, worship heathen gods and offer sacrifices to idols – actions which the poet condemns and which have led modern scholars to ask why the presumably Christian Danes relapse to heathenism.

Faced with this dilemma, Brodeur, after discussing earlier solutions, writes:

> This clearly describes a general and undivided appeal by the great men of the Danes to their pagan gods, not the apostasy of a mere faction led by heathen priests.... Nor can the idol-worship of the Danes be explained as a relapse.... The poet tells us in the plainest terms that the Danes – all of them – were heathen.... We are, then, compelled to the conclusion that the poet knew the Danes were, and always had been, pagan ... sinners not from intent, but from inherited ignorance.[10]

I cannot discuss all the details of Brodeur's argument. But the presence of *hwilum* in l. 175 and the absence of *næfre* from ll. 180–3, where the only negative is *ne*, shows that there are no linguistic grounds for his quoted statement that this cannot 'be explained as a relapse'. And it is certainly possible – if not, as Ushigaki put it, 'highly probable' – that 'the Excursus [*Beowulf* ll. 175–88] refers obliquely, but critically, to the current religious reality' (Ushigaki 1985b, p. 50); Wentersdorf has attested to that.[11] But even if we accept Brodeur's quoted view that 'the poet knew the Danes were, and always had been, pagan', the inconsistency remains but in reverse; the question is no longer 'Why did the Christian Danes worship idols?' but 'Why did the heathen Danes have a Christian *scop*?' It will not do to say with Brodeur (p. 217) that the Danes 'were in fact pagans.... But in spirit, as their words and acts reveal them, they are essentially Christian.'

So Brodeur has not convinced me that I cannot continue to believe in the possibility of a relapse, especially when my personal response to Brodeur's statement (p. 185) that *Beowulf* was 'composed in an effectively converted England' is the reflection 'Has there ever been such a place?' Two sensitive scholars have recently proposed other ways of looking at it. First, Ushigaki

[8] See p. 33.
[9] See p. 30, fn. 1.
[10] Arthur Gilchrist Brodeur *The Art of* Beowulf (Berkeley, Cal., 1959) (hereafter cited as Brodeur), pp. 198, 198, 199, 199, and 205.
[11] Karl P. Wentersdorf '*Beowulf*: The Paganism of Hrothgar's Danes', *SP* 78.5 (1981), 91–119.

(1985b, pp. 51–2), discussing the shift from pagan to Christian in Anglo-Saxon England, suggests that

> in the process of this epochal change, there could be broadly two possible alternatives open to the Christian poet: one being to modify the heathen world in the light of Christian sense of values and ideals, to blend the two so that they might not conflict with each other, though there would necessarily be some cases in which the poet would have difficulty in bringing about an ideal amalgamation of heroic ethos and Christian morality and have no other choice but to remain equivocal, and the other being to set forth the hopefulness of Christian faith by rejecting heathenism once for all as an evil way of life; in this case condemnation and religious didacticism will often be at the cost of the poetic integration. The most probable suggestion in all this is that the *Beowulf*-poet's general principle of composition was basically the former but in the Excursus at issue he made an exceptional choice.... Hence an inconsistency in description and artistic blemish.

This explanation asks us to accept the relapse of the Danes and to explain it as an inconsistency due to what I have called elsewhere 'the poet's frequent concern with the effect of the moment'[12] – a remedy also invoked by Irving in an interpretation previously rejected by Ushigaki (1985b, pp. 46–7).

Second, Robinson has recently given what I would characterize as the most convincing expression of a proposition – a proposition which I accept – that amphiboly (a word defined in *OED* as 'ambiguous discourse; a sentence which can be construed in two distinct senses; a quibble') can be present in OE poetry and has provided us with the concept of 'apposed meanings', an original and fruitful term which will – or ought to – become an accepted and valuable part of our critical vocabulary; for an impressive illustration see his remarks on *Beowulf* l. 2469 (pp. 51–2). The last paragraph of his Preface demands – repeat demands – the close attention of all Old English scholars. Indeed, what he says of the meanings of words, of punctuation (including capitalization), and of syntax, holds also in my opinion for inflexions; see *OES* §§14–15 and 18–20 and the General Index s.v. 'emendation'. Writing about *Beowulf* l. 92, Robinson remarks (p. 37):

> The only interpretation of *se ælmihtiga* that would be logically impossible is the one most commonly held by modern students and scholars of the poem, who assume from editors' capitalization of *Ælmihtiga* that this is an unambiguous reference to the Christian Deity and therefore evidence that the scop in Heorot is a Christian. *Beowulf* takes place in a heathen realm in a heathen age, and the scop's creation hymn is one that any pious

[12] See p. 33, fn. 8.

heathen might sing. The assumption that now and again the heathen characters turn Christian and address themselves to the Christian Deity makes a muddle of the poet's artful strategy of using inherent ambiguities in the Christianized Old English vocabulary to present the men of old favorably and yet honestly to a Christian Anglo-Saxon audience.

This is an imaginative solution and I have no doubt that, of the poet's hearers or readers, some of those who held Christian beliefs understood the passage in Robinson's way. But the intensity of belief among those hearers and readers must have varied and I have the uneasy feeling that it is unlikely that what he calls 'the poet's artful strategy' was apprehended by even all those who had some acquaintance with or some belief in Christianity. Such a concept inevitably involves some element of circular argument in that it rests on assumptions about the poet's 'intentions'. Indeed, attractive and brilliant as Robinson's presentation is, I find it hard to believe that the poet was always in such firm control of his material and always had such a clear understanding of the strategy as Robinson suggests.

Hence I conclude that there is no 'right answer' and allow myself to continue to believe in the possibility that the poet is describing a relapse in *Beowulf* ll. 175–88. Here I have chosen to go through a different gate. As always, which gate I choose will help to determine which view of *Beowulf* I adopt (or is it *vice versa?*). There are many such gates for the reader of *Beowulf*, but perhaps the most crucial choice concerns the exit gate, which is marked *lofgeornost*. Here again my choice differs from that of Stanley and Robinson.

Anyone discussing the meaning of *lofgeornost* or any other OE compound must now heed Robinson's warning (Preface, second page): 'Often and unconsciously readers have had their interpretations of the poem restricted or even predetermined by glossaries and dictionaries which arbitrarily disambiguate the grammar of nominal compounds and the meanings of polysemous words.' As he suggests by precept and example throughout the book, all meanings of a word are available wherever it occurs and the context activates one meaning or more and leaves others inert. This flexibility, he argues, is present in the superlative *lofgeornost*, which follows three superlatives expressing approval. The question is: does *lofgeornost* express approval or disapproval? Or is that too stark an opposition?

Stanley plumps for disapproval. After observing that *mildust*, *monðwærust*, and *liðost*, express praise, he writes (pp. 147–8):

> The word *lofgeornost* has different associations. If the word had been *domgeornost* we might have been able to think of Beowulf as a man who, having lived the life of a virtuous pagan, is not afraid of judgment, but seeks it most eagerly, full of hope in justice, and therefore hope of glory.

> But the word is *lofgeornost*. Perhaps it can be used as a superlative of praise as the editors and commentators think. ...
> Perhaps the word *lofgeorn* too had a favorable sense of which no example survives, unless it be the use of the superlative at the end of *Beowulf*. In an unfavorable sense the word occurs often.

But he goes on to imply that 'perhaps' is to be understood as a negative and that the poet is expressing Christian disapproval. Robinson (pp. 81–2) agrees, with the comment that 'Stanley ... discusses *lofgeornost* with insight and accuracy' (p. 103, n. 55):

> But the *Beowulf* poet apposes one final superlative to make the last word of his poem: Beowulf was *lofgeornost*, 'the most eager for praise' or 'most vainglorious'. Far from the name of a Christian virtue, this word occurs most often in Anglo-Saxon homiletic discussions of the cardinal sins. Bosworth-Toller, it is true, tries to set up a positive sense for the word ('most eager to deserve praise'), but the only documentation for this meaning is the last line in *Beowulf*. Even if there were a positive, Christian sense of *lofgeorn*, would a contemporary of the poet's have thought such a meaning available to the hero's pagan mourners? The audience is by this time far too well-practiced in discriminating between pagan and Christian senses of words, far too aware of how the language of the poem bears witness to the theological predicament of the people described by that language. In *lofgeornost* they could only have seen that the hero lived and died in ignorance of Christian truth. He was gentle, kind, and self-sacrificing and had almost every other virtue. By any human standard of judgment he would seem deserving of a place in Heaven. But human standards are of no consequence in circumstances such as these. It is the judgment of another, more mysterious power that matters here. ...

I concede that any positive Christian sense of *lofgeorn* would not have been available to the hero's pagan mourners. However, this is also true of negative Christian meanings. And both propositions would hold for the poet's pagan hearers or readers.

As far as I can see, there are three possible (or proposed) meanings for *lofgeornost* awaiting activization. They are (1) 'most eager for pre-Christian, pagan *lof*'; (2) 'most eager for Christian *lof*' (*Seafarer* ll. 72–80a); (3) 'most vainglorious', as proposed by Stanley and accepted by Robinson. (It is perhaps worth noting here that meanings (1) and (2) seem to imply the form *lof-geornost*, as opposed to meaning (3) *lofgeorn-ost*.) I am very uneasy about meaning (3) and hope to demonstrate why by an examination of the ten instances of the positive form *lofgeorn* recorded in the *Microfiche Concordance*. All these are late – so anyone opting for an earlier date for *Beowulf* (as Robinson (p. 6) is 'inclined' to do) has to explain why they are necessarily relevant to *Beowulf* – and all are in what can be called Christian texts: five from the *Benedictine Rule*, three *iactantia* examples (three manuscripts of *ÆLS* 16. 300), *WHom* 10c. 128, and *WPol* 4 (ed. Jost, p. 262) 2. There are no comparatives and the only superlative is that in *Beowulf* l. 3182.

I have not yet found any evidence or seen it suggested that the simplex *lof*, its derivatives, or its compounds apart from *lofgeorn*, imply something bad or undesirable. What is the evidence that *lofgeorn* means 'vainglorious'? Whitelock, cited by Robinson, is incomprehensible for our purposes; it is not clear whether she is referring to *lofgeorn* in *ÆLS* 16. 300 or to some other word like *gilpgeorn*.[13] Where is the evidence for Stanley's statement (p. 148) 'In an unfavorable sense the word occurs often' and in particular for the sense 'vainglorious'?

Four of the *Benedictine Rule* examples occur in chapter 31 *De cellarario monasterii qualis sit Be mynstres hordere*: *BenR* 31. 1, 31. 16. All represent Latin *prodigus* 'spendthrift, wasteful'; Hanslik records no variants.[14] *BenRGl* 61. 6 and 62. 3 read *cystig*, which is glossed by Bosworth-Toller as '*munificent, benevolent, bountiful, liberal, generous, good*; munificus, largus, probus, bonus'. It is hard to see 'vainglorious' here. Indeed, as the Revd Dunstan Adams OSB, Monk of Ampleforth, has suggested to me in a private communication, better links between *prodigus* and *lofgeorn* can be found in either the sense 'recklessly wasteful' – the cellarer of the monastery's good, Beowulf of his life – or the sense 'recklessly generous of self', 'prodigal' in the best sense – compare the 'prodigal father' of Luke 15. 11–32 – for St Benedict goes on to exhort the cellarer to humility and selfless concern for the well-being of the brethren collectively and individually. Both these senses bring to mind Christ the Saviour-Champion of his people – as Klaeber has it, 'we might even feel inclined to recognize features of the Christian Savior in the destroyer of hellish fiends, the warrior brave and gentle, blameless in thought and deed, the king that dies for his people'[15] – and will remind those who heard it of the paper given by Thomas D. Hill at the 1985 ISAS conference[16] in which he argued that the 'variegated obit' was a sign of approbation, that *Beowulf* ends with one, and that therefore the poet thought that Beowulf, like the patriarchs, was saved. I do not stress the point but it is a tantalizing ambiguity.

The last example from *BenR* is *BenR* 18. 17 *Ne sy nan lofgeorn ne wilnigende þæt his dæda halige gesæde sien ær hie halige weorðan* . . . representing Latin *Non velle*

[13] See Robinson, p. 103, n. 55. On *gilpgeorn* see Stanley, p. 148.

[14] Rudolph Hanslik *Benedicti Regula* (Corpus Scriptorum Ecclesiasticorum Latinorum 75, Vienna, 1960).

[15] Klaeber ed. *Beowulf*, 3rd edn (Boston, 1941), p. li.

[16] 'The "Variegated Obit" as an Historiographic Motif in Old English Poetry and Anglo-Latin Historical Literature.'

dici sanctum antequam sit, rendered by *BenRGl* 22. 3 *na nellan beon gesæið halig ærðampe he sig.* Here *lofgeorn* seems to sum up or to be glossed by what follows. It can mean 'eager for praise, for a good reputation'. But 'vainglorious' seems to be stretching it a bit. The same can be said of *WHom* 10.c 127 *Se ðe wære idelgeorn weorðe se notgeorn. Se ðe wære lofgeorn for idelan weorðscype weorðe se carfull hu he swypast mæge gecweman his drihtne,* where one would expect the compounds *idelgeorn, notgeorn,* and *lofgeorn,* to be similarly interpreted – 'idleness-eager', 'employment-eager', and 'praise-eager' – and where, I would argue, the phrase *for idelan weorðscype* would be tautologic if *lofgeorn* meant 'vainglorious'. In *WPol* 4 (ed. Jost, p. 262) 2 *sume we synt gewunode þæt we syn to liðie and to lofgeorne and we willwyrdað mannum æfter freondscipe and þurh þæt olæcað oftost on unnyt* 'some of us are accustomed to be too pliant and too eager for praise', *to* must mean 'too'; there is no negative and so 'not at all' (*OES* §§1142–3) is impossible. Is Wulfstan really saying that it is a good thing for bishops to be somewhat vainglorious but that they should not overdo it? (I intend this as a rhetorical question demanding the answer 'No'.)

This leaves *ÆLS* 16. 300 *Se seofoða leahter is iactantia gecweden þæt is ydel gylp on ængliscre spræce þæt is ðonne se man bið lofgeorn and mid licetunge færð and deð for gylpe gif he hwæt dælan wile and bið þonne se hlisa his edlean ðære dæde and his wite andbidað on ðære toweardan worulde,* together with the parallel passages in MSS D and U. Of this, Stanley writes (p. 148): 'In an unfavorable sense the word [*lofgeorn*] occurs often. One example will suffice.... The implications are ominous.' He seems to have chosen the example most favourable to his purpose. But here Ælfric says that *iactantia* is *ydel gylp* and goes on to give a definition of *ydel gylp* in a series of clauses in cumulative coordination. If *lofgeorn* meant 'vainglorious', why did he go on to say *mid licetunge...for gylpe*? I would suggest that *lofgeorn* means 'eager for praise, for a good reputation' here too and that the rest of the sentence is essential to the explanation of *ydel gylp.*

So I find the evidence for *lofgeorn* 'vainglorious' at best very flimsy. The irony – as I see it – is that there was no need for Robinson to follow Stanley in this interpretation. The two-fold apposed meanings of *lofgeornost* he needs could arise quite naturally in the hearers or readers capable of grasping them – *lof* is a proper aim for heroic warriors but not for Christians and Robinson could have written 'But it was not the kind of praise which a Christian could seek or approve' instead of 'or "most vainglorious"' at the end of the first sentence of the passage quoted on p. 47. Some indeed who knew the *iactantia* passage might even have seen 'most vainglorious' as a possible extension. But it is not essential. For me at any rate the importation of the idea of vainglory diminishes the effect of the moving sentences with which Stanley (p. 151) and Robinson (p. 82) end: 'That is why we reread the poem with sadness and compassion of an ideal that avails nothing' and 'All the poetry of *Beowulf* can do is bring the two together in a brief, loving and faintly disquieting apposition.'

But even without the sense 'most vainglorious' for *lofgeornost*, Stanley and Robinson can continue to argue that in one way or another the word carried pejorative implications. Such implications are essential if the poet's 'message' is that *paganus est perditus* and that, being *paganus*, Beowulf is damned. Is it?

Stanley believes that it is, quoting Alcuin's famous letter of 797 and 2 Corinthians 6. 14–15, with the comments 'Alcuin's words make it clear that *paganus* and *perditus* are cause and effect, that to be heathen is to be damned' (p. 149) and 'Christ has no concord with Belial; to be heathen is sin enough. That was Alcuin's view. Nothing in *Beowulf* contradicts it' (p. 150). The statement 'Nothing in *Beowulf* contradicts it' is not only inconclusive – I could write 'Nothing in *Beowulf* supports it except the feelings of those who believe it and interpret *lofgeornost* to suit that belief' – but also dubious – it is possible to interpret *Beowulf* ll. 2819–20 and 3107–9 (both quoted below) as contradicting it.

Godfrey has written

> The English Church on the whole did not produce philosophers or original thinkers, still less heretics, but rather guardians of a tradition, a sacred trust to be maintained for future generations. Bede himself was essentially a traditionalist, and even more so was Alcuin.[17]

But it is not clear that the equation *paganus est perditus* was regarded by Anglo-Saxons as an essential part of the tradition. Despite his protestations (pp. 149–50), Stanley has not established that the Anglo-Saxon Church taught the doctrine uniformly and without dispute. 1 Peter 4. 5–6 reads

> οἳ ἀποδώσουσι λόγον τῷ ἑτοίμως ἔχοντι κρῖναι ζῶντας καὶ νεκρούς. εἰς τοῦτο γὰρ καὶ νεκροῖς εὐηγγελίσθη, ἵνα κριθῶσι μὲν κατὰ ἀνθρώπους σαρκί, ζῶσι δὲ κατὰ Θεὸν πνεύματι.

The Vulgate has

> Qui reddent rationem ei qui paratus est judicare vivos et mortuos.
> Propter hoc enim et mortuis evangelizatum est, ut judicentur quidem secundum homines in carne, vivant autem secundum Deum in spiritu

and *The New English Bible*

> but they shall answer for it to him who stands ready to pass judgement on the living and the dead. Why was the Gospel preached to those who are dead? In order that, although in the body they received the sentence common to men, they might in the spirit be alive with the life of God.

'Who are the dead?' is a difficult question. Selwyn reports the view of some scholars that, taken in conjunction with 1 Peter 3. 18–19

[17] C. J./John Godfrey *The Church in Anglo-Saxon England* (Cambridge, 1962), p. 215.

ὅτι καὶ Χριστὸς ἅπαξ περὶ ἁμαρτιῶν ἔπαθε, δίκαιος ὑπὲρ ἀδίκων, ἵνα ἡμᾶς προσαγάγῃ τῷ Θεῷ, θανατωθεὶς μὲν σαρκὶ ζωοποιηθεὶς δὲ πνεύματι, ἐν ᾧ καὶ τοῖς ἐν φυλακῇ πνεύμασι πορευθεὶς ἐκήρυξεν,

where the Vulgate has

> Quia et Christus semel pro peccatis nostris mortuus est, justus pro injustis, ut nos offerret Deo, mortificatus quidem carne, vivificatus autem spiritu,
> In quo et his, qui in carcere erant, spiritibus veniens prædicavit

and *The New English Bible*

> For Christ also died for our sins once and for all. He, the just, suffered for the unjust, to bring us to God. In the body he was put to death; in the spirit he was brought to life. And in the spirit he went and made his proclamation to the imprisoned spirits,

1 Peter 4. 6 refers to all the dead. Selwyn gives good linguistic reasons for rejecting this view – in the twentieth century.[18] But, I would argue, the possibility cannot be dismissed out of hand that such an interpretation may have been in the mind either of the *Beowulf* poet or of some of his hearers or readers; that of the three possible senses of *lofgeornost* noted above it was the first alone – 'most eager for pre-Christian, pagan *lof*' – which was activated in the minds of some hearers or readers; and that Beowulf was to some of these a virtuous heathen who, like Enoch, was with God, even though the manner of his going was different, for Enoch, in the mysterious words of Genesis (AV) 5. 24, 'walked with God: and he was not; for God took him'. This is perhaps not as outrageous as it seems for (as Kenneth Sisam writes) 'Genesis was in the forefront of Christian teaching to laymen.'[19] [I add as an afterthought the possibility that Matthew (AV) 10. 15 'Verily I say unto you, It shall be more tolerable for the land of Sodom and Gomorrha in the day of judgement, than for that city' – a statement repeated with minor variations in Mark 6. 11 and Luke 10. 12 – could have been interpreted as implying that those who had not had the opportunity of accepting Christ could expect to be treated more mercifully than those who had.] But Stanley assumes that the poet was a man of deep Christian belief and purpose, that the Church taught *paganus est perditus*, and that the poet accepted this. There is no proof that he did. Acquiescence – thinking or unthinking – in religious observances and doctrines has not been a marked characteristic of individual English Christians through the ages. I think of the disputes about the two *ASB*s now authorized for use in the Church of England – *The Abandoned Service Book 1662*, formerly known as *The Book of Common Prayer*, and *The*

[18] Edward Gordon Selwyn *The First Epistle of St Peter* (London, 1947), pp. 213–16 and 337–9.
[19] *The Structure of* Beowulf (Oxford, 1965), p. 76.

Alternative Service Book 1980. I perceive the irony of opponents of the ordination of women within the Church of England threatening to join the Roman Catholic Church, which refuses to allow its own ordained priests to marry yet ordains married priests converted from the Church of England. I note that the Church of England has room for those who believe in the Resurrection of Christ's material body and for those who – in the teeth of Luke 24. 36–43 – do not. It were no difficult task to multiply examples from earlier periods; they would include the controversial introduction of the Authorized Version of the Bible (1611) and of *The Book of Common Prayer* (1662). So I neither feel nor think myself under any obligation or compulsion to accept the proposition that the poet's concern was with the notion that *paganus est perditus*. The burden of proof, as I see it, rests on Stanley. He himself admits (p. 149) that his rejection of Schücking's interpretation is a matter of choice, not necessity: 'Schücking saw in the figure of Beowulf Saint Augustine's *rex iustus*; *it seems possible* [my italics] to look upon him rather as Alcuin's *rex perditus*.' Wallace-Hadrill on the other hand looks with some favour on Schücking's interpretation:

> What, then, was the poet's idea of a good king? Up to a point, the answer has already been provided in a few pages by Professor Schücking, and his conclusions can be summarized thus: Beowulf is himself the embodiment of the Christian kingly virtues and at the same time of those traditional pagan kingly virtues that were compatible with Christianity. He was the *rex justus*: wise, pious, kind and humble, careful of and considerate for those he ruled; the dragon-slayer is in effect the Good Shepherd who perishes in protecting his flock.[20]

So, bearing in mind the penultimate paragraph of item 4 above, I would suggest that it is possible to believe that Beowulf was after all saved and that the poet meant the words he put in the mouth of Wiglaf

Beowulf l. 3107   ond þonne geferian   frean userne,
                     leofne mannan   þær he longe sceal
                     on ðæs Waldendes   wære geþolian

and the words he himself spoke

Beowulf l. 2819   him of hræðre gewat
                     sawol secean   soðfæstra dom.

The *possibilities* then are many. I cannot, however, conclude without nailing my own colours to some sort of a mast. In one mood, I see *Beowulf* as a poem whose theme is summarized by Bede's story of the sparrow,[21] a poetic explora-

[20] J. M. Wallace-Hadrill *Early Germanic Kingship in England and on the Continent* (Oxford, 1971), p. 121.
[21] *Historia Ecclesiastica Gentis Anglorum* 2. 13.

tion of the life of man in this world, of the blind forces of nature and the dark passions of men against 'our little systems [which] have their day and cease to be' – a meaning all the more poignant to me at the moment of writing, as I prepare to leave the room in St Edmund Hall in which I have taught for the last twenty years. In another, I share the view expressed by Tolkien in a treasured private letter:

> This then is a story of a great warrior of old, who used the gifts of God to him, of courage, strength and lineage, rightly and nobly. He may have been fierce in battle, but in dealings with men he was not unjust, nor tyrannical, and was remembered as *milde* and *monðwære*. He lived a long while ago, and in his time and country no news had come of Christ, God seemed far off, and the Devil was near; men had no hope. He died in sorrow, fearing God's anger. But God is merciful. And to you, now young and eager, death will also come one day; but you have hope of Heaven. If you use your gifts as God wills. *Bruc ealles well*!

In yet another, I hear the *Beowulf* poet speaking with the voice of Tennyson's Ulysses:

> Tho' much is taken, much abides; and tho'
> We are not now that strength which in old days
> Moved earth and heaven; that which we are, we are;
> One equal temper of heroic hearts,
> Made weak by time and fate, but strong in will
> To strive, to seek, to find, and not to yield.

But I dare not say that the poet 'meant' any of these. Wilfrid Gibson wrote:

> 'Poetry should be *this* –
> Not *that*!'
> 'Poetry should be *that* –
> Not *this*!'
> The little critics hiss
> And contradict each other flat;
> While, careless of *what* poetry should be,
> The poet goes on writing poetry.

I accept that some Anglo-Saxon hearers or readers thought that because *paganus est perditus*, Beowulf was damned. (In fact, I am prepared to concede that most modern interpretations of *Beowulf* might have been felt or thought by one Anglo-Saxon or another.) But I cannot accept that all did; some, I believe, would have found a message of hope, not despair. As Tolkien wrote in the letter already referred to, 'I think we fail to grasp imaginatively the pagan "heroic" temper, the almost animal pride and ferocity of "nobles" and champions on the one hand; or on the other hand the immense relief and hope of Christian ethical teaching amidst a world with savage values.' And what of those who had not accepted Christianity? Bewildered by the Christian moralizing of *Beowulf*, they could at least have comprehended Beowulf's nobility and could have seen him as an example to be followed. The assertion that one of these rather than another must have been what the poet 'meant' is a claim I could not make and a claim I cannot accept. So in the end I return to Robinson's sensitive and valuable book by suggesting that *Beowulf* itself is a major example of amphiboly, a poem which can be appropriately characterized in the words penned by Gaule in 1642 and quoted by *OED* s.v. *amphibolical*: 'œnigmaticall, obscure, amphibolicall, ambiguous, and equivocating'. To vary the words of Dr Johnson in the Preface to his *Dictionary*: 'To enchain poetry, and to lash the wind, are equally the undertakings of pride, unwilling to measure its desires by its strength.'

6
Reviews

(a) *Twelve* Beowulf *Papers 1940–1960*. With Additional Comments by Adrien Bonjour, Neuchatel: Faculté des Lettres; Geneva: Librairie E. Droz, 1962*

Professor Adrien Bonjour has long been gratefully known as one who thinks of *Beowulf* as a poem rather than as a collection of cruxes or an archaeological or historical treatise *manqué*; *The Digressions in* Beowulf (1950) has influenced many subsequent writers. Here he reprints with further comments eleven articles published between 1940 and 1957 and adds a new one. Some scarcely warrant reprinting, e.g. VI. 'Young Beowulf's Inglorious period', VII. 'Monsters Crouching and Critics Rampant: or the *Beowulf* Dragon Debated', and IX. '*Beowulf* and the Snares of Literary Criticism'. They serve to fan the embers of controversies now dead or dying – not always, one fears, with the friendliness the author promises (p. 121), and sometimes in a florid and over-metaphorical style.

On the other hand, I. 'The Use of Anticipation in *Beowulf*', II. 'Grendel's Dam and the Composition of *Beowulf*', III. 'The Technique of Parallel Descriptions in *Beowulf*', VIII. 'On Sea Images in *Beowulf*', and X. '*Beowulf* and the Beasts of Battle', exemplify M. Bonjour's gift for casting new light on the poet's brilliance. Inevitably, room exists for disagreement on matters of detail. Thus the claim that Beowulf's narrow escape in the fight against Grendel's dam 'gives us a first intimation of his ultimate vulnerability' (p. 36) hardly squares with p. 37, n. 1 or with the *scop*'s song of Sigemund and Heremod, and, since Beowulf too is mortal, seems to deny the poet's audience powers of deduction with which it is elsewhere credited (e.g. p. 64).

Elsewhere, too, M. Bonjour sometimes seems to want it both ways. In IV. 'Beowulf and Heardred', he cannot really explain Beowulf's part in, and after, Hygelac's last raid. Hence at pp. 75–6 he asks: 'If so, was not the poet justified in leaving his hero's part in the Heardred conflict out of focus, if not entirely in

---

* Reprinted from the *Review of English Studies* 15 (1964), 306–7. In self-defence, I have to say that I still feel much the same as I did when I wrote the last paragraph of this review. But the encouragement of people whom I must presume to be wiser than I am has induced me to recant.

the dark – even at the unexpected risk of having rationalistically-minded critics ask insidious questions about the minutiae of Beowulf's historical connections?' Yet, after reading V. 'The Problem of Dæghrefn', we might retort in the same emotive terms by asking whether this is not a case of an artistically minded critic making insidious explanations about the minutiae of Beowulf's historical connexions.

XI. 'Poésie héroïque du moyen âge et critique littéraire' contains an interesting analysis of the 'oral-formulaic' theory and its application to *Beowulf* and the *Chanson de Roland*; M. Bonjour takes a sensible line against the view that formulaic poems must be 'oral'. XII. '*Beowulf* et le démon de l'analogie' (hitherto unprinted) amusingly exposes the weaknesses in a typewritten paper by D. W. Lee which apparently suggests that Alcuin wrote *Beowulf* on 16 or 17 April 789 or 790 (p. 181). It then argues that McNamee's theory that *Beowulf* is an allegory of salvation cannot be accepted because the divergences between *Beowulf* and the Christian story outweigh the parallels. This is a telling point and might be applied to allegorical interpretations of other Old English poems. Whether or not M. Bonjour finally demolishes McNamee's theory is, however, a matter for the individual reader.

M. Bonjour spends much time and ingenuity on comparatively minor problems which trouble only those who pursue an unjustified search for literal consistency, e.g. pp. 39–40 and 77–88. He is forced to admit one flaw (p. 96), almost concedes another (pp. 74–6), and overlooks or ignores some which have been noted by Sisam, Smithers, and others. While, therefore, it may be true that he is 'not tempted to save the dogma of the poet's infallibility at any cost' (p. 95), he certainly presents us with a more favourable impression of the poem's structure than seems warranted.

This is one result of the piecemeal approach. A second – and more serious – is that major difficulties are overlooked. After hesitating, M. Bonjour concludes in a rather shrill voice that the Grendel tribe and the dragon are kin (pp. 112–13). (Here he is in danger of arguing from analogy – which he condemns so eloquently in XII.) If there is doubt about the nature of the dragon, this is either a serious artistic blemish or the result of our ignorance, a possibility which M. Bonjour treats somewhat lightly (p. 125). Again, M. Bonjour thinks *Beowulf* a pessimistic poem. Its mood is one of grief and sadness (p. 20). Beowulf died in vain (p. 28). (But only, it seems to me, in the sense that we all die in vain.) M. Bonjour does not really face the difficulty inherent in the belief that an accomplished Christian artist would write such a poem (p. 46). And many modern readers find grounds for optimism in *Beowulf* without destroying its greatness.

'At the risk of bruising my humpty-dumpty toes in another pitfall' (to quote M. Bonjour, p. 125), I feel compelled to express the hope that volumes of this type – collecting the articles of a lifetime with comments and qualifications from an older and wiser author – will not become the accepted thing. Thanks to M. Bonjour and others like him, *Beowulf* has been 'rehabilitated'; perhaps the time has come when it should be allowed to speak for itself.

(b) *An Anthology of Beowulf Criticism* ed. Lewis E. Nicholson, Notre Dame: University of Notre Dame Press, 1963*

The idea of producing an anthology of *Beowulf* criticism is an excellent one, in view of the ever-increasing spate of articles about *Beowulf* and the rapidly growing number of new universities which are finding it impossible to obtain full runs of out-of-print periodicals. Mr Nicholson certainly had the second point in mind, for he tells us that 'the purpose of this anthology is to bring together in convenient form some of the best scholarly and critical essays on *Beowulf* to appear in recent years, some of which are not available in small libraries.' This purpose he has achieved well enough, though it is inevitable that his choice will not satisfy all. Some will regret the absence of an account of the excavations at Yeavering and of articles such as those by Rosemary Cramp (*Mediaeval Archaeology* 1 (1957), 57–77) and Adrien Bonjour (*PMLA* 72 (1957), 563–73). This reviewer at any rate would have dispensed with Mrs Goldsmith's article, which presents what is for him a sadly distorted view of the hero of the poem. Others, doubtless, will have their own candidates for omission. But these are matters of taste.

However, other matters are also at stake. For whom is the book intended? Subject to the reservations made above, it is certainly a handy compilation for the teacher. But did Mr Nicholson have the undergraduate in mind? It would seem so, from the outside of the back cover. Has he then given him enough help? He has presented him with eighteen papers, some of which are (to say the least) controversial, and some of which contradict others. Yet the preface as a whole is little more than a series of summaries strung together by such remarks as 'A notably contrary point of view is offered by Schücking and Hamilton' (p. ix), 'Unlike Goldsmith, Malone sees the poet as . . .' (p. x), or the observation that Magoun's article is 'important, but controversial' (p. xi). This is satisfactory as far as it goes. But does it go far enough? I very much fear that those able to profit from the anthology will scarcely need it, while those who need it will be unable to profit from it. The beginner is likely to get mental indigestion from this necessarily arbitrary selection of scholarly articles, some of which are guilty of special pleading.

In my opinion, the book would have been more useful if Mr Nicholson had aimed at producing a historical anthology of *Beowulf* criticism along the lines of Hugh Sykes Davies's *The Poets and their Critics*, which first appeared as a

* Reprinted from the *Review of English Studies* 15 (1964), 414–15.

Penguin in 1943 and has since been reprinted in an enlarged version by Hutchinson of London. We should then have had a general introduction to *Beowulf* criticism, followed by key extracts from important articles and books, with brief comments from the editor where necessary. Such a historical outline might have started from the view that *Beowulf* was a translation of a Scandinavian poem, moved briefly through the theories of multiple authorship and the mythological interpretations, quoted W. P. Ker's famous judgements in *The Dark Ages* and *Medieval English Literature*, and given us (as Mr Nicholson does) Professor Tolkien's lecture in full. By judicious summarizing of the articles presented, it could have included extracts from T. M. Gang's criticisms of Professor Tolkien (*RES* 3 (1952), 1–12) and from K. Sisam's article in *RES* 9 (1958), 129–40, and could have found room for Professor Whitelock's view that the poem may have been intended for oral recitation in three sittings. And so on.

Such a book would have given 'undergraduate students meeting *Beowulf* for the first time' an interesting historical perspective and the information on which they could make up their own minds about the poem instead of being tossed like a *pilche clut* from critic to critic until they are forced to take refuge in a bewildered and uncritical acceptance of the views of their teacher or of one of the contributors to Mr Nicholson's anthology.

(c) *The Structure of* Beowulf by Kenneth Sisam, Oxford: Clarendon Press, 1965*

This book – in my opinion the most challenging and tonic discussion of *Beowulf* since Professor Tolkien's Academy Lecture and Professor Whitelock's *The Audience of* Beowulf – shows clearly why Dr Sisam once described himself as 'not among the whole-hearted admirers of the construction of the poem'. It should cause whole-hearted admirers to do some soul-searching.

Dr Sisam sees the *Beowulf* poet as primarily a storyteller appealing to the *heorðwerod* in an Anglo-Saxon hall. The lack of 'certain forward references from one main adventure to another' (p. 4, n. 2[1]) suggests that the plot was 'built up to meet the demand for another story about the hero who destroyed Grendel' (p. 5). Hence we should not expect literal consistency or architectural perfection; at times we have to do with primitive narrative, as in the Return from the Mere, ll. 837–927 (p. 31), or with a 'poet who has temporarily lost his inspiration', as in Beowulf's Return to Geatland, ll. 1888–2199 (p. 45). Such

* Reprinted from the *Review of English Studies* 17 (1966), 190–1.

[1] Does the argument in this note – and at times elsewhere – depend on the assumption that everything in *Beowulf* was designed to make its full impact on first hearing or reading? Is this consistent with Dr Sisam's observations that *Beowulf* 'has many of the marks of premeditated art' (p. 3, n. 4) and that 'enjoyment of poetry does not require the understanding of every allusion' (p. 9, n. 1)? See also (3) below.

weaknesses in the structure of this and other Old English poems 'suggest that a keen sense of literary form . . . was not widespread among the Anglo-Saxons' (pp. 65–6).

There is perhaps nothing very revolutionary here. The great merit of the book is its plea for a Return to the Poem. 'The pressure to find something new is strong', says Dr Sisam, 'and one of its consequences is a tendency to speculate on the things that are not expressed in *Beowulf*' (p. 27). Because, 'for many modern critics, *Beowulf* in its plain meaning does not come up to the ideal standards they have set' (pp. 26–7), ingenious theory follows ingenious theory, Time elevates unjustified assumptions into firm facts, there is a 'tendency to read too much trouble into the text' (p. 42), and the poem is lost in the 'literature' surrounding it.

Among other things, Dr Sisam calls into doubt current views on such important topics as the Finn Episode, the fate of the Geats, and the place of Christianity in the poem. Only the first can be discussed here. The belief that Hroðulf was a traitor is an unsupported assumption – 'in all sources, early and late, he is a character to be admired' (p. 36). Hence no parallel is intended between Hildeburh and Wealhþeow. Again, since Freawaru is not mentioned in this part of the poem, there is no parallel between her and Hildeburh (pp. 48–9). Dr Sisam, indeed, writes 'That dramatic irony was used in Anglo-Saxon heroic poetry is an assumption. Where it has been detected, the Anglo-Saxon audience is supposed to have known something conjectured by a modern critic' (p. 36, n. 2) and admits his assumption 'that this kind of poetry depended on expression, not on silences, dark hints or subtle irony' (p. 60).

Several points can be made here:

1 Since the *Beowulf* poet differs from all other sources in making Scyld, not Sceaf, the mysterious voyager and since he alone gives Sigemund a dragon, the argument that Hroðulf must be good in *Beowulf* because he is good in all the sources is perhaps not conclusive.
2 Does the irony usually detected in references to the burning of Heorot (ll. 81–5 and 778–82) and to Hygelac's possession of the *Brosinga mene* when he was killed (ll. 1202–14) really depend on 'something conjectured by a modern critic'?
3 Dr Sisam writes 'To remind the audience of Sigemund's more complete success was not the happiest way of praising Beowulf' (p. 4, n. 2). Could the points mentioned in (2) give some support to the view that the poet was at least capable of such a reminder?
4 The idea that a contrast between Beowulf and Heremod is intended at ll. 901–15 is dismissed at p. 29, n. 2 as 'too slight to be effective'. Is this dismissal a little summary in view of the parallel paratactic sentences beginning *He* (Beowulf) l. 913 and *hine* (Heremod) l. 915?

5 Does it therefore remain a *possibility* (despite Dr Sisam's note C) that ll. 1162–5, placed as they are immediately after the climax of the Finn Episode, could imply that Hroðulf was a traitor?² If so, Dr Sisam's question 'How did this set of traitors get the reputation of heroes?' (p. 43) has to be answered.

Whether these objections are the last desperate mouthings of a critical dragon slain by Dr Sisam or whether the dragon still lives to launch a counter-attack, I am not sure. But I am sure that Dr Sisam's criticisms must be answered if some current opinions about *Beowulf* are to be maintained. This is a book which must be taken seriously by all who talk or write about *Beowulf*; to vary R. W. Chambers's words, I would not sell it for a wilderness of articles.

(d) *A Reading of* **Beowulf by Edward B. Irving Jr, New Haven and London: Yale University Press, 1968***

I read this book with mixed feelings. Professor Irving is sensitive and on the whole sensible. He believes that '*Beowulf* is fundamentally heroic poetry, not theology' (p. 93), and is more concerned with increasing 'a reader's respect for the poet's artistry' (p. 56) and illuminating old truths than with producing new interpretations. He has succeeded in doing this in prose which is clear, graceful, and at times almost poetic. He writes illuminatingly on general problems (e.g. p. 205 the tone of the Old English *Ubi sunt* passages and p. 208 Beowulf's 'greed') and on individual lines or words (e.g. pp. 159 and 175), and offers us new ways of looking at things (e.g. p. 209 the notion of the dragon as a mock king). The last chapter seems to me particularly helpful.

That there is room for qualification and disagreement is inevitable. Mr Irving's remarks on pp. 25–6 about the delay in Grendel's realization of Beowulf's power are contradicted in part at least by the text of the poem and by his own comments on p. 25 itself and on pp. 105–6 and 109. (His importation of 'suddenly' into the translation on p. 25 is partly responsible for this and exemplifies the rather peculiar remarks about translation on p. viii. How can a translation support an argument?) That Unferth murdered his kinsmen (p. 6) we know from the poem (pp. 75–6). To say that Grendel 'is Death' (p. 111) seems to me to weaken the effect of p. 213. The human laws by which Grendel will not abide (p. 20) are not observed by many humans in the poem (pp. 34 and 178–9). Mr Irving is a little fond of words like 'of course', 'must', 'certainly', and 'surely'. More line references would have been helpful, e.g. pp. 8, 14, and 20. The translation on p. 54 disregards the change of tense in the original; Klaeber's punctuation seems preferable here. Note 23 on p. 171 is rather violently

² [1987. But it is a *possibility* which I myself do not accept. See *OES* §3955.]
* Reprinted from the *Review of English Studies* 20 (1969), 202–4.

expressed; Klaeber has only two emendations more than Dobbie. In n. 4 on p. 134 the emendation *sēðan* will be felt by some to involve something even more 'extremely unusual' than the manuscript *syððan*.

Sometimes Mr Irving accepts without comment interpretations which have been questioned by recent writers: e.g. p. 163 (Beowulf cuts the dragon in half), pp. 169 and 178–80 (the Ingeld story is 'Beowulf's prediction'), p. 223 (Beowulf's spirit is 'restless and on the verge of death'), and p. 224 ('the imagined example'). Some of his own observations are likely to be questioned. Does the coastguard falter (p. 52)? Lines 407–55 should be read in conjunction with lines 372–85 (p. 62). Is it true that 'Beowulf's thoughts are scarcely mentioned' (p. 103)? Not all Christian moralizers adopt a 'smug I-told-you-so' tone (p. 91). In what sense are the Geats 'men of... piety' (p. 51)? Is the physical encounter between Beowulf and Grendel really 'reduced to an almost symbolic minimum' (p. 28)?

Miss Beatrice White once spoke of some Old English literary critics as 'insistent sleuth-hounds [who] push their detective faculties to the limit ... according to them examples of litotes and meiosis seem to catapult from every situation' (*Anglia* 78 (1960), 287). Mr Irving seems to have joined their ranks. On p. 2 he speaks of 'the impression of a persistent tone of irony and understatement that *modern readers* [my italics] receive from this poetry'. But by the time we get to p. 6 this has become an accepted feature of the poet's style: 'this remark by the poet, couched as it is in the habitual ironic mode of understatement,...'. And so we read on – e.g. pp. 6 n. 5, 7, 14, 16, 19, 20, 30, 66, 103–6, 107 – until we reach pp. 111–12 where we learn that the poet has exorcized Grendel 'by bringing him into the sunlit world of laughter' and has contrasted him with a Beowulf of 'ironic wit and a grave gaiety'. While not seeking to deny the possibility that the poet may sometimes have intended some irony, I must say that Mr Irving's fluent pen here seems to have run away with him.

The bibliography cites Kenneth Sisam's *The Structure of* Beowulf. One might therefore have expected some reference to Dr Sisam's discussion of the Geats after Beowulf's death (*Structure*, pp. 51–9) in Mr Irving's last chapter, where much is made of 'eventual and inevitable national death' (pp. 243ff.). But Mr Irving plays a somewhat equivocal game with Dr Sisam. At pp. 10–12 it seems to be taken for fact that Hrothulf was a traitor. Yet in n. 3 on p. 132 'the cautious reader' is advised to consult Dr Sisam's book 'for a pertinent warning that *Beowulf* scholars may have created their own convenient legend on the basis of very little evidence in the poem or elsewhere'. Why this observation did not appear on p. 10 is a puzzle. It is hard to see why it is only the cautious reader who will benefit from Dr Sisam's observations. (Is the reader who believes Mr Irving necessarily imprudent?) I accept the possibility that Hrothulf may have been a traitor (see *RES* 17 (1966), 190–1). But since Mr Irving accepts that he was (p. 132), he should have paid some attention in chapter four to Dr Sisam's question 'How did this set of schemers get the reputation of heroes?' (*Structure*, p. 43).[1] As it is, we are back in a pre-Sisam state of innocence – Wealhtheow and Hildeburh are 'peace-weavers' (pp. 134, 137, and 179) along with Freawaru (p. 169); the Danes are traitors (pp. 136, 138, 141, 144, and 195); ll. 1228–31, with their indicatives, 'become pure incantatory prayer' (p. 144). And Hrothulf's treachery is used to suggest the possibility that Heoroweard 'may also have been eying his uncle's throne' (pp. 10–11). This opens up a fruitful field for fresh speculation – soon perhaps Hrothgar, Heoroweard, and Hrothulf will equal Onela, Eanmund, and Eadgils, while Hrothgar's seizure of Heoroweard's throne will parallel Hrothulf's seizure of Hrethric's, but will be contrasted with Beowulf's treatment of Heardred and perhaps even with Hrothulf's nobility in striving to restore Heoroweard to his rightful seat.

But it would be wrong to end on an ungracious note. Most of the matters I have aired are matters of opinion and in those places where I detect faults they are often the faults of enthusiasm and of love for the poem. The book has heightened my appreciation of *Beowulf*. I am grateful and am confident that many readers will lay it down with the same feeling.

---

[1] [1987. But see item 6c above, fn. 2.]

Part II
Cædmon

7
Bede's *Habere* = Old English *Magan*?

In the well-known account of the poet Cædmon in book IV, chapter 24 of his *Historia Ecclesiastica*, Bede reports the conversation between the angel and Cædmon in the following words:

> 'Cædmon,' inquit, 'canta mihi aliquid.' At ille respondens: 'Nescio,' inquit, 'cantare ...' ... 'Attamen,' ait, 'mihi cantare habes.' 'Quid,' inquit, 'debeo cantare?'[1]

The Old English translation reads:

> Cedmon, sing me hwæthwugu. Þa ondswarede he 7 cwæð: Ne con ic noht singan ... Hwæðre þu meaht singan. Þa cwæð he: Hwæt sceal ic singan?[2]

It is generally agreed that *nescio* and *debeo* are accurately translated by *ne con ic* and *sceal ic* respectively. But the identity of *habes* and *þu meaht* is less certain. Thus, in his Sir Israel Gollancz Memorial Lecture, read to the British Academy on 19 February 1947, Professor C. L. Wrenn observed:

> It is also to be considered whether the rendering in the Alfredian versions of Bede's *mihi cantare habes* in the speech of the being who spoke with Cædmon in his dream by *þu meaht me singan*, does not imply some corroboration of a separate English tradition independent of Bede: for *habes* does not seem to have the meaning of the Anglo-Saxon *meaht*.[3]

But is it true that the Ecclesiastical Latin *habere* and Old English *magan* have no meaning in common? I doubt it; indeed, there are three possible solutions to the equation.

Reprinted from *Neuphilologische Mitteilungen* 66 (1965), 107–11.

[1] Quoted from volume I of C. Plummer's edition (Oxford, 1896), p. 259, ll. 24ff.

[2] Quoted from T. Miller's EETS edition, p. 342, ll. 29ff. In omitting *me* Miller follows T. Its absence is due to a scribe rather than to the translator, for it appears before *miht* in B. and before *singan* in O. and Ca. [1987. On this see now item 9 below and Raymond J. S. Grant 'Bede's *Mihi Cantare Habes* Revisited', *NM* 84 (1983), 159–62.]

[3] *Proceedings of the British Academy* 32 (1946), p. 284.

The first is that both have the sense *posse* 'to be able to'. This is, of course, the commonest meaning of OE *magan*. Lewis and Short cite examples of *habere* in this sense from classical authors,[4] while A. Blaise in his *Dictionnaire Latin-Français des Auteurs Chrétiens* (Strasbourg, 1954) notes *habere* in the sense 'avoir, pouvoir (av. inf., cl.): (emplois plus étendus)', and cites examples from Tertullian, Irenaeus, Cyprian, and others.[5] However, of all the sentences from Bede's *Ecclesiastical History* in which any form of the verb *habere* is followed by an infinitive,[6] the only other one in which it might mean 'to be able to' is in book III, chapter 25, where King Oswy speaks to Colman: *'Habetis,' inquit, 'uos proferre aliquid tantae potestatis uestro Columbae datum?'* [7] Here Sherley-Price's translation reads: 'Can you show that a similar authority was given to your Columba?'[8] Unfortunately, this passage is not represented in the Old English version, for it comes from one of the chapters omitted by the translator. The only passage from Bede in which *habere* + infinitive is translated by *magan* is the one specifically under discussion. It can scarcely be called in evidence here. But it remains an example.

The second possibility is that both have the sense 'to be obliged to, must'. Lewis and Short note this sense of *habere* as ante-classical and post-Augustan.[9] Blaise cites examples of *habere* meaning 'devoir, avoir à (faire) ($μέλλω$)' from Tertullian and Augustine and further examples of the sense 'devoir (av. idée plus prononcée d'obligation, de nécessité)' from Tertullian, Irenaeus, Cyprian, Lactantius, Ambrose, and others.[10] This sense is firmly attested in Bede in two places: book I, chapter 7 ... *quaecumque illi debebantur supplicia, tu soluere habes*, where the OE has *þu scealt ðam ylcan wite onfon, ðe he geearnode*[11] and book III, chapter 22 *tu in ipsa domu mori habes*, where the OE reads *þu scealt in þæm sylfan huse sweltan 7 deaþ þrowigan*.[12] That *magan* can carry this sense is not so well-attested. But Bosworth-Toller cites the use in legal statutes of *magan* meaning

---

[4] S.v. *habeo* I. A. 2. ($β$) and II. A. 2.

[5] S.v. *habeo* 10.

[6] I acknowledge here my debt to P. F. Jones *A Concordance to the Historia Ecclesiastica of Bede* (Cambridge, Mass. 1929).

[7] Plummer, p. 188, l. 23 ff.

[8] Penguin Classics, 1955.

[9] S.v. *habeo* I. A. 2. ($β$).

[10] S.v. *habeo* 11. Du Cange notes '1. HABERE. Velle, vel debere.' See also H. P. V. Nunn *An Introduction to the Study of Ecclesiastical Latin* (Eton, 1951), p. 42.

[11] Plummer, vol. I, p. 19, ll. 9ff. and Miller, p. 36, l. 7 respectively.

[12] p. 174, l. 9 and p. 228, ll. 22ff. respectively. There are two other examples of *habes* + infinitive: book IV, chapter 14 (Plummer, p. 234, l. 10), which is not represented in the OE version, and book IV, chapter 24 (Plummer, p. 261, ll. 30ff.), where the OE translator translates freely: (Miller, p. 348, ll. 2ff.) *Ne þinre forþfore swa neah is.* This is a pity, since the passage comes in the account of Cædmon's death. Thus all the examples which bear on our problem have the second person verb forms *habes* or *habetis*. The examples with *necesse habere* at Plummer p. 314, l. 11 and p. 343, l. 14 are not strictly relevant.

'shall' or 'must' and translating *debere*.¹³ The permissive use of *magan* is, of course, well-known.¹⁴

The third solution to the equation is that both refer to the future. This too is attested for *habere* by Blaise, who remarks 'de l'idée de nécessité, on passe à l'idée de futur, d'avenir prochain ...' and gives examples from Tertullian, Cyprian, and others.¹⁵ Examples in which *magan* at least approximates to a future sense have been quoted and discussed by Standop.¹⁶ However, there does not seem to be any example of this usage in the Latin Bede – unless we agree with Blaise, who cites our 'mihi cantare habes, Bed. Hist. 4, 22' as an example and then observes 'd'ailleurs il est parfois difficile de distinguer l'idée d'obligation de l'idée de futur.'¹⁷

As far as I can see, the Latin *mihi cantare habes* can have no meaning other than one of the three suggested above. Hence we must accept *either* that one of the three equations suggested above is right, *or* that the Old English translator was at fault (a possibility which cannot be denied, for he makes mistakes elsewhere), *or* that the variation was deliberate. This last is possible; it might have been an attempt to distinguish *habes* from *debeo*. But there is no evidence to support Professor Wrenn's idea that the translator deliberately made the Old English mean something other than what he thought the Latin to mean or the conclusion that the variation is proof of his knowledge of an oral tradition independent of Bede. That such a tradition existed is, of course, certain – unless all the by-standers except Bede or his informant(s) were deaf-mutes, or unless no one else ever bothered to mention the matter. But the belief that it differed in any important detail or that it ever reached the Old English translator of Bede's *History* is not strengthened in any way by the point under discussion here.

No final solution is possible. But it seems not unlikely that the Old English translator meant to translate accurately and thought that he had. If he did translate accurately, one of the three equations suggested above is right. Any one of them would fit the context but, in view of the uses of OE *magan*, the sense 'to be able to' seems most acceptable. If he did not translate accurately, the most likely possibility (having regard to the predominant meanings of *habere* + infinitive and of *magan*) is perhaps that *habes* meant 'you must', and that the translator, confused by the following *debeo*, translated it *þu meaht* 'you can'. If we are humble enough to believe that the translator understood Bede's intention better than we do and was more familiar with the uses of *habere* and

---

[13] Supplement, s.v. *magan* IV. a.

[14] See E. Standop *Syntax und Semantik der modalen Hilfsverben im Altenglischen* (Bochum-Langendreer, 1957), pp. 27–9.

[15] S.v. *habeo* 11. This use, as Professor Mustanoja has pointed out to me, is illuminated by the composition of the Romance future tense; see M. K. Pope, *From Latin to Modern English* (Manchester, 1952), §872. 3 and *passim*.

[16] Standop *Syntax und Semantik*, pp. 21–4.

[17] S.v. *habeo* 11.

magan than we are – a not unlikely hypothesis, for (as Professor Whitelock has observed) 'he was very familiar with the text'[18] – we may even be able to accept this as evidence for the view that *habere* could equal *magan* in the sense 'to be able to' as well as *sculan*, in the sense 'must, to be obliged to'. Such overlaps of meaning occur in Old English; compare the uses of *magan* and [*motan*] in *The Battle of Maldon* ll. 14 and 235 and ll. 83 and 272 respectively, and note the various meanings cited by Standop for these verbs, and for *sculan* and *willan*.[19] That they occur also in Bede's Latin need scarcely surprise us; we have Blaise's testimony to their existence in other writers of Ecclesiastical Latin,[20] and they are the very stuff of any living language.

---

[18] Dorothy Whitelock *The Old English Bede* (Sir Israel Gollancz Memorial Lecture, British Academy, 1962), p. 62.
[19] Standop *Syntax und Semantik, passim.*   [20] See above.

8
Swa in Cædmon's *Hymn*, Line 3

The meaning of *swa* in Cædmon's *Hymn*

> Nu scylun hergan   hefaenricaes uard,
> metudæs maecti   end his modgidanc,
> uerc uuldurfadur,   sue he uundra gihuaes,
> eci dryctin,   or astelidæ ...

and its exact relationship to the *quomodo* of Bede's Latin rendering of the *Hymn* in his *Historia Ecclesiastica Gentis Anglorum*, book IV, chapter 24,

> Nunc laudare debemus auctorem regni caelestis, potentiam Creatoris et consilium illius, facta Patris gloriae, quomodo ille, cum sit aeternus Deus, omnium miraculorum auctor extitit ...

has long been a source of difficulty. My purpose here is not to re-stage the controversy by summarizing the previous suggestions and arguments, but to make three more or less speculative points in the hope of throwing some light on the problem.

I

Swa might be explained as an anticipatory adverb 'so, thus, in this way':

> Now ought we to praise the Lord.... Thus (in this way, order), he established ... his wonders.... First the heavens ... then the earth....

This anticipatory use of *swa* can, I think, be found in Old English poetry,[1] but the Latin *quomodo* suggests that Bede did not understand it this way; *quomodo* is not so used in any of the other seventeen places where it occurs in his *Historia Ecclesiastica*.[2]

Reprinted from *Notes and Queries* 212 (1967), 203–4.

[1] I hope to discuss this point more fully elsewhere in connexion with *swa* in *Wanderer*, l. 6. [1987. See now item 12. II below.]

[2] See below.

II

Swa is explained by E. E. Ericson as meaning 'how', presumably because it is represented by Latin *quomodo*.[3] Such a sense for *swa* has not been attested elsewhere in Old English; in Ericson's second example,

> 7 he swutelice sæde on his gesetnisse be Cristes acennednisse, *swa swa* he com to mannum ... ,[4]

the clause which he translates '*how* he should come to mankind' means 'just as he did come to mankind' – *com* is indicative, not subjunctive, and it is the actual fulfilment of Daniel's prophecy which is being stressed.

The sequence *sicut... swa...* 'how' at the beginning of verse 2 of the following Psalm is, however, interesting:

> Roman Psalter 131
> Memento, Domine, David, et omnis mansuetudinis ejus
> Sicut juravit Domino: votum vovit Deo Jacob. ...[5]

> Paris Psalter 131 1. Gemune þu, drihten   mærne Dauid
>   and ealle his mannþwærnesse   micle and goode.
>   2. Swa ic æt frymðe geswor   ferhðe wið drihten
>   and gehat gehet,   he geheold teala
>   wið Iacobes   god þone mæran. . . .

> Authorized Version (Psalm 132)
> 1. Lord, remember David, and all his afflictions:
> 2. How he sware unto the Lord, and vowed unto the mighty God of Jacob....

At first glance, it seems possible that we have here an example of *swa* 'how'. But it is, I think, more than unlikely that the Old English poet of the *Paris Psalter* understood it as such; his *swa* is a literal rendering of the Latin *sicut* for which (as far as I can discover) the sense 'how' is unattested in either classical or ecclesiastical Latin. The Latin *sicut* appears to derive from the ὡς of the Septuagint. This in its turn represents the Hebrew *asher*, a word of many functions which is adequately represented here by the Greek ὡς and by MnE 'how'.[6] It is the Latin *sicut* which is at fault. Greek ὡς numbers among its

---

[3] *The Use of* Swa *in Old English* (Hesperia Ergänzungsreihe, XII, 1932), p. 12. See also C. L. Wrenn in *Proceedings of the British Academy* 32 (1946), 282, and *YWES* (1932), 72.

[4] Quoted (with Ericson's italics) from S. J. Crawford *The Old English Version of* The Heptateuch (EETS, o.s. 160), p. 43, ll. 648–51.

[5] Migne *Patrologia Latina* XXIX, col. 390.

[6] This is the usual rendering. It is found, for example, in the Authorized Version and in the English text of the Scriptures adopted by the Jewish Publication Society of America and reproduced by A. Cohen in his edition of *The Psalms* (London, 1945).

meanings both 'as' and 'how'[7] and the Latin translator wrongly chose to translate it here as *sicut*.[8] So the faint hope that *Paris Psalter* 131. 2 could throw some light on *swa* in Cædmon's *Hymn* must be dismissed, for the verse does not contain an example of *swa* as an interrogative adverb 'how'. We can not only agree with Miss Daunt that this category postulated by Ericson is 'somewhat too frail to stand alone';[9] we can dismiss it altogether.

III

Swa can also be explained as causal 'because, inasmuch as'. It has been so taken[10] and the usage is attested.[11] The difficulty, of course, is again *quomodo*. However, there is a recorded example of *quomodo* itself meaning 'since, as, seeing that'; Blaise glosses it as *puisque* and refers us to a passage from Tertullian (born c. AD 150).[12] I have not been able to trace further examples of this use, but if it were attested in later ecclesiastical Latin, it might provide a solution.

It is, however, possible that the citation from Tertullian is an example of *quomodo* in error for *quoniam* through wrong resolution of the abbreviation $\overline{QVO}$.[13] The same explanation could, of course, hold for Bede's *quomodo*. It must be admitted that there is no evidence for such an error in the *Historia Ecclesiastica*.[14] And since *quomodo* in the example under discussion is common to all the extant Latin versions (Plummer records no variants), the error – if it occurred at all – would need to have taken place in a manuscript 'more ancient than any which we possess, and which cannot be very far removed from an autograph of Bede'.[15]

The whole line of argument is therefore speculative. But at least it provides

[7] See Liddell and Scott *A Greek-English Lexicon*, new edn, ed. H. S. Jones (Oxford, 1925–40), s.v. ὡς Ab. ὡς (without accent) of the Relat. Pron. ὅς *as*. Ac. ὡς Relat. and Interrog., *how*.

[8] I am indebted to H. R. Moehring, Department of Religious Studies, Brown University, Providence, R.I., for his generous help with this paragraph.

[9] *YWES* (1932), 72.

[10] See *YWES* (1932), 72.

[11] I hope to discuss this point more fully elsewhere in connexion with *swa* in *Wanderer*, l. 43. [1987. See now item 12. IV below.]

[12] See A. Blaise *Dictionnaire Latin–Français des Auteurs Chrétiens* (Strasbourg, 1954), s.v. *quomodo* 7.

[13] See A. Souter *Glossary of Later Latin* (Oxford, 1949), s.v. quomodo. This work goes as far as AD 600.

[14] P. F. Jones in his *Concordance to the Historia Ecclesiastica of Bede* (Cambridge, Mass., 1929) records thirteen examples of *quoniam*, all without textual variants. There are seventeen examples of *quomodo*, excluding that under discussion. Of these, nine introduce questions (dependent or non-dependent), seven introduce comparative clauses, one is adverbial. Textual variants are recorded in two places – *quando* (Plummer, p. 69, l. 2) and *quoquo modo* (the sole adverbial example, Plummer, p. 121, l. 32); in both *quomodo* seems to be the aberrant reading. In addition, one manuscript has *quomo* in error at Plummer, p. 102, l. 19.

[15] C. Plummer *Venerabilis Baedae Opera Historica* (Oxford, 1896), I. xcii.

us with one way (if not two) of explaining the equation *swa*: *quomodo* in Cædmon's *Hymn* as causal 'because'. Some thirty-five years ago Miss Daunt wrote that 'many people translate [this *swa*] as a causal conjunction'. We can, I think, agree that they were not without some justification.[16]

---

[16] *YWES* (1932), 72.

9
Postscript on Bede's *Mihi Cantare Habes*

In the 15th edition of Sweet's *Anglo-Saxon Reader*, Professor Dorothy Whitelock's note on this problem reads:

> 33. *mē āht singan*. This, the reading in T, represents closely *mihi cantare habes*, provided we take *āht* as an old second person singular form of *āgan*. The reading in other MSS. would stem from their taking *me aht* as *meaht*, which would then necessitate the addition of a pronoun.[1]

This suggestion was put forward by Fr Klaeber in 1901[2] and, in a postscript provoked by an article by John M. McBryde,[3] in 1938.[4] There can be no doubt that it is a possibility. But one or two points should perhaps be made before it receives 'tenure' at the expense of the other possibilities adumbrated in my previous discussion.[5]

Professor Whitelock's compressed note conceals four things – T does not read *mē āht singan*; it is by no means established that the translator had *mihi* in his Latin text; the equation suggested does not rest on impregnable foundations; to explain the variant readings of the manuscripts is most complicated if we accept *me aht singan* as the original.

That T reads *meaht* is agreed by Miller and Klaeber, confirmed by my own inspection of the MS and by Dr Neil Ker, and acknowledged by Professor Whitelock in her footnote to the text.[6] However, as Dr Ker has reminded me, the presence or absence of gaps in this manuscript is of little significance – in this very sentence *meahtsingan* appears to be written as one word and on the same page we find *ende byrd nesse*.[7] Hence Professor Whitelock may be justified in printing what she does. But even if she is, her note on p. 243 is likely to

Reprinted from *Neuphilologische Mitteilungen* 70 (1969), 369–80.

[1] *Sweet's Anglo-Saxon Reader*, 15th edn, revised throughout by Dorothy Whitelock (Oxford, 1967), p. 243.
[2] *JEGP* 3 (1901), 497–500.
[3] *MLN* 52 (1937), 412–13.   [4] *MLN* 53 (1938), 249–50.
[5] See *NM* 66 (1965), 107–11 [item 7 above]. This 'Postscript' owes a lot to Edward Wilson of St Edmund Hall, Oxford. I am grateful.
[6] Whitelock *Sweet's Anglo-Saxon Reader*, p. 46, fn. 11.   [7] Tanner MS 10, f. 100r.

mislead some by seeming to imply that there is a gap between *me* and *aht* in the manuscript.

Did the translator have *mihi* in his Latin text? Plummer distinguished two types of manuscript – the M-type (in his view, the earlier) and the C-type[8] – and argued that the Anglo-Saxon translator used a manuscript of the C-type.[9] Professor Sir Roger Mynors of Corpus Christi College, Oxford, has kindly allowed me to say that his investigations confirm Plummer's findings. He further tells me that all surviving Latin manuscripts in England are of the C-type and points out that, while there may still have been manuscripts of the M-type in ninth-century England, they have left no trace.[10]

Now MS C lacks *mihi*. That this is a characteristic of the C-type manuscripts is shown (Professor Mynors has told me) by the fact that MS K – another manuscript of the C-type in an eighth-century Northumbrian hand – also lacks *mihi*.[11] If this absence of *mihi* is the result of omission, the omission would have to be pushed a long way back, perhaps even to Bede's study. On the other hand (and here again I am indebted to Professor Mynors), there is little evidence to support a suggestion that *mihi* in manuscripts of the M-type could be an addition. If it were, it too would go a long way back. Thus we cannot be absolutely sure that the translator's text did not have *mihi* in it. But since *mihi* is not in either C or K, it ought not to have been in the C-type text used by the translator.

This uncertainty about the Latin text the translator had in front of him is an unfortunate complication. If the Tanner MS 10 depends on a C-type manuscript, there is something to be said for the reading *þu meaht singan = cantare habes*.[12] But, as Klaeber has pointed out,

> still, granting the proposition that the particular MS. used by the translator did not contain the pronoun, the addition of *me* (which actually appears in O, Ca, B) would not be more remarkable in this place than in the following line, where all the MSS. read *sing me frumsceaft*, as over against the Latin *canta principium creaturarum*. This could easily have been suggested by the foregoing *canta mihi aliquid*.[13]

---

[8] C. Plummer *Venerabilis Baedae Historiam Ecclesiasticam Gentis Anglorum* (Oxford, 1896), I. xciv–xcvii.

[9] Plummer, p. cxxix. See also T. Miller's EETS edition, I. xxiii–xxiv.

[10] I am deeply grateful to Professor Mynors for allowing me to see in proof the relevant passages in his text, from the late Bertram Colgrave's edition of Bede's *Ecclesiastical History of the English People* which is shortly to appear in the Oxford Medieval Texts, and for his generosity in giving me so much time and help. [1987. The book was published as Bede's *Ecclesiastical History of the English People* ed. Bertram Colgrave and R. A. B. Mynors (Oxford, 1969).]

[11] K = Kassel Landesbibliothek 4° MS theol. 2 (CLA, VIII, no. 1140).

[12] For *habere = magan*, see *NM* 66 (1965), 108–9 [item 7 above].

[13] *MLN* 53 (1938), 250.

This would suppose that the translator rendered *habes* by *aht* and added *me* of his own volition (rather than from an M-type manuscript). Then later a scribe or scribes, faced with *þu meaht singan*, added another *me*, either in imitation of the phrase *Cedmon, sing me hwæthwugu* or by dittography or from (memory of) a Latin text containing *mihi*.[14] In the first and last cases, there would presumably have been some equivalence in mind between *habes* and *meaht*.[15] The variation in the position of *me* (both positions are syntactically possible) could be accounted for in at least three ways:

a scribal accident. It is not difficult to see how a scribe faced with *me meaht* could produce *meaht me* (or vice versa);
b deliberate variation of position by a scribe who wished to change the emphasis of the sentence;[16]
c independent insertion of *me* in the different positions by two different scribes. If we are prepared to admit independent insertions of *me* by the translator and by one script, we need not boggle at a third.

We are thus in a position to account for all the variants if we assume that the Anglo-Saxon translator wrote *þu me aht singan*.

Is he likely to have done this? There can be no objection to the word-order or to *aht* as a second person singular present indicative.[17] But the word *aht* raises a syntactic and a semantic problem. Can it be followed by an uninflected infinitive? Can it mean 'must' at this time?

The first problem was tackled by Klaeber:

Is the construction of *āht* with the pure infinitive to be conceded? *Āgan* with *tō* and the inflected infinitive is recorded a number of times.... We do not remember any other instance of *āgan* with the simple infinitive. But this construction may, without any difficulty, be accounted for by the Latin model, which was unhesitatingly copied. The pure infinitive in this case is not more suspicious than after *geearnian* (= *mereri*) 350, 23; 372, 34; 406, 15; 470, 8; *forhycgan* (= *contemnere*) 76, 29; 464, 10; or *gearo bēon* (roughly corresponding to: *uelle*) 56, 20. (Cf. also Wülfing, §§480 f.; 487.) – That the construction of *āgan* may nevertheless be considered even as a syntactical idiom accordant with Teutonic traditions, appears from the

---

[14] This would seem to be the only situation which could 'necessitate the addition of a pronoun'. Even here, 'necessitate' is a strong word.

[15] I recapitulate the readings of the MSS:

T *þu meaht singan*
B *þu me miht singan*
N, O, Ca *þu meaht me singan*

[16] This must be conceded as a possibility, though our ignorance of Anglo-Saxon intonation patterns forbids a detailed demonstration.

[17] See A. Campbell *Old English Grammar* (Oxford, 1959), §767.

parallel use of *āga* in Old Frisian, and *haban* in Gothic. (See Richthofen, *Altfriesisches Wörterbuch*, p. 592; J. Grimm, *Deutsche Grammatik* IV (1837), p. 93; Balg, *The First Germanic Bible*, pp. 367 f.; also Blackburn, *The English Future; its Origin and Development*, pp. 7 f., 14.)

If we add that in Middle English the present as well as the preterite of *aȝen* are found with the pure infinitive, just as *ought* occasionally in Early Modern English writings, we may safely regard all possible doubts disposed of.[18]

I fear that we can do no such thing. The three Old English verbs which Klaeber cites are all recorded with both inflected and uninflected infinitives.[19] The only example of an uninflected infinitive after *āgan* in the collections of Bosworth-Toller,[20] Callaway,[21] *OED*,[22] and Ono,[23] is from Homily LVII in Napier's edition of Wulfstan (a homily not accepted by Miss Bethurum):

> ac man ah cyrican and haligdom to secanne
> and þær hine georne inne to gebiddanne
> and mid eadmodnysse hlystan....[24]

This example is much later than that under discussion and merely serves to demonstrate the strength even then of *āgan*'s preference for the inflected infinitive. The pure infinitive in the Bede passage is much more suspicious than those in Klaeber's other examples and gains little real support from examples from other Germanic languages or from later stages of English itself. It is, of course, possible for an editor to follow Klaeber and to read *þu me aht singan* on the assumption that *singan* was put down as an unthinking crib for *cantare*.[24a]

To turn to the second problem. There is no doubt that *habeo* was sometimes used by Bede to mean 'must, have to',[25] though one might perhaps ask why he

---

[18] *JEGP* 3 (1901), 499–500.

[19] See Morgan Callaway, Jr *The Infinitive in Anglo-Saxon* (Washington, 1913), pp. 44 and 54 (*geearnian* and *forhycgan*) and pp. 150–1 and 152–3 (*gearo bēon*).

[20] There are no examples of *āgan* + infinitive in the Dictionary proper. All those s.v. *āgan* IV in the Supplement have the inflected infinitive.

[21] Callaway for once lacks his usual clarity and incisiveness: despite his blanket observation (pp. 79–80), he does recognize *āgan* as an exception: 'with all the strict auxiliaries except *agan*, the predicative infinitive is normally uninflected...' (p. 82). He quotes the Wulfstan example on p. 80.

[22] There are none s. vv. *owe*, *ought*, or *own*.

[23] Shigeru Ono 'The Early Development of the Auxiliary *Ought*', *Hitotsubashi Journal of Arts and Sciences* 1 (1960), 47.

[24] Arthur Napier *Wulfstan* (Berlin, 1883), p. 294, ll. 24–6.

[24a] [1987. On the question which infinitive *agan* prefers, see now *OES* §§932–3 and 996, and Shigeru Ono 'Old English *agan* + Infinitive Revisited', *Journal of Social Sciences and Humanities* (*Jimbun Gakuko*) (Tokyo), 191 (March 1987), 33–48.]

[25] See *JEGP* 3 (1901), 498 and *NM* 66 (1965), 109.

used *debeo* in the next speech if *habes* implies obligation in the passage under discussion. But is it equally certain that his translator could have used *āgan* in this sense with the infinitive of a verb like *singan*? The primary sense of *āgan* during the Old English period was 'to have, to possess'.[26] According to the *OED*, it also had the sense 'to have to pay'. The first supporting example is from the tenth-century Northumbrian glosses to the Lindisfarne Gospels:

[*c* 950 *Lindisf. Gosp.* Matt. xviii. 28 ʒeld þæt ðu aht to ʒeldanne]
[*Vulg.* debes *Rushw.* and *Ags. G.* scealt, *Hatt.* scelt].[27]

(The full Vulgate reading is *Redde quod debes.*) The other *OED* examples are on a par with this.[28] None of them gives any support to the notion that *āgan* alone means 'to be obliged to'; the sense of the Old English is 'You have something to pay. Pay it.' In other words, *āgan* means 'to possess' and the inflected infinitive qualifies the object. The comparison is with MnE 'I have my house to let', not with MnE 'I have to let my house'.[29]

The first examples in the *OED* of '*āgan* + infinitive' in the sense 'to have it as a duty or obligation' are from '*c* 1175 *Lamb. Hom.*'.[30] The Bosworth-Toller Supplement cites six Old English sentences in which *āgan* is said to be used 'of obligation, *to have* to do something'.[31] Four of these involve the infinitive *to geldanne*, two the infinitive *to donne*. All of them show a syntactical pattern like that of the passage from Lindisfarne Matthew 18. 28 above. The sense is 'to have something to pay' or 'to have the duties of a priest (or thane) to do'. The Bosworth-Toller entry should read 'to have something to do'; *āgan* again denotes possession, not obligation.

Callaway notes thirty-two Old English examples where an infinitive is used with 'agan (nagan), *owe* (*not*), *ought* (*not*)'.[32] In the four which do not belong to the late tenth or to the eleventh century, *āgan* once again has the sense of possession.[33] It must be admitted that some of the remaining twenty-eight

[26] See Bosworth-Toller s.v. *āgan* and *OED* s.v. *owe*.
[27] S.v. *owe* B. II. 2.
[28] S.vv. *owe* B. II. 2 and *ought* A. II. 2.
[29] Cf. the following versions of Luke 7. 40:
Greek: Σίμων, ἔχω σοί τι εἰπεῖν.
Vulgate: Simon, habeo tibi aliquid dicere.
Old English (Thorpe): Simon, ic hæbbe þe to secgenne sum þing.
New English Bible: Simon, I have something to say to you.
[30] S.vv. *owe* B. III and *ought* A. III. 5b. (a).
[31] S.v. *āgan* IV.
[32] Callaway, pp. 80–1.
[33] They are (quoted after Callaway, p. 81):
Laws 30, Ælfred, Intr., c. 12ᵃ: *nage he hie ut on elðoedig folc to bebycgganne.*
— *Ib.* 48, Ælfred, c. 2: *age he ðreora nihta fierst him to gebeorganne* (or final?).
— *Ib.* 116, Ine, c. 62: *nah ðonne self nane wiht to gesellanne* beforan ceape.
Wærf. 241. 18: ðæt se ðe agymeleasede, ðæt he heolde his lichaman forhæfednesse, *nahte* sona na ma *to sprecenne* ðæs wundorlican mægnes word buton lichamlicre tungan = 296 A²: ut qui carnis continentiam servare neglexerat, sine lingua carnea non *haberet verba* virtutis.

examples quoted by Callaway suggest that the *OED* is in error in noting no examples before *c.* 1175 of '*āgan* + infinitive' meaning 'to have it as a duty or obligation'. Ono seems justified in his claim that 'it was towards the end of the eleventh century that the meanings "to have to pay" and "to have as a duty (*to do*)" became prevalent. In the earlier periods these meanings were usually expressed by *sculan*.'[34] The implication that the usage was in existence *c.* 1000 is supported by some of the examples from Wulfstan. But even this lends little support to the notion that the ninth-century translator of Bede wrote *þu me aht singan* with the feeling that it meant 'You must sing to me' – though of course the absence of examples is not conclusive, since arguments based on silence are notoriously dangerous.

It is possible that *aht* may be an unthinking crib for *habes* just as *singan* may be for *cantare*. Professor Whitelock has suggested elsewhere that the translator of Bede was 'influenced by the practice of interlinear glossing of a text'[35] and was 'unable to shed the habits of a school of interlinear glossing'.[36] That he occasionally misunderstood the Latin is well-known, and Miss Whitelock's own note in the *Reader* on ll. 48ff. of this same text explains an example where his undue respect for, or his inability to cope with, the original produced violations of Old English idiom (which, interestingly enough, led the scribe of T to make an error). But how likely is it that he so misunderstood (*mihi*) *cantare habes* that his tendency to 'translate over-literally'[37] led him to produce a direct crib of the words and yet to use the appropriate Old English word-order and not that of the Latin? If such an assumption lies behind the acceptance of the reading *þu me aht singan*, it should be stated, as it was by Klaeber. But Professor Whitelock does not seem to be making this assumption; her Glossary gives *aht* as 'must'.

The table on p. 79 summarizes and comments on the possible meanings of *habes*, *aht*, and *meaht*.

In making our choice, we must consider the three possibilities I have already outlined:[38]

a one of these equations is right and was intended by the translator;
b the translator was in error. Perhaps he made an unthinking literal translation. Perhaps he was confused by the following *debeo* and translated *habes* 'you must' by *þu meaht* 'you can';
c the translator made a deliberate variation, perhaps in an attempt to distinguish *habes* from *debeo* or, as Professor Wrenn has suggested, under the influence of 'a separate English tradition independent of Bede'.[39]

[34] Ono, p. 48.   [35] *Proceedings of the British Academy* 48 (1962), 76.
[36] *Proceedings*, pp. 76–7.   [37] *Proceedings*, p. 76.
[38] *NM* 66 (1965), 110–11 [item 7 above].
[39] *Proceedings of the British Academy* 32 (1946), 284.

Meaning	habes	aht	meaht
'you must, have to ...'	(i) Not disputed. Examples in Bede. See *JEGP* 3 (1901), 498 and *NM* 66 (1965), 109 [item 7 above]. (ii) Why *debeo* in next speech if *habes* implies obligation?	(i) Can it mean this? (ii) Should it have inflected infinitive? See above.	Possible. See *NM* 66 (1965), 109 [item 7 above].
'you can ...'	Possible. See *MLN* 52 (1937), 413 and *NM* 66 (1965), 108–9 [item 7 above].[40]		The commonest sense.
'you shall ...' (future)	Possible. See *NM* 66 (1965), 110 [item 7 above][41]		Perhaps just possible but unlikely. See *NM* 66 (1965), 110 [item 7 above].
'you have [something] ...'	A common meaning. But there is no object. Could we understand *aliquid* from the visitor's first speech? Possible, but unlikely?	The commonest meaning. But the absence of an object is a difficulty. It can scarcely mean 'You have [a song] to sing to me'. Could we understand *hwæthwugu* from the visitor's first speech? Possible, but unlikely?	

Little more can be said about (b). On (c) see the last paragraph of this 'Postscript'. If we accept (a) in the belief that the Old English translator knew better than we do what he was up to, can we decide objectively in favour of one of the equations set out in the table?

---

[40] Klaeber overstated his case when he wrote '*þu meaht* ("you can", "you may") as translation of *habes* is quite unintelligible' (*JEGP* 3 (1901), 498). On p. 499 he said 'The chance of *magan* having been chosen as the English equivalent of *habere* is infinitesimal.'

[41] Professor Mynors has told me that, while this usage is not good Latin, Bede might easily have used it when representing conversation.

Not, I think, on syntactic or semantic grounds. Nor is the context decisive. Klaeber wrote in 1901 'The traditional *meaht* disturbs the context very seriously and makes the spirit's reply little short of incongruous. By the reintroduction of the original reading [*me aht*] perfect order and logical harmony are restored.'[42] John M. McBryde, however, objecting to the rendering 'you must' and pleading for 'you can', tells of his 'surprise' on discovering 'how a palpable error in the rendering of a single word has obscured the significance of the lovely story which tells how Cædmon received the gift of song'.[43] Moved, no doubt, by this, Klaeber admitted in 1938 that the choice is, 'of course, a matter of opinion'.[44] We must, I think, agree.

Professor Whitelock takes her text 'from the Tanner MS., which has several superior readings; but in a few places where it is in error, readings of other manuscripts are substituted'.[45] So T may be in error here; Miller notes that 'B. constantly sides with C. O. Ca. against T. in cases of omissions by T.'[46] But even if we accept T, we are not obliged to accept *þu me aht singan*.

I have already shown above that we can account for all the variants if we assume that the Anglo-Saxon translator wrote *þu me aht singan*. But it would seem that the acceptance of this reading involves a more complicated series of explanations than the acceptance of any other. If we assume that T omitted *me* (wherever he got it from) by haplography, we have to explain only the variation in the position of *me*. There are three ways of doing this; see p. 75 above. If we assume that T's *meaht* = 'can' is right, we have to account for the addition of *me* in another manuscript or in other manuscripts (bearing in mind that *þu meaht singan* makes sense without *me*), and for the variation in position. For ways of doing this see pp. 74–5 above.

To accept *þu me aht singan* as the original reading, we have to assume that *me aht* was written as *meaht* in the original manuscript or that it was misread as *meaht* or that it was a *lectio difficilior* not understood by a scribe and therefore written as *meaht*. Then we have to account as above for the addition of *me* and the variation in its position. All this is certainly possible. But it is a more complicated chain of misunderstanding than is necessary for any other reading.

The acceptance of *þu me aht singan* is therefore not as easy and obvious a solution as might at first appear:

    a there is some doubt about the presence of *mihi* in the Latin text;
    b the syntax of *aht* + the simple infinitive is questionable;
    c the equation *þu aht* = 'you must' is questionable;

---

[42] *JEGP* 3 (1901), 500.
[43] *MLN* 52 (1937), 412.
[44] *MLN* 53 (1938), 250.
[45] *Sweet's Anglo-Saxon Reader*, 15th edn, p. 45.
[46] EETS, o.s. 95, 96. xxv. The problem of contamination arises; see D. Whitelock *Proceedings of the British Academy* 48 (1962), 81, n. 22.

d that T's reading is necessarily superior textually has yet to be demonstrated;
e a complicated explanation is required to account for the other variant readings;
f the case for any of the three variants (*þu meaht singan*; *þu me miht singan*; *þu meaht me singan*) seems no less strong syntactically, semantically, contextually, and palaeographically.

I have to admit (as now appears to be my wont) that this investigation has produced no positive conclusion about these readings. All seem possible. No one of them can be proved right. My own inclination at the moment is still to print anything but *þu me aht singan*. However, the real point of my first article was to suggest that this particular passage provided no evidence for the view that an oral tradition about Cædmon independent of Bede reached the Old English translator of Bede's *History*. This conclusion, I believe, still stands whichever of the four readings we adopt.[47]

---

[47] Ono may be right in suggesting that the use of *āgan* (for *sculan*) = *debere* in the Lindisfarne Glosses may be a Northumbrian characteristic (p. 48, n. 11). At first glance, this might support the notion that *aht* was a relic of Northumbrian, orally transmitted. But the Glosses are some two centuries after Bede himself and appreciably later than the Old English *Bede*. And, as I have already shown, even in them *aht* alone does not mean 'must'. To claim oral transmission from the early eighth century of a tenth-century usage dubious in itself and dubiously Northumbrian would be too much.

10
Bede's Account of the Poet Cædmon: Two Notes

In the course of his account of the poet Cædmon in book 4, chapter 22 (24) of his *Historia Ecclesiastica Gentis Anglorum*, Bede remarks:

At ipse cuncta, quae audiendo discere poterat, rememorando secum, et quasi mundum animal ruminando, in carmen dulcissimum conuertebat, suauiusque resonando, doctores suos uicissim auditores sui faciebat.[1]

The Old English version as published by T. Miller (MS T) reads:

Ond he eal, þa he in gehyrnesse geleornian meahte, mid hine gemyndgade; 7 swa swa clæne neten eodorcende in þæt sweteste leoð gehwerfde. 7 his song 7 his leoð wæron swa wynsumu to gehyranne, þætte seolfan þa his lareowas æt his muðe wreoton 7 leornodon.[2]

Two points of interest emerge from this.

I

The first is the syntactical problem presented by the Old English version of the Latin *doctores suos uicissim auditores sui faciebat*. As we have seen, MS T (which, according to Miller, 'may claim to represent the archetype most faithfully')[3] has *seolfan þa his lareowas æt his muðe wreoton 7 leornodon*. None of the remaining manuscripts reads *seolfan þa his lareowas*. MS B (the connexion of which to MS T 'is illustrated by common faults')[4] has *þa sylfan lareowas*. MS C (which offers 'independent testimony on any question of reading'[5] to MS T) has *þa seolfan his lareowas*, a reading shared (with minor spelling

Reprinted from *Iceland and the Mediaeval World: Studies in Honour of Ian Maxwell* ed. Gabriel Turville-Petre and John Stanley Martin (Melbourne, 1974). This article was written in 1967 when the author was at Brown University, Providence, Rhode Island.

[1] C. Plummer *Venerabilis Baedae Opera Historica* (Oxford, 1896), 1. 260. [So also the 1969 edn of Colgrave and Mynors.]
[2] EETS, o.s. 95, 96, p. 346, ll. 1–5.
[3] EETS, p. xxviii.   [4] EETS, p. xxv.   [5] EETS, p. xxvi.

variations) by MSS O and Ca. – MS C is the 'elder brother in the family to which these three belong'.[6] The following table sets out these variations:

MS T   seolfan þa his lareowas
MS B   þa sylfan lareowas
MS C   þa seolfan his lareowas
MS O   þa sylfan his lareowas
MS Ca. ða sylfan his lareowas.

C. T. Onions in his revised edition of Henry Sweet's *Anglo-Saxon Reader* prints *þā sylfan his lārēowas*.[7] His note reads: '*þā sylfan* can only mean "the same". It is possible, however, that the original reading was *selfe*, "his teachers themselves".'[8] It is not clear whether he is suggesting that we read *þa selfe his lareowas* or *selfe his lareowas*. Are these possible readings?

Neither Grein-Köhler nor Bosworth-Toller seems to cite any similar examples of the combination 'demonstrative + strong form of *self*' except *þæs sylfes* in *Soul and Body* i. 55–6:

... syððan ic ana of ðe   ut siðode
þurh þæs sylfes hand   þe ic ær onsended wæs,[9]

where *þæs sylfes* refers back to *gode* in *Soul and Body* i. 46: *ond ic wæs gast on ðe fram gode sended*,[10] and means 'of the (self-)same (*or* of that very) [God] by whom I had been sent'; it is far from clear to me why both dictionaries gloss this example under 'self' rather than 'same'. I have as yet found nothing similar myself. It would therefore seem that there is little point in reading *þa selfe*; it is ill-attested and would still mean 'the same'.

Although the strong form of *self* does occur alone in the meaning 'self',[11] the closest parallel I know to the reading *selfe his lareowas* is *sylfes þæs folces* in *Riddle* 64. 6, where we have a demonstrative instead of a personal pronoun. This reading then would (I suppose) adequately represent *doctores suos*, but the arrangement is again ill-attested and the exact significance of *selfe* cannot be determined with any certainty.

In view of this, we should ask whether there is anything really wrong with *þa sylfan*, which appears in all the manuscripts except T. (The reading of T

[6] EETS, p. xxvi.
[7] I quote from the 12th edn (Oxford, 1950).
[8] Op. cit., p. 207.
[9] See Grein-Köhler, s.v. *self* 1 (p. 595 top right), and Bosworth-Toller, s.v. *self* A. II. (2). The same two lines occur in *Soul and Body* ii. 52–3, with minor spelling variations.
[10] Cf. *Soul and Body* ii. 43.
[11] Bosworth-Toller, s.v. *self* A. III.

seems unacceptable.)[12] B's *þa sylfan lareowas* is a well-attested construction and would give good sense. It could mean 'those very teachers', 'the same teachers', or perhaps even 'the teachers themselves' – it is hard to see why Bosworth-Toller and Grein-Köhler differentiate between *se sylfa cyning* in *Christ* l. 1208, which they both gloss as 'self', and *se sylfa god* in *Paris Psalter* 107. 10, which both take as 'the same'.[13]

However, the fact that all the other manuscripts, including T, read *his* suggests that the Sweet *Reader* was right to prefer *þa sylfan his lareowas*, on which C, O and Ca. agree, with spelling variations. But is the note in the *Reader* right in claiming that '*þā sylfan* can only mean "the same"'? Bosworth-Toller, which accepts this reading, disagrees – it glosses the passage under 'A. *self, very, own*' (not under 'B. (*the*) *same*') and translates 'his very teachers learned from his mouth'.[14] As we have seen above, there is no real evidence that *þa sylfan* must mean 'the same'. And even if, despite this, we insist that it must, the translation 'the same ones his teachers' is not so very far from *doctores suos* (especially when we consider that there are mistranslations and variations elsewhere in the Old English version). The real point at issue is perhaps, not whether *þa sylfan* must mean 'the same', but whether there is any real distinction between these two translations. Here too, it is difficult to see on what principle Bosworth-Toller distinguishes the Bede passage, which it glosses under 'A. *self, very, own*', from some of those which it glosses under 'B. (*the*) *same*', e.g. *Leechdoms* i. 190. 18: *Heo tofereþ ðæt sar; ðæt sylfe heo deþ mid wine gecnucud*.[15] What is needed is a rethinking of the basic division in the articles on *self* in Bosworth-Toller and Grein-Köhler rather than argument about the Bede passage.

---

[12] Postscript (January 1968). Dorothy Whitelock in her revision of *Sweet's Anglo-Saxon Reader* (15th edn, Oxford, 1967) prints the reading of T (p. 48, l. 73) with the note (p. 243): '73. *þætte seolfan þā his lāreowas* "that his very teachers". The use of the demonstrative along with possessives is particularly common in Anglian: cf. l. 17 above.' The reference at p. 46, l. 17 reads *his þā ǣfestan tungan*. But, while this might justify us in reading *his þā seolfan īāreowas* (which no manuscript has), it provides no real support for T's version, with the syntactically suspicious weak form *seolfan* standing alone.

[13] See Bosworth-Toller, s.v. *self* A. I. (*ð*) and B. (*a*) and Grein-Köhler, s.v. *self* 2. and 3., respectively. Both strong and weak forms of *self* can mean 'self', e.g. Genesis ll. 139, 570. But both Sweet and Grein-Köhler seem to have in mind the notion that the strong form of *self* cannot mean 'the same' – the former opposes *selfe* 'themselves' to *þa sylfan* 'the same' and the latter has, s.v. *self*, three divisions – 1. *starke Flexion, ipse* ... 2. *schwache Flexion, ipse* ... 3. *schwache Flexion, derselbe, idem*. ... That this is not true is suggested by *Leechdoms Wortcunning and Starcraft of Early England* ed. T. O. Cockayne (rev. edn, London, 1961), ii. 72. 17, *on selfe wisan* 'in the same fashion' quoted after Bosworth-Toller, s.v. *self* B. (*β*). Such examples are naturally rare. We shall, theoretically, look in vain for examples of 'demonstrative and strong form of adjective and noun' in either sense – hence perhaps the fluctuating attitude of Bosworth-Toller and Grein-Köhler to examples like *Christ* l. 1208 and *Paris Psalter* 107. 10. On *-an/-um* confusion, see C. L. Wrenn in *PST* (1943), pp. 29–30.

[14] S.v. *self* A. I. (*ð*).

[15] Quoted from Bosworth-Toller, s.v. *self* B. (*α*).

II

The second point of interest is the Old English translator's use of the phrase *æt his muðe wreoton 7 leornodon*. This is found, with spelling variations, in all the manuscripts except B, which has *æfter* for *æt*, and C, where f. 15ª ends at *æt his* and f. 15ᵇ begins *leornodon*.[16] The translator's use of the word *wreoton* is a filling-out of the Latin similar to his representation of *cantare* by *be hearpan singan* in the same chapter; both seem to depend on personal knowledge of the circumstances under which Anglo-Saxon poetry was delivered. It is interesting that C. L. Wrenn did not discuss *wreoton* when he suggested that the addition of the words *for sceome*[17] and the representation of the Latin *mihi cantare habes* by *þu meaht me singan*[18] might 'imply some corroboration of a separate English tradition independent of Bede'.[19] However, it seems clear that *wreoton* could not strengthen the weak case for such a tradition; indeed, it might further weaken it.

F. P. Magoun Jr is, I think, correct in dismissing *wreoton* as evidence for the present existence of 'other songs or substantial remnants of songs'[20] by Cædmon. But the addition is perhaps evidence for something else, for it seems to suggest that in the late ninth century, when the translation appears to have been made,[21] people were still taking down orally composed poetry (whether during performance or by slow dictation afterwards is not clear) or were aware that this had been a practice in the past. That such versions may have been intended for memorization and subsequent rote delivery by other entertainers is suggested (as Magoun has pointed out[22]) by Cynewulf's prayer in *Juliana* ll. 718–22:

> Bidde ic monna gehwone
> gumena cynnes,   þe þis gied wræce,
> þæt he mec neodful   bi noman minum
> gemyne modig,   ond meotud bidde
> þæt me heofona helm   helpe gefremme....

But these passages also suggest that we are not bound to accept the view that *Beowulf* must have been an orally composed poem with no fixed text; it could

---

[16] See EETS, o.s. 110, 111, p. 412.
[17] *Proceedings of the British Academy* 32 (1946), 281.
[18] *Proceedings*, p. 284. But see *NM* 66 (1965), 107–11 [item 7 above].
[19] *Proceedings*, p. 284.
[20] *Speculum* 30 (1955), 61.
[21] See *Proceedings of the British Academy* 48 (1962), 77–8.
[22] *Speculum* 28 (1953), 460, n. 25. This is not the time to discuss Magoun's notion of Cynewulf as at times a 'writing' poet and at times an 'oral' poet later dictating to himself or someone else. But I may say that I disagree with it.

have been orally composed and then, at the first public performance or before, *æt þæs scopes muðe writen 7 eft gemunen*, or it could have been composed in writing for subsequent memorization.[23]

But – whatever the method of composition or delivery – the fact that poems were still being produced in correct metre in the late tenth century seems to cast doubt on Magoun's suggestion that the writing of Anglo-Saxon poetry as prose in the great codices was not 'a measure of economy' but was 'merely because neither scribes nor singers understood in a formal sense the metrics of the verse ...'.[24] This seems to contradict the testimony of the *Chronicle* poems of which A. Campbell has written:

> The *Battle of Brunanburh* is, accordingly, one of a group of poems preserved in the *Chronicle* (937, 941, 973, 975 lines 1–12, and 1065), which are to be described as panegyrics upon royal persons, arising out of the commemoration of events in which they were concerned. Each poem takes its rise from a single event, in the first two a victory, in the third a coronation, in the last two a death. Such poems must have been a popular form of composition with certain poets of the age ... would appeal only to courtly circles, and cultured monks. They are extremely careful in metre and style, full of evidence that the poets had meticulously studied earlier Old English verse, and are equally distant from the doggerel of the popular poems of the *Chronicle*, and the vigorous, but often careless, verse of the *Battle of Maldon*. In the two latter styles of writing we have natural, unfettered developments of the old style, but in the poems now under consideration we have an artificial preservation, or rather, perhaps, resurrection of the old style.[25]

For these poems were being composed just when the miscellanies of Anglo-

---

[23] For justification of the view that 'lettered' poets could use 'oral' formulae, see now Larry D. Benson's important article in *PMLA* 81 (1966), 334–41.

Another point may perhaps be made here. In *Early English and Norse Studies Presented to Hugh Smith* ed. Arthur Brown and Peter Foote (London, 1963), p. 129, F. P. Magoun Jr writes 'In view of a general lack of cyclic composition in oral singing the apparent cyclic character of the Beowulf material in Brit. Mus. MS Cotton Vitellius A. xv is *a priori* immediately suspect and a close examination of the material strengthens the suspicion that this is not a single poem, no continuum produced by a single singer singing on a single occasion.' The conclusion he draws is not the only possible one. Even if we assume, as he does, that *Beowulf* was orally composed, we could argue that it was an orally composed exception to the 'general lack of cyclic composition in oral singing'; note the first three words in Magoun's remark (on p. 128 of the same work) 'Seldom if ever does a folk-singer, composing extemporaneously without benefit of writing materials, compose a cyclic poem, that is, sing in a single session or series of sessions a story which he or she feels is a unit dealing with several consecutive events in a character's life.' But it would also be possible for us to argue that, since *Beowulf* is an exception to this 'general' rule, it could not have been orally composed.

[24] *Speculum* 28 (1953), 462–3.

[25] A. Campbell *The Battle of Brunanburh* (London, 1938), pp. 37–8.

Saxon poetry were being written. It seems less hazardous to stick to the view that the reason for writing poetry as prose was economy – parchment was precious and tenth-century bursars were probably no different from their twentieth-century successors.

11

Cædmon's *Hymn*, Line 1: What Is the Subject of *Scylun* or Its Variants?

1   The question posed in my title has the obvious answer *we* in

Cæd(H) l. 1   Nu we sculan herian   heofonrices weard,
metudes myhte   7 his modgeþanc,
wurc wuldorfæder,   swa he wundra gehwilc,
ece drihten,   ord astealde;
he ærest gesceop   ylda bearnum
heofon to hrofe,   halig scyppend,
middangearde   mancynnes weard;
ece drihten   æfter tida
firum on foldum,   frea ælmyhtig,

an answer which is of course supported by *debemus* in Bede's Latin paraphrase:

Hic est sensus, non autem ordo ipse uerborum, quae dormiens ille [Cædmon] canebat; neque enim possunt carmina, quamuis optime conposita, ex alia in aliam linguam ad uerbum sine detrimento sui decoris ac dignitatis transferri.

Reprinted from *Sources and Relations: Studies in Honour of J. E. Cross, Leeds Studies in English* 16 (1985), 190–7.

Notes: The abbreviations for the names of texts are those proposed by Christopher Ball, Angus Cameron, and myself, in *ASE* 4 (1975), 207–21 and 8 (1979), 331–3. *Beowulf* is cited from Klaeber (3rd edn), the remaining verse texts from the Anglo-Saxon Poetic Records, abbreviated to ASPR.
    The Latin of Bede's account of the poet Cædmon is quoted from Bede's *Ecclesiastical History of the English People* ed. Bertram Colgrave and R. A. B. Mynors (Oxford, 1969), the Old English from the Old English version of Bede's *Ecclesiastical History of the English People* ed. Thomas Miller, EETS o.s. 95, 96, 110, 111.
    The names of the authors serve as cue-titles for the following works:
Three Northumbrian Poems ed. A. H. Smith (London, 1933);
The Anglo-Saxon Minor Poems ed. E. V. K. Dobbie, ASPR vi (New York and London, 1942);
D. R. Howlett 'The Theology of Cædmon's *Hymn*', *Leeds Studies in English* 7 (1974), 1–12;
Bruce Mitchell 'Bede's Account of the Poet Cædmon: Two Notes', *Iceland and the Mediaeval World: Studies in Honour of Ian Maxwell* ed. Gabriel Turville-Petre and John Stanley Martin (Melbourne, 1974), pp. 126–31 [item 10 above].

The nominative *we* or something like it appears in a majority of the seventeen versions of the *Hymn* listed by Dobbie (pp. xciv–x). Two of the four Northumbrian versions (*Di* and *P*) have *Nu pue*. The eight West-Saxon versions in Latin manuscripts of Bede's *Ecclesiastical History* – *H, W, Bd, Ln, Mg, Tr 1, Ld 1*, and *Hr* – all have *Nu we*. Three of the five versions in manuscripts of the 'Alfredian' translation also have *Nu we* – *Ca, O* (where *we* is added above the line) and *B*. *C* has *Ne*, which Smith (p. 3) and Dobbie (p. xcix) took as an omission of the pronoun *we* but which is perhaps better regarded as a scribal conflation of *Nu* and *we*.

2   But the same question provokes no obvious answer in the three remaining manuscripts – the two 'oldest Northumbrian texts' and 'the best West Saxon text' (Howlett, p. 6):

Cæd(M) l. 1   Nu scylun hergan   hefaenricaes uard,
                 metudæs maecti   end his modgidanc,
                 uerc uuldurfadur,   sue he uundra gihaues,
                 eci dryctin,   or astelidæ.
                 He aerist scop   aelda barnum
                 heben til hrofe,   haleg scepen;
                 tha middungeard   moncynnæs uard,
                 eci dryctin,   æfter tiadæ
                 firum foldu,   frea allmectig,

Cæd(L) l. 1 *Nu scilun herga* ..., and

Cæd(T) l. 1   Nu sculon herigean   heonfonrices weard,
                 meotodes meahte   and his modgeþanc,
                 weorc wuldorfæder,   swa he wundra gehwæs,
                 ece drihten,   or onstealde.
                 He ærest sceop   eorðan bearnum
                 heofon to hrofe,   halig scyppend;
                 þa middangeard   moncynnes weard,
                 ece drihten,   æfter teode
                 firum foldan,   frea ælmihtig.

The noteworthy absence of *we* from these manuscripts – I deliberately avoid the pre-emptive term 'omission' – has in my opinion been too easily brushed aside by scholars who are apparently content to accept the implication of Smith's gloss (p. 53): '*scylun, lpl.* Cl'. It is the initial purpose of this paper to enter a syntactical caveat against this attitude, which seems to me a remarkable one in view of the fact that 'it is a peculiarity of the Ingvaeonic languages that there is only one form for the three persons of the plural' in verbs.[1]

[1] A. Campbell *Old English Grammar* (Oxford, 1959), §729.

3   Smith (pp. 3-4) offers the following comment:

> The other important difference is that D [= *ASPR Di*] P have *we* (line 1), but ML omit it. The latter versions give no indication of the original reading, for two manuscripts of the OEBede (which in respect of reading *eorþan* follow DP) omit *we*, whilst the remaining manuscripts, both HE and OEBede, insert it. It is probable that *we* was added independently (like *on*) in the prototype of the later HE group (for they also agree in reading *gehwilc* for *gehwæs* and *tida* for *teode*), but otherwise we must suppose that addition or omission of *we* depended largely upon individual scribes. In early Northumbrian such pronouns were sometimes omitted,[1] as in ML, and the fact that DP have *we* but that two of the related OEBede versions omit it rather indicates that *we* was in *Y but not in *Y's prototype from which the OEBede versions are ultimately derived.

Smith's footnote reads:

> Cf G. Sarrazin, ESt xxxviii. 183 ff. The addition of *we* is more likely than its omission in later recensions and there was, as Frampton, *op. cit.* 9, shows, a strong tendency to begin OE poetry with a pronoun (e.g. *Beowulf*, *Exodus*, *Daniel*, &c.). The 'modernizing' tendency is noticed also in later versions in the substitution of *ord* for the earlier *or* (MLDP) (cf Frampton 6).

The implications of this and his glossary entry above are that it was immaterial whether *we* was there or not; that *debemus* was an acceptable translation, whether Bede's version had *we* or did not have it; and (one must presume) that any native speaker of Old English hearing a vernacular version of the *Hymn* without *we* would without blinking take it to mean the equivalent of 'we are obliged to, we must'. Somewhat similar attitudes seem to me to be implied in Dobbie's note (p. 198):

> Nu] The omission of the pronoun subject *we* [in M and L of the Northumbrian version, and T and C of the West Saxon *eorðan*-group) is not unparalleled in early Northumbrian (see Genesis 1098, where *ic* is omitted in the MS., and also Genesis 828, 885, where *ic* has been added above the line) but may well have seemed, to the later scribes, to require emendation.

But the notion that the 1st pers. nom. pl. pron. *we* could be unexpressed at the beginning of a poem in which it does not occur and in which there was therefore no first person grammatical referent derives no support from *GenA* l. 870, *GenA* l. 1098, *GenB* l. 828, or *GenB* l. 885,[2] and virtually none from *And* l. 1487,[3]

[2] G. Sarrazin *EStudien* 38 (1907), 183 and Dobbie's ASPR note quoted above.
[3] A. Pogatscher *Anglia* 23 (1901), 285.

where there is a clear sequence *And* 1. 1478 *ic* . . . 1. 1481 *Mycel is to secganne* . . . 1. 1483 *þæt scell æglæwra / mann on moldan þonne ic me tælige* . . . , to justify the non-expression of *we*, the subject of *sceolon*, in *And* 1. 1487 *Hwæðre git sceolon //* . . . *reccan*. I cannot accept Smith's notion, tentatively endorsed by Dobbie (pp. xcix and 198), that 'the addition of *we*' can be explained away as the result of a '"modernizing" tendency' when there is no evidence that *scylun* alone can mean 'we must' in *Cæd(M)* 1. 1; see 6 and 8 below.

4   It is, however, possible to argue that the absence of *we* in three manuscripts of such authority as *M, L*, and *T*, is proof that the first sentence of the *Hymn* gave good sense without *we*. It could indeed be claimed that to believe it was unacceptable Old English or that it made nonsense without *we* would involve accepting unacceptable coincidences. If so, another subject for *scylun* must be found. Here I am grateful to Christopher Ball, of Keble College, Oxford, for allowing me to make use of an idea which he first propounded in the late 1960s: that the original subject of *scylun* was *uerc uuldurfadur* and that *we* is a later insertion which changed the meaning of the sentence. We need look no further than *Beo* 1. 395 *Nu ge moton gangan* . . . to establish that *Cæd(H)* 1. 1 *Nu we sculan herian* . . . is acceptable Old English. Further examples of this pattern appear in *And* 11. 595, 811, and 1517, *Dream* 1. 78, *El* 1. 511, and *GuthB* 1. 6. For variations of it, see *inter alia GenB* 1. 816, *ChristC* 1. 1327, and *Fast* 1. 39. Although I have at the moment no exact parallels for the adverb–verb–triple object–subject pattern involved in Ball's interpretation, I am confident that it is good Old English and that the different intonation patterns which the language then had – capable as they must have been of distinguishing the object–verb–subject/subject–object pattern in *GenA* 1. 2887 *Wudu bær sunu, / fæder fyr and sweord* – would have permitted a *scop* to make such a relationship clear. The closest example I have so far found is

PPs 133. 1   Efne bletsien nu   bliðe drihten
                    ealle his agene   onbyhtscealcas.

For variations, see *Beo* 1. 337, *Sat* 1. 579, and *Met* 4. 47.

5   We have Bede's testimony that Cædmon based his later poems on the scriptures and we find in the Psalms sound scriptural basis for both the interpretations so far proposed. We animate beings are called upon to praise God in *Ps(A)* 94. 1 *cumað gefen we dryhī wynsumie we gode*, Latin *uenite exultemus dño iubilemus dō*, and to praise His works in *Ps(A)* 20. 13 *we singað 7 singað megan ðin*, Latin *cantabimus et psallimus uirtutes tuas*. God's inanimate creations are called upon to praise Him in *Ps(A)* 102. 21 *bledsiað dryhī all werc his*, Latin *benedicite dñm omnia opera eius*, and in *Ps(A)* 144. 10 *ondettað ðe dryhī all werc ðin*, Latin *confiteantur tibi dñe omnia opera tua*. But a third possibility – suggested by Howlett (p. 6) in 1974

– is that those who heard *we* construed *uerc uuldurfadur* as a nominative appositional variant of it, 'assuming that *we* are part of God's handiwork, the creatures who should praise Him'. This interpretation too makes good Old English – such appositional variants play a vital role in the weaving of Old English poetry – and draws scriptural authority from passages in which inanimate creations of God are exhorted in the imperative to praise Him and are thereby personified; these include *Ps(A)* 102. 21 and 144. 10 (the last two examples quoted), the whole of *Ps(A)* 148, and *PsCa6* 8, the *Hymnvm Trivm Pverorvm* or *Benedicite*, which begins *bledsiað all werc dryhtnes dryhten* ..., Latin *benedicite omnia opera dñi dñm*. ... But if it is to be accepted for MSS *M*, *L*, and *T* – those without *we* – this last interpretation too must clear the hurdle 'Can *scylun* alone mean "we must"?' So, for what remains of this argument, it can be subsumed under the two main divisions *we*/no *we*.

6 We must now ask whether there are any arguments by which it can be proved that, despite the syntactical difficulties raised in 3 above, *scylun* alone can mean 'we must'. The absence of *we* in MSS *M*, *L*, and *T*, can of course be attributed to scribal omission. Such omission is well attested in manuscripts of Old English poetry – but this is merely the dishonoured argument 'There are examples of *x*. Therefore this must be one' – and the addition of *we* above the line in MS *O* may be regarded as an actual example – but since it cannot be proved as one because it is 'a corrector's addition' (Dobbie, p. xcix) and therefore may be due to the influence of another version with *we* or of Latin *debemus*, it may equally well be regarded as another testimony to the existence of an independent version without *we*. One can see that, if the Latin version with *debemus* had come first, *scylun* alone could be explained as a careless gloss for it; compare *Coll* 253 *wyllaþ wesen wise*, Latin *uolumus esse sapientes*, and see *NM* 70 (1969), 376 [item 9 above], where I discuss the possibility that there are unthinking cribs in the Old English *Bede*. But this is out of the question, for there is no doubt that the Old English *Hymn* came first; see Smith, pp. 12–13, and Dobbie, pp. xcix–c. The possibility that *scylun* without *we* is due to the influence of *debemus* seems to me so remote that it too can be dismissed, even (I believe) in MS *L*, where 'the hymn is written in the lower margin of fol. 107*a* below the relevant passage in the Latin text, and in the same hand' (Dobbie, p. xcv), for here the readings of MSS *M*, where 'the text of the hymn is added on fol. 128*b*, the last page of the manuscript' (ibid.), and *L* support one another. It can scarcely be said to arise in MS *T*, where the *Hymn* is an integral part of the Old English text.

7 We are left then with the possibility that Cædmon sang *we* and that scribal omission accounts for its absence from manuscripts *M*, *L*, and *T*. But there is another possibility: that Cædmon did not sing *we* and that its appearance in the

majority of manuscripts is the result of later insertion in one or more than one prototype. Now the fact that Bede wrote *debemus* means either that the version he heard or read had *we* or that it did not and that – since in my opinion *scylun* cannot mean 'we must' – he misunderstood or was misled by his immediate informant(s). Is such a misunderstanding likely? One could suppose that Bede and his fellow monks might have been unfamiliar with Old English poetry and were misled by the difficult element order involved in taking *uerc uuldurfadur* as subject; see 4 above. Or one could suppose that they were more accustomed to thinking 'we must praise God' than 'God's inanimate creations must praise Him' and were misled by anticipating the former. But Howlett (p. 6) gives good reasons why we should think better of Bede's understanding of Old English poetry and Colgrave and Mynors (p. xix) state that his book 'became a pattern and gave a new conception of history to western Europe', which suggests that he was not easily misled. So I am forced to conclude that Bede's source in all probability had *we* and from now on will assume that it had.

8   If this conclusion and the arguments I have so far advanced be accepted, it follows that *we* cannot be properly described as a later addition brought about by the '"modernizing" tendency' discussed in 3 above. So we seem bound to conclude either that the absence of *we* in MSS *M*, *L*, and *T*, is the result of omission after Bede's time or that there were two separate forms of the text – one with *we* and one without *we* – before Bede's time. When discussing the possible meanings of Bede's *mihi cantare habes*, I wrote in *NM* 66 (1965), 110 [item 7 above] that the existence of 'an oral tradition independent of Bede ... is, of course, certain – unless all the by-standers except Bede or his informant(s) were deaf-mutes, or unless no one else ever bothered to mention the matter'. I now carry this further by suggestion that the presence or absence of *we* be traced back to the initial, or to an early, recital of the *Hymn*. We can postulate either that Cædmon himself delivered two versions or, given the excitement of the occasion described by Bede and the inherent unreliability of human witnesses, that some of those present heard *we* and some did not, depending on which of the two ideas discussed in 5 above – 'we must praise God' or 'God's inanimate creations must praise Him' – was uppermost in their minds. While it is impossible to believe that Cædmon sang the *Hymn* only once to a human audience – both the *tungerefa* and the Abbess Hild are likely to have had a private performance before what must have been only the first public one – I am inclined to give Cædmon the benefit of the doubt: Bede does say that *exsurgens autem a somno, cuncta quae dormiens cantauerat memoriter retenuit* and I am reluctant to allow human frailty to obtrude into this sacred moment. But the possibility of error on the part of one or more of the hearers is a very real one. For, while Bede's description of the first public performance neither supports nor rules out the possibility that a written version was made more or less on the

spot – on this see 9 below – it does not rule out the possibility of independent oral performances by excited bystanders rushing off to infirmary, cottage, or the study of a dedicated scribe or mystic left unmoved by such worldly excitements. And independent oral performance inevitably carries with it the possibility of textual corruption; witness the well-known story of how the message 'We are going to advance. Can you send us reinforcements?' was passed down along a line of advancing troops and reached its ultimate recipient in the form 'We are going to a dance. Can you lend us three and fourpence?' and see the work of Alison Jones/Gyger on the Old English *Daniel* and *Azarias*[4] and on the two versions of *Soul and Body*.[5]

9   This suggestion of misunderstanding at the initial, or at an early, recital of the *Hymn* is in my view rendered more plausible and more attractive by the consideration that it might also account for other variations, including those typified by the reading *Cæd(M)* l. 5 *aelda barnam* where *Cæd(Di)* l. 5 has *eordu bearnum*, and for the fact that this variation cuts across the *we*/no *we* variation in the various manuscripts. If accepted, it also means that arguments about which version came first will have to be rephrased in some such way as this: Did Cædmon sing *we* or did he not? Did he sing *aelda* or *eordu*? Here we can, I think, dismiss some arguments for the idea that he sang *we*, including the fact that the majority of manuscripts read *we* and the parallels gathered by F. P. Magoun, Jr,[6] for these are relevant both here and in Magoun's general argument only if we accept the idea that Cædmon was not the first to use Germanic alliterative verse for Christian purposes, an idea which Magoun 'proves' by using these same parallels; compare here Smith, pp. 14–15. We will perhaps continue to argue about the respective value of Bede's readings – *debemus* supports *we scylun* and *filiis hominum aelda barnum* – and of the *lectio difficilior* principle – which supports *scylun* and *eordu bearnum*, but this can be countered by the argument that the change from *aelda* to *eordu* could have been made by a hearer who had in mind some such phrase as *homo ex humo*,[7] and the non-expression of *we* by a hearer who had in mind some such verse as *Ps(A)* 102. 21 *bledsiað dryhī all werc his*, Latin *benedicite dnm omnia opera eius*. However, the idea of initial or early misunderstanding makes it difficult to sustain arguments about the primacy of particular readings. So I will not pursue them here. Nor will I attempt to draw a stemma, although I will voice my surprise that the presence or absence of *we* has not been taken more seriously in the discussion of the relationships between the various manuscripts of the *Hymn*. But I have to agree that there are very real difficulties. I have, I hope, established the pos-

[4] *MÆ* 35 (1966), 95–102.
[5] *MÆ* 38 (1969), 239–44. [1987. But see P. R. Orton *MÆ* 48 (1979), 173–97.]
[6] *Speculum* 30 (1955), 62.
[7] See John Golden *NM* 70 (1969), 627–9.

sibility that oral versions with and without *we* existed before Bede's time. Both may have been committed to writing, although it is to be noted that the Old English *wreoton* in *Bede* (T) 346. 4 ... *seolfan þa his lareowas æt his muðe wreoton 7 leornodon* is not supported by the Latin ... *doctores suos uicissim auditores sui faciebat* – a point overlooked (conveniently, it may seem, since it hardly supports his notion of oral tradition) by C. L. Wrenn;[8] see my comments in Mitchell 1974 [item 10 above]. On the other hand, it is arguable that only a version with *we* was written down and the absence of *we* in MS *T* is a genuine instance of scribal omission; see 6 above. Here I must leave the reader, for I find myself in a predicament reminiscent of that which led Dr Johnson to write: 'Some words there are which I cannot explain because I do not understand them.'

[8] *Proceedings of the British Academy* 32 (1946), 277–95.

Part III

The Wanderer, *The Seafarer*, and Other Poems

12

Some Syntactical Problems in *The Wanderer*

I. Lines 1–5

One of the most argued questions about *The Wanderer* has been whether the first five lines portray the *anhaga* as still looking for consolation or as having achieved it. Of course the problem diminishes in importance – or disappears – if we accept the attractive suggestion of John C. Pope that there are two speakers – the wanderer and the wise man.[1] For then we can agree that the first five lines are spoken by the wanderer and that 'the opening clause keeps the consoling possibility of God's ultimate mercy in view without assuring us that the speaker has already obtained mercy'.[2] But it continues to trouble R. F. Leslie, who rejects Pope's suggestion and sticks to the view that, apart from the poet, there is a single speaker, the wanderer. Leslie thinks that this man has experienced God's mercy[3] and is prepared to 'grant him the percipience in the first five lines to see the grace of God operating to counter the otherwise fixed course of events . . .'.[4]

However, ll. 1–5 do not offer conclusive evidence that the grace of God has operated to console Leslie's wanderer. Leslie notes: 'The sense "experiences" rather than "awaits" or "expects" is to be preferred here, because the prefix *ge-* denotes completion and the adverbial clause beginning *þeahþe* "even though" implies fulfilment rather than expectation in the verb *gebīdeð*.'[5] This is confusing. The principal clause admits what cannot be denied – that *gebidan* can mean 'wait for, expect' (see *Beowulf* l. 2452) as well as 'experience' (cf. *Beowulf* l. 2445); note also Leslie's own glossary, where *gebidan* l. 70 is correctly glossed 'to wait'. Yet the subordinate clause seems to deny this by its claim that the

---

Reprinted from *Neuphilologische Mitteilungen* 69 (1968), 172–98. This article was written before items 13 and 14 but appeared after them because it was rejected by *Anglia* with no reason given.

[1] 'Dramatic Voices in *The Wanderer* and *The Seafarer*' in *Franciplegius Medieval and Linguistic Studies in Honor of Francis Peabody Magoun, Jr* ed. J. B. Bessinger and R. P. Creed (New York, 1965), pp. 164–93 (hereafter cited as Pope). [1987. Pope retracted this suggestion in *ASE* 3 (1974), 75–86.]

[2] Pope, p. 167.

[3] R. F. Leslie *The Wanderer* (Manchester, 1966), p. 65, note to l. 1. The passage is quoted below. Hereafter, this work is cited as Leslie.

[4] Leslie, p. 10.

[5] Leslie, p. 65, note to l. 1.

prefix *ge-* denotes completion. What can this remark mean? EITHER 'the prefix *ge-* denotes completion *here* because it fits my theory about the poem.' An editor is entitled to express a personal preference. But he ought to make what he is doing absolutely clear. Editors and critics of Old English often avoid this responsibility. OR 'the prefix *ge-* must imply completion here because it does everywhere else.' But Leslie can scarcely mean this, since he denies it by implication in the principal clause. And the proposition is quite untenable. A study of the Bosworth-Toller Supplement s.v. *gebidan* is sufficient to establish this. The meaning 'to await' is clear enough in the shortened version of Lindisfarne Luke 2. 38 quoted in the Supplement: *þa þe gebiodon lesing qui expectabant redemtionem*, but is even clearer in the full text printed by Skeat: *ðaðe ge-biodon ł bidendo woeron lesing ł lesnis hierusalem.* Even in *Beowulf* l. 1060 – cited by Leslie[6] and also by B. J. Timmer[7] as a presumably clear example of *gebidan* 'to experience' – the sense 'expect' is by no means impossible. That *ge-* does not always denote completion has now been confirmed by J. W. R. Lindemann, who writes:

> Now, if Old English simplexes, as we have just seen, are capable of expressing *perfective* aspect as well as imperfective, and if *ge-* compounds are capable of expressing *imperfective* aspect as well as perfective, then *ge-* cannot be a 'formal', preverbal tag indicating perfective aspect.[8]

The second half of Leslie's 'because' clause is also open to objection. Why does the *þeah þe* clause imply fulfilment rather than expectation in the verb *gebideð*? One possible line of argument is that *sceolde* is past tense and therefore denotes that the misery is over. This might be Leslie's point, for he uses this argument about *sceolde* l. 8.[9] But there, as in his discussion of *gewitan* in *Ruin* l. 9,[10] his reluctance to translate an Old English preterite as a perfect causes him to go wrong. In *Wanderer* l. 3, too, *sceolde* can mean 'has had to' and therefore cannot prove that the misery is over.

However, Leslie's reference to S. B. Greenfield's article suggests that he might be following Greenfield, who argued that *gebidan* must mean 'to experience' because the combination 'seek ... though' is not a logical unit.[11] If we are to translate *gebideð* as 'seeks', says Greenfield, 'a conjunction meaning "while, because" would be required instead of one meaning "although"'.[12] This seems scarcely tenable. Even if we admit that the sequence is illogical (which I do not), the argument is irrelevant, for Christian belief does not always seem

[6] Leslie, pp. 65–6.
[7] *Neophilologus* 26 (1941), 221.
[8] *JEGP* 64 (1965), 82.
[9] Leslie, p. 4. This point is to be discussed elsewhere.
[10] See *Neophilologus* 49 (1965), 44–6. (Leslie has withdrawn these remarks in the revised edition of *Three Old English Elegies*.)
[11] *JEGP* 50 (1951), 464–5.
[12] *JEGP* 50 (1951), 464.

logical. The martyr in the Coliseum and the Christian who died painfully of cancer yesterday undoubtedly shared a steadfast hope and faith in God's mercy without experiencing relief from the cares of this world and the agonies of a cruel death. This argument therefore also fails. Since I can think of no others, I am left with no proof for the proposition that the *þeah þe* clause implies fulfilment rather than expectation, though of course I do not seek to deny the possibility, or for the view that there are any ungrammatical reasons why the sense 'experiences' for *gebideð* 'is to be preferred here'. Such negative conclusions (and this paper reaches little else) are certainly most unsatisfactory. But when evidence is not forthcoming, it is our duty to reach them.

II. *Swa*, line 6

On this point, Leslie writes:

> The wanderer's monologue has frequently been held to begin, not with the opening lines of the poem, but with line 8, because at this point the pronoun in the first person is introduced after the *swā cwæð* construction in lines 6–7. But a construction of this type normally has a summary or retrospective function: there is no clear evidence that it can point exclusively forward.[13]

It is probably true that *swa* points back more often than it points forward. But there are clear examples in which *swa* is used before a speech; we can cite among others

Panther l. 66 Siþþan to þam swicce   soðfæste men
              on healfa gehwone   heapum þrungon
              geond ealne ymbhwyrft   eorþan sceata.
              Swa se snottra gecwæð   sanctus Paulus:
              'Monigfealde sind   geond middangeard
              god ungnyðe   þe us to giefe dæleð
              ond to feorhnere   fæder ælmihtig,
              ond se anga hyht   ealra gesceafta,
              uppe ge niþre.'   þæt is æþele stenc,

Azarias l. 67 ff., and the corresponding passage in

Daniel l. 356   þær þa modhwatan
              þry on geðancum   ðeoden heredon,
              bædon bletsian   bearn Israela
              eall landgesceaft   ecne drihten,
              ðeoda waldend.   Swa hie þry cwædon,

[13] Leslie, p. 3.

> modum horsce, þurh gemæne word:
> 'Ðe gebletsige, bylywit fæder,
> woruldcræfta wlite and weorca gehwilc!...'[14]

So the fact that *swa* occurs in *Wanderer* 1. 6 cannot be taken even as an argument (let alone as proof) that ll. 1–5 must be in inverted commas. Equally, of course, it does not prove that they cannot be. Pope's more moderate statement expresses the situation more accurately: 'And the *Swa cwæð eardstapa* at line 6, though there is precedent for such an expression (under somewhat different circumstances) as an introduction to a speech, is much more likely to refer to something already said.'[15]

But the problem should perhaps be stated differently: it is not necessarily a question of whether *swa* 'can point exclusively forward' (as Leslie has it) or whether *swa* can introduce speeches (as Greenfield and Pope have it). Thus in

> *Beowulf* 1. 18   Beowulf wæs breme – blæd wide sprang –
> Scyldes eafera Scedelandum in.
> Swa sceal geong guma gode gewyrcean,
> fromum feohgiftum on fæder bearme,
> þæt hine on ylde eft gewunigen
> wilgesiþas, þonne wig cume,
> leode gelæsten; lofdædum sceal
> in mægþa gehwære man geþeon,

swa clearly points forward. But it does not introduce a speech and does not point exclusively forward; it has a resumptive – almost causal – function.[16] A similar explanation is possible in *Daniel* 1. 360 and in *Wanderer* 1. 6, where 'And so, thus, for this reason' would fit the context without demanding inverted commas.

W. S. Mackie had another argument: 'The past tense *cwæð* must refer to what precedes, and lines 1–5 should be placed within inverted commas, as the beginning of the Wanderer's soliloquy. Contrast *ācwið*, present tense, referring to what follows, in line 91.'[17] Presumably the same argument would apply in *Wanderer* 1. 111 *Swa cwæð snottor on mode*.... However, it cannot stand as proof

---

[14] It would seem that Leslie silently rejected these examples without mentioning them. It is hard to believe that he could have overlooked them because: (1) Greenfield had already cited those from *Panther* and *Azarias* in *JEGP* 50 (1951), 456, in the course of a discussion to which Leslie refers in connexion with these very lines and on the very page where he made the remark quoted above. See Leslie, p. 3 *passim* and nn. 1 and 2; (2) This very article and these two examples were again referred to by Pope (p. 189, n. 10) in the article from which my next quotation is taken and to which Leslie refers on p. 10 of his edition.

[15] Pope, p. 168.
[16] Further on this usage, see §IV below.
[17] *MLN* 40 (1925), 92.

in view of the first three examples quoted in this note, for in all of them the past tense refers to a following speech. The fact that the present tense *acwið* in *Wanderer* l. 91 refers forward is no proof that the past tense *cwæð* in *Wanderer* ll. 6 and 111 must refer exclusively to what has gone before. The 'rule' adumbrated by Mackie cannot therefore solve the difficulty of whether to put inverted commas around ll. 1–5 of *The Wanderer*. Similar problems, of course, occur elsewhere, in the absence of inverted commas from the manuscripts.[18]

Such problems are, in a sense, artificial. The Anglo-Saxon *scop* would, one presumes, have made clear by his performance of *Wanderer* ll. 66–72 whether he expected the audience to take *ær he geare cunne* (l. 69b) as modifying ll. 66–9a, l. 69a alone, or ll. 70–2, or whether it was used *apo koinou*. The language of the poetry may not have been as formal and as 'grammatical' as that of the prose. As J. G. Leyerle of Toronto has reminded me, connexions are made differently in spoken language, and modern punctuation of Old English poems forces a necessarily modern interpretation on a language which may have worked differently. Since we cannot hear a *scop* perform and cannot interrogate a native speaker of Old English, we lack the vital clue of intonation. Hence we must be prepared to admit that there are some questions we can never answer, some problems we can never solve, some propositions we can never prove. This truth, trite as it may seem, is sadly in need of recognition by students of Old English language and by critics of Old English literature alike.

III. Lines 37–44 and 29b–33

There is a lot to be said for Leslie's suggestion that ll. 39–44 are in some sense the object of *wat* (l. 37);[19] indeed, a case could be made for extending this to include more of the wanderer's experiences, possibly even as far as the end of l. 57.

But his explanation calls for comment. He writes

> *Hū* (cf. lines 29–30) or perhaps *þæt*, is to be understood, for to put a conjunction before *þinceð* (41) would be misleading, because the *ðonne* clause is part of the larger clause after *wāt*, and to place it before *ðonne* would give an awkward juxtaposition of conjunctions; the poet therefore leaves it out as in the syntactically similar construction in *Vainglory* 77–80....[20]

---

[18] In this connexion, the following observation by Pope is not without interest (Pope, p. 187): 'In the dialogue of Joseph and Mary in the *Christ* there are no explicit identifications, and we must judge, as in *The Seafarer*, entirely by what the speakers say (that is, until Mary's carefully introduced speech at the end), though I must add that I do not myself believe in the rapid interchange of speeches attributed to Joseph and Mary in our editions.'

[19] Leslie, pp. 72–3, note to ll. 37ff.

[20] Leslie, p. 73.

There is little or no justification for understanding *hu*; I know of no examples in Old English where an interrogative conjunction or pronoun is unexpressed. To understand *þæt* presents little problem, as the following series will show:

Maldon l. 5   þa þæt Offan mæg   ærest onfunde,
         þæt se eorl nolde   yrhðo geþolian ... ,

Solomon and Saturn l. 204
         Wat ic ðonne, gif ðu gewitest   on Wendelsæ
         ofer Coforflod   cyððe secean,
         ðæt ðu wille gilpan   ðæt ðu hæbbe gumena bearn
         forcumen and forcyððed,

Beowulf l. 798   Hie þæt ne wiston,   þa hie gewin drugon,
         heardhicgende   hildemecgas,
         ond on healfa gehwone   heawan þohton,
         sawle secan: þone synscaðan
         ænig ofer eorþan   irenna cyst,
         guðbilla nan   gretan nolde,[21]

and (the example quoted by Leslie after Bosworth-Toller and Grein-Köhler[22])

Vainglory l. 77   Wite þe be þissum,
         gif þu eaðmodne   eorl gemete,
         þegn on þeode,   þam bið simle
         gæst gegæderad   godes agen bearn... .[23]

But, while agreeing that *þæt* can be understood, I do not think that an Anglo-Saxon poet would have shared Leslie's feeling that 'to put a conjunction before *þinceð* (41) would be misleading, because the *ðonne* clause is part of the larger clause after *wāt* ... ',[24] for that is exactly where he would have put the *þæt* if he had put it in. The example from *Solomon and Saturn* quoted above illustrates the point and confirming examples will be found in *Beowulf* ll. 1477ff., *Beowulf* ll. 1846ff., *Elene* ll. 576ff., *Guthlac* ll. 1159ff., and *Juliana* ll. 334ff. There are no examples in Old English poetry of the arrangement postulated by Leslie – of putting *þæt* before *ðonne* (l. 39) – possibly for the reason he suggests, that it would give an awkward juxtaposition of conjunctions.[25] Hence the ambiguity in

[21] Cf. *Beowulf* ll. 2200-14.
[22] S.v. *witan* I. (5) (a) and *witan* 4. respectively.
[23] Cf. Kenneth Sisam's version of *Seasons for Fasting* ll. 168ff. in *Studies in the History of Old English Literature* (Oxford, 1953), p. 51.
[24] Leslie, p. 73.
[25] Here Leslie (rightly) disregards the fact that in MnE 'that' would precede the 'when' clause and would therefore be placed in the position which he claims would give an 'awkward juxtaposition' in OE. Yet, since at the end of his note on l. 37 he wants to understand *þæt* before *gif* in *Vain-*

Beowulf l. 272

　　　　　　　　　　þu wast, gif hit is
swa we soþlice　　secgan hyrdon,
þæt mid Scyldingum　　sceaðona ic nat hwylc,
deogol dædhata　　deorcum nihtum
eaweð þurh egsan　　uncuðne nið,
hynðu ond hrafyl,

where it is not certain whether *gif* introduces a dependent question 'whether ...' or a conditional clause.[26]

However, it may be questioned whether it is necessary to understand *þæt* in *Vainglory* ll. 77–80 or in *Wanderer* ll. 37–44. Grein-Köhler explains the passage from *Vainglory* (and others in which there is no subordinate clause to complicate the issue) as examples in which we have 'statt des abhängigen Satzes ein Satz in direkter Rede'.[27] If we accept this view, we can place a colon after *forþolian* l. 38. The object of *wat* will then be the direct speech in ll. 39–44 (or 39–57).[28]

A somewhat similar problem exists in *Beowulf* ll. 2200–14. But we need not venture so far afield, for we can perhaps find another in ll. 29b–33 of *The Wanderer*. Leslie is worried about the apparent absence of an object for *wat* in l. 37. What about *wat* in l. 29b? It is true that we can construe the *hu* clause as the object of *wat*, and this is what is usually done. But in that case we may merely be transferring the difficulty to *cunnað*, also in l. 29, for it, too, regularly

glory l. 78, he presumably wants to understand *þæt* before *ðonne* in *Wanderer* l. 39 – in both cases following the MnE practice and creating what he has already objected to as an 'awkward juxtaposition'. His sensitive feeling for OE idiom was a better guide than his reliance on MnE usage; if *þæt* is to be understood, it should be understood after (and not before) the subordinate clause. It is interesting that J. H. Gorrell made a similar mistake by equating OE and MnE syntactical practice. Gorrell claims that the arrangement postulated by Leslie for *Vainglory* ll. 77–80 is 'naturally of frequent occurrence' (*PMLA* 10 (1895), 347). It is in MnE. But unfortunately the only example he cites – *Cura Pastoralis* (ed. Sweet), p. 85, l. 4 – does not illustrate his point, for the subordinate clause comes after the subject of the *þæt* clause. There are (as pointed out above) no examples in the poetry of the type Gorrell is trying to illustrate. As yet, I have noted none in the prose.

[26] A similar example is to be found in *Andreas* l. 271 ff., where the *þeh* clause may modify the principal clause or the noun clause. C. Schaar, in *Critical Studies in the Cynewulf Group* (Lund, 1949), pp. 53–4, followed by K. R. Brooks in his edition of *Andreas and The Fates of the Apostles* (Oxford, 1961), p. 78, note to ll. 474f., rejects Krapp's punctuation of *Andreas* ll. 474–80. If we accepted their reasoning, we would be forced to conclude that the *þeh* clause in *Andreas* ll. 271–2 must belong in the dependent speech. But I hope to show elsewhere that their arguments are not conclusive and that, while in both passages the *þeh/þeah* clauses can be construed with either the preceding or the following clauses, they are perhaps best taken *apo koinou*. [1987. See *NM* 70 (1969), 78–81.]

[27] S.v. *witan* 4.

[28] This is in essence the solution adopted in Henry Sweet's *Anglo-Saxon Reader* (revised by C. T. Onions). But here the colon is placed after *gebindað* l. 40. This is an error, for the reason given by Leslie, p. 72, note to ll. 37ff. Similarly, we must reject the full-stop after *gebindað* in the Anglo-Saxon Poetic Records iii. Further on the punctuation of this passage, see §V below.

takes an object, as in *Maldon* l. 215 *nu mæg cunnian hwa cene sy*.[29] The problem of *wat/cunnað* in l. 29 may therefore be parallel to that of *wat* in l. 37. Hence it could be urged that, if Leslie has a comma after *forþolian* in l. 38, he should also have one after *geholena* in l. 31 and should take the *hu* clause as the object of *cunnað* and ll. 32–3 (or 32–6) after *wat*. But here too I would happily settle for a colon, this time after *geholena* – the punctuation in C. T. Onions's revision of Sweet's *Reader*. Either way, we would have another parallel construction to add to the many already present in the poem.

IV. *Swa*, line 43

Here Leslie, following Miss Kershaw and others, observes:

> There appears to be some ellipsis here, *swā* being used with both adverbial force meaning 'just as' (cf. Bosworth-Toller IV (1) (a)) and with the force of a temporal conjunction 'when' (cf. Bosworth-Toller V (8)); cf. *Andreas* 926–7:
>
> Nō ðū swā swīðe   synne gefremedest
> swā ðū in Achaia   ondsæc dydest.[30]

There can be no dispute that *swa* can mean both 'as' and 'when'. But that it means both at the same time is unlikely; the meaning 'as when' is both unparalleled and unnecessary. It cannot be justified by citing the composite meaning 'as if' which *swa* can have in Old English. This sense – which would not be possible here because of the indicative *breac*,[31] even if the context were held to permit it – is an extension of the comparative use of *swa* 'as' and can nearly always be so translated, e.g.

> *Christ* l. 1376   Onginneð sylf cweðan,
> swa he to anum sprece . . .

which probably meant (originally at least) 'He begins to speak as he would speak to one person. . . .'[32] The example in

---

[29] The only possible example of *cunnian* used absolutely which I have been able to trace is that cited in the Bosworth-Toller Supplement s.v. *cunnian* II:
Cht. Th. 171. 19 *Ða cwæð ic þæt he wolde cunnigan.*
But here a pronoun object is implied and may be understood from what has gone before.
We could adopt a similar solution here by taking the *hu* clause (l. 30) as the object of both *wat* and *cunnað*.
Another possibility, which G. N. Garmonsway pointed out to me, would be to take *wat* in l. 29 as being used absolutely, in emphatic anticipation of *wat* in l. 37: 'He knows. . . . Assuredly he knows. . . .'
[30] Leslie, p. 75, note to l. 43.
[31] *Swa* 'as if' is followed in the poetry by only subjunctive or ambiguous verb forms. I have as yet found no exceptions to this rule in the prose.
[32] The present subjunctive is idiomatic: see *A Guide to Old English* (Oxford, 1965), §177. 4.

Wanderer 1. 95   Hu seo þrag gewat,
                genap under nihthelm,   swa heo no wære

is one of four in the poetry where 'as if' seems to be required, but it may still have seemed a comparative clause to an Anglo-Saxon – 'How the time has passed, just as it were not'. However, along with *Christ* ll. 179 ff., *Wife's Lament* ll. 23 ff., and *Paris Psalter* 77. 65, it provides some justification for F. Behre when he speaks of 'the sense-change of *swa*, so that it comes to mean no longer "in the same way as" but "in the same way as if"'.[33]

But there is no evidence that *swa* was undergoing a 'sense-change' from 'as' to 'as when' in Old English. In the *Andreas* example cited by Leslie, the sense is 'The sin you have committed was not as great as the denial you made in Achaia, that you did not know how to journey into distant parts ...' and the *swa* clause is one of comparison.

That in *Wanderer* l. 43 can be similarly explained; *swa* gives good sense as a conjunction 'as, just as' if we translate '... he is embracing and kissing his liege lord, and laying hands and head on his knee, just as from time to time he used to make use of the throne in days of old ...'. If we take ll. 43b–4 as parenthetic, we will get similar sense with *swa* meaning 'so, in this way'. With these versions, *giefstolas breac* must be synonymous with *clyppe ond cysse* etc.[34] This is perhaps not impossible if we look upon the whole ceremony of homage and gift-giving – retainers' demonstration of loyalty and lord's response – as one.[35]

But if it seems objectionable, we can establish a causal relationship between the homage and the receiving of gifts. There are two alternatives. The wanderer can do homage because he has made use of the throne, in other words because he has accepted the gifts and privileges bestowed by the lord. In this case, *swa* will mean 'because'[36] and we can translate: '... he is embracing and kissing his liege lord and laying hands and head on his knee, because from time to time in days of old he enjoyed the privileges of the throne'.

Alternatively, the wanderer can enjoy the privileges because he has paid homage. In this case, we can again take lines 43b–4 as parenthetic, but explain *swa* as an adverb expressing a causal connexion 'so, therefore, on that account',

[33] F. Behre *The Subjunctive in Old English Poetry* (Göteborg, 1934), p. 282.
[34] I owe this observation to A. J. Bliss in a private communication. I am grateful to him for the great stimulus I have received from discussion and correspondence with him about *The Wanderer*.
[35] Cf. *Maxims* i. 67–8 quoted by Leslie in his note on ll. 41b–4 (Leslie, p. 74). His whole note is relevant here.
[36] The causal use of *swa* 'marking the grounds of action, *as*, *since*' is mentioned by Bosworth-Toller s.v. *swa* V. (9). One example is cited – *Lord's Prayer* ii. 115 ff. Others from the poetry will be found in *Beowulf* ll. 3096 ff., *Genesis A* ll. 1018 ff., *Andreas* ll. 1114 ff., etc. Such a use is another of those extensions to which the basically modal conjunction *swa* is liable; see Quirk and Wrenn *An Old English Grammar* (London, 1955), p. 101. Miss E. M. Liggins has discussed the causal use of *swa* in prose in *The Expression of Causal Relationship in Old English Prose* (Unpublished Ph.D. dissertation, London, 1955), pp. 334–54.

i.e. 'because he has paid homage'. The *OED* gives no examples of this sense before 1200.[37] But Bosworth-Toller provides support; among the examples it cites are *Genesis B* 1. 381, *Andreas* 1. 1328, and

Genesis B l. 288
Ic mæg hyra hearra wesan,
rædan on þis rice.   Swa me þæt riht ne þinceð,
þæt ic oleccan   awiht þurfe
gode æfter gode ænegum.   Ne wille ic leng his geongra wurþan.[38]

Others could be cited.

If we can take *swa* as 'because', another possibility arises. It is well-known that Anglo-Saxon writers had difficulty in indicating a change of subject. Thus in

Maldon l. 285   þa æt guðe sloh
           Offa þone sælidan,   þæt he on eorðan feoll ...

we are bound to agree (unless our sense of humour is over-developed) that *he* in l. 286 refers to *þone sælidan* and not to Offa.[39] Similarly, it is syntactically possible that *he* in *Wanderer* l. 43 refers to *mondryhten* – the lord who performed the duties of the throne in the same way as Zacharias performed the duties of the priesthood in Luke 1. 8 '... *Zacharias his sacerdes hades breac*.[40] We could thus translate '... he is embracing and kissing his liege lord and laying hands and head on his knee, because from time to time in days of old the lord had performed the duties of the throne'. These duties, of course, are clearly defined in *Beowulf* ll. 18–25 (quoted in section II above) and the translation of *Wanderer* ll. 41–4 proposed above would fit quite well with Leslie's notion that

> it may be that the exile in his dream is not thinking of his initiation into the *comitatus*, but of one of the periodical distributions of treasure, at which a ceremonial demonstration of loyalty and affection was the retainer's response to his lord's generosity.[41]

But it is offered here merely as a syntactical possibility.

If it is accepted that *he* in *Wanderer* l. 43 refers to the lord, it may be thought by some that *swa* could mean 'who'. As I have already pointed out, it is my opinion that *swa* is never so used.[42] None of the other meanings which *swa* can

[37] S.v. *so* II. 10 (b).
[38] S.v. *swa* IV. (1) (c) and V. (6).
[39] For further examples and a discussion of the problem, see my note in *RES* 15 (1964), 132–3.
[40] Quoted from the Bosworth-Toller Supplement, s.v. *brucan* III. Further examples of this use are given there.
[41] Leslie, p. 74, note to ll. 41b–4.
[42] See *Anglia* 81 (1963), 300, and *RES* 15 (1964), 140. This opinion still stands, despite K. R. Brooks's treatment of *swa* in the Glossary to his edition of *Andreas and The Fates of the Apostles* (Oxford, 1961). I hope to explain in detail elsewhere why I believe him to be wrong. [1987. See *NM* 70 (1969), 75–8.]

have seems to fit *Wanderer* l. 43. The sense 'when' is not suitable, whether we take *he* as the lord or the wanderer. The sense 'so that' (consecutive) would fit if *he* referred to the lord, but is ruled out by the sequence of tenses, and 'so that' final – which would presumably require the subjunctive – is not firmly attested in the poetry.[43]

But even after we dismiss all these possibilities, *swa* in *Wanderer* l. 43 can still be explained quite regularly and quite acceptably in several ways. Thus, although I have no objection to admitting *hapax* usages when necessary,[44] I do not feel that I need accept 'as when' for *swa* in *Wanderer* l. 43, despite the fact that it gives excellent sense.[44a]

V. Lines 37–57

How should we punctuate these lines? The conventional punctuation can be seen in Sweet's *Reader* and in ASPR.[45] They have only minor variations such as full-stops for semi-colons except in ll. 51–3.

The *Reader* has comma at end of l. 51;
full-stop at end of l. 52;
comma at end of l. 53.

ASPR has semi-colon at end of l. 51;
nothing at end of l. 52;
full-stop in middle of l. 53;
exclamation mark at end of l. 53.

I prefer a colon after *forþolian* (l. 38) and a comma after *gebindað* (l. 40).[46]
This conventional interpretation of ll. 37–51 can be set out thus:

ll. 39ff. As often as misery and sleep bind him ..., he dreams ...
ll. 45ff. When he awakes again ..., he sees ...
l. 49 Then the wounds of his heart are more grievous ...

Here we have parallelism between ll. 39–40 and l. 45, parallelism between l. 41 and l. 46, with poignant and emphatic contrast between *þinceð* and *gesihð*, and the whole thing summed up effectively in ll. 49ff.

[43] On this point see my discussion in *Neophilologus* 49 (1965), 51–5.
[44] See my note X in *RES* 15 (1964), 137. I think it not unjust to state here that the responsibility for the unfortunate misprint in the last line of that note is not mine.
[44a] [1987. I returned to this question in item 17; see pp. 152 and 167–70 below.]
[45] Sweet's *Anglo-Saxon Reader*, revised by C. T. Onions (Oxford, 9th edn or later), and Anglo-Saxon Poetic Records iii.
[46] For a fuller discussion on this point, see §III above.

This interpretation gives us in:

ll. 39–40 þonne S. . . . V.[47] in a subordinate clause;
l. 45 ðonne V. S. in a subordinate clause;
l. 49 þonne V. S. in a principal clause;
l. 51 þonne S. . . . V. or O. S. V. in a subordinate clause.[48]

Thus we have an inconsistency between l. 45 and l. 49 which we would not expect in Old English prose, where the opposition S. . . . V. (or S. V.)/V. S. works pretty well to distinguish subordinate from principal clauses. But it has not been established that it works in the poetry; there (in my opinion) these word-orders are not conclusive. Leslie writes in his note on l. 39:[49]

> Boer points out that the feelings of the *winelēas guma* are narrated in chronological order and supports this observation by noting that each section is introduced by *ðonne* (39, 45, 49, 51). He claims that this parallelism indicates clearly the correct punctuation of lines 39–40, and that in each section a new sentence is begun with *ðonne*. The parallelism is incomplete, however, for Boer ignores the word order. His claim is valid for lines 45 and 49, where *ðonne* is followed by inversion of subject and verb,[50] indicating that it is to be taken adverbially and so begins a new sentence; but in lines 39 and 51 the verb is at the end of the clause, signifying subordination and the interpretation of *ðonne* as the conjunction 'when'.[51]

I cannot accept the view that this and similar problems in the poetry 'may be solved on syntactical grounds alone'.[52] That the order V. S. does not prove a clause is principal is suggested by examples like the following:

> *Beowulf* l. 2542   Geseah ða be wealle   se ðe worna fela
> gumcystum god   guða gedigde,
> hildehlemma,   þonne hnitan feðan,[53]
> stondan stanbogan,   stream ut þonan
> brecan of beorge,

---

[47] S. = subject, V. = verb, O. = object.
[48] The subject is usually taken as *gemynd*. But it could be *mod*, as A. J. Bliss has pointed out to me privately.
[49] Leslie, p. 73.
[50] The same argument is used by Leslie on p. 72, note to ll. 37ff.
[51] The same argument is used by Leslie on p. 76, note to ll. 50b–5.
[52] Leslie, p. 76, note to ll. 50b–5.
[53] Here the finite verb alliterates in a half-line containing a noun. As A. Campbell points out in *English and Medieval Studies presented to J. R. R. Tolkien* ed. Norman Davis and C. L. Wrenn (London, 1962), p. 16, this is perhaps a licence inherited from the poetic technique of the Germanic lay; he compares *Finnsburh* ll. 7, 11, 12, 13, and 17.

Some syntactical problems in The Wanderer

Whale l. 24

> þonne gefeleð   facnes cræftig
> þæt him þa ferend on   fæste wuniaþ,
> wic weardiað   wedres on luste,
> ðonne semninga   on sealtne wæg
> mid þa noþe   niþer gewiteþ
> garsecges gæst,   grund geseceð,

and

Wanderer l. 11

>   Ic to soþe wat
> þæt bið in eorle   indryhten þeaw....

Similarly, the order S. . . . V. does not prove that a clause is subordinate, e.g. *Whale* l. 24 (quoted above),

Wanderer l. 1   Oft him anhaga   are gebideð . . . ,

Wanderer l. 82

>   sumne se hara wulf
> deaðe gedælde;   sumne dreorighleor
> in eorðscræfe   eorl gehydde.

Indeed, Leslie departs from his own rules by taking as principal

Wanderer l. 62

>   Swa þes middangeard
> ealra dogra gehwam   dreoseð ond fealleþ,

which Miss Kershaw took as subordinate. The choice is clearly a deliberate one on his part.[54]

Nor can I accept Leslie's further claim in his note on l. 103b:

> The clause *þonne won cymeð* is often taken as parenthetic, e.g. by Krapp–Dobbie; but it is more closely linked in sense with the following lines than with those which precede it, and it is syntactically linked with the principal clause *nīpeð nihtscūa* by reason of the inversion of subject and predicate in the latter. A semi-colon therefore appears preferable to a comma after *wōma*.[55]

The initial verb does not prove that the two clauses must be syntactically linked. Disregarding clauses beginning with *ne* + verb (*Wanderer* ll. 15, 66) we have verbs standing at the very beginning of a sentence in *Wanderer* ll. 29, 32, 34, 78, 85, 97, and 107.

It thus seems clear to me that word-order is not conclusive in the poetry, that it cannot be used to prove that a certain clause must be subordinate and another principal. But this, of course, does not stop an editor from suggesting

[54] See Leslie, p. 81, note to ll. 62b–3. He had a choice here which he did not have in *Wanderer*, ll. 1 and 82.
[55] Leslie, p. 87.

that a poet may deliberately have arranged his clauses so that those with S. . . . V. were subordinate and those with V. S. were principal. Nor does it mean that such a suggestion is wrong; it merely means that it cannot be proved right. What is probably the best punctuation I have yet seen of *Wanderer* ll. 37–57 is based on the proposition that the *þonne* clauses with S. . . . V.[56] in ll. 39 and 51 are subordinate and those with V. S. in ll. 45 and 49 are principal. It will, I hope, be discussed (if it is not adopted) in a forthcoming edition of *The Wanderer* by A. J. Bliss and T. P. Dunning.[56a]

VI. Lines 65b–72

Here Leslie writes: 'After discussing the prerequisite for gaining wisdom, the wanderer enumerates the elements of which it consists (65b–72), the principal stress being laid on the value of moderation.'[57] I should like to examine the evidence for the view that 'moderation' is implied here.

The word *to* in Old English certainly has the sense 'too', e.g. *Cura Pastoralis* 449. 14 *Hi sellaþ wið to lytlum weorðe* . . . and

Fortunes of Men l. 48   Sumum meces ecg   on meodubence
yrrum ealowosan   ealdor oþþringeð,
were winsadum;   bið ær his worda to hræd.

Hence it is clearly possible that the wanderer is stressing the value of moderation. But there is an alternative – that he is implying that the wise man should not possess these qualities at all. If this is so, we have a series of examples of understatement or meiosis similar perhaps to that by which the *Beowulf* poet tells us that the messenger who announced Beowulf's death was speaking the truth:

Beowulf l. 3028   Swa se secg hwata   secggende wæs
laðra spella;   he ne leag fela
wyrda ne worda.

An examination of the Old English examples cited by Leslie in defence of his view may help to show whether this is possible.[57a]

[56] Or O. S. V. in the case of l. 51; see above.

[56a] [1987. It was both discussed and adopted; see *The Wanderer* ed. T. P. Dunning and A. J. Bliss (London, 1969), pp. 19–21. I am, however, less enthusiastic about it than I was in 1968 and in particular do not accept their claim on p. 17 that 'the fact remains that the text of *The Wanderer* does contain some elaborately articulated periods which in no way depend on the policy of the editor.']

[57] Leslie, p. 13.

[57a] [1987. L. G. Downs 'Notes on the Intensive Use of Germanic *Te, *To, "To : Too"', *JEGP* 38 (1939), 64–8, had already advanced the idea that *to* could express absolute negation. But I was unaware of his article when I wrote what follows; see *OES* §1143.]

The example from *Andreas* comes from the passage where God is comforting the imprisoned Matthew:

Andreas 1. 97   'Ic þe, Matheus,   mine sylle
           sybbe under swegle.   Ne beo ðu on sefan to forht,
           ne on mode ne murn.   Ic þe mid wunige ...'

Is one really to imagine that God is saying 'Don't be too afraid'? The Christian belief is that 'perfect love casteth out fear' and it seems more reasonable to suppose that God is saying 'Don't be at all afraid'. This feeling is reinforced by the direct prohibition which follows – 'Do not grieve', not 'Do not grieve too much'.

The other OE parallels offered by Leslie are from Miss Bethurum's edition of Wulfstan.[58] They read:

Homily VIIIc, ll. 168–73:[59]

Ne beon ge ofermode ne to weamode ne to niðfulle ne to flitgeorne ne to felawyrde ne ealles to hlagole ne eft to asolcene ne to unrote. And ne beon ge to rance ne to gylpgeorne ne færinga to fægene ne eft to ormode, 7 ne beon ge to slapole ne ealles to sleace, ac scyldað eow georne wið deofles lare

and

Homily Xc, ll. 97–100:
Ne ænig man to hlagol sy ne færinga to fægen ne eft ne beo to ormod. Ne ænig man oþerne bæftan ne tæle ne hyrwe to swyðe. Ne ænig man andan ne healde on his heortan ealles to fæste.

After citing these passages and referring to some articles which compare them to the Golden Mean, Leslie observes: 'Miss Bethurum notes that the idea of the Golden Mean was not found by Wulfstan in his sources, nor was this manner of expression.'[60]

It is worth quoting more fully the relevant notes from Miss Bethurum's edition. Of the passage from Homily VIIIc she writes:

In this concluding section Wulfstan is freely reworking material from Xc, and a part of the Canons of Edgar.... What he adds to his sources is the idea of the Golden Mean, as he contrasts in ll. 169–70 and 171–2 the extremes of loquacity and frivolity on the one hand with sloth and despondency on the other....[61]

[58] Oxford, 1957 (hereafter cited as Bethurum).
[59] Leslie (p. 13, n. 1) cites only ll. 168–71, but the next two lines seem relevant.
[60] Leslie, p. 13, n. 1.
[61] Bethurum, p. 318, note to ll. 156–74. I agree with Miss Bethurum that *hlagol* implies 'frivolity' and is therefore an undesirable quality; see below.

The source of this passage in Xb. 101 has no hint of the idea of moderation implied in Wulfstan's contrasts.[62]

In her note on the passage from Homily Xc, we read:

> Wulfstan adds the idea of the Golden Mean, which he did not find in his sources for Xb. In VIIIc he elaborates it further and makes several contrasts....[63]

In clarification of these notes, the relevant paragraph (ll. 94–111) of the Latin Homily Xb must be quoted:

> Quiescite igitur agere peruerse; discite benefacere. Legem Domini caute custodite. Sepe per annum ad communionem corporis Cristi uos preparate. Nolite, fratres, nolite tardare conuerti ad Dominum. Sed qui fuit cupidus, sit in elemosinis largus. Qui fuit ebriosus et gulosus, sit sobrius et abstinens. Qui fuit fornicator, sit purus et castus. Qui fuit iracundus, sit patiens. Qui fuit tristis pro secularibus causis, sit hylaris et gaudens. Qui fuit tediosus, quod est otio uacans, sit propriis manibus operans uel Deo seruiens. Qui pro uana gloria aliquid faciebat, incipiat soli Deo placere. Qui fuit superbus, sit humilis. Qui fuit latro, sit idoneus. Qui fuit somnolentus, sit uigil. Qui fuit bilinguis, sit boniloquus. Qui fuit detractor, sit benignus. Qui fuit in uerbis otiosus, sit eloquiis bonis intente perseuerans. Qui in causis iniustis se implicabat, orationibus sanctis se occupet. Qui fuit incredulus, sit fidelis. Sic et contra singula uitia uel peccata pugnandum est, quia prius oportet derelinquere malum et deinde facere bonum.

In the light of all this, it seems reasonable to ask whether Wulfstan really was referring to the Golden Mean. The notion that he was rests entirely on his use of the word *to*, since both Leslie and Miss Bethurum admit (as they are bound to do) that he did not find the idea in his sources. We may note first that Wulfstan frequently uses *to* in a way which suggests that he did not always mean it to imply moderation. Thus in *Sermo Lupi* we read:

> Understandað eac georne þæt deofol þas þeode nu fela geara dwelode to swiðe, 7 þæt litle getreowða wæron mid mannum, þeah hi wel spræcon, 7 unrihta to fela ricsode on lande. And næs na fela manna þe hogode ymbe þa bote swa georne swa man scolde, ac dæghwamlice man ihte yfel æfter oðrum, 7 unriht arærde 7 unlaga manega ealles to wide geond ealle þas ðeode.[64]

Here (as in the passage from *Andreas*) the implication is that these things

[62] Bethurum, p. 320, note to ll. 170–3.   [63] Bethurum, p. 330, note to l. 98.
[64] Quoted from MS C (Bethurum, p. 261, ll. 12–18).

should not be happening at all. It seems a very dubious compliment to suggest that Wulfstan was ready to tolerate the devil, lack of faith, and wickedness, in moderation. Is one supposed to believe that *ealles to wide geond ealle þas ðeode* means that a little sin in Canterbury was a good thing as long as there was none in Wulfstan's own diocese? Similarly, in the sentence which immediately follows the passage cited from Homily Xc, we read (ll. 100–4):

Ne ænig man oðerne ne hatie to swyðe. Ne ænig man ne gewunie þæt he mid yfelum wordum to wyriende weorðe. Ne ænig man ne sy to sacfull ne ealles to geflitgeorn. Ne ænig man ne lufige druncen to swyðe ne fule oferfylle.

Can we reconcile the notion that Wulfstan approved of some hatred (but not too much, of course) with Christ's injunction 'But I say unto you: "Love your enemies"'? Did Wulfstan wish his flock to curse and to quarrel in moderation? Was he foolish enough to believe that one can love drunkenness in moderation? Again it seems more likely that we have to do with a rhetorical use of *to*, in other words with a form of meiosis.

Secondly, an examination of the passages in which Wulfstan is supposed to be advocating moderation scarcely bears out the hypothesis. In both, all the qualities mentioned are undesirable (especially for Christians) – with the possible exception of *fægen* (see below). Further, not all the pairs in either passage consist of opposing qualities. In the second, the only contrast is in the phrase *ne færinga to fægen ne eft ne beo to ormod*. This appears word for word (apart from variations in person and number) in the first passage, where we find other contrasts possible between *ofermod* and *weamod*[65] and in the sequence *ne to felawyrde ne ealles to hlagole ne eft to asolcene ne to unrote*.[66]

Thirdly, we may note that both these passages are preceded by a series of direct prohibitions and that the first is followed by a series of positive injunctions and the second by more direct prohibitions; cf. *sceal* in *Wanderer* ll. 65 and 70.

Thus we find that neither the idea of the Golden Mean nor the manner of expression is found in Wulfstan's sources and that neither passage is systematically made up of pairs of opposites. This comes out clearly if we note the specific opposition in each line of the Irish gnomic passage quoted by Leslie because it is 'similar in content and form to that in *The Wanderer*'.[67] One feels

---

[65] The word *weamod*, which does not seem to occur in the poetry, is glossed by Bosworth-Toller as 'angry, wrathful'. If the sense 'woe-minded, dispirited' were possible, there might be a contrast with *ofermod* 'overbold, presumptuous'.

[66] Miss Bethurum's comment on this passage has been quoted above. The contrast between *felawyrde* and *asolcene* is perhaps not very pointed – the idle are often talkative. But it may be intended.

[67] Leslie, p. 13. The similarity is therefore not as great as it might seem.

that, if Wulfstan had intended to stress the value of moderation, he would have made a better job of it by more careful use of contrasted pairs. He was not unaware of the value of antithesis to an orator. And, as already noted, only bad qualities are mentioned (possibly excluding *fægen*, which is discussed below), qualities which it is unlikely Wulfstan would want his flock to have even in moderation; cf. Ephesians 4. 31–2 where we read:

> Let all bitterness, and wrath, and anger, and clamour, and evil speaking, be put away from you, with all malice: And be ye kind one to another, tenderhearted, forgiving one another, even as God for Christ's sake hath forgiven you.

In view of all this, there is at least some doubt whether Wulfstan is advocating moderation in these passages. Hence they lend but dubious support to Leslie's interpretation of the passage from *The Wanderer*.[68]

When we turn to *The Wanderer*, we again find that the qualities mentioned are (in the context in the case of *gielpes . . . georn*; see below) undesirable, with the possible exception of *fægen*, and that the passage contains no series of opposite qualities, indeed no contrasts at all apart from *forht* and *fægen*.[69] The occurrence of *fægen* in all three passages is noteworthy, and there may be something in Miss Suddaby's notion that the three are 'based on a similar tradition of gnomic wisdom'.[70] That *fægen* appears in all three certainly argues against the emendation to *fæge* in the sense 'over-bold, like a man who is *fæge*' which has been suggested for *Wanderer* l. 68 in an attempt to remove the apparent anomaly that *fægen* is the only good characteristic mentioned.[71] The emendation cannot be entertained for the Wulfstan passages because it makes nonsense of them; the sequence *færinga . . . eft* demands antonyms, not synonyms. And it is unnecessary in *The Wanderer* even if we demand a bad sense for *fægen*, for Bosworth-Toller's gloss *elatus* 'elate'[72] will provide the

---

[68] The use of *to* in the passage from *Blickling Homilies* which begins at p. 109, l. 25 of Morris's edition with an injunction that it is needful and profitable for all men to observe well their baptismal vows can, I think, be similarly explained.

[69] If we take *wac* to mean 'wanting in courage' rather than 'lacking in moral strength' (as Leslie does), it provides much the same contrast with *wanhydig* as *forht* does with *fægen*; cf. Pope's translation quoted below. But the lack of a series of oppositions seems to me to deal a pretty considerable blow to Miss Suddaby's conviction that 'the main point is obviously that extremes of all kinds are to be avoided' (*MLN* 69 (1954), 465). 'Obviously' is not a word I should use myself in this situation – or, indeed, in many such.

[70] *MLN* 69 (1954), 465.

[71] This suggestion has been discussed in Oxford on several occasions. But I have not succeeded in discovering for certain the identity of its first proposer. It is, of course, palaeographically possible (cf. the emendations involving *n* in ll. 14, 22, 28, 59, 89, and 102) and could be accounted for by postulating an error in the common source. But it is difficult to accept it, for the reasons given above.

[72] S.v. *fægen*.

meaning 'over-confident'. Thus we would get the same contrast between 'over-confidence' and 'lack of spirit or courage' in each of the three passages. But since this is the only contrast in *The Wanderer* and since here again all the qualities are bad ones, undesirable in wise men, either pagan or Christian, it is possible that here too we have examples of meiosis.

But there is no proof, as I see it now, and the exact sense of *to* in these passages remains unestablished. The same difficulty occurs in the much-discussed

Maldon l. 89   Ða se eorl ongan   for his ofermode
                 alyfan landes to fela   laþere ðeode.

Are we to believe here that the poet is implying that Byrhtnoth should not have allowed the Danes to cross the causeway at all or that his error lay in allowing them 'too much land', i.e. in giving them enough room to manoeuvre and deploy instead of hemming them in from all sides as they crossed? Yet, be that as it may, the more I ponder, the less likely it seems to me that the wanderer's experiences led him to believe that a wise man should be impulsive, hasty of speech, lacking in moral strength, reckless, afraid, over-confident,[73] avaricious, eager for glory[74] – even in moderation.

These remarks still apply if we accept Pope's view that these words were spoken by a wise man who is not the wanderer and if we adopt his translation of the individual qualities:

> A wise man must be patient, must not be too hot of heart or too hasty of speech, nor too weak a fighter nor too reckless, nor too fearful nor too sanguine, nor too greedy for money, nor ever too eager to boast before he knows for certain. A fighting man must wait, when he is to speak his vow, until, bold of spirit, he knows for certain whither the purpose of (men's) breasts will turn.[75]

---

[73] For *fægen*. This is the only word for which I have not followed Leslie's glossary.

[74] If we accept 'glory' for *gielp* (rather than Pope's 'to boast'), we must, I think, assume that pagan *lof* is meant; cf. J. Leyerle's development in *MÆ* 34 (1965), 89–102, of J. R. R. Tolkien's suggestion that Beowulf is being criticized for his excessive pride and desire for glory. The Christian form of *lof* described in *Seafarer* ll. 72–80 would scarcely fit the context of *The Wanderer*; it is hard to imagine any Christian urging either moderation in one's eagerness for Heaven or a complete lack of such eagerness. But there remains the possibility that *lofgeornost* in *Beowulf* l. 3182 may refer to the Christian form of *lof*; see *Neophilologus* 47 (1963), 130–2 [pp. 8–10 above].

[75] Pope, p. 169.

13
An Old English Syntactical Reverie: The Wanderer, Lines 22 and 34-36

In defence of the emendation of MS *mine* to *minne* in *Wanderer* l. 22, R. F. Leslie suggests that we compare 'the unambiguously singular *goldwine*'[1] in

Wanderer l. 34　　Gemon he selesecgas　　ond sincþege,
　　　　　　　　　hu hine on geoguðe　　his goldwine
　　　　　　　　　wenede to wist.　　Wyn eal gedreas!

Since *goldwine* can be nominative singular or nominative plural of a masculine *i-* noun, the verb *wenede* is presumably the basis for this observation. This form is not in itself unambiguously singular – as well as preterite singular indicative or subjunctive, it can be preterite plural subjunctive; cf. also in The Exeter Book,

Descent into Hell l. 82　　...hwonne we word godes
　　　　　　　　　　　　þurh his sylfes muð　　secgan hyrde.[2]

In view of this, I wrote the following in a very condensed review of Leslie's edition: 'Since dependent questions after *gemunan* sometimes have subjunctive verbs, *wenede* does not certify *goldwine* (l. 35) as "unambiguously singular" (p. 69).'[3] The key word here is 'certify'. It is certainly possible, and perhaps even probable, that *wenede* is preterite indicative and therefore singular. But, for the reasons set out below, I cannot at present accept that it must be.

It is now generally agreed that remarks such as that of A. S. Cook – 'certainty is rendered by the indicative'[4] – are unwarranted and enshrine an oversimplified view of the difference between the indicative and the subjunctive. Thus in *þæt* clauses after *gemunan* – the verb governing the *hu* clause in *Wanderer* l. 35 – we find both the indicative, e.g.

Reprinted from *Neuphilologische Mitteilungen* 68 (1967), 139-49.

[1] R. F. Leslie *The Wanderer* (Manchester, 1966), p. 69, note to l. 22.
[2] Cf. *Daniel* l. 101 *dæde* (preterite subjunctive plural) and *Order of the World* l. 7 *bringe* and *Riddle* 26. 16 *mære* (both in Exeter Book and both present subjunctive plural). See further A. Campbell *Old English Grammar* (Oxford, 1959), §§472-3 and 735 (g).
[3] To appear in *RES*. [1987. *RES* 18 (1967), 104.]
[4] *First Book in Old English* (London, 1921), p. 104.

Christ and Satan l. 723   Ða he gemunde   þæt he on grunde stod,
                            locade leas wiht   geond þæt laðe scræf,
                            atol mid egum . . .[5]

and the subjunctive, e.g.

Daniel l. 624   Gemunde þa on mode   þæt metod wære,
                  heofona heahcyning,   hæleða bearnum
                  ana ece gast.

There is no doubt that Satan was in hell. But equally there is no doubt – in the mind of either the poet or of Nabochodonossor – that the *metod* is *ana ece gast*; it was part of the poet's belief and the king had learnt in his seven years of exile that He 'was', not that He 'might be', the King of Kings. Nor can *wære* imply that He 'will be'; the reference is not to the future-in-the-past.

There is one example in the poetry of a dependent question or exclamation[6] after *gemunan* with the preterite indicative, viz.

Juliana l. 624   Ic þa sorge gemon,
                   hu ic bendum fæst   bisga unrim
                   on anre niht   earfeða dreag,
                   yfel ormætu.

Here, as in *Christ and Satan* l. 723, the reference is to the past. But there are no examples like *Daniel* l. 624 in which the preterite subjunctive is used with reference to a completed and undisputed act or state in the past. The only unambiguous preterite subjunctive in d.q./d.e. after *gemunan* in the poetry is

Soul and Body i. 19   Lyt ðu gemundest
                        to hwan þinre sawle þing   siðþan wurde,
                        syððan of lichoman   læded wære!

Here the reference is to the future-in-the-past.[7]

---

[5] Anglo-Saxon Poetic Records has a full stop after *stod*. Since Satan is already aware that he is in hell (l. 718), a comma seems preferable. This punctuation is perhaps another example of the curious 'superstition, which disallows subordination in a clause preceding the principal sentence' referred to by S. O. Andrew in his *Postscript on* Beowulf (Cambridge, 1948), p. 21. It is more than time that his remarks on this and on some other points were taken seriously instead of being brushed cavalierly aside on the strength of such comments as that of Kemp Malone in his review of Andrew's *Syntax and Style in Old English* in *MLN* 60 (1945), 557: 'until he can bring himself to make a really detailed investigation he should not expect his results to be accepted, or even taken seriously'. As a result of the attitude which finds expression there, the warning of the anonymous reviewer of the same work in *The Times Literary Supplement* has already come true: 'any future editor of an OE text will neglect Mr. Andrew's book at his own peril.' They have.

[6] Hereafter abbreviated to 'd.q./d.e.'. No satisfactory criterion for distinguishing the two has emerged.

[7] The remaining nine verbs in the preterite in d.q./d.e. after *gemunan* have ambiguous verb

In the present tense, we have

Paris Psalter 88. 41   Gemune, mære god,   hwæt si min lytle sped,

Judgement Day ii. 123
    Ic bidde, man, þæt þu gemune   hu micel bið se broga ... ,

Christ and Satan l. 644   Georne þurh godes gife   gemunan gastes bled,
                         hu eadige þær   uppe sittað
                         selfe mid swegle,   sunu hælendes!

and *Judgement Day* ii. 92 where the imperative *gemyne* is followed by three indicatives and one ambiguous verb form. We can explain the subjunctive *si* in the first example as due to the imperative in the principal clause. But in the third and fourth examples, in the same or very similar circumstances, we have the indicative. These examples show an inconsistency of mood after *gemunan* like that already noted in the *þæt* clauses in *Christ and Satan* l. 723 and *Daniel* l. 624.

All the examples of d.q./d.e. after other words of remembering must now be considered. After *gemyndigian* we find an ambiguous preterite form referring to the past in *Paris Psalter* 142. 5. The noun *gemynd* is followed by a preterite indicative referring to a completed act in the past in

Andreas l. 960   læt ðe on gemyndum   hu þæt manegum wearð
                  fira gefrege   geond feala landa,
                  þæt me bysmredon   bennum fæstne
                  weras wansælige

(note here the imperative in the principal clause) and by an ambiguous preterite with a similar time reference in *Paris Psalter* 77. 42. After the adjective *gemyndig* we find a present subjunctive preceded by an imperative equivalent in the principal clause and by a purpose clause with the present subjunctive in *Paris Psalter* 82. 4, and three ambiguous preterite forms – *Andreas* l. 163 and *Paris Psalter* 73. 20 (both referring to actions completed in the past, but with an imperative in the principal clause in *Paris Psalter* 73. 20), and *Judith* l. 75 (where the future-in-the-past is expressed by *mihte*).

Where does all this leave us in regard to *wenede* in *Wanderer* l. 36? The contrast between *Juliana* l. 624 and *Soul and Body* i. 19 might lead us to argue that, since *wenede* is a preterite referring to an act or series of acts completed in the past, it is therefore indicative singular and that *goldwine* is therefore 'unambiguously singular', as Leslie suggests. But 'unambiguously' is a strong word in forms referring to something which happened, or which was, in the past – *Beowulf* l. 1186, *Andreas* l. 639, *Wanderer* l. 35 (the example under discussion), *Riddle* 83. 7, *Paris Psalter* 104. 5, *Charm* 2. 1, 2, 23, 24. (On the ambiguity of the *-est* ending in the last four examples, see Campbell *Old English Grammar*, p. 325, §752(3).)

view of the inconsistent use of indicative and subjunctive in the *þæt* clauses and in the d.q./d.e. after *gemunan* already discussed.[8] The preterite indicative after the imperative in *Andreas* l. 960 might be advanced in favour of the view that the indicative was so strongly the mood of certainty that it overcame the tendency of the imperative to produce a subjunctive in the subordinate clause. But we have already seen the distinction breaking down in the present and we find the *Andreas* poet himself using the preterite subjunctive after an imperative in

> *Andreas* l. 557   Saga, þances gleaw   þegn, gif ðu cunne,
> hu ðæt gewurde   be werum tweonum,
> þæt ða arleasan   inwidþancum,
> Iudea cynn   wið godes bearne
> ahof hearmcwide.

In view of these inconsistencies and of the paucity of examples of d.q./d.e. after *gemunan* and other words of remembering, some examination of the use of moods in d.q./d.e. after other verbs is called for. After verbs of thinking or considering in the poetry, there are two preterite subjunctives in which the reference is to the future-in-the-past – *Beowulf* l. 173 (after *eahtian*) and *Soul and Body* ii. 19 (after *geþencan*).[9] This, of course, merely underlines what we know – that the Old English preterite subjunctive could be so used – despite F. Behre's confident assertion to the contrary: 'in OE. as well as in other Old Germanic languages the "prospective" subjunctive does not exist.'[10] But again we find the preterite subjunctive referring to the past, and not to the future-in-the-past – this time after *ahicgan* in

> *Daniel* l. 130   Hu magon we swa dygle,   drihten, ahicgan
> on sefan þinne,   hu ðe swefnede,
> oððe wyrda gesceaft   wisdom bude,
> gif þu his ærest ne meaht   or areccan?[11]

The only other preterite subjunctive in d.q./d.e. after verbs of thinking and

---

[8] Such inconsistencies are not peculiar to clauses governed by *gemunan*.

[9] This is the same example as *Soul and Body* i. 19 already cited. The Exeter Book has *geþohtes* where the Vercelli Book reads *gemundest*.

[10] *The Subjunctive in Old English Poetry* (Göteborg, 1934), p. 185.

[11] Grammatically *bude* here could be second singular preterite subjunctive with an understood [*þu*] (meaning Nabochodonossor) as subject. But in private communications R. T. Farrell has argued that this is impossible within the context of the poem, since the king is not portrayed as a revealer of wisdom at this point in either the poem or the Vulgate. Farrell takes *wisdom* as the subject of *bude*. In his opinion 'the whole structure of the poem is based on an opposition of wise Jews and unwise heathens, one of whom, Nabochodonossor, becomes wise by a long process of conversion. The only exception to the rule is a counsellor to the king who speaks in lines 416–429, but *he is invented by the poet* (his italics).'

considering occurs in *Paris Psalter* 76. 10, where *geheolde* probably refers to the future-in-the-past.[12]

We turn now to verbs of saying. Here again we find the preterite subjunctive used of the future-in-the-past, e.g.

Beowulf l. 3069   Swa hit oð domes dæg   diope benemdon
                    þeodnas mære,   þa ðæt þær dydon,
                    þæt se secg wære   synnum scildig....

But we also find both preterite indicative and preterite subjunctive used of states or completed actions, e.g. (*ge*)*cyðan*

Elene l. 175   ...ðæt hie for þam casere   cyðan moston
                godspelles gife,   hu se gasta helm,
                in þrynesse   þrymme geweorðad,
                acenned wearð,   cyninga wuldor,...

but

Andreas l. 796   Sceoldon hie þam folce gecyðan
                 hwa æt frumsceafte   furðum teode
                 eorðan eallgrene   ond upheofon,
                 hwær se wealdend wære   þe þæt weorc staðolade,

and after *secgan*

Beowulf l. 50   Men ne cunnon
               secgan to soðe,   selerædende,
               hæleð under heofenum,   hwa þæm hlæste onfeng

but

Elene l. 157   Ða þæs fricggan ongan   folces aldor,
               sigerof cyning,   ofer sid weorod,
               wære þær ænig   yldra oððe gingra
               þe him to soðe   secggan meahte,
               galdrum cyðan,   hwæt se god wære,
               boldes brytta,   þe þis his beacen wæs....

Examples could be multiplied.

Here then we have further evidence to show that both preterite indicative and preterite subjunctive could be used of states or completed actions in the past. These variations can be plausibly explained thus:

[12] But cf. *heolde* probably referring to the past in a *þæt* clause in *Paris Psalter* 118. 55 (Latin *Memor fui in nocte nominis tui, Domine; et custodivi legem tuam*).

The *indicative* is used when the content of the noun clause is presented as a fact, as certain, as true, or as a result which actually has followed or will follow.

When the *subjunctive* is found, some mental attitude towards the content of the noun clause is usually implied: one of the following ideas may be present – condition, desire, obligation, supposition, perplexity, doubt, uncertainty, or unreality.[13]

But to say this is not to agree with Cook that 'certainty is rendered by the indicative'[14] or with F. Mossé: 'Mais, toutes les fois qu'il s'agit d'un fait, d'une constatation, d'une réalité, on emploie l'indicatif. . . .'[15] We cannot argue that because the wanderer actually was entertained by his lord in the past, *wenede* in *Wanderer* l. 36 must be indicative. We cannot argue that, because to us in the twentieth century – more than a thousand years since the sentence was conceived – this looks like an objective statement, *wenede* must therefore be indicative. For, when we examine the context more closely, we find that there is another possibility.

In ll. 39–57, the solitary, lordless wanderer dreams that he is back in the hall with his lord. He dreams that he sees his former companions. But he awakes and finds it all a dream; the reality is misery. Here we find elaborated the ideas already expressed in ll. 34–6: he remembers his companions and his lord, but *wyn eal gedreas*; the reality is misery. Lines 37–8 connect the two in an explanatory way: 'For this is his experience who . . .'. Thus I cannot see how we today can rule out the possibility that the wanderer – in his loneliness, distress or perplexity[16] – begins to doubt whether these people ever existed. He dreams he sees his lord and his former companions. But they melt away. How do we know that in his clouded mind the realities of the past – the hall-retainers, the receiving of treasure, the feasting – were not equally felt as figments of the imagination? To concede this possibility is to concede that *wenede* may be subjunctive and therefore may be plural. We are in no position to be dogmatic.

Nor is our procedure beyond reproach. We separate examples with the preterite indicative from those with the preterite subjunctive and say that the indicative presents the content of the noun clause as a fact and that, when the subjunctive is used, some mental attitude towards it is implied. We then say 'Here is an example with the indicative. The speaker must have been certain about that!' Or we say 'Here is an example with the subjunctive. Obviously the

---

[13] These conclusions are based on a complete study of the poetry and on systematic samplings of the prose. Complete collections from the prose may add some telling examples. But I am not hopeful that they will resolve the question discussed below.
[14] *First Book in Old English*, p. 104.
[15] *Manuel de l'anglais du moyen âge* I *Vieil-anglais* (Paris, 1945), p. 159.
[16] Or other emotion; the list given above is not exhaustive.

speaker was doubtful.' No deep discrimination is needed to see that this argument involves some degree of circularity.

And then, despite the fact that we cannot listen to speakers of Old English or ask them why this clause has the indicative and that one the subjunctive, we press on to apply our own conclusions to clauses with ambiguous verbs and try to decide whether they are indicative or subjunctive. The problem of the mood of *wenede* would not, I imagine, have detained Alfred or Ælfric for very long. But I cannot see how we can presume or pretend to decide when we lack the vital clue of intonation, when we do not have the *Sprachgefühl* of the native speaker, and when we do not know what ancient fears or primitive taboos lurk behind the use of the subjunctive. Hence I believe that the secret of *wenede* lies buried with the poet of *The Wanderer*.

Thus the emendation of *mine* to *minne* in *Wanderer* l. 22 does not, in my opinion, derive any support from

Wanderer l. 35   hu hine on geoguðe   his goldwine
                    wenede to wiste.

It is, of course, quite an acceptable emendation. But *goldwine mine* is plural in form. The wanderer could have had more than one lord, as many a follower of King Æthelwulf of Wessex and his sons could have testified.[17] The word *winedryhtnes* in *Wanderer* l. 37 is not evidence against this; it could be a generic reference to any follower deprived of any lord. And *wenede* could be subjunctive plural. So it is just as possible – and just as logical – to argue that 'since *mine* is plural, *wenede* must also be plural' as to argue that 'since *wenede* is singular, we must read *minne*'.

This discussion may seem a classic example of a nut cracked by a steam roller. However, a reverie is defined in the College Edition of Webster's *New World Dictionary of the American Language* as 'dreamy thinking or imagining, especially of agreeable things; fanciful musing ... a dreamy, fanciful or visionary notion or daydream'. And in this reverie we have travelled a long way – not, I hope, altogether without reason or justification – from Leslie's apparently clinching observation: cf. the unambiguously singular *goldwine* in l. 35. For it is not merely the emendation of *mine* to *minne* which is at stake; whether the wanderer had one lord or more than one lord is of little importance for our approach to the poem. Nor is it merely the significance of the Old English subjunctive. It is a larger question – that of the use of syntax as a tool by editors of Old English texts. Syntax is of course an essential tool. But in our present state of knowledge, it must not be used without as full an understanding as is possible of the issues involved. Syntax and semantics are

[17] Æthelwulf died 858. His sons included King Æthelbald (died 860), King Æthelbert (died 866), King Æthelred (died 871), and King Alfred.

still the Cinderellas of Old English studies.[18] Perhaps fairy godmothers are near at hand? However that may be, *This was my sweven; now hit ys doon.*

---

[18] G. N. Garmonsway's recent comments on the word *wæfre* give a startling glimpse of how much there is to be done in semantics; see *Franciplegius: Medieval and Linguistic Studies in Honor of Francis Peabody Magoun, Jr* (New York, 1965), pp. 143-4.

14
More Musings on Old English Syntax

I. *The Wanderer*, lines 8—11

Of this passage, R. F. Leslie writes:

> The wanderer's monologue is resumed on a more personal note, recounting in lines 8–9a his own former friendless state. It is important to note the use of the past tense here; the wanderer no longer 'stands in the midst of sorrow' as has been claimed. It is the failure to recognise that the wanderer's troubles are over and done with which weakens Elliott's claim that we have to deal with a particular history rather than a personal but typical fate in the lament of the wanderer. He believes that the wanderer has a guilty secret which he dare not acknowledge to anyone. Although this interpretation seems to find support in the verb *durre* 'dare' (10), it overlooks the force of *nū* (9). There is no longer anyone left alive to whom he dare speak openly because he has outlived his friends, the men of his own generation.[1]

The argument hinges on *sceolde* l. 8 and *nu* l. 9. I have shown elsewhere in a discussion of *Wanderer* ll. 1–5 that *sceolde* can be either a preterite or a perfect.[2] If the adverb *nu* can be used to 'prove' anything, it would seem to me to argue for R. W. V. Elliott rather than for Leslie, since it suggests to me that *sceolde* is perfect: 'Often I have had to bewail my sorrow alone at break of each day; there is now no longer any man alive to whom I dare reveal my heart openly.' The sequence 'Often I had to ... there is now no one' seems somehow less satisfactory. We may also note that *ana* is stressed while *nu* is not.

Leslie spins what seems to me a somewhat complicated tissue of conjecture in arguing against Elliott. In support of the latter some rebutting questions and observations can be put – on the same speculative level. Leslie argues: 'Elliott's supposition that he dare not speak because of the guilt he hides would be more cogent if he were surrounded by his own friends, which he is not.'[3] In reply to

---

Reprinted from *Neuphilologische Mitteilungen* 69 (1968), 53–63.

[1] *The Wanderer* (Manchester, 1966) (hereafter cited as Leslie), pp. 4–5.
[2] To appear in *NM*. [1987. See item 12. I above.]
[3] Leslie, p. 5.

this, one might ask: 'Since the wanderer's friends and companions would presumably know of his guilt, is he not more likely to remain silent among strangers?' Leslie's claim is that 'he has become a wise man with a good share of years in the world, and he must follow the code of behaviour of such.'[4] Would not the *geoguþ* as well as the *duguþ* be expected to observe the heroic virtues? Is silence necessarily a proof of old age? Are last survivors necessarily old? Osric's godson in the famous Chronicle annal for 755 comes to mind. Leslie further writes:

> Insufficient attention has been paid to *geāra iū* in line 22. These emphatic adverbs make clear that all these things happened a long time ago, and underline his present ripeness in years and experience.[5]

Such phrases, however, might be merely conventional; cf. *Dream of the Rood* l. 28 *þæt wæs geara iu, (ic þæt gyta geman)* ..., where it is not necessary to believe that a long period has elapsed. We are not forced to place much importance on what might be merely the equivalent of 'It's ages since I saw you'. And loneliness often leads to emotional exaggeration.

But it seems unprofitable to continue arguments of this kind, begotten of attempts to give a local habitation and a name to something which can never be localized or defined.

II. *Oft*, *The Wanderer*, line 53

Here Leslie retains the MS *oft* in preference to the emendation to *eft*.[6] His comparison with the *oft* of l. 40 might be countered by a comparison with the *eft* of l. 45 and there are certainly contextual arguments for the emendation. But Leslie makes a good point when he says: 'The retention of MS. *oft* ... emphasises that the dream-like state described is a recurrent one, as is also made clear by *swiþe geneahhe* (56).'[7] He could have strengthened his case by citing the use of *beoð* (l. 49) and *bið* (ll. 50 and 55) and by pointing out that these confirm the repeated *þonne*'s as frequentative (though to be sure *þonne* would still have been used even if the happenings had occurred only once, since *þa* is used only of a single act in the past).[8] These are the syntactical devices which tell us that the dream-like state is a recurrent one.

III. *The Wanderer*, lines 58-9

Leslie writes: 'The verb *gesweorcan* clearly implies change of state, but the subjunctive form *gesweorce* in the indirect question clause in line 59 leaves open the

[4] Leslie, p. 5. [5] Leslie, p. 6.
[6] Leslie, p. 78, note to l. 53. [7] Leslie, p. 78, note to l. 53.
[8] See *Neophilologus*, 49 (1965), 46–7, and compare the combination *oft* ... *þonne* discussed there.

question whether the wanderer's *mōdsefa* "mind" *does* or *might well* "become dark".[9] Even granting that these words are spoken by the wanderer, I can see little point in speculating on this question. It is certainly true that the present subjunctive form of the verb *gesweorce* could mean either 'does become dark' or 'may (shall) become dark'[10] and could therefore leave open the question whether the wanderer's mind is or is not dark, for the present subjunctive is the mood in the other three dependent questions in the poetry after *geþencan* in which some aspect of the answer is still in doubt for the original speaker and/or the reporter:

    Seafarer l. 117   Uton we hycgan   hwær we ham agen,
                                      ond þonne geþencan   hu we þider cumen ...

    Riddle 41. 8   þæt is to geþencanne   þeoda gehwylcum,
                                      wisfæstum werum,   hwæt seo wiht sy,

and

    Judgement Day i. 77   Lyt þæt geþenceð
    . . . .
    hu him æfter þisse worulde   weorðan mote.

These examples contrast with dependent questions or exclamations in which the situation is clear, for there we find the indicative, e.g.

    Soul and Body i. 25   Hwæt, ðu on worulde ær
                                 lyt geþohtest   hu þis is þus lang hider!

and

    Christ l. 370   Ara nu onbehtum   ond usse yrmþa geþenc,
                             hu we tealtrigað   tydran mode,
                             hwearfiað heanlice.[11]

Whether the wanderer's mind is or is not dark at the time he speaks seems to me to depend on whether or not we accept the emendation of *mod sefan minne* to *modsefa min ne* before *gesweorce* in l. 59. If we reject the negative as a repetition of the *ne* of l. 58 or as the result of some other scribal confusion and read *modsefa min gesweorce*, we can translate either 'I can think of no reason why my mind becomes dark' or 'I can think of no reason why my mind may (or 'shall') become dark.' In this case, the question is open. But both these translations run

[9] Leslie, p. 79, note to ll. 58–9.
[10] The translations proposed by Leslie ('might well ...') and Gordon ('should ...') – see Leslie, p. 79, note to ll. 58–9 – scarcely fit the present subjunctive.
[11] This example is sufficient to disprove the proposition that the subjunctives in *Seafarer* l. 117 and *Riddle* 41. 8 are the automatic result of the imperative or imperative equivalent in the principal clause.

contrary to the sense of the passage – that there is every reason for his mind becoming dark is the whole point. Thus sense requires the negative and supports the emendation adopted by Leslie.

If then we accept the negative, we can translate either 'I can think of no reason why my mind does not become dark' or 'I can think of no reason why my mind may not (or 'shall not') become dark.' In this case, there is no need for speculation about the present state of his mind: it is not dark. To speculate about whether if will eventually become dark seems to me to be carrying the question a little far.

But Leslie maintains that

> the case for the mind of the wanderer actually becoming dark can only be firmly maintained if the phrase *geond þās woruld* is put inside the subordinate *for hwan* clause as in Mrs. Gordon's translation 'Therefore I can think of no reason in this world why my heart should not grow dark . . .'.[12]

There is no doubt that the phrase *geond þas woruld(e)* – both here and in *Christ and Satan* 1. 642, which Leslie cites[13] – can be taken as part of the subordinate clause; cf.

Juliana l. 32   Ða wæs sio fæmne   mid hyre fæder willan
welegum biweddad;   wyrd ne ful cuþe,
freondrædenne   hu heo from hogde,
geong on gæste.   Hire wæs godes egsa
mara in gemyndum,   þonne eall þæt maþþumges-
teald
þe in þæs æþelinges   æhtum wunade,

where *freondrædenne* (taken by Kock as parallel to *wyrd* 'the fact, her love')[14] is better explained as dependent on *from hogde* 'despised', i.e. as part of the subordinate clause placed before the conjunction.[15] Thus C. W. Kennedy translates 'Nor did he fully know her destiny, how she, young in heart, despised his friendship. . . .'[16] But this whole argument seems to me unnecessary, even on Leslie's premiss that the speaker is the wanderer:

> God moves in a mysterious way
> His wonders to perform,

[12] Leslie, p. 79, note to ll. 58–9. [13] Leslie, p. 80, note to ll. 58–9.
[14] *Jubilee Jaunts and Jottings* (Lund, 1918), p. 53.
[15] The construction (or poetic licence) can still be found in the alliterative verse of the fourteenth century; cf. *Sir Gawain and the Green Knight* l. 903 *þat he biknew cortaysly of þe court þat he were*. For the reverse phenomenon – part of the principal clause within a following subordinate clause – see *swa godes* in *Genesis B* l. 620 and *sweartra* in *Juliana* l. 468. [1987. See *OES* §1921a.]
[16] A better rendering for *wyrd* might be 'his destiny' or perhaps 'how things stood'. [1987. The placing of material belonging to the subordinate clause before the subordinating conjunction is further discussed and exemplified in *OES* §1920.]

and the mere fact that the wanderer can think of no reason why he does, may, or will, not despair can scarcely be accepted as proof that he eventually does. If his mind has not already darkened after all that he has experienced, it is hard to imagine the circumstances under which it will. The argument is, of course, completely unnecessary if we accept John C. Pope's view that ll. 58–110 were spoken, not by the wanderer, but by the *snottor on mode* of l. 111. As Pope writes:

> There are several ways in which this passage [ll. 58–63] gains by being attributed to the second speaker. It was always a little puzzling to find the wanderer giving reasons for the darkening of his mind, as if it had not been darkened long ago by the death of his kinsmen. But the thinker, if he is to feel an answering sadness, must explain the ground for it. In the second line, the possessive *min* now takes on the extra meaning that explains why it is carrying the alliteration: 'why *my* mind should not grow dark', that is, 'my mind also, like the wanderer's'.[17]

IV. *The Seafarer*, lines 33–5

Views about the exact grammatical status of the first *þæt* clause in

Seafarer l. 38
          Forþon cnyssað nu
    heortan geþohtas,   þæt ic hean streamas,
    sealtyþa gelac   sylf cunnige;
    monað modes lust   mæla gehwylce
    ferð to feran,   þæt ic feor heonan
    elþeodigra   eard gesece

have varied. Miss Kershaw translated it 'until' – a reasonable rendering in the light of examples like

Beowulf l. 358   eode ellenrof,   þæt he for eaxlum gestod
                        Deniga frean,

where we find a temporal element in what is formally a result clause. Her translation reads:

> But assuredly even now my thoughts are making my heart to throb, until of my own accord I shall venture on the deep waters, the tossing of the salt waves. At every opportunity a yearning impulse incites my heart to set forth and seek the land of strangers far away.[18]

What R. K. Gordon thought it was is not immediately apparent from his translation:

[17] *Franciplegius: Medieval and Linguistic Studies in Honor of Francis Peabody Magoun, Jr* (New York, 1965), p. 168. [1987. Pope has now retracted; see *ASE* 3 (1974), 75–86.]
[18] *Anglo-Saxon and Norse Poems* (Cambridge, 1922), p. 23.

And yet the thoughts of my heart are now stirred that I myself should make trial of the high streams, of the tossing of the salt waves; the desire of the heart always exhorts to venture forth that I may visit the land of strange people far hence.[19]

He may have thought of it as a noun clause or a purpose clause. But this is, I think, a purely terminological question. In such translations as those of W. W. Lawrence

> Even I myself, who have endured so much hardship, am impelled to make trial of the mighty waves again[20]

and of Miss Whitelock

> Therefore my heart's thoughts constrain me to venture on the deep seas, the tumult of the salt waves[21]

we have the same problem in different terms: is the infinitive used in an accusative and infinitive construction or to express purpose?

Mrs Gordon, however, translates

> And so the thoughts trouble my heart now that I myself am to venture on the deep (or towering) seas.[22]

J. C. Pope, after objecting to other aspects of her translation, goes on:

> Her 'now that' further weakens the effect. But this interpretation of *nu... þæt* is abnormal (the ordinary idiom being *nu... nu*) and is rendered very improbable by the seeming parallelism of the clause of purpose[23] in the next sentence. (She is probably right, however, though this does not affect the argument, in taking *heortan* as the object of *cnyssað*.)[24]

In view of this difference of opinion, it may be useful to cite those examples from the poetry in which *nu* in a main clause is followed by a temporal *þæt* clause.

If we exclude examples like

> *Beowulf* l. 2646 Nu is se dæg cumen,
> þæt ure mandryhten mægenes behofað,
> godra guðrinca,

[19] *Anglo-Saxon Poetry* (London, n.d.), p. 85.
[20] *JEGP* 4 (1902), 467.
[21] In *Early Cultures of North-West Europe: H. M. Chadwick Memorial Studies* (Cambridge, 1950), p. 264, n. 19.
[22] *The Seafarer* (London, 1960), pp. 37–8.
[23] Or noun clause – another example of the terminological problem referred to above.
[24] *Franciplegius*, p. 190, n. 25.

where the *þæt* clause refers to a noun – compare

Maldon l. 104
        Wæs seo tid cumen
  þæt þær fæge men feallan sceoldon,

where there is no *nu* – there are four. The rendering 'now that' in the sense in which Mrs Gordon uses it is impossible in *Genesis B* ll. 498–9 and in

Seasons for Fasting l. 152
    Nu wæs æt nehstan þæt us nergend Crist,
    halig heofenes weord, heolp and lærde.

(This latter example seems to me to destroy the faint possibility that *Christ and Satan* ll. 40–3 and *Guthlac B* ll. 1166–71 might support Mrs Gordon's rendering of *The Seafarer* passage; in both of these, as in *Beowulf* ll. 2646–7, *þæt* refers to a noun and not to *nu*.) This leaves us with two –

Metres of Boethius 8. 42
            Ac hit is sæmre nu,
    þæt ðeos gitsunc hafað gumena gehwelces
    mod amerred, þæt he maran ne recð,
    ac hit on witte weallende byrnð

and

Metres of Boethius 10.57
            Ac hit is wyrse nu,
    þæt geond þas eorðan æghwær sindon
    hiora gelican hwon ymbspræce,
    sume openlice ealle forgitene,
    þæt hi se hlisa hiwcuðe ne mæg
    foremære weras forð gebrengan.

The translation 'because' for *þæt* would fit these sentences very well, but the evidence for this sense in the poetry is very flimsy indeed.[25] To take *þæt* as introducing a noun clause in apposition to *hit* is very strained. Here then the translation 'now that' seems to me at the moment the most convincing possibility. But we must note that in both these examples *þæt* immediately follows *nu*, as in MnE 'now that', whereas in *The Seafarer* passage the two are separated.

Pope therefore is clearly on good ground when he observes that the construction postulated by Mrs Gordon is abnormal. As far as the poetry is concerned, he could have said 'unique' – a claim which, on the negative evidence of Bosworth-Toller, might be extended to Old English as a whole.[26] Thus, even

[25] I hope to examine it elsewhere. [1987. See *OES* §§3118–27.]

[26] It may also be noted that Bosworth-Toller cites no examples like *Metres of Boethius* 8. 42 and 10. 57 and that *OED* has no examples of 'now that' before 1530.

if we think it safer to keep an open mind until the complete evidence from the prose is available, and even if we believe that uniqueness cannot automatically be equated with impossibility when the question is one of syntax, we must agree that the available evidence gives no support at all to Mrs Gordon's interpretation of *nu... þæt* in *Seafarer* ll. 33–4.[27]

---

[27] The other twelve examples in the poetry of the combination 'adverb of time + *þæt*', e.g. *gearu iu... þæt* (*Dream of the Rood* ll. 28–9), do not seem to me in any way parallel to the construction postulated by Mrs Gordon. [1987. See *OES* §§2591–3.]

15
The Narrator of *The Wife's Lament*: Some Syntactical Problems Reconsidered

The syntactical cockles of the heart of Professor Tauno F. Mustanoja (in whose honour I am glad to write these words) must have been warmed by the problem which Martin Stevens raises in his article 'The Narrator of *The Wife's Lament*'.[1] Mr Stevens deserves our gratitude for seizing a weapon whose potential power had been neglected and for mounting with it a bold assault on the firmly entrenched proposition that syntactical reasons compel us to accept that the narrator of *The Wife's Lament* must be a woman. I do not think that Mrs Angela M. Lucas's foray has driven off the besiegers.[2] Here I try to answer the question 'Has the citadel really fallen?'

A few preliminary comments on some syntactical observations made by Mr Stevens and Mrs Lucas will clear the way for a discussion of the main problem – *minre sylfre sið* (l. 2). First, Mr Stevens has misunderstood *Genesis B* l. 611a, which he quotes in isolation. There we read

> *Genesis B* l. 611
> þu meaht nu þe self geseon,   swa ic hit þe secgan ne þearf,
> Eue seo gode,   þæt þe is ungelic
> wlite and wæstmas,   siððan þu minum wordum getruwodest.

The object of *geseon* is not *þe self*, as Mr Stevens seems to think,[3] but the noun clause beginning in l. 612b. The question of an acc. form of *self* agreeing with *þe* does not arise, for *self* is nom. sg. fem. (declined like *blind*[4]) agreeing

Reprinted from *Neuphilologische Mitteilungen* 73 (1972), 222–34.

[1] *NM* 69 (1968), 72–90 (hereafter referred to in the footnotes as S.).
[2] *NM* 70 (1969), 282–97 (hereafter referred to in the footnotes as L.). Her first sentence in IV (L., p. 289) seems unfair to Mr Stevens. At no point does he claim to have produced 'grammatical proof' that the narrator must be male.   [3] S., pp. 76–7.
[4] See A. Campbell *Old English Grammar* (Oxford, 1959) (hereafter cited as *OEG*), §639. Certainly, if *þe* and *self* were to agree in acc. sg. fem., we should need *þe selfe*. But would we not equally need *þe selfne* if they agreed in acc. sg. masc.?

with þu and þe is a (possibly pleonastic) reflexive dat. after *geseon*.[5] So this example is irrelevant.

Irrelevant too (and perhaps worse) is Mr Stevens's argument about the agreement of *bi me ful geomorre* (l. 1) if *geomorre* is taken as an adj. Whether *eadig* in *Catholic Homilies* (ed. Thorpe) i. 202. 22 *eadig eart þu* should be described as having common gender or as an idiomatically uninflected form is perhaps a terminological problem.[6] But I cannot see how this sentence leads Mr Stevens to the following conclusion: 'The point is that an Old English audience would not inevitably have understood *geomorre* as a feminine adjective because it allegedly referred to a feminine speaker (who was already disguised and obscured by the masculine *scop*).'[7] This seems to mean that, even if it is an adj. and not an adv., *geomorre*, with the distinctive fem. inflexion -*re*, would not necessarily have been taken as fem. because *eadig* appears instead of *eadigu* in the example quoted above, but might have been felt as either masc. or neut. – even though it ends in -*re*. This seems so absurd that I must be mistaken.[8]

Thirdly, Mr Stevens argues that, if the narrator had been a woman, the poet 'would surely have used the feminine *ane* for the masculine *ana* to reinforce the identification' in *þonne ic on uhtan ana gonge* (l. 35).[9] He goes on to 'prove' this proposition in a somewhat repetitive footnote:

> Alistair Campbell points out that in the adjectival sense of 'alone', *ana* may be used to refer to a feminine pronoun (see *Old English Grammar*, p. 282). The feminine form *ane*, however, would have been the established usage and, in this instance, surely the one the poet would have chosen, as is argued in behalf of *geomorre* in line 1, had he wanted to speak in the person of an exiled wife.[10]

I do not see the point of the remark 'The feminine form *ane*, however, would have been the established usage'. *Ana* and (less frequently to the best of my knowledge[11]) *ane* are both 'established' usages for the nom. sg. fem. of

---

[5] On this well-attested construction see J. M. Farr *Intensives and Reflexives in Anglo-Saxon and Early Middle English* (Baltimore, Md, 1905), pp. 26–8.

[6] See *A Guide to Old English*, 2nd edn (Oxford, 1968), §187. 1(d); the rule stated there for ptcs. can be extended to adjs. *Eadig* is scarcely masc., as Mrs Lucas suggests (L., p. 288). *Riddle* 33 offers an instructive comparison. The speaker of ll. 9–13 is fem. – *hio* (l. 5) and *wrætlicu* (l. 1). But l. 5a reads *Wæs heo hetegrim*, with an uninflected adj. So we can resist the temptation to argue that *Wife's Lament* l. 29b *eal ic eom oflongad* proves that the speaker is not a woman.

[7] S., p. 81.

[8] Mrs Lucas rather understates it (I think), when she writes 'Therefore the fact that *geomorre* has a feminine ending rather increases the possibility that the speaker is a woman than the reverse' (L., p. 288). That *geomorre* may be an adverb is admitted below.

[9] S., p. 83.   [10] S., p. 83, fn. 1.

[11] M. Rissanen, in a private communication, has kindly supplemented the paragraph on this point in his *The Uses of* One *in Old and Early Middle English* (Helsinki, 1967), p. 134, where he cites

'alone'.[11a] All Mr Stevens is doing is claiming that *ana*, which could refer to a woman, would 'surely'[12] not have been used by the poet to refer to a woman – 'surely'.[13]

Fourthly, there is the remarkable tangle woven by Mr Stevens in his defence of Conybeare's reading of l. 18 *ðaicmefulgemæc/nemonnanfunde* instead of the usually accepted *ðaicmefulgemæcne/monnanfunde*. 'The separation of *gemæc* and *ne*', remarks Mr Stevens, 'is, of course, an editorial privilege.'[14] Of course. But what sort of an editor would want to use his privilege to produce a line which may be impossible metrically[15] and is certainly impossible syntactically.

one example each of *ana* and *ane* as nom. sg. fem. I quote from his letter of 31 Dec. 1970 these references to 17 more examples of *ana* as nom. sg. fem. (abbreviations as in his book):

Wærf. Greg. 54, 1; 211, 16.
Hept. 385, VI, 17.
Ælfric Lives II, 224; VII, 199; X, 238.
Ælfric Hom. I, 184, 19; 552, 33; II 62, 26; 102, 5; 346, 28.
Hom. Assmann 33, 221, 223.
Wulfstan Napier 149, 21; 197, 23.
Verc. Hom. 80, 77.
Byrhtferth 128, 2.

On the use of *ane* as a nom. sg. fem., he writes:

At the moment I can only find the following four in addition to Ælfric Lives 33, 107 quoted in my thesis:

ne miht þu ane wunian Ælfric Lives 33, 150.
his fostormoder ane wæs him fylgende Wærf. Greg. 96, 21.
(But some other MSS read *ana*)
næfre ne mihte me nan man ofercuman buton þu ane Hom. Assmann 176, 235.
and þu ane from fæder and fram modor... to gode þu gehwurfe ibid. 177, 249.

But the last two examples are probably from a very late MS and perhaps show the EME levelling of the ending.

[11a] [1987. See *OES* §539 for my withdrawal of my statement that *ane* is an 'established' usage for the nominative singular feminine of 'alone'.]

[12] S., p. 83.   [13] S., p. 83, fn. 1.   [14] S., p. 87.

[15] There would be no point in discussing the metrical validity of a syntactically impossible line were it not that it illustrates neatly why I am becoming increasingly reluctant to admit metre as a criterion in situations like this. Mrs Lucas says 'In fact, on metrical grounds alone the emendation implied by Conybeare is untenable. The *a*-verse thus emended could be an example of type e (a rarity in itself which would be dubious), but the possibility of its occurring need not be considered, as the emended *b*-verse will not scan at all' (L., p. 295). As far as the *a*-verse (for which Mr Stevens has a different explanation; S., p. 88, fn. 1) is concerned, I have already condemned the bizarre proposition that the fact that something is rare proves that the case in point cannot be an example; see *Neophilologus* 52 (1968), 297. The *b*-verse raises a question of a different kind. Mr Stevens (S., p. 88, fn. 1) describes it as an *a*-type with anacrusis – *ne mónnan fúnde*. Mrs Lucas does not state her grounds for rejecting this, but her metrical authority is A. J. Bliss *The Metre of* Beowulf (Oxford, 1958). On pp. 40ff., Bliss rejects the possibility of scanning *Beowulf* l. 414a *under heofenes hador* as *a*-type with anacrusis and caesura in position (i), and is therefore able to say 'It appears, then, that anacrusis is not permissible when the caesura is in position (i)' (p. 41). This is presumably Mrs Lucas's reason for rejecting Mr Stevens's scansion here. It is, however, an interesting fact that, of the 130 patterns which appear in Bliss's table II of Appendix C (excluding item 50), 29 occur only

Ne must immediately precede the verb it negates; otherwise it is a conjunction,[16] which it cannot be in *The Wife's Lament* l. 18. Even those who are unwilling to accept the metrical and other arguments advanced by Mrs Lucas[17] will, I think, have to agree that this is conclusive.

Nor is this the only syntactical objection to Conybeare's reading, for it leaves *gemæc* without the acc. sg. masc. *-ne* which is required if we are to accept the view of Bosworth-Toller and the editors that *gemæc* is an adj. It is clear that Mr Stevens would like to follow Conybeare in taking *gemæc* as a noun. But he lacks the courage to defy Bosworth-Toller and so comes up with 'at least the possibility, if not the probability, that *gemæc* in a construction of this type has prepositional force in the sense of modern English "like"'.[18] This amazing proposition is reinforced by the remark that

> in such a construction, *gemæc* seems to resemble *gelic* as used in the following passage from *Juliana*:
>
> Ic to soþe wat
> þæt ic ær ne sið   ænig ne mette
> in woruldrice   wif þe gelic.   (547b–549b)
>
> In this passage *gelic* has prepositional force (even though *Bosworth-Toller* classifies it under the general label of adjective; s.v. *gelic* adj.). Indeed, if used adjectively, *gelic* could only with difficulty be taken as a modifier of *þe*. Concordance in such a case would call for *gelicum*, not *gelic*. (S., p. 88)

The word *gelic* in the *Juliana* passage is the acc. sg. neut. of an adj. agreeing with *wif* and governing the dat. *þe*.[19] The idea that it is a modifier of *þe* is wrong; the suggestion that we need *þe gelicum* is impossible.[20]

---

once. Why should *Beowulf* l. 414a not be a thirtieth? [1987. On this point, see my 1987 addition to fn. 6 in item 17 below.] This question derives added point from three *b*-verses cited by Mr Stevens (p. 88, fn. 1): *The Wife's Lament* l. 27b *on wuda bearwe* (this, I expect, will be explained as *c*-type with resolution), and *Phoenix* l. 47b *oð bæles cyme* and l. 53b *ne laþes cyme* (short stressed syllable in *cyme*, or resolution?).

[16] See S. O. Andrew *Syntax and Style in Old English* (Cambridge, 1940), p. 62, and *A Guide to Old English* §§184. 4(d).

[17] L., pp. 292–5.   [18] S., p. 87.

[19] B-T properly glosses this as an adj. (not 'under the general label of adjective') and indeed translates the passage. See H. Sweet *Cura Pastoralis* (EETS, o.s. 45), Preface, p. ix.

[20] Similarly, Mr Stevens wrongly suggests (S., p. 88) about the sentence *Hi wif habbaþ him gemæc* that 'if *gemæc* were adjectival here, it would have to be emended to *gemæcum* to agree with dative plural *him*'. The problem here is that one would expect *gemacu*, *gemæcu* as acc. pl. neut. agreeing with *wif* if B-T is right in taking the vowel as short. But we can perhaps call to our aid the principle set out in *A Guide to Old English* §§187. 1(e) and 200 by extending it to adjs.; cf. p. 135, fn. 6, above. To call *gemæc* a noun would not help here; it would still have an inflexional ending, whatever gender we made it, if it were acc. pl. But we would expect *to* + dative. Another solution is to take *wif* and *gemæc* as acc. sg. neut. Each man could have one wife, and OE can have either

So far then Mr Stevens has only been marching round the citadel. His first real attack is his attempt to justify Thorpe's view that *geomorre* is for *geomore* adv. 'sadly'.[21] As Mrs Lucas hints, he hovers between explaining *-rr-* as a scribal error made in anticipation of the two *-re* inflexions which follow or as a genuine orthographic variant of *-r-*.[22] Such doubling might be explained by reference to the simplification of double consonants in syllables not carrying full stress which produced *opera* and *æftera* for *operra* and *æfterra*;[23] this could be the basis of an inverted spelling *-rr-* for *-r-*.[24] Mr Stevens claims that to take *geomorre* as a modifier of *me* is a 'clumsy interpretation'.[25] We could compare *Juliana* l. 449 *þæt þu miltsige me þearfendum* and *Judith* l. 85 *me þearfendre* and could claim that to take *geomorre* as an adverb is even clumsier. This is a matter of opinion. But Mrs Lucas goes too far when she says 'When eminently good sense can be made of the text as it stands, such suggestions cannot seriously challenge the woman-speaker interpretation.'[26] All Mr Stevens wants us to do is to agree that *geomorre could* (not *must*) be an adverb. We are, I think, bound to admit that Mr Stevens has re-opened an old breach here.

But the corner-stone of the view that the narrator must be a woman is l. 2a *minre sylfre sið*. It is against this that Mr Stevens's main battering-ram – the example *minre seolfre nidþearfe* used by a male speaker – is directed. Has he dislodged the stone?

No one will deny the proposition that in *mines felaleofan* (l. 26) and *for minre weaþearfe* (l. 10), where we have the combination possessive + noun, the possessive agrees with the noun in gender, number, and case.[27] But it is dangerous to deduce from this, as Mr Stevens does, that '*minre* in the second line of "The Wife's Lament" is singular, dative, and feminine not because the speaker is a woman but because it agrees syntactically with its headword

singular or plural in such circumstances; cf. *bedde* and *wifum* in *Lives of the Saints* (ed. Skeat) ii. 318. 75 ... *þæt ic ana ne belife æfter minum leofum þegnum þe on heora bedde wurdon mid bearnum and wifum færlice ofslægene*. (Some MSS indeed read *beddum* here.)

[21] S., pp. 81–2.
[22] L., pp. 288–9. Mr Stevens (S., p. 82, fn. 3) refers to p. 138 of J. and E. M. Wright *Old English Grammar*, 3rd edn (Oxford, 1961). It is not clear how anything on this page is relevant. Nor do pp. 137 and 139–40 help. All the examples have to do with doubling at the end of a stressed syllable. None involve doubling of *r*.
[23] *OEG* §457 and fn. 4; see also *OEG* §643 (4). The illogical doubling of consonant symbols referred to in *OEG* §65 is a less likely source – it is Northumbrian, it involves consonants at the end of a stressed syllable, and no examples with *-rr-* are cited.
[24] R. T. Farrell has privately drawn my attention to another possible example of *-rr-* for *-r-*. This is *Daniel* l. 392 where MS *herran þinne* may be for *heran þine* (with *heran* a form of **hera* 'servant') = Latin *servi Domini*, rather than for *hearran sinne*; see his forthcoming edition of *Daniel and Azarias* (Methuen OE Library). This, however, differs in that the doubling (if such it is) takes place after a stressed syllable. The only such example in those mentioned by Campbell in *OEG* §457 and fn. 4 is *tydde* 'instructed' from the OE Bede.
[25] S., p. 82.   [26] L., p. 289.   [27] S., p. 75.

sið'.[28] Mr Stevens speaks of *minre* as a 'possessive adjective'.[29] Yet he goes on to quote the views of Sweet, Bosworth-Toller, and Ingerid Dal,[30] all of whom speak of *self* agreeing with a *personal pronoun*, not with a 'possessive adjective'. I believe they are right – firstly because of what I think to be the origin and history of the idiom (see below) and secondly because, if Mr Stevens's emendation *minre sylfre siðe* is right, he has to explain the violation of another basic rule of Old English syntax – that in the combination possessive + adj. + noun, the adj. is normally declined weak; on this too see below.

Let us start by examining combinations of possessive + *self* in 1st pers. gen. pl.[31] Here we find *Cura Pastoralis 220. 7 þone anwald ure selfra*, Wulfstan's *Homilies* (ed. Napier) 1. 3 *for his synnum and ure selfra*, and (with the noun following) *Christ* l. 362 *þurh ure sylfra gewill* (*gewill* acc. sg. neut.), and *Judith* l. 285 *ure sylfra forwyrd* (*forwyrd* nom. sg. fem.). This usage is, I believe, the original one. What we have is the gen. pl. of the group *ic self*, where both *ic* and *self* can be described as pronouns. In the two prose examples *ure* cannot be a declined form of the possessive agreeing with the noun (*urne* and *urum* respectively would be required). It is unlikely to be one in the two examples from the poetry, though the form would be right.

When we turn to the singular we find both Mr Stevens and Mrs Lucas quoting Campbell's observation that 'the sg. of this construction requires the poss. adj. agreeing with *selfes*, *-re*, or with the noun possessed, e.g. *mines selfes sunu, on minne selfes dom*'.[32] Both these constructions of course occur; see further below. But I must take issue with the word 'requires'. I can see no reason why the singular form of the construction should have been any different originally from the plural. My opinion is that we see the original construction in *Christ* l. 254 *þurh þin sylfes gong* (*gong* acc. sg. masc.), where the declined form of the possessive would have to be *þines* or *þinne*; the only possible explanation is that *þin sylfes* is the gen. sg. masc. of *þu self* referring to Christ. We probably have the same construction in *Genesis A* l. 2922 *þin sylfes bearn* (*bearn* nom. sg. neut.) and *Christ* l. 9 *þin sylfes weorc* (*weorc* acc. sg. neut.), though here *þin* could be the neut. sg. of a possessive agreeing with *bearn* or *weorc*, and *self* could be used

---

[28] S., p. 75. That it is dative is, of course, one of the points in dispute.

[29] S., p. 74. I prefer to dispense with the terms 'possessive adjective' and 'possessive pronoun' because of their ambiguity. In MnE we can say that 'my' in 'These are my books' is an adjective and 'mine' in 'These books are mine' a pronoun. But we can find inflected and uninflected forms in both places in OE. It would appear that an OE possessive is called an adjective when it is inflected to agree with a noun, a pronoun when it is not – no matter what its function in the sentence. 'Possessive' will serve as a blanket term. When necessary we can distinguish between the gen. of a pers. pron. and a declined form of the possessive.

[30] S., pp. 75–6.

[31] The 3rd pers. forms *his, hire, hira* are not considered because they are indeclinable. By chance, my collections do not at present include examples of this sort with 2nd pers. pl.

[32] *OEG* §705, fn. 3.

independently; see below. Another unambiguous example – this time of the gen. dual of *ic self* – is *Genesis B* l. 792 *uncer sylfra sið* (*sið* acc. sg. masc.), where the inflected form of the possessive would have to be *uncerne* or *uncra/ uncer(r)a*.

But since we cannot be sure in some of these examples whether we have the gen. of the pers. pron. or a declined form of the possessive identical with it, it is clear that there was a possibility of confusion in the minds of native speakers. If for example we start with *Christ* l. 254 *þurh þin sylfes gong* and substitute an inflected form of the possessive for *þin*, we can decline *þin* to agree with *sylfes* or with *gong*. These are the two constructions cited by Campbell. Other examples of the first pattern are *Christ and Satan* l. 684 *on þines seolfes dom* and *Andreas* l. 1417 *on þines sylfes hand*.[33] That the analogy I am suggesting here – the inflecting of what was properly the gen. of the pers. pron. under the influence of the inflexion of a word which followed – did in fact operate in Old English can be seen from examples like *Cura Pastoralis* 63. 1 . . . *gif hwelc forworht monn cymð, 7 bitt urne hwelcne ðæt we hine læden to sumum ricum menn*, *Cura Pastoralis* 211. 13 *Forðæmðe* [*on eo*] *werre towesnesse ge habbað gecyðed ðæt ge ures nanes ne siendon*, and *Blickling Homilies* 185. 1 *þu forleosest þin rice 7 þines sylfes feorh*. It is this analogy which produces *Orosius* 48. 21 *iowra selfra anwaldes* – the example quoted by Campbell to illustrate his remark that 'pl. poss. adjs. are unusual with *self*'[34] – and *Cura Pastoralis* 220. 5 *ðæt we sceoldon urra selfra waldan*.

But if *þin* in *Christ* l. 254 *þurh þin sylfes gong* were declined to agree with *gong*, we would produce the idiom seen in *Beowulf* l. 2147 *on* [*min*]*ne selfes dom*, the example quoted by Campbell and the only one of its kind so far known to me. This could also be explained as a blend of two other constructions – that seen in *Beowulf* l. 2652 *mid minne goldgyfan* and the absolute use of *self* seen in *Beowulf* ll. 894–5 *þæt he beahhordes brucan moste // selfes dome*. But however it is explained, this traditional restoration should probably be regarded as tentative until supporting examples are found.

Unfortunately no feminine equivalents of *Christ* l. 254 *þurh þin sylfes gong* or of *Beowulf* l. 2147 *on* [*min*]*ne selfes dom* have come to my notice. But on the

---

[33] In these examples *selfes* could be explained as a noun. Though such constructions are possibly one source of the substantival use of *self* (see *OED* s.v. *self* C. I), *self* was not, I think, felt as a noun in OE. Wherever there is a difference between the paradigm of the noun and the corresponding form of an adj. or pron., *self* always (as far as I know) has the latter, e.g. *selfne, selfre, selfra*, not *self, selfe, selfa*.

[34] *OEG* §705, fn. 3. Two other examples may be mentioned here – *Lives of the Saints* ii. 342. 109 . . . *gelicode me þæt ic eowerne sum me to begeate* and *Ælfric's Homilies* (ed. Pope) i. 242.272 *gif hwylc-eowres assa fylþ*, where (as Pope points out in his note on p. 246) *Li Mark* 14. 5 has *huelc uel huæs iueres* and the WS version *hwylces eowres* (which seems to be on all fours with the examples quoted above; one would expect *hwylces eower). In *eowerne sum* the wrong word seems to have been inflected, and we could explain *hwylc eowres* in the same way if we did not wish to follow Pope in taking it as a compound; I would not think the *Li* gloss conclusive evidence for his view.

analogy of the first and of examples like *Elene* l. 222 *hiere sylfre suna* (*suna* gen. sg. masc.) and *Riddle* 33. 8 *ymb hyre sylfre gesceaft* (*gesceaft* acc. sg. fem./neut.),³⁵ we could postulate a hypothetical **þurh þin sylfre gong* which would produce *Christ* l. 339 *þinre sylfre sunu* (*sunu* acc. sg. masc.), (where, as Mr Stevens agrees,³⁶ the speaker is and must be feminine) and *Wife's Lament* l. 2 *minre sylfre sið*.

Now if Mr Stevens's reading of *Wife's Lament* l. 2 – **minre sylfre siðe* (*siðe* dat. sg. fem.) with *bi* understood from the preceding line – were produced on the analogy of *Beowulf* l. 2147 *on* [*min*]*ne selfes dom*, we should still have to do with a feminine speaker, for *minre* would be dative with *siðe* and *sylfre* would be gen. sg. fem. of *sylf* used independently. But this does not dispose of the matter, for (as Mr Stevens has acutely observed) there is another possible analogy – the phrase from *Alexander's Letter to Aristotle* (EETS o.s. 161) 14. 1 *be minre seolfre nedþearfe* Latin 84. 8 *de proprio meo... periculo*. He could have strengthened this weapon by adding *Bede* 480. 21 *of minre sylfre cyþeþe* Latin (ed. Colgrave and Mynors) 566. 18 *ex mea ipse cognitione*. In both places we have a male speaker, with *minre seolfre* (*sylfre*) agreeing in gender, number, and case, with a feminine noun. Both are direct translations from Latin. In both, the Latin has a possessive agreeing with the noun, and another word which the OE translator has represented by *seolfre* (*sylfre*). That in the first (*proprio*) agrees in gender, number, and case, with the possessive and the noun; *seolfre* does too. That in the second (*ipse*) seems to be nom. in the printed versions. But the translator represented it by *sylfre* (agreeing with the possessive and the noun) either because his Latin version had an ablative *or* because he made a mistake and took *ipse* as an ablative *or* because he was glossing rather mechanically and the nom. *self* would not have been possible between *minre* and *cyþeþe*.

The equivalent of *on minne sylfes dom* here would be **minre selfes nedþearfe* (*cyþeþe*); what we have is a feminine equivalent of **on minne selfne dom*.³⁷ That such a combination – either masc. or fem. – is native OE is extremely dubious. *Self* can be declined strong or weak, and the rules of OE syntax would lead us to expect a weak form of *self* after a possessive, just as occurs after the demonstrative in, for example, *Christ* l. 1208 *se sylfa cyning* and *Metres of Boethius* 25. 54 *on ðisse selfan bec*.³⁸ This suggests to me that the two examples primarily under

---

³⁵ As will be seen from fn. 31, above, I take the point made by Mr Stevens in his footnote 2 on p. 78. But I think my analogy legitimate.

³⁶ S., p. 76.

³⁷ Strictly speaking, the masc. equivalent should be dat. **minum selfum dome*. Such a combination can be paralleled because in the dat. sg. masc. and neut., the difference between strong and weak forms is blurred by the ambiguity of the *-um/-an* ending; see *PST* (1943), 29–30. It would not justify *minre sylfre nedþearfe*, where the weak form would be *selfan*.

³⁸ I must admit that there are examples involving adjectives other than *self* in which a strong form of the adj. comes between a possessive and a noun. I hope to publish a full discussion elsewhere. [1987. See *OES* §§121–2.] The salient points are perhaps: (1) Unambiguous examples occur

discussion here are not native, but were produced under Latin influence. This is far from unlikely; indeed, Professor Dorothy Whitelock has suggested that the translator of Bede was 'influenced by the practice of interlinear glossing of a text' and was 'unable to shed the habits of a school of interlinear glossing'.[39] There are no parallel examples (as far as I now know) in the poetry. The possibility of Latin influence in *The Wife's Lament* seems remote. So Mr Stevens is asking us to believe that an OE poet used a syntactically most unusual and (I think we can say) irregular construction which is based on Latin and is not found in the poetry. He asks us to do this when it involves our accepting a not particularly convincing emendation of a passage which makes good sense as it stands. He asks us to do this when an obvious analogy to the unamended passage presents itself from the poetry – *Christ* l. 339 *þinre sylfre sunu*. And he asks us to do this because to admit the syntactical equivalence of *Christ* l. 339 and *Wife's Lament* l. 2 would be to admit that a woman is speaking in *The Wife's Lament* – which he does not want to admit.

I do not propose to review what Mr Stevens calls 'the contextual and semantic evidence'.[40] It is inconclusive and in the end individual preference must decide between Mr Stevens – 'the traditional interpretation ... as a woman's monologue ... is not sustained by the context, the setting, or the diction of the poem'[41] – and Mrs Lucas – 'the mood and tone of the poem, ... if attentively read as poetry, suggests that its narrator is *not* a man'.[42] But we may note that Mr Stevens quotes with apparent approval Mr Bambas's suggestion that the rarity of examples argues that this cannot be one[43] and speaks of 'the tenuous identification of three inflectional endings'.[44] One ought to have been enough for any self-respecting speaker of Old English; after all in *Wulf and Eadwacer reotogu* (l. 10) is the only clue that the speaker is a woman, apart from the implication of phrases like *uncerne earne hwelp* (l. 16).[45] Mr Stevens claims that as a result of his work 'few difficulties remain'[46] in the way of those who wish to

in Alfredian prose, e.g. *Cura Pastoralis* 393. 8 *his getreowne ðegn*, *Gregory's Dialogues* 212. 17 *mid hire scamleasre bælde*, and *Bede* 238. 22 *his unrihtes sleges* where the later MS B has the expected weak form *unrihtan*. (2) The only example known to me in the poetry where the possessive and the adj. occur *in the same half-line* (on the basic principle involved, see L. Fakundiny in *RES* 21 (1970), 129–42 and 257–66) is from *The Later Genesis* l. 654 *his holdne hyge*. (3) The only examples known to me in Ælfric's *Catholic Homilies* involve the ambiguous *-an/-um* ending. (4) Some authorities hold that examples of this kind are survivals of an earlier idiom.

[39] *PBA* 48 (1962), 76 and 76–7. See also *NM* 70 (1969), 376.
[40] S., p. 73.
[41] S., p. 90.
[42] L., p. 297. See also *NM* 70 (1969), 104, where Dr Rissanen can 'by no means exclude the possibility that the poet made use of a traditional theme in composing a poem with a new motif – a lament of the wife for her lost husband'.
[43] S., p. 72. See fn. 15, above.
[44] S., p. 82.
[45] What exactly does Mr Stevens mean when he says that *Wulf and Eadwacer* is 'reputedly also spoken by a woman' (p. 81)?
[46] S., p. 90.

dispose of the woman narrator. That those based on literary considerations are more formidable than he suggests has been shown by Mrs Lucas and by Dr Rissanen.⁴⁷ But the decision cannot be made on literary grounds alone while the grammatical citadel still stands; Mr Stevens has struck it only a glancing blow, while one of his weapons – his interpretations of l. 18 – lies splintered beyond repair.

For he relies on too great a combination of improbabilities. If we are to accept that the speaker is not a woman we must accept all the propositions which follow. First, we must accept that *minre* and *sylfre* are both in agreement with a feminine noun; my reasons for thinking this most unlikely are given above. Second, we must accept the emendation *siðe* for MS *sið*. Mrs Lucas has offered metrical objection to this, the gravamen of which is, not that the type is rare in itself (see fn. 15, above), but that it would be an odd hypermetric half-line in a context of normal half-lines.⁴⁸ Third, we must accept that a feminine noun *sið* does in fact exist. This seems at best an open question.⁴⁹ But since the justification for it is *Riddle* 64. 2 *on sibþe*, ought Mr Stevens not to have explained how he can read *siðe*? (I suppose some sort of simplification – graphic or phonetic – is possible.⁵⁰)

Fourth, we must accept that an emendation is necessary and that the MS reading – which Mr Stevens describes as a 'wrenched construction' on p. 77 and as 'inexplicable' on p. 82 – is in fact 'wrenched' and 'inexplicable'. To reach this conclusion, Mr Stevens has resorted to the time-honoured (but no more valid for that) practice of translating the Old English into Modern English – 'I recite this tale, my own journey'⁵¹ – and saying 'Hey presto! See how wrenched this construction is.' But the semantic fields of OE *wrecan* and MnE 'recite' do not overlap completely and a study of the passages which follow suggests that *sið wrecan* is just as acceptable as the *soðgied wrecan, siþas secgan* of *Seafarer* ll. 1–2, for one can no more 'say a journey' in MnE than 'recite one':

Seafarer l. 1   Mæg ic be me sylfum   soðgied wrecan,
                   siþas secgan,

Order of the World l. 8   Is þara anra gehwam   orgeate tacen,
                            þam þurh wisdom   woruld ealle con
                            behabban on hreþre,   hycgende mon,
                            þæt geara iu,   gliwes cræfte,
                            mid gieddingum   guman oft wrecan,
                            rincas rædfæste,

---

⁴⁷ L., *passim*, and 'The Theme of "Exile" in *The Wife's Lament*', NM 70 (1969), 90–104, respectively.
⁴⁸ L., pp. 287–8.   ⁴⁹ See S., p. 79, and L., p. 287.
⁵⁰ See *OEG* §§66 and 457.   ⁵¹ S., p. 77.

and

> *Menologium* l. 68
> Sculan we hwæðere gyt
> martira gemynd ma areccan,
> wrecan wordum forð, wisse gesingan,
> þæt embe nihgontyne niht and fifum,
> þæs þe Eastermonað to us cymeð,
> þæt man reliquias ræran onginneð,
> halige gehyrste.

And there can be no grammatical or stylistic objection to *giedd* and *sið* being in apposition.

Fifth, we must accept that *geomorre* is an adverb, not an adjective; that this is possible is admitted above. And sixth, we must accept that *bi* can be understood at the beginning of l. 2 from the preceding *bi*. This point awaits further examination,[51a] but my own feeling is that, if the poet had intended *bi* to govern line 2a, he would have repeated it, especially if the intervening *geomorre* was an adverb. We may compare here

> *Elene* l. 294
> þa ge wergdon þane
> þe eow of wergðe þurh his wuldres miht,
> fram ligcwale, lysan þohte,
> of hæftnede,

> *Deor* l. 5
> ... siþþan hine Niðhad on nede legde,
> swoncre seonobende on syllan monn,

> *Waldere* ii. 27
> Se ðe him to ðam halgan helpe gelifeð,
> to gode gioce,

and

> *Maldon* l. 318
> ac ic me be healfe minum hlaforde,
> be swa leofan men, licgan þence.[52]

All this is too much. Personally, I shall be content to go to the grave believing that the narrator is a woman. But such is the ingenious desperation of some present-day critics of OE literature that (as I write in December 1970) I await with confident horror an overtly homosexual interpretation of this poem, based in particular on lines 33–6

[51a] [1987. See *OES* §§1170–6.]

[52] I hope to discuss elsewhere my reasons for suspecting Mrs Gordon's interpretation of *eorþan sceatas* in *Seafarer* l. 61, which would support Mr Stevens's [*bi*] in *Wife's Lament* l. 2. [1987. See *OES* §§1174–5. I now accept Mrs Gordon's interpretation of *eorþan sceatas* but no longer believe that it supports Mr Stevens's.]

The narrator of The Wife's Lament

Frynd sind on eorþan,
leofe lifgende, leger weardiað,
þonne ic on uhtan ana gonge
under actreo geond þas eorðscrafu.[53]

---

[53] It goes almost without saying nowadays that it has been explained as Christian allegory; see, for example, M. J. Swanton in *Anglia* 82 (1964), 269–90, and M. H. Landrum in *A Fourfold Interpretation of* The Wife's Lament (Ph.D. dissertation, The State University, Rutgers, 1963).

16
The *Fuglas Scyne* of *The Phoenix*, Line 591

Phoenix l. 583   Swa nu æfter deaðe   þurh dryhtnes miht
somod siþiaþ   sawla mid lice,
fægre gefrætwed,   fugle gelicast,
in eadwelum   æþelum stencum,
þær seo soþfæste   sunne lihteð
wlitig ofer weoredum   in wuldres byrig.
Ðonne soðfæstum   sawlum scineð
heah ofer hrofas   hælende Crist.
Him folgiað   fuglas scyne,
beorhte gebredade,   blissum hremige,
in þam gladan ham,   gæstas gecorene,
ece to ealdre.   þær him yfle ne mæg
fah feond gemah   facne sceþþan,
ac þær lifgað a   leohte werede,
swa se fugel fenix,   in freoþu dryhtnes,
wlitige in wuldre.

The words *fuglas scyne* in l. 591b of this passage have long caused difficulty to interpreters of *The Phoenix*. Ettmüller suggested reading *fiðrum scyne*, Emerson explained that the phoenix was Christ and that the *fuglas scyne*, which he equated to the birds which follow the phoenix (see ll. 158–67), were 'the throngs of blessed souls which follow the Lord', while Dobbie noted that 'the reference here seems to be to angels, but the poet may simply have become confused by his Phoenix-symbolism'.[1] Blake accepts Emerson's explanation of ll. 591–4a but sees a 'shift in the allegory', in that in ll. 583–90 and again in ll. 594b–8 Christ is represented by the sun and the phoenix betokens the blessed who worship him, as the phoenix worships the sun (ll. 120–4, 288, and

Reprinted from *Old English Studies in Honour of John C. Pope* ed. Robert B. Burlin and Edward B. Irving, Jr (Toronto, 1974), pp. 255–61.

[1] L. Ettmüller *Engla and Seaxna Scôpas and Bôceras* (Quedlinburg and Leipzig, 1850), p. 276; O. F. Emerson 'Originality in Old English Poetry', *RES* 2 (1926), 30; E. V. K. Dobbie, note to *Phoenix* l. 591 in Anglo-Saxon Poetic Records (New York, 1936), iii. 279.

elsewhere). Thus 'the blessed are sometimes compared with the phoenix and sometimes with the birds which follow the phoenix', and there is 'a certain amount of confusion' and 'a slight harshness'.[2]

Cross, however, in rejecting this explanation along with those of Ettmüller and Dobbie, writes:

> But there may be a simpler explanation that credits the poet with better control. Throughout the anagogical interpretation Christ is clearly the sun and the Phoenix is each good Christian and all good Christians. As the poet says, *þær lifgað a leohte werede, / swa se fugel fenix* 'they [*gæstas gecorene* 'chosen spirits' (593b)] live there [in heaven], always clothed in light, like the Phoenix bird' (596-97a) and, as I have suggested above, the righteous appear to simulate one feature of the Phoenix' beauty in *se beorhta beag* 'the bright ring' (602a), which adorns each of them in heaven. Since the *fuglas scyne* are *beorhte gebredade* 'brightly restored' (592a), a verb used of the Phoenix (372b) to describe its resurrection, *fuglas* must refer to the Phoenix. If the text is not corrupt, it seems to me that the plural *fuglas* may well have been written under the grammatical influence of plural *sawlum* 'souls' within the preceding lines.[3]

I agree with Cross that there is no need to accept a shift in the allegory here. Later on (ll. 637b ff) Christ is indeed represented – on the typological or allegorical level – by the phoenix. But it is unnecessary to import this parallel here – on the anagogical level.

It is, however, a nice point whether a poet who makes the grammatical error of writing a plural when he means to write a singular is showing 'better control' than one who confuses his allegory. Moreover, while the last-ditch desperation of a 'corrupt' text or the notion of confusion in allegory does offer some sort of solution, I doubt whether the idea that the poet accidentally wrote a plural for singular in l. 591b solves anything beyond explaining the plural *folgiað* in l. 591a; it merely postpones the problem until we get to *gæstas gecorene* (l. 593), which is in apposition with *fuglas scyne* and would therefore presumably have to be read as singular too, referring to one single spirit following Christ, as the phoenix followed the sun. Can we really accept this?

I think not, for it runs contrary to the whole logic of the poet's treatment of the allegory on the anagogical level, which, following Cross (ll. 141-3), I take as running from l. 474 to the end of the anthem to the Father/Son at l. 631 and perhaps to l. 633 or l. 637a.[4] Throughout this section, the blessed in Heaven are

---

[2] N. F. Blake ed. *The Phoenix* (Manchester, 1964), pp. 33 and 85.
[3] J. E. Cross 'The Conception of the Old English *Phoenix*' in *Old English Poetry: Fifteen Essays* ed. R. P. Creed (Providence, R.I., 1967), pp. 142-3. I acknowledge gratefully my debt to Mr Blake and Professor Cross. Without their work, this note would obviously never have been written.
[4] Lines 632-3 (and perhaps 634-7a) seem to be used *apo koinou*, pointing both back to the

always referred to or thought of in the plural, starting with 'him' (l. 474) – which refers back to the nominative plural *Meotudes cempan* (l. 471) – and ending with the verb *reordiað* (l. 632) or *singað* (l. 635). Apparent exceptions fall into three groups.

First, there are collective nouns. *Gæsta gedryht* (l. 615) and *sibgedryht* (l. 618) are both construed first with singular verbs (*hergað* and *swinsað*) and then with plural verbs (*mærsiað*, *singað*, and *bletsiað*). If we include in this section ll. 632–7a

> Ðus reordiað ryhtfremmende
> manes amerede in þære mæran byrig,
> cyneþrym cyþað, caseres lof
> singað on swegle, soðfæstra gedryht,
> þam anum is ece weorðmynd
> forð butan ende,

there is also *soðfæstra gedryht* (l. 635). The use of plural verbs throughout this passage suggests that the collective is in apposition with *ryhtfremmende* (l. 632) and does not directly govern any of the verbs. Hence I use above Blake's punctuation in preference to that in Anglo-Saxon Poetic Records iii, which has a semi-colon after *byrig* (l. 633) and no comma before *soðfæstra* (l. 635).

Second, there are the expressions in which the singular of an indefinite pronoun is used with the genitive plural of *an* or of an adjective. In four of these the reference is to some aspect of mortal man as an individual in this world, before death or before the Last Judgement: his life in l. 487, *ealdor anra gehwæs*; his fear in ll. 503–4, *Weorþeð anra gehwylc / forht on ferþþe*; the heat he will feel before the Last Judgement in ll. 521–5:

> Hat bið monegum
> egeslic æled, þonne anra gehwylc,
> soðfæst ge synnig, sawel mid lice,
> from moldgrafum seceð meotudes dom,
> forhtafæred;

and his work in l. 598, *weorc anra gehwæs*. In the remaining three the reference is to a reward which each individual will win in Heaven: a noble and perpetually young body in ll. 534–7:

> Swa bið anra gehwylc
> flæsce bifongen fira cynnes,

preceding speech and forward to ll. 637b–54, which can be taken as 'represented speech'; see O. Jespersen *The Philosophy of Grammar* (London, 1924), pp. 290–2, though C. W. Kennedy, in both his prose and verse translations, put ll. 636–54 in inverted commas. Examples of this sort are relevant to the problem of *swa cwæð* in *Wanderer* ll. 6 and 111; see *The Wanderer* ed. T. P. Dunning and A. J. Bliss (London, 1969), pp. 30–6.

>   ænlic ond edgeong,   se þe his agnum her
>   willum gewyrceð ...

and a radiant crown, mentioned *twice* in ll. 602–7:

> þær se beorhta beag,   brogden wundrum
> eorcnanstanum,   eadigra gehwam
> hlifað ofer heafde.   Heafelan lixað
> þrymme biþeahte.   Ðeodnes cynegold
> soðfæstra gehwone   sellic glengeð
> leohte in life. ...

But even in these the genitive plural emphasizes the fact that the poet is thinking, not just of one individual who is capable of joining the blessed, but of all such individuals. This is of course also implicit in the use of *gehwa* and *gehwylc*, to which (as Campbell, *Old English Grammar*, §719 observes) 'a general inclusive sense is given ... by the prefix *ge-*'.

Third, there are two sentences with a gnomic ring in which the poet is thinking of the individual in this world, of the human being who will or can win here the reward of the righteous. Lines 482–5:

> þus eadig eorl   ecan dreames,
> heofona hames   mid heahcyning
> earnað on elne,   oþþæt ende cymeð
> dogorrimes ...

and ll. 516–17: *Wel biþ þam þe mot / in þa geomran tid gode lician.*

The first two of these three groups lend positive support to the notion that the poet of *The Phoenix* is likely to think of all blessed souls rather than of one individual soul when he turns his mind to Christ in Heaven followed by the company of blessed ones, the soldiers of Christ who have earned their reward. The third group shows that, on the rare occasions when he uses the singular alone (without a genitive plural) in the anagogical section, he is referring (quite naturally) to an individual on earth who must win by his own deeds his share in the collective reward reserved for the souls of all the blessed.

The same distinction obtains in the other allegorical sections. In the typological or allegorical (ll. 632 or 637b–77), all the relevant references are in the plural, and all are to the blessed in Heaven. In the moral or tropological (ll. 381–473), we have two singular references, both to the individual in this world. The first is ll. 381–6, where we are told that *eadigra gehwylc* will win eternal life as the reward for his deeds. The second is ll. 451–65, where we have a catalogue of the deeds by which a *dryhtnes cempa* on this earth will win the protection of God. But significantly this same expression is used in the plural in ll. 470–3 when the transition is being made from the moral to the anagogical level and the poet's interest switches from the temporal world to the heavenly, from the individual on earth to the company of the blessed ones in Heaven:

> Swa nu in þam wicum willan fremmað
> mode ond mægne meotudes cempan,
> mærða tilgað; þæs him meorde wile
> ece ælmihtig eadge forgildan.

The other relevant references in this section are plural ones, again to the heavenly host.

All this accords with Cross's contention (ll. 142–3) that 'throughout the anagogical interpretation Christ is clearly the sun and the Phoenix is each good Christian and all good Christians'. But it also suggests that his postulated singular for *fuglas scyne* (l. 591) would be out of place in the context of ll. 583–98. For, if he were right, we would not only have to take *gæstas gecorene* (l. 593) as singular (see above); we would also be left without a plural antecedent for *him* (l. 594) and a plural subject for *lifgað* (l. 596), and so (as far as I can see in the absence of any explanation from Cross) would be forced to extend the poet's error of singular for plural to these lines. Cross's interpretation would then leave us with the phoenix (= *fuglas scyne* and the subsequent plurals taken as singulars) being *swa se fugel fenix* (l. 597). This seems rather pointless and almost as confused as the explanations it attempts to replace.

If, however, we follow the poet's argument in ll. 583–98, we find that in ll. 583–8 and again in ll. 594b–8 he compares the souls of the blessed bright in the protection, the glory, the sunshine, of Christ the Sun to the phoenix, *þære sunnan þegn* (l. 288). What happens in the intervening ll. 589–94a? I suggest that Cross is right in thinking 'that the plural *fuglas* may well have been written under the grammatical influence of the plural *sawlum* "souls" within the preceding lines' (l. 143), but wrong in implying that this was a mistake by the poet. It is my feeling that the plural *fuglas scyne* is an integral part of the plural sequence *sawla* (l. 584) ... *soðfæstum sawlum* (l. 589) ... *gæstas gecorene* (l. 593) ... *him* (l. 594) ... *lifgað* (l. 596) and has the same referent – the blessed souls which follow Christ.

We will, I believe, pay the poet the compliment he deserves if we credit him with saying what he meant rather than if we blame him for an error in his allegory or a slip in his syntax. For in *fuglas scyne* (l. 591), the *comparison* made in *fugle gelicast* (l. 585) – which is taken up again in *swa se fugel fenix* (l. 597) – gives way to a firm albeit momentary *identification* of the souls of the blessed following Christ with so many bright phoenixes following the sun. This identification is the culmination of one of the images which have been in the poet's mind, and it has in it the very essence of poetic kennings like that in *Christ B* ll. 858–63:

>   þa us help bicwom,
> þæt us to hælo   hyþe gelædde,
> godes gæstsunu,   ond us giefe sealde
> þæt we oncnawan magun   ofer ceoles bord
> hwær we sælan sceolon   sundhengestas,
> ealde yŏmearas,   ancrum fæste –

unconscious perhaps and incongruous when over-analysed, but spontaneous and poetically effective when accepted 'with a gladsome mind'.

We can if we wish accept the notion that the poet is 'confused'. If we do, it is the 'confusion' of a poet's imagination, a sort of Old English equivalent of the 'jumping of the points' from one line of imagery to another seen in the switch from 'gun' to 'dog' at the word 'muzzled' in *The Winter's Tale* I. ii. 153–7:

> Looking on the lines
> Of my boy's face, methoughts I did recoil
> Twenty-three years and saw myself unbreeched
> In my green velvet coat; my dagger muzzled
> Lest it should bite its master.

POSTSCRIPT, APRIL 1972

I completed the original manuscript of this article in August 1971. In March 1972, I read in A. A. Lee's *The Guest-Hall of Eden* (New Haven and London, 1972) the following passage (p. 121): '... *The Phoenix*, where faithful and heroic souls from middle-earth come as perfume-bearing phoenixes to share in the *dreama dream* (658, joy of joys) with "the best of princes" (621)'. Although it is not clear that the phrase 'perfume-bearing phoenixes' is a reference to *fuglas scyne* (l. 591), it would seem possible that Lee has independently reached a conclusion similar to mine about this expression.

17
Linguistic Facts and the Interpretation of Old English Poetry

In their admirable edition of *The Wanderer* Dunning and Bliss give the meaning 'as when' for *swa* in l. 43b

Wanderer l. 41 þinceð him on mode   þæt he his mondryhten
             clyppe ond cysse,   ond on cneo lecge
             honda ond heafod,   swa he hwilum ær
             in geardagum   giefstolas breac

and defend their gloss in the following words: 'Here literary considerations must outweigh linguistic arguments.'[1] And in his latest book, Stanley B. Greenfield approves: 'Thus Bliss–Dunning... can properly say that though usage of *swa* meaning "as when" here "would be unique", but [*sic*] "literary considerations must outweigh linguistic arguments".'[2] I do not approve. I would say that Dunning and Bliss have let literary considerations outweigh not linguistic *arguments*, but linguistic *facts*. Hence my title.[3]

Reprinted from *Anglo-Saxon England* 4 (1975), 11–28.

[1] *The Wanderer* ed. T. P. Dunning and A. J. Bliss (London, 1969), p. 113.
[2] *The Interpretation of Old English Poems* (London and Boston, 1972), pp. 118–19.
[3] The word 'linguistic' is used in its ancient sense – 'of language' – and has no reference to its present-day use by practitioners of a 'science' which has hijacked the word and which in many of its aspects will (I believe) prove to be one of the great non-subjects of the twentieth century – though I do not deny that it has valuable techniques in the analysis and teaching of current languages. [1987. This 'singular footnote' not unnaturally attracted adverse comment. It was indeed, and was intended to be, 'an exquisitely passionate attack on contemporary linguistics'. (Both quotations are from Matthew Marino in *Mediaevalia* 5 (1979), 1.) I plan to discuss elsewhere this issue, which I raised again in *OES* (i, pp. lxii–iii) and which has been pursued by several reviewers of that book. But I have not changed 'my opinion that, on the evidence so far available to me, the techniques of the various forms of linguistics fashionable today have little to offer students of OE syntax' (*OES* i, p. lxii) and, bearing in mind Dr Johnson's observation that 'I soon found that it is too late to look for instruments, when the work calls for execution', do not see the justice of E. G. Stanley's claim that 'Dr Mitchell himself might have been looked to, by some users at least, to make current linguistic methodologies productive for Old English syntax' (*RES* 37 (1986), 235). That is the responsibility of those who believe in them – a responsibility which they have yet to meet.] It is with pleasure and gratitude that I acknowledge my debt to Professor Peter Clemoes for his cogent criticisms of earlier drafts of this paper.

What, then, is a linguistic fact for the reader of Old English poetry? We can perhaps say generally that it is a statement which limits his choice of interpretations; for example, that a particular metrical pattern is impossible, that a given inflexional ending is unambiguous, that the word being discussed means 'x' and not 'y',[3a] that a conjunction expresses a particular relationship – contrast *oþþæt* and *þenden* – or that a certain word-order is found only in principal clauses. We might agree that general statements such as these – and any particular statements about individual examples properly based on them – are, or could be, linguistic facts. We might also agree that we are entitled to expect consistency in their application. This is not the case in the Dunning–Bliss edition of *The Wanderer*, where the editors accept *swa*, 'as when', while admitting that it is unique, but in ll. 53–4 reject certain figurative meanings of *swimman* and *fleotan* because they are unique. Greenfield condemns what he calls this 'double-dealing'.[4]

But how reliable are these linguistic facts when we really need them? Are we like the critic of whom A. E. Housman said 'all the tools he uses are two-edged, though to be sure both edges are quite blunt'? In seeking to use facts, we have to discover first what generalization (or generalizations) is (or are) relevant to the problem (or problems) before us and second what relationship exists between the generalization(s) and the particular instance we are considering. These two questions demand separate discussion.

Establishing acceptable generalizations about the Old English language is less easy than is sometimes believed. We are perhaps most aware of difficulty in the realm of semantics. But even here assumptions are too often regarded as facts. Fred C. Robinson has recently warned us how a lexicographer, by the way in which he treats a certain word in his dictionary, can become a literary interpreter and influence generations of critics.[5] A particular case in point is whether the last word in *Beowulf* – *lofgeornost* – must be pejorative. I do not propose to go into this much discussed topic. But it is noteworthy – in view of *mildust ond monðwærust* in the preceding line – that even now no one discussing this word seems to have mentioned the fact that in *Blickling Homily* vi Christ is called *milde ond monðwære*.[6] Opinions may differ about the significance of this, but it is hard to deny that the fact ought to be mentioned. The new *Dictionary of Old English*, to be edited by Christopher Ball and Angus Cameron, will of

---

[3a] [1987. Such statements cannot, of course, always be made; as Dr Johnson has it, 'such is the exuberance of signification which many words have obtained, that it is scarcely possible to collect all their senses'. The discussion on *lofgeornost* in item 5 above demonstrates this. But our difficulties with that word arise in part at least from the linguistic fact that the other three superlatives in *Beowulf* ll. 3181–2 all imply praise.]

[4] *NQ* 215 (1970), 115.

[5] 'Lexicography and Literary Criticism: a Caveat', *Philological Essays: Studies in Old and Middle English Language and Literature in Honour of Herbert Dean Meritt* ed. J. L. Rosier (The Hague, 1970), pp. 99–110.

[6] But see below, Postscript, pp. 170–1.

course be invaluable. Meanwhile, a little less anxiety to *prove* – or to assume that it has been proved – that a word *must* mean 'x' and not 'y' would be welcome.

The danger of treating *assumptions* about the meaning of a series of individual words as if they were *facts* is that the process gets cumulatively more and more out of hand and leads ultimately to what I must describe as the arrogance implicit in such titles as 'The Meaning of *The Seafarer* and *The Wanderer*' and *The Mode and Meaning of* Beowulf, which seem to me to involve the further assumptions that every poem has one fixed meaning and that that meaning has been revealed to a modern Cædmon.

Another assumption which, I believe, is too easily accepted is that there are rules which hold for Old English metre. I am becoming increasingly reluctant to admit metre as a decisive criterion, especially when it comes to dismissing the reading of a manuscript in favour of an editorial emendation. I am going to content myself here with one statement and one question on this topic. First, then, the statement. In table II of Appendix C of his book on the metre of *Beowulf*,[7] A. J. Bliss lists all the types of half-lines in *Beowulf*. If we exclude

---

[7] *The Metre of* Beowulf (Oxford, 1962), pp. 123–7. [1987. I have already admitted with an apology – see item 4, fn. 4 and *OES* §2780 – that this paragraph misrepresented Bliss's position. But I have not yet accepted that my comments 'miss the mark', as T. F. Hoad claimed in *RES* 28 (1977), 193–4, although I certainly used a shotgun instead of a sniper's rifle. I said:

> In Table II of Appendix C of his book on the metre of *Beowulf*, A. J. Bliss lists all the types of half-lines in *Beowulf*. If we exclude hypermetric lines, we find that there are 130 acceptable types, of which twenty-nine occur only once. But Bliss also has eleven half-lines which he classifies as 'remainders' and eight which he calls 'defective'.

These statements are true. The rest of the paragraph was carelessly misleading. But Hoad's comment too was in part misleading:

> Bruce Mitchell is inspired by what he considers to be some critics' brushing aside of linguistic evidence for literary convenience to write on 'Linguistic Facts and the Interpretation of Old English Poetry'. The article has a substantial discussion of the expression (or non-expression) of a pluperfect time-relationship in Old English. The polemics, which seem less important, miss the mark once, since it is not the case that Professor A. J. Bliss 'finds in *Beowulf* forty-eight half-lines which occur only once, of which twenty-nine are acceptable and nineteen are not' (p. 13). The eight 'defective' half-lines are at points where the text is irretrievably lost. Six of the 'remainders' are not 'half-lines which occur only once' but a group sharing one metrical pattern, and far from finding them 'unacceptable' Professor Bliss considers that 'the fact that they are all *b*-verses and have such a clearly defined structure suggests that they do belong to a type of some kind, and are not merely corrupt'. The other five 'remainders', one of which (2488a) again involves textual corruption, are all discussed by Bliss and reasons given for their special treatment (on all the 'remainders' and 'defective' half-lines see Bliss's *The Metre of* Beowulf, §§84, 86, 87).

(Let me digress briefly here by saying that I do not agree that 'the polemics' are 'less important'; I still believe – perhaps even more strongly as Time's winged chariot sounds louder in my ears – that what I said needed saying and needs to be taken seriously.) I accept what Hoad said about 'the eight "defective" half-lines', about 'six of the "remainders"', and about l. 2488a. But Hoad evaded

hypermetric lines, we find that there are 130 acceptable types, of which twenty-nine occur only once. But Bliss also has eleven half-lines which he classifies as 'remainders' and eight which he calls 'defective'. This seems to mean that he finds in *Beowulf* forty-eight half-lines which occur only once, of which twenty-nine are acceptable and nineteen are not. Now the question. If twenty-nine acceptable types occur only once, on what grounds can we be sure that one of the remaining nineteen is not an acceptable thirtieth?

There are superstitions about word-order too. Some six years ago I wrote:

[it] seems clear to me that word-order is not conclusive in the poetry, that it cannot be used to prove that a certain clause must be subordinate and another principal. But this, of course, does not stop an editor from suggesting that a poet may deliberately have arranged his clauses so that those with S. . . . V. were subordinate and those with V. S. were principal. Nor does it mean that such a suggestion is wrong; it merely means that it cannot be proved right.[8]

I still believe this and remain unconvinced by arguments that, for example, the word-order Subject–Noun Object–Verb proves that a clause in poetry must be subordinate. They can still be heard. But one has only to point to the opening of *Beowulf* to see the folly of this:

Beowulf l. 1   Hwæt, we Gardena   in geardagum
              þeodcyninga   þrym gefrunon. . . .

In using this argument, critics are relying on a useful guide inherited from their student days which does not always hold even in Old English prose. On the other hand, a tendency to rely too much on the modern feeling that the subject comes first concealed the meaning of l. 51 of *The Wanderer* – *þonne maga gemynd mod geondhweorfeð* – and created consequent difficulties until it was suggested that *mod* was the subject, not the object, of *geondhweorfeð*.[9] There are sentences

the issue in respect of the remaining four – ll. 2435b, 2717b, 2093a, and 3056a (see Bliss, §87) – by using the words 'reasons [are] given for their special treatment'. Bliss says (§87) that these 'have nothing in common but their refusal to conform to any recognized type' and his 'special treatment' is nothing more than an explanation of why they do not conform. Yet they are good Old English and were acceptable to Klaeber and at least some other editors. None of them is specifically rejected by Bliss. So in 1987 I stand by what I said in 1985 in *OES* §2780 and repeat that 'I have so far failed to get what I think is a straight answer to a straight question.' For what it is worth, I note a new puzzle which I have not discussed before but which might have some relevance to my argument: of the twenty-nine patterns which occur only once, four (types 12, 17, 30, and 49) are the only example of their 'type'.]

[8] 'Some Syntactical Problems in *The Wanderer*', *NM* 69 (1968), 190–1. [1987. See pp. 111–12 above.]

[9] This conclusion was reached simultaneously and independently by Dunning and Bliss (*The Wanderer*, pp. 21–3) and by Peter Clemoes ('*Mens absentia cogitans* in *The Seafarer* and *The Wanderer*', *Medieval Literature and Civilization: Studies in Memory of G. N. Garmonsway* ed. D. A. Pearsall and R. A. Waldron (London, 1969), pp. 74–5).

with the order Object–Verb–Subject, which runs directly counter to the instinct of modern readers. One such occurs in *Genesis A* l. 2887b, where the poet is describing the approach of Abraham and Isaac to the mountain where the latter was to be sacrificed: *Wudu bær sunu, / fæder fyr and sweord* (ll. 2887b–8a).

This particular example provides a striking illustration of a difficulty which dogs the student of Old English syntax and indeed literature. One can readily see that Anglo-Saxon hearers used to the word-order Object–Verb–Subject, alive to variations of intonation, and familiar with the book of Genesis, would have had no doubt that *wudu* was the object of *bær*. A few ignoramuses may have missed the point, and very likely at the other extreme, there were a few theologically trained hearers (or perhaps more likely readers) on the alert for subtle implications who would have relished the ambiguity detected by R. P. Creed:

> *Wudu*, placed first for purposes of alliteration, is generally and correctly translated as an accusative. But it can also be translated – or rather, *heard* momentarily in Old English – as a nominative. The case of *sunu* is similarly ambiguous. The verse, then, can be caught both ways: 'son bore wood' and 'wood bore son'; or 'the Son bore the Cross', and 'the Cross bore the Son'. In this remarkable punning line the offering of Isaac not only prefigures the crucifixion of Christ, it sharply figures – images – the later drama of Christianity. Isaac becomes the Son sacrificed in order to mediate between man and God.[10]

What we must not assume is that such a reading was intended by the poet. Alliteration (as Creed says) and rhetorical chiasmus would be enough to account for the word-order Object–Verb–Subject. But it would be hazardous indeed to claim that no Anglo-Saxon ever read the passage in the way Creed does. We have no native informants for Old English. This is difficulty enough. We make things even worse by tacitly assuming that there was one standard *mann on þæm Cloppames wæne* who represents all Anglo-Saxons of all periods. Such assumptions seem to me implicit in remarks about the effect of a certain word or phrase on 'the audience of the poem' and in the two titles quoted above.

Difficulties can arise even in the realm of inflexions, where we might think that the generalizations were fairly firmly established. The intractable riddle of *hryre* in *The Wanderer* l. 7b

> *Wanderer* l. 6   Swa cwæð eardstapa,   earfeþa gemyndig,
> wraþra wælsleahta,   winemæga hryre

is one. The adjective *gemyndig* can take the dative, e.g. *gif we gemyndige beoð*

---

[10] 'The Art of the Singer: Three Old English Tellings of the Offering of Isaac', *Old English Poetry: Fifteen Essays* ed. R. P. Creed (Providence, R.I., 1967), p. 80.

Cristes bebodum,[11] as well as the genitive. But the genitives which precede *winemæga hryre* in the passage from *The Wanderer* seem to rule out the possibility (suggested in the Bosworth-Toller Supplement, s.v. *gemyndig* IV (1) (b)) of taking it as a dative on *gemyndig*. We must agree with Dunning and Bliss that Old English idiom is against the simple emendation to genitive plural *hryra* – the distributive singular seen in *æfter deofla hryre* (*Beowulf* l. 1680a) is the norm – and that to emend to *hryres* is too violent.[12] Their unwillingness to take *hryre* as accusative after *cwæð* is understandable. Examples like ... *lofsang cweðan*, *Ðrihten cwæþ word*, and ... *of ðam welerum ðe wom cweðen* – all cited by Bosworth-Toller, s.v. *cweðan* I – offer indifferent support for *cweðan hryre*, 'to speak the fall', because the accusatives describe what is uttered – words, a song, or the like – and not the topic or theme of the utterance. The closest parallel is perhaps Ælfric's *Arrius se gedwola cwæþ gemot ongean ðone bisceop*,[13] 'Arrius proclaimed a synod' (again from Bosworth-Toller). But it smacks of Latin influence. Dunning and Bliss accept as 'the most plausible explanation'[14] Miss Kershaw's notion that '*hryre* can hardly be taken otherwise than as a loose causal or comitative dative',[15] and offer the translation '"remembering the fierce battles accompanying the deaths of his kinsmen", i.e. "the fierce battles in which his kinsmen died"'. I should like some evidence for the proposition that it can be so taken. However, the mention by Dunning and Bliss of the 'possibility ... of taking both *hrusan* for *hruse* in [*The Wanderer*] l. 23 and *hruse* for *hrusan* in l. 102, as examples of the levelling of endings in late Old English'[16] provides a speculative foundation for further speculation. If such confusion between *-e* and *-an* is possible in the weak feminine noun *hruse*, is it possible that the strong masculine noun *hryre* acquired analogical weak forms in the oblique cases and that *hryre* is in fact a levelled form of an aberrant genitive singular *hryran*?

Those whose immediate reaction is to utter a snort of disbelief are invited to consider the various forms recorded in Bosworth-Toller and A. Campbell's *Old English Grammar* for words like *ewe* and *wange*, to remember that the masculine forms *sunna* and *mona* exist alongside the feminine *sunne* and *mone*, and to note that Bosworth-Toller distinguishes the words *will, well, wyll,-es* (masc.); *will,-an* (fem.); and *willa,-an* (masc.). To this last group J. E. Cross rightly adds the proviso 'if these distinctions are valid'.[17] But even if we reject them, the confusion of forms remains real. Of course, if we took literally the

---

[11] *The Homilies of the Anglo-Saxon Church: The First Part Containing the Sermones Catholici or Homilies of Ælfric* ed. Benjamin Thorpe, 2 vols (London, 1855–6) (hereafter cited as Thorpe) i. 312. 34.
[12] *The Wanderer*, p. 106.   [13] Thorpe i. 290. 12.   [14] *The Wanderer*, p. 106.
[15] *Anglo-Saxon and Norse Poems* ed. N. Kershaw (Cambridge, 1922), p. 162.
[16] *The Wanderer*, p. 108.
[17] 'The Metrical Epilogue to the Old English Version of Gregory's *Cura Pastoralis*', *NM* 70 (1969), 382, n. 4.

surprisingly suspicious remark made by Klaeber that 'lack of concord as shown in the interchange of cases ... should cause no surprise or suspicion',[18] the problem would disappear. So too would much else.

No matter how we solve it, we must agree that *hryre* is a real difficulty. But there are times when failure to apply a simple and obvious generalization leads to the creation of a pseudo-problem. This, I believe, is the case with *bræc* in *Beowulf* l. 1511b

Beowulf l. 1509b   ac hine wundra þæs fela
           swencte on sunde,   sædeor monig
           hildetuxum   heresyrcan bræc,
           ehton aglæcan

and with *wehte* in *Beowulf* l. 2854a

Beowulf l. 2852b   He gewergad sæt,
           feðecempa   frean eaxlum neah,
           wehte hyne wætre;   him wiht ne speow,

in both of which Klaeber detects an 'imperfective' use, translating *bræc* as 'was in the act of breaking', 'tried to pierce' and *wehte* as 'tried to rouse'.[19] These man-made difficulties, arising as they do from unwillingness to accept the linguistic facts, demonstrate the soundness of Zandvoort's observation that 'the attempt to transfer the category of "aspect" from Slavonic to Germanic, and from there to Modern English grammar, strikes one as an instance of misplaced ingenuity.'[20] Klaeber's suggestions embody not only the transfer of the notion of 'aspect' to Old English but also a violent extension of the idea of 'imperfective' as opposed to 'perfective' so that it embraces 'non-perfection' in the sense of failure. But they need not be accepted. There is no real reason why *bræc* should not be translated 'broke' or 'pierced' – the objections are those of a modern scholar who, having swallowed the idea that Beowulf could descend for *hwil dæges* without a snorkel outfit,[21] cavils at the suggestion that the seamonsters' tusks achieved what the fingers of Grendel's dam could not – while in *wehte... speow* 'rousing him with water, but without success', it is clear that *wehte* cannot mean 'succeeded in rousing', and unnecessary to think that it ought to; compare the Modern English sentence 'He gave him the kiss of life,

[18] *Beowulf and the Fight at Finnsburg* ed. Fr. Klaeber, 3rd edn (Boston, 1936), p. xciii.
[19] *Beowulf* (ed. Klaeber), pp. 186 and 221.
[20] R. W. Zandvoort 'Is Aspect an English Verbal Category?', *Contributions to English Syntax and Philology* ed. F. Behre (Göteborg, 1962), 19.
[21] I must now say (June 1974) that I am convinced by F. C. Robinson's defence of S. O. Andrew's explanation of *hwil dæges* in *Beowulf* l. 1495b as 'daytime'; see *Old English Studies in Honour of John C. Pope* ed. Robert B. Burlin and Edward B. Irving, Jr (Toronto, 1974), pp. 121–4. But this does not affect my point; as Robinson rightly says, most critics have explained *hwil dæges* as either 'the space of a day' or 'the large part of a day'.

but without success.' In the first instance we can do with a less shrill demand for literal consistency, in the second with deeper consideration of the semantic fields of *weccan*.[21a]

Whatever the obstacles, however, we neglect the search for sound generalizations at our peril. Let me illustrate this from two past tense verb forms – *Ongunnon* and *Het* in *The Wife's Lament* ll. 11a and 15a:

Wife's Lament l. 6   Ærest min hlaford gewat   heonan of leodum
ofer yþa gelac;   hæfde ic uhtceare
hwær min leodfruma   londes wære.
Ða ic me feran gewat   folgað secan,
wineleas wræcca,   for minre weaþearfe.
Ongunnon þæt þæs monnes   magas hycgan
þurh dyrne geþoht,   þæt hy todælden unc,
þæt wit gewidost   in woruldrice
lifdon laðlicost,   ond mec longade.
Het mec hlaford min,   herheard niman,
ahte ic leofra lyt   on þissum londstede,
holdra freonda.   Forþon is min hyge geomor,
ða ic me ful gemæcne   monnan funde,
heardsæligne,   hygegeomorne,
mod miþendne,   morþor hycgendne.

Both have been explained as pluperfects. Here we must ask: what general statements can be made about the use of a simple past tense to express a pluperfect sense?

The standard comment on this problem is typified by the laconic observation in my own *Guide to Old English*: 'The preterite indicative is used ... for the pluperfect, e.g. *sona swa hie comon* "as soon as they had come" and (with a strengthening *ær*) *and his swura wæs gehalod þe ær wæs forslægen*.'[22] There are similar remarks by P. S. Ardern,[23] N. Davis,[24] and R. Quirk and C. L. Wrenn.[25] All the examples of a past tense without *ær* as a pluperfect which are given by these writers and by F. Th. Visser[26] are in subordinate clauses, where (as Quirk

---

[21a] [1987. On this point see further *OES* §§872 and 3980a, and *Archiv* 214 (1977), 136, where E. G. Stanley in a generous appraisal of my article, argued against my interpretations of *bræc* and *wehte*. I respect his arguments but remain unconvinced. For *bræc*, I urge that *Beowulf* is not a poem distinguished by internal consistency because of what I have described in item 4, fn. 8 above as 'the poet's frequent concern with the effect of the moment'; see also p. 166 below. For *wehte*, I repeat that *weccan* need not mean 'to succeed in rousing'.]

[22] 2nd edn (Oxford, 1968), §197.
[23] *First Readings in Old English* (Wellington, 1948), §40.
[24] *Sweet's Anglo-Saxon Primer*, 9th edn (Oxford, 1953), §92.
[25] *An Old English Grammar*, 2nd edn (London, 1958), §127.
[26] *An Historical Syntax of the English Language* II (Leiden, 1966), §808.

and Wrenn point out) 'the pluperfect time-relation is often implicit by reason of the type of clause'.

On the strength of these observations or others like them, readers of Old English poetry (including myself) have in the past been willing – sometimes indeed eager – to accept that any Old English past tense can be taken as the equivalent of a Modern English pluperfect in any kind of clause whenever it suits a reader's interpretation of the passage in question. So it is perhaps not surprising that I was comparatively unmoved when I first read the following statement by Douglas D. Short:

> With its sophisticated system of verbal phrases, Modern English can accommodate elaborate inversions of chronology without confusing a listener, but Old English had to function with a far simpler system and therefore was not nearly so flexible a language in indicating time relationships. The pluperfect time relation was usually expressed in Old English by the use of the preterit of *habban* with the past participle of transitive verbs and the preterit of *wesan* with the past participle of intransitive verbs, although as the language developed *habban* gradually began to be used with intransitive verbs as well. Occasionally, in certain adverbial clauses where the adverb actually indicates the time relationship, a simple preterit can have a pluperfect sense. Similarly, in a non-adverbial dependent clause in which the action clearly precedes the action of the independent clause, a preterit alone has the force of a pluperfect. However, in line 11 of *The Wife's Lament* none of these conditions exists.[27]

After giving this what seemed to me at the time proper consideration, I still had the feeling that *Ongunnon* in *The Wife's Lament* l. 11a could be taken as a pluperfect; the examples in subordinate clauses already mentioned and the fact that the periphrasis with *wæs/hæfde* was not completely established in Old English provided, I felt, a *prima facie* case for this view. But I am now beginning to realize that I failed to appreciate both the acuteness and the importance of Mr Short's remarks. For, when recently (November 1972) pressed by a pupil to agree that this *Ongunnon* could indeed imply – as Pei and Gaynor have it in *A Dictionary of Linguistics* (New York, 1954) – that 'the action was completed by the time another action occurred', I came out with the old platitudes and the answer 'yes'. But, as I walked home, I pondered: 'Did I have any indisputable parallels?' I did not. So my search began.

There is no doubt that the Old English past tense can be used where today we would or could use a *perfect*. Often an adverb makes this time reference clear, e.g. *nu* in *Beowulf* ll. 1337b–9a[28] and *ær* in *Beowulf* ll. 655–7. But there are

[27] 'The Old English *Wife's Lament*: an Interpretation', *NM* 71 (1970), 588–9.

[28] To economize in space I give only the line references to the numerous illustrative passages from *Beowulf* which follow. So those accompanying me further will need a copy of the text. I ask their indulgence.

numerous examples with no adverbs both in principal clauses, e.g. *Beowulf* ll. 38 and 247b–8, and in subordinate clauses, e.g. *Beowulf* ll. 426b–30 and 442–5a. But the undoubted existence of examples without an adverb in which a past tense expresses what we may take as a perfect relationship cannot be used as an argument for the unrestricted use of the past tense as the equivalent of a pluperfect.[29]

I have two reasons for this statement. First, the distinction between the past tense implying that an action is completed and the perfect implying that the state resulting from an action still continues seems not to have been felt by the Anglo-Saxons as fully as it is today; compare *Beowulf* ll. 1–3 with *Beowulf* ll. 443–4, and the verb in the *nu* clause in *Genesis B* ll. 730b–31a

> *Genesis B* l. 729b Him is unhyldo
> Waldendes witod, nu hie wordcwyde his,
> lare forleton

with that in *Genesis B* ll. 836b–7a

> *Genesis B* l. 835b Nis me on worulde niod
> æniges þegnscipes, nu ic mines þeodnes hafa
> hyldo forworhte, þæt ic hie habban ne mæg,

and note that Ælfric gives the following glosses in his *Grammar*: 'PRAETERITVM TEMPVS ys forðgewiten tid: *steti* ic stod'[30] and

ac swa ðeah wise lareowas todældon þone PRAETERITVM TEMPVS, þæt is, ðone forðgewitenan timan, on þreo: on PRAETERITVM INPERFECTVM, þæt is unfulfremed forðgewiten, swilce þæt ðing beo ongunnen and ne beo fuldon: *stabam* ic stod. PRAETERITVM PERFECTVM ys forðgewiten fulfremed: *steti* ic stod fullice. PRAETERITVM PLVSQVAMPERFECTVM is forðgewiten mare, þonne fulfremed, forðan ðe hit wæs gefyrn gedon: *steteram* ic stod gefyrn. forði is se forðgewitena tima on ðreo todæled, forðan ðe naht ne byð swa gemyndelic on gecynde, swa þæt ys, þæt gedon byð.[31]

I shall discuss the pluperfect gloss later. But let us note that, when glossing the perfect *steti*, Ælfric does not use a periphrasis with *wesan/habban* – which he does use in his homilies – and that, when he writes *ic stod fullice* for the perfect, he is using a pedagogic formula which, as far as I know, occurs nowhere else in Old English. My second reason is that no displacement in time of the events described is involved by taking a past tense as a perfect. The usual translation of *Næfre ic... geseah* in *Beowulf* l. 247b is 'I have never seen...', but 'I never saw

[29] On the use of a past indicative to refer to a future perfect, as in *The Ruin* 9, see Bruce Mitchell 'Some Problems of Mood and Tense in Old English', *Neophilologus* 49 (1965), 44–6.
[30] *Ælfrics Grammatik und Glossar* ed. Julius Zupitza (repr. Berlin, 1966), p. 123, ll. 15–16.
[31] *Ælfrics Grammatik*, p. 124, ll. 1–11.

...' is (almost) equally acceptable and its adoption has no effect on meaning or time sequence.

What limitations, then, are there on the use of the Old English past tense as a pluperfect? There is no doubt that the simple past tense can have a pluperfect sense in the situations outlined by Mr Short in the passage already quoted. However, I would augment these undisputed categories and state the position thus. (My main concern at the moment is with the poetry, so my examples are taken from *Beowulf*. But I have the impression that what I set out below applies to the prose too.)

The past tense may serve as a pluperfect in:

a a principal clause when the time relationship is expressed by an adverb, e.g. ll. 1612–16a, or by another clause, e.g. ll. 262–5a, or by a *habban* periphrasis in a parallel sentence, e.g. ll. 828b–31a;

b in an *ac* clause, either without an adverb, e.g. ll. 2826b–9, or with one, e.g. ll. 2971–3;

c in a parenthesis, either without an adverb, e.g. ll. 53–7a, or with one, e.g. ll. 898–902a;

d in an adverb clause of time, e.g. ll. 115–16a, 138–42a, and 716b–17;

e in other types of subordinate clauses, either without an adverb, e.g. ll. 142b–3, 841b–6, 1333b–7a, and 1397–8, or with one, e.g. ll. 756b–7, 1355b–7a, 1465–7a, and 1618–19;

f in a conditional clause, where a past subjunctive may express impossibility in the past, e.g. ll. 963–6 and 1550–3a.

The category missing is the principal clause with a simple past tense which occurs in a sequence of such clauses with no specific indication of a change in the time relationship, the category to which, if pluperfect, *Ongunnon* and *Het* in *The Wife's Lament* ll. 11a and 15a would belong. Is it possible for us to decide whether such isolated forms can be taken as pluperfect or, in other words, whether such forms can disrupt the obvious time sequence without any contextual or grammatical hint?

Let us here reconsider the statement by Mr Short above. Two points arise. First, it seems possible that for certain clauses at least (for example, those introduced by *siþþan*) the adverb 'occasionally' can be replaced by 'often' and perhaps even by 'regularly'. Second, we may note the ambiguity of the word 'usually'. Does this mean that the only exceptions are those specified in the sentences beginning 'Occasionally' and 'Similarly'? Or does it mask the old fallacy that 'because something is rare, this cannot be an example'?[32] Mr Short

---

[32] I have drawn attention to two specific examples of this fallacy in operation in the sphere of Old English syntax in 'Two Syntactical Notes on *Beowulf*', *Neophilologus* 52 (1968), 297, and 'The Narrator of *The Wife's Lament*', *NM* 73 (1972), 224, n. 4. [1987. See respectively p. 22 and item 15, fn. 15 above.]

has clearly done us a service by showing that we have too easily taken for granted the proposition that one simple past tense in a series of past tenses can – with no immediate contextual or grammatical hint – interrupt the narrative flow by referring further back in time. He has not, however, succeeded in demonstrating that we are wrong to do so.

It may be difficult for us – lacking as we do intonation patterns and native informants – to make such a demonstration. Indeed Visser shows clearly that there is a difference of opinion about how the past tense and the pluperfect are used in Modern English.[33] But two questions can be asked. First, exactly how widespread is the use of the *habban* periphrasis for the pluperfect? Second, are there any examples in which the wider context of a poem demonstrates that the simple past tense can be used as a pluperfect in a principal clause without any immediate contextual hint? I hope it will not be taken as an indication of idleness or lack of interest if I confess that I have not the time at present to re-read the Old English corpus with a view to answering these questions fully. I have already confessed to neglecting them in the past. But I can assay tentative answers.

As to the first, the *Beowulf* poet uses the periphrasis with *hæfde/hæfdon* thirty-three times. Twice, at ll. 202–9 and 1292–5, it can be taken as the equivalent of a past tense because it does not seem to denote a break in the time sequence (though I would not press the point in either example).[34] That it is sometimes used *metri causa* is suggested first by ll. 3074–5 and 3164b–5, where it is reinforced by *ær*, and second by ll. 2103b–4, where the periphrasis and the past tense are used in parallel clauses, both with a pluperfect reference.

Analysis of the thirty-three examples shows that (*mutatis mutandis*) the periphrasis appears in *Beowulf* in the six situations described above in which the past tense functions as a pluperfect – with the exception of (c). Examples follow. Only two – both of them in category (e) subordinate clauses – have *ær*. It is important to note that in category (a) principal clauses, none of the periphrases is accompanied by *ær*.

a   In principal clauses the periphrasis *alone* denotes a change in time sequence. Good examples are ll. 665b–7a and 893–5a;

b   so also in *ac* clauses, e.g. ll. 691–6a. The periphrasis also occurs after *ond* in ll. 2706–8a and after *nealles* in ll. 2144–6a;

c   the absence from *Beowulf* of examples in this category is the result of chance. The nearest example is ll. 2401–5, where the *hæfde* clause is semi-subordinate rather than semi-parenthetical;

d   we find the periphrasis in adverb clauses of time in ll. 106–7a and 219–20;

[33] *An Historical Syntax* II, §810.
[34] We may note here Davis's observation (*Sweet's Primer*, §92) that 'even the form with *hæfde* sometimes has the sense of a simple past'.

e it occurs in other subordinate clauses in ll. 1166b–17, 1598b–9 and (with *ær*) in ll. 3074–5 and 3164b–5;

f it expresses impossibility in the past in ll. 1550–3a.

For the convenience of any reader who wishes to pursue the matter, I list below all the examples of the periphrasis in *Beowulf*.[35]

But the fact that in principal clauses the simple past tense has a pluperfect reference only when this is made clear by a grammatical or contextual hint, whereas the *hæfde* periphrasis needs no such hint, emphasizes the obvious fact that the Old English past tense was not a direct equivalent of what we think of as a pluperfect. This is confirmed by Ælfric's use of *ic stod gefyrn* – not *ic stod* – for *steteram*.[36] A comparison of this gloss with *Widewe wæs ðeos Anna, þe we gefyrn ær embe spræcon*,[37] where a past tense + *gefyrn ær* has a past or perfect – not pluperfect – reference, suggests that the phrase *ic stod gefyrn* was a pedagogic device rather than an idiomatic equivalent of *steteram*. That Ælfric did not use a periphrasis *ic wæs/hæfde gestanden* to explain *steteram* supports the proposition already advanced that even the periphrasis itself was not specifically pluperfect, though it could serve alone to indicate a change in time sequence just as the pluperfect does. (The Old English periphrasis is, I believe, of native origin and not the result of Latin constructions like *urbem captam habet*.[38] So it does not seem to me arguable that Ælfric avoided the Old English periphrasis in the *Grammar* because he thought of it as the equivalent of the Latin one – which he does not mention.) One is driven to the scarcely surprising conclusion that there was in Old English no perfect or pluperfect in the sense in which modern grammarians understand the terms and that the Old English past tense alone is unlikely to convey a pluperfect time reference.

I turn now to the second question: are there any examples in which the wider context of a poem – here *Beowulf* – demonstrates that the simple past tense can be used as a pluperfect in a principal clause without an immediate contextual hint? To answer this we have to fall back on individual examples. But the dangers involved for a modern reader in the analysis of particular examples can be demonstrated by considering two selected at random. *Hwær cwom mearg?* (*The Wanderer* l. 92a) is usually translated 'Where has the horse gone?' But this (as I have suggested above) may be a concept not always present to the Anglo-

---

[35] (a) In principal clauses (15): ll. 205, 665, 743, 825, 828, 883, 893, 1294, 2321, 2333, 2381, 2397, 2844, 2952, and 3046; (b) in *ac* clauses (2): ll. 694 and 804; in an *ond* clause (1): l. 2707; after *nealles* (1): l. 2145; (c) in parenthesis (1): ? l. 2403; (d) in adverb clauses of time (6): ll. 106, 220, 1472, 2104, 2630, and 3147; (e) in other subordinate clauses (6): ll. 117, 1599, 2301, 2726, 3074, and 3165; (f) expressing impossibility in the past (1): l. 1550. Total 33.

[36] *Ælfrics Grammatik*, p. 124, l. 9.   [37] Thorpe, i. 148. 10.

[38] The evidence which leads me to this belief is based on a long and complicated argument which is intended to form part of my *Old English Syntax*, now in progress. [1987. See *OES* §§702–33.]

Saxon mind. Why not 'Where did the horse go?' The *Exodus* poet's epitaph on the Egyptians drowned in the Red Sea is *Hie wið God wunnon!* (l. 515b). This could be translated 'They had contended against God!' But since their contending ended when they died 'they contended' – or even 'were contending' – 'against God [at the moment of their death]' cannot be ruled out. We must however attempt what may be impossible.

My rapid re-reading of *Beowulf* produced no convincing examples of principal clauses in which a past tense conveyed a pluperfect time reference with no immediate hint. What seemed to me the five most likely ones all proved illusory. In ll. 12–16a and 415–21a a subordinate clause certifies the time reference of *ongeat* and *ofersawon*. In ll. 2117b–20a the *fornam* clause is a parenthetic explanation for the actions of Grendel's dam and belongs, I think, in category (c). In ll. 884b–9 we may take *wiges heard* as referring to Sigemund or – by interpreting *æþelinges bearn* as 'the son of Sigemund' – to Sigurðr-Sigfrit. But whichever we do, *geneðde* takes its time reference from *acwealde*, a pluperfect equivalent after *syþðan*; see category (d). A fifth example is ll. 1584b–8a, which contain (it is said) the only instance in Old English poetry of *to ðæs þe* meaning 'to the point where, whither' not preceded by a verb of motion. This has caused editors some concern; Dobbie indeed is 'tempted to believe that some of the text, containing a verb of motion, has been lost before 1585b'. This is quite unnecessary. Beowulf did not conduct his fight against Grendel from an armchair. We can take *forgeald* as pluperfect, *to ðæs þe* as 'to the extent that, so that', and translate – as Wrenn and Clark Hall have it – 'He, wrathful warrior, had given him his reward for that, so that he now saw Grendel lying in his restingplace, worn out with fighting, destitute of life, as he had been maimed erewhile in fight at Heorot.' But this does not justify our taking *Ongunnon* or *Het* in *The Wife's Lament* as pluperfect, for the preceding reference to Grendel's raids prepares us for a change in time reference and this is clinched by the *swa* clause in ll. 1587b–8a.

So in the event I was left with no principal clauses in *Beowulf* in which a simple past tense interrupted the time sequence and so functioned as a pluperfect without any immediate grammatical or contextual hint. Is this really so surprising? Why should an Anglo-Saxon poet use a simple past tense in such circumstances rather than a past tense + *ær* or a *wæs/hæfde* periphrasis? Let those who believe that *Ongunnon* or *Het* could be pluperfect produce a Modern English principal clause in which a simple past tense in a sequence of simple past tenses has a pluperfect reference with no grammatical or contextual hint.

It is obvious that more work needs to be done before it can be said that this is the rule in either prose or poetry. And we must, I think, admit the possibility that the poet intended *Ongunnon* or *Het* to be taken as pluperfect by hearers whom he knew, or assumed, to have previous knowledge of a story of two lovers now lost to us, though here too I should like to see a modern example. But I must say that at the moment I have a lot of sympathy with Mr Short's proposition that *Ongunnon* in *The Wife's Lament* l. 11a cannot be pluperfect. The same applies to *Het* in l. 15a.

My use of evidence in this discussion demands a comment. The dangers of using material from one poem to *prove* something about another are – or ought to be – obvious. To some Americans ex-President Nixon was hounded out of office by his enemies. Imagine that in a thousand years' time the only surviving account of his resignation was one which took this line. We are in a similar position regarding Byrhtnoth's *ofermod* at the Battle of Maldon, for we have the testimony of only one man – the poet. What he says may give a distorted picture and seems uncertain evidence on which to base a theory about Beowulf's conduct when faced with the menace of the dragon. Yet parallels have been drawn. It is even dangerous to use one passage from a poem in an attempt to *prove* something about another passage from the same poem, for this involves the assumption that Old English poems were conducted on the lines of James Joyce's *Ulysses*. It is clear that this is not true of *Beowulf* at any rate. It is difficult to reconcile the accounts of Beowulf's youth in ll. 2183 ff. and 2428 ff.; Hrothgar's claim in ll. 1331 ff. that he does not know where Grendel's mother has gone contrasts strangely with his remark in ll. 1357 ff. that she and Grendel dwell in the haunted mere and with what seems to me the suggestion in ll. 1377 ff. that Beowulf will be able to find her there;[38a] and the statement at ll. 2777 ff. that Beowulf's sword had wounded the dragon is contradicted in ll. 2904 ff., where the poet says that Beowulf could not inflict any wound on the monster with a sword. Finally, I must admit that I remain dubious about the validity of the time-honoured method of using material from the prose homilists to *prove* that a passage in the poetry must have Christian overtones when specific Christian references are lacking.

I would argue, however, that these instances concern literary matters and that linguistic facts are different in kind. *Beowulf* may not belong to the same period as *The Wife's Lament*. Ælfric almost certainly does not. Yet each offers evidence about the Old English language at a particular time. There are no examples in which the simple past tense expresses a pluperfect sense without any contextual feature to make that sense explicit in *Beowulf*, in Ælfric, or (as far as I know) in the earlier prose or in the later poetry. The idea that there could be runs contrary to English usage of all periods. It seems to me reasonable to regard it as a strong linguistic probability, to put it no higher, that such a usage is not and never has been English. None the less, we must bear in mind the point already made: that, while there are no examples to support the notion that *Ongunnon* and *Het* could have a pluperfect sense, the possibility exists that there was contextual evidence in a background story known to the original audience but now lost.

[38a] [1987. See now item 1, fn. 9a above.]

The absence of any firm examples will not deter those who are willing to tread the slippery path down which Dunning and Bliss have already taken a tentative step, and down which Greenfield beckons us to follow,[39] towards the proposition that there are times when 'literary considerations must outweigh linguistic arguments'. There are times when a refusal to be so deterred is justified. There are others when it is not.

Dame Helen Gardner's handling of an Old English phrase in her superb translation of *The Dream of the Rood* provides us with a useful case in point. In the course of her commentary she writes:

> The word 'alone' occurs at the close (line 126) referring to the dreamer and the *litotes* 'with a small company', meaning 'with nobody', or 'alone', is used of Christ in the tomb (line 72). For this reason I have accepted the reading of the runic inscription on the Ruthwell Cross in place of the reading of the manuscript [*to þam æðelinge*] at line 61 [= OE line 58], though it has been argued that there is no parallel for its syntax in extant Anglo-Saxon poetry.[40]

I think Dame Helen slightly mis-states the nature of the problem. It is true that there is no parallel in the poetry for the Ruthwell Cross's *æþþilæ til anum*. But M. Rissanen quotes sufficient parallels in the prose to make it (I should say) obligatory for us to agree that the *reading* is possible (though not necessarily preferable to that of the manuscript). The point is one of *meaning*. Rissanen carries conviction when he asserts that in view of the examples he quotes '– and in view of the total lack of such instances where *an* would be used as an exclusive pronoun "a solitary person" – it seems that *til anum* in *Ruthwell Cross* III. 3 means "together", "to the same place", rather than "to the solitary one"'.[41] Yet, while the linguistic facts are on his side, Dame Helen could attempt to justify her translation by arguing either that poets sometimes use irregular syntax or that this happens to be the only surviving example of a construction which later became more common in the sense 'to a lone one'. But this is not really necessary. The fact that 'noble ones came together' could be said to emphasize by contrast the loneliness and aloneness of Christ on the cross. There is no contradiction here between literary considerations and linguistic facts. What Dame Helen has done is to emphasize her literary interpretation at the expense of literal translation when she renders *hweþræ þer fusæ fearran kwomu / æþþilæ til anum* by 'yet warriors from afar eagerly came speeding / to where he hung alone'. Here we can almost have our cake and eat it.

The problem which faces us when we turn to the passage which prompted

---

[39] See *The Wanderer*, pp. 112–13 and *Interpretation*, pp. 118–19.

[40] *Essays and Poems presented to Lord David Cecil* ed. W. W. Robson (London, 1970), p. 33. The line numbers are those of Dame Helen's translation.

[41] 'Old English *þæt An*, "Only"', *NM* 68 (1967), 286.

Dunning and Bliss's remarks, *The Wanderer* ll. 41–4, is quite different. At the end of my 1968 note on *swa* in *The Wanderer* l. 43,[42] I said that 'although I have no objection to admitting *hapax* usages when necessary, I do not feel that I need accept "as when" for *swa* in *The Wanderer* l. 43, despite the fact that it gives excellent sense'. Dunning and Bliss agree that their interpretation involves the acceptance of an assumption suggested by Leslie.[43] It is not immediately apparent to me why this assumption is so much less objectionable than some of those I suggested. But the important point is that, if we translate *swa* 'as when', we allow literary considerations to do impossible violence to linguistic facts. If this were a plausible use of *swa* and it were by chance that we have no examples of it (as Greenfield seems to imply in the passage I quote below), then we could accept it. But the notion that *swa* could mean 'as when' runs contrary to the whole pattern of English conjunctions at all periods of the language. The only single-word conjunction which has a composite meaning in Old English is admittedly *swa* – in the sense 'as if'. But I think I have shown in the note referred to that this is merely a convenient translation for an extended use of *swa*, 'as', in a comparative clause with a subjunctive expressing hypothesis, and that it provides no justification for *swa*, 'as when'. I do not believe that *swa* could have that double meaning.

In my opinion, we have here modern critics deliberately and unnecessarily flying in the face of linguistic probability because they like their interpretation better than any of those which the syntax suggests the Old English poet actually meant. Is there not a danger that, if this attitude spreads and is adopted by less reputable and sensitive scholars, it will harden into a form of impertinent (if not arrogant) sentimentality in which anything goes?

Greenfield does not seem to think so:

> It might be well to emphasize here that, the corpus of the poetry and prose being relatively small in size, textual and analytical critics are often glad to find even *one* parallel syntactic or semantic instance to support their interpretation, let alone a 'norm'! Going further, we may note that statistically there is very little difference between one example and none. Thus Bliss–Dunning, after presenting and rejecting the various extant meanings Bruce Mitchell has ferreted out [!] for the conjunction *swa* in connection with lines 41 ff. –
>
> > þinceð him on mode   þæt he his mondryhten
> > clyppe ond cysse   ond on cneo lecge
> > honda ond heafod   *swa* he hwilum ær
> > in geardagum   giefstolas breac
>
> (it appears to his mind that he embraces and kisses his liege-lord, and

---

[42] 'Some Syntactical Problems', pp. 182–7. [1987. See item 12. IV above.]
[43] *The Wanderer* ed. R. F. Leslie (Manchester, 1966), p. 74.

lays hands and head on his knee *swa* he enjoyed favours from the throne formerly in bygone days) –

can properly say that though usage of *swa* meaning 'as when' here 'would be unique', but 'literary considerations must outweigh linguistic arguments' (pp. 112–13). In advancing this proposition, Bliss–Dunning are making an important point about the relation between textual, syntactic and literary concerns which bring us, in a way, back to the historical versus present meaning considerations raised in the first chapter. This is a point they make on several occasions, including the emendation to the singular *goldwine minne* in line 22, rather than accepting the syntactically possible MS. plural:

> a decision must be made on literary rather than linguistic grounds. In line 22 the emendation to *minne* (a plausible emendation, since the scribe has made mistakes involving *n* in lines 14, 59, 89, and 102) seems desirable in the light of the meaning of the following line; though the wanderer may have lost more than one lord, he is not likely to have buried more than one (p. 108).[44]

Two points must be made here. First, the choice between the manuscript reading *goldwine mine* and the emendation *goldwine minne* in l. 22b

Wanderer l. 22   siþþan geara iu   goldwine min[n]e
hrusan heolstre biwrah,   ond ic hean þonan
wod wintercearig   ofer waþema gebind...

is, as Greenfield acknowledges, a choice between two syntactical possibilities. It is not a question of literary considerations outweighing linguistic 'arguments' here. It is merely a matter of allowing literary considerations to decide in favour of one syntactic possibility against another. The decision cannot be made on linguistic grounds. But taking *swa* to mean 'as when' is an entirely different kettle of fish. It means preferring a syntactical *impossibility* to several syntactical *certainties*.

As my second point will show, I do not use the word 'impossibility' lightly. I am not a statistical expert. My own view is that the importance of the difference between one example and none will vary with the circumstances; we may be more inclined to accept an inherently probable nonce-usage than an inherently improbable one. Linguistic expectation must come into it. If I have examples like *ic mæg beon geclænsod* and *he mæg beon geclænsod*, it is reasonable for me to argue that **þu miht beon geclænsod* was a living form and its absence is the result of chance. Here, I agree, the difference between no examples and one is not

---

[44] *Interpretation*, pp. 118–19. (Perhaps I may say that the logic of the Dunning–Bliss argument about the unlikelihood of the wanderer burying a second dead lord eludes me. [1987. On this point see item 13 above, p. 124 and fn. 17.])

very significant. Indeed, I have already accepted this by saying that the absence of the *hæfde* periphrasis in parentheses in *Beowulf* 'is the result of chance'. At the other extreme, however, there are things which are contrary to the run of the language and to our expectation. *Swa*, 'as when', is, I believe, one. Here the finding of a single example would be decisive.

The importance of this can be illustrated from life. Ohthere and Wulfstan clearly had more justification for believing that they would find different ploughs, ships, garments, and customs as they sailed north than for believing that they would find a dragon. Our attitude to the existence of the Loch Ness monster or the Abominable Snowman would be vastly different if we had one example rather than none.

There are, then, varying relationships between a generalization and any particular instance of it. One proposed solution may be the only possible one; for example *gemæcne* in *ða ic me ful gemæcne monnan funde* (*The Wife's Lament* l. 18) must be acc. sg. masc.[45] Another may be impossible; for example Conybeare's reading *ða ic me ful gemæc ne monnan funde* of the same line.[46] In between there is a wide spectrum ranging from 'very likely' through 'possible' to 'very unlikely'. As an example of the 'very likely' I would cite Fred C. Robinson's defence of the manuscript reading *þone* in *Beowulf* l. 70a;[47] as an example of the 'very unlikely' the pluperfect interpretation of *Ongunnon* and *Het* in *The Wife's Lament* ll. 11a and 15a. For the rest, argument will continue about such matters as the interpretation of *hryre* in *The Wanderer* l. 7b, the punctuation of *The Wanderer* ll. 37–57 and the exact status of metrical 'rules'. This is as it should be; in Old English studies as in real life there is room for honest difference of opinion. The role of linguistic (and other) facts is to delimit this area.

POSTSCRIPT ON *MILDE OND MONÐWÆRE* (above, p. 153)

While this volume was in the press, the article by Mary P. Richards, 'A Reexamination of *Beowulf*, ll. 3180–3182', *ELN* 10 (1973), 163–7, came into my hands. In it the author notes that in *Anglia* 50 (1926), 223–4, Klaeber drew attention to the fact that *milde ond monðwære* is used in the *Blickling Homilies* of Christ and elsewhere of saints or other good Christians. She interprets the phrase in *Beowulf* as a 'religious formula' and observes that 'the ending of the poem does not reveal a blend of Christian and pagan Germanic ideals. Rather,

---

[45] See my 'The Narrator', pp. 224–6. [1987. See item 15, pp. 136–7.]
[46] See my 'The Narrator', pp. 224–6.
[47] 'Two Non-Cruces in *Beowulf*', *Tennessee Studies in Literature* 11 (1966), 151–5.

the poem concludes with the suggestion that Beowulf was as excellent a Christian as possible here on earth.' Obviously this is a possibility, but equally obviously it is not a certainty. (Reference to Mary P. Richards's article and to a short discussion on the same point in 1965 by Rowland L. Collins has now been made in *Old English Newsletter* 8. 1 (1975), 35.)

18
The Dangers of Disguise: Old English Texts in Modern Punctuation

I. General considerations

1 The author of *The Seafarer* observed that it is uncertain which one of three things – disease, old age, or violence – will take a man's life. Even the most profound pessimist must take comfort in the fact that, in this respect at any rate, things have not got worse. But the most determined optimist needs all his resolution as he contemplates the three things which are certain about punctuation in manuscripts of Old English: there is often not much of it; there is little agreement about its significance; it is not the punctuation of modern English or of modern German. For the rest there is uncertainty, dispute, and difference of opinion, about its nature – syntactical and grammatical or rhythmical and rhetorical? – and about how OE texts should be punctuated today. So we have scholarly disagreement, with each writer interpreting the same facts differently and too often believing that he or she alone is right – a dilemma in which Skeat and Murray once found themselves during and after a tandem tricycle ride to Eynsham and from which they were rescued only by the intervention of Mrs Murray.[1]

But is the intervention of modern editors of OE texts always helpful or necessary? It is clear that modern *readers* cannot always grasp the exact nuance an Anglo-Saxon author, reader, or reciter, conveyed to his *hearers*. Even if we assume that there is only one such nuance and that the modern editor has grasped it, he cannot always convey it to others by modern punctuation, which is concerned with modern English as a written rather than as a spoken language, whereas in Old English (one ventures to think) we may sometimes have to do with the rhythms and clause terminals of something closer to speech than to writing. We all know the interchange which runs 'X is his own worst

Reprinted from the *Review of English Studies* 31 (1980), 385–413.

[1] K. M. E. Murray *Caught in the Web of Words: James A. H. Murray and the Oxford English Dictionary* (London, 1977), p. 327.

enemy'. 'Not while I'm alive!' I am beginning to think that the worst enemy of those trying to appreciate OE prose and poetry is the unmodified use by editors of a system of punctuation designed for an entirely different language, either modern German (as in Klaeber's *Beowulf*) or modern English (as in Dobbie's *Beowulf*). I am increasingly coming to believe that the use of modern punctuation – the function of which is syntactical – is forcing editors into unnecessary decisions and is distorting the flow of OE passages in both prose and poetry.

2 There are two distinct problems. First, the punctuation in manuscripts of OE prose is generally much fuller than that in manuscripts of OE poetry. Second, the needs of scholars, of ordinary readers, and of beginners, differ. This paper, which is suggestive rather than prescriptive, is not primarily concerned with the needs of scholars. But the failure of editors to give the manuscript punctuation of OE prose texts means that sometimes at any rate syntactical evidence is suppressed. Thus C. G. Harlow reports that in his Ælfric manuscripts 'there is generally no punctuation before an objectival noun clause', whereas '*þæt* expressing consequence or purpose is normally punctuated ... and thus stands in strong contrast ... with *þæt* introducing a noun clause'.[2] He cites other such cases. Malcolm Godden, in his paper 'Old English', independently and strikingly confirms this:

> Normalizing spellings has never been part of the tradition except in texts for beginners. On the other hand it has been customary, since the nineteenth century, to modernize the punctuation of Old English texts. The editors of the Anglo-Saxon Poetic Records series and of some individual poems have faithfully recorded the presence of capitals separately, though not of points; in most editions of prose texts, however, the original punctuation is not recorded at all and the editors simply supply their own. The omission is particularly disturbing because it represents a deficiency which the interested reader cannot supply himself by consulting a facsimile or microfilm: often only the ink colour distinguishes original punctuation marks from later additions, and only the manuscript itself provides evidence of that nature. In some manuscripts punctuation may be eccentric and unhelpful, but in others it has considerable bearing on the difficult problem of Old English syntax and sentence structure; some of the suggestions that S. O. Andrew made for repunctuating Thorpe's text of the *Catholic Homilies*, for instance, are in fact supported by the manuscript punctuation, though Andrew hadn't as far as I know, consulted the manuscript.[3]

[2] *RES* 10 (1959), 6 and 8.
[3] *Editing Medieval Texts: English, French and Latin Written in England* ed. A. G. Rigg (New York and London, 1977), p. 19.

If we had Wulfstan's *Homilies* in the original punctuation, with the most important manuscripts printed at one opening (as in Skeat's *Gospels*), we would be better equipped to judge how far the scribes were aware of, and how consistently they marked, the 'continuous series of two-stress phrases' detected by Angus McIntosh:

> If I begin by asserting that Wulfstan's prose consists of a continuous series of two-stress phrases related in structure to the classical half-line, and severely restricted in somewhat the same fashion to certain rhythmical patterns, I shall run the risk of having concocted some fabulous abstraction. So having stated what I believe to be the fact, I should like to present some of the grounds on which what I say is based.[4]

My limited random samplings show some inconsistencies. Even McIntosh's own evidence shows some; see his n. 14, which reveals (among other inconsistencies) that in the thirty-four two-stress phrases which occur in all manuscripts of a passage from *Sermo Lupi*, 'only three have no punctuation at all, a proportion which roughly applies to the *Sermo* as a whole'. There are also three which have punctuation in only one manuscript. Both these represent over 8.8 per cent. Such inconsistencies, the fact that McIntosh seems to recognize only two degrees of stress, and my general reluctance to impose this two-stress pattern on the varied syntactic and rhythmic structures in Wulfstan's prose, are among my reasons for wanting to see further work on what I am, I fear, still inclined to view if not as 'some fabulous abstraction', then as 'unserviceable simplifications',[5] adherence to which often 'does violence to the natural emphasis'.[6]

3   But the value of printed editions of texts for the use of scholars (as opposed to general readers) is now questionable. The point has been well made by L. P. Harvey in a recent review:

> V. K. would clearly set himself the highest of standards in producing a 'careful edition', and would strive to indicate all the peculiarities of the MS so as to enable the reader to draw his own conclusions and judge for himself. The objective commands our admiration, but we must ask ourselves whether it is one which is either in theory or in practice realizable, and whether it still makes sense in a world of colour microfilms and slides, and all the other scientific paraphernalia (amongst which we must surely soon count the hologram), without which no responsible scholar would nowadays wish to operate. Modern textual editors have developed refined conventions for registering in print almost all the characteristics

---

[4] 'Wulfstan's Prose' *Proceedings of the British Academy* 35 (1949), 114.
[5] J. Turville-Petre *MÆ* 19 (1950), 90.
[6] D. Whitelock *RES* 12 (1961), 66.

of a MS which could possibly be relevant to any student (and indeed, many might think, quite a number of little conceivable interest to anybody). Thus have been brought almost to perfection the editorial methods first developed at the Renaissance, when humanist scholars undertook systematic editions of ancient texts for the benefit of the world of scholars. We have arrived at near perfection paradoxically just at the time when these editorial methods have become, for many purposes, quite obsolete. Certainly the Leiden glossary is a MS which can now never be edited to our satisfaction in black printed letters on white pages, for, as the author has carefully pointed out (e.g. p. 33), choice of various colours of ink is of vital importance in distinguishing between various hands etc., and indeed in places it is not only necessary to know that a letter is of a particular colour, but also that it has been partly toned up with a second colour. To render all this relevant evidence (at least as important as the actual size of the letters etc.) in print would be well-nigh impossible, and in any case prohibitively expensive. It is at least open to debate whether a profusion of finicking detail is really required, whether it is even desirable, when a colour slide (so easily magnified as many times as one could wish) will put at the reader's disposal all sorts of detail (fine *gradations* of colour for example) which letterpress could never convey.

Nobody subjecting the Leiden glossary, or any similar text, to detailed analysis will in the future be content with a printed edition, and so we must ask what the purpose of the sort of ultra-refined edition of the kind envisaged by V. K. could be. Are not 'palaeographical' editions now obsolete? The wheel may have turned full circle, and the sort of sound common-sense edition executed by Seybold may well serve our purpose, which is to make accessible in easily-legible form one suggested possible reading of a MS that the modern scholar will, in case of need, naturally consult in full colour reproduction, should actual physical examination of the document not be possible. The ease with which a scholar can travel nowadays to see his sources is yet another important new factor which would make it sensible to modify editorial practices first developed for the very different networks of communications which existed in the world in the days of J. J. Scaliger, and, indeed, of C. F. Seybold.[7]

I certainly agree that future workers on OE prose syntax will need to make more use of manuscripts or of colour facsimiles than has hitherto been the case and will have to beware of over-reliance on computer print-outs. But the problem raised by Harvey lies outside my self-imposed sphere of reference. So

[7] *Journal of the Royal Asiatic Society* (1978), 174. I am grateful to Professor Harvey for drawing my attention to this review and for supplying me with a copy of it.

too does the presentation of prose texts for beginners – the question of normalization, the wisdom or otherwise of providing Latin originals and/or later English versions of a text for comparison purposes, and the value of manuscript facsimiles, all arise. What punctuation to use, if any – none may be a justifiable pedagogic device at times[8] – must also be considered. Some of the points I make in the course of this article seem to me relevant here. With these passing observations, I turn to the presentation of OE prose for those who no longer need normalized texts, but have not yet acquired full familiarity with the language.

II. The presentation of prose texts for ordinary readers

4   Assuming, as seems reasonable, that we need some punctuation, we have three possibilities: the manuscript punctuation, modern punctuation, or a compromise between the two. Editions of OE prose texts published by the Early English Text Society fluctuate between the manuscript punctuation – Rypins, *Three Old English Prose Texts* (1924), Henel, *De Temporibus Anni* (1942), Kenneth and Celia Sisam, *The Salisbury Psalter* (1959), Godden, *Ælfric's Catholic Homilies: Second Series* (1979) – and modern editorial punctuation – Napier, *Chrodegang* (1916), Crawford, *Heptateuch* (1922), Crawford, *Byrhtferth's Manual* (1924), and Pope, *Homilies of Ælfric: A Supplementary Collection* (1967 and 1968). It would appear that the Early English Text Society has no fixed policy for the punctuation of OE texts which appear under its imprint, but is content to leave it to individual editors to decide which to use. No doubt each text presents its peculiar problems. But sometimes, for example in the case of Ælfric, it is hard to see any particular reason for the different treatment accorded to similar texts. While both W. W. Skeat (*Lives of the Saints*, 1881 and 1890) and J. C. Pope print the alliterative prose in metrical lines – a decision I regret because of my naïve fear that other beginners will share my experience of believing for quite a long time that Ælfric wrote bad poetry rather than good prose – they differ in their treatment of punctuation. Skeat printed the text 'precisely as it stands in the MS., unless in any case express notice to the contrary is given. This remark applies particularly to the accents and the punctuation.'[9] (Godden agrees: 'The punctuation and capitalization are those of the manuscript and any emendations are indicated in the footnotes.'[10]) But in Pope's edition 'the punctuation has been modernized throughout. Sentences, however, accord with the capitals and punctuation of the basic manuscript unless otherwise stated.'[11] I prefer the procedure adopted by Skeat and Godden.

5   Kenneth and Celia Sisam give as their reason for printing the *Salisbury Psalter* 'as it stands in the manuscript' the fact that 'a word-for-word rendering

[8] See below III. 9.   [9] EETS o.s. 76, p. vii.
[10] EETS s.s. 5 (1979), xciv.   [11] EETS o.s. 259 (1967), 188.

has no literary quality'.[12] I cannot accept the implied suggestion that the fact that Ælfric's *Homilies* have 'literary quality' is a valid reason for printing them with modern punctuation. Why not? Let me in reply ask what Pope meant by 'sentences' in the remark quoted in the previous paragraph. Are they OE sentences? Or MnE sentences? Or is it assumed that there is no difference? This is no mere debating point. P. A. M. Clemoes, whose edition of Ælfric's *Catholic Homilies: First Series* – with its manuscript punctuation – is so eagerly awaited, has kindly supplied me with the Cambridge University Library MS Gg. 3. 28 punctuation of *ÆCHom* i. 2. 11.[13]

> Ic ælfric munuc 7 mæssepreost swaðeah waccre þonne swilcū hadum gebyrige . wearð asend on æþelredes dæge cyninges fram ælfeage biscope aðelwoldes æftgengan to sumū mynstre ðe is cernel gehatén þurh æðelmæres bene ðæs þegenes . his gebyrd and goodnys sind gehwær cuðe;

Here . represents a *punctus* and ; a *punctus versus*. The word immediately following the *punctus versus* is *þa*, not capitalized. The passage quoted is clearly not a MnE sentence, for *his* is not a relative pronoun in Modern English, though it may have been in danger of becoming one in Old English. But could it be an OE sentence? Harlow tells us that in the Ælfric manuscripts he studied (which include Gg. 3. 28) 'the *versus* is like a full stop and regularly ends the sentences, except in certain limited circumstances where lighter punctuation is allowed. Only rarely does the *versus* occur elsewhere' and 'a capital letter is commonly used to begin a new sentence after a *versus*, and only rarely elsewhere'.[14] But even the one example so far quoted shows that it is dangerous to believe that every *punctus versus* in every OE manuscript is the exact equivalent of a MnE full stop. There are numerous such examples. One is *ChronA* 87. 4 (894)

> þa se cyning hine þa west wende mid þære fierde wið Exan cestres. swa ic ær sæde, 7 se here þa burg be seten hæfde; þa he þær to gefaren wæs, þa eodon hie to hiora scipum.

(The commas and the semi-colon are editorial.) Two more involving *his* (quoted in Godden's text) are *ÆCHom* ii. 96. 19 (Thorpe) *ÆCHom* II. 6. 168 (Godden)

> Hé cwæð þæt hé cuðe sumne man on romebyrig. his nama wæs Seruulus. ðearfa on æhtum. and welig on geearnungum; Se læg bedryda fram

[12] EETS o.s. 242 (1959), v.
[13] I use throughout the short titles of OE texts proposed by Christopher Ball, Angus Cameron, and myself, in *ASE* 4 (1975), 207–21 and 8 (1979), 331–3. *Beowulf* is cited from Klaeber (3rd edn), the remaining verse texts from the Anglo-Saxon Poetic Records (hereafter abbreviated to ASPR).
[14] *RES* 10 (1959), 5 and 3, n. 1.

cildháde. oð his geendunge; He læg singallice and næfre sittan ne mihte.
ne híne on oðre sidan bewendan. ne his handa to his muðe geræcan;

and *ÆCHom* ii. 510. 31 (Thorpe) *ÆCHom* ii. 34. 204 (Godden)

> Martinus eac cóm to anes mannes huse his cnapa wæs awed wunderlice
> ðurh deofol. and árn him togeanes mid gyniendum muðe, þa bestáng se
> halga his hand him on múð. het hine ceowan / mid scearpum toðum. his
> liðegan fingras. gif him alyfed wære;

A Latin *cuius* may lie behind *his* in these two examples and in *ÆCHom* i. 2. 11
above. But even if this could be demonstrated, I would not regard it as proof of
the proposition that the punctuation in this or in other OE prose manuscripts
was Latin based and so as alien to OE as MnE punctuation is. I am indebted to
Godden for the following comments on the two passages from *ÆCHom* ii:

> In the first passage, all nine manuscripts are in impressive agreement. All
> have small *h* on *his* but large *S* on *Se* (except for Bodley 343 which has
> *He* for *Se*). Those which (like Gg. 3. 28) use the *punctus* and *punctus versus*
> have *punctus* before *his* and *punctus versus* before *Se*, and those which use
> only the *punctus* have none before *his* but one before *Se*. Large initial *S*
> appears in odd places in Gg. 3. 28, as on *Sumne* here, but not in the other
> manuscripts. In the second passage, the other two manuscripts do not
> use the *punctus versus* and hence have *wæs*. and *muðe*. but no original
> punctuation after *huse*.[15]

The appearance of *He* for *Se* after *geearnungum;* in MS Bodley 343's version of
ÆCHom ii. 96. 19 and the similarity of punctuation before *He* and *Se* in all
other versions of the same passage also warn of the dangers of attempting to
draw precise grammatical boundaries in a language for which we have no
native informants and no intonation patterns. Robert Foster puts the point well
when he observes

> that many Old English narrative passages are composed of strings of
> largely independent units marked and coordinated by *þa*, which is used
> here as an infinitely repeatable marker of temporal sequentiality and
> carries little or no information about the grammatical relation of clauses.
> Each of these *þa*-headed discourse units is composed of one or more
> independent clauses. Within each unit, there may be found both co-
> ordination and subordination, and even cases of subordination by the *þa*
> ... *þa* 'when ... then' construction. These passages, then, can be
> examined from a broader perspective than the level of grammatical rela-
> tions, namely that of the organization of narrative material.[16]

[15] Private communication.
[16] *NM* 76 (1975), 406. This article will repay study.

6   That Old English and Modern English do not share identical sentence structure in the prose is also clear from an analysis of the Parker Chronicle annal for 1001, which (according to Zuck) 'has a cluster of thirty-four clauses, the longest in the corpus'.[17] I make it thirty-three, with two in the later addition. But the clauses beginning 7 ðær or 7 þær in ChronA 132. 5, 9, 20, and 23, may (Malcolm Parkes has suggested to me in a private communication) exemplify scribal confusion between the *positura* – which according to Isidore was a *nota sententiarum* used to mark the end of something, to separate it from what followed – and the Tironian sign for the Latin word *et* used in OE manuscripts for *ond*. If so, we could distinguish five sentences or 'clause-clusters'. If not, the same might still be true, for *ond* could well begin a sentence for an Anglo-Saxon hearer or reader who, being familiar with the intonation patterns and syntax of the language, would have unwittingly solved the problems of punctuation presented to a modern reader by a series of *ond* clauses.[18] More such examples could be produced to strengthen the impression that in OE prose, as in modern spoken English, sentence boundaries in the strict sense are not always well defined. Thus MS Bodleian, Laud Misc. 509 has *nytenū . Swa* in *Exod*(*L*) 9. 10–11 . . . *7 swellende blæddran 7 wunda wurdon on ðam mannum 7 on þam nytenum . Swa þæt ða dryas ne mihton standan beforan Moise.* . . . Crawford prints *nytenum, Swa*; Klaeber reports Grein as having . *Swa*,[19] although my edition (1872) has , *Svâ*. The difference is, I suspect, immaterial. It is more than likely that different Anglo-Saxon readers would have given different intonation to this and similar sentences as they read them aloud. I feel and think that the 'black/white' distinction between parataxis and hypotaxis is too simple for Old English. Some independent confirmation that this is true for the prose – on the poetry see III below – comes from Ruth Waterhouse, who suggests that in a chapter opening like *ÆLS* 31. 366

>   VIIII. Æft on sumne sæl siðode martin*us*
>   on his bisceop-rice . þa bær man þær an lic
>   anes hæðenes mannes þ*æt* hi hine be-byrigdon .

---

[17] Louis Zuck *The Syntax of the Parker Manuscript of the Anglo-Saxon Chronicle from the Year 892 through 1001* (Michigan diss., 1966; *Dissertation Abstracts* 27 (1967), 2143A), p. 91.

[18] Cf. here Joan Turville-Petre's suggestion that *ond þa* in the Parker Chronicle annal for 755 is 'emphatically sequential ("next" or "straightway")' and introduces 'principal statements', *Iceland and the Medieval World Studies in Honour of Ian Maxwell* ed. G. Turville-Petre and J. S. Martin (Melbourne, 1974), pp. 121 and 116.

There is room for work on this point. It is a commonplace that *ond* frequently affects the element order of a clause which follows it; see *NM* (1966), 87–8. Yet, if one studies the *ond*-clauses which editors punctuate as principal in such Chronicle annals as those for 755, 871, 878, and 1001, one must be struck by the frequency with which they have the element order which would be regular if the *ond* were not present.

[19] *Anglia Beiblatt* 52 (1941), 216.

Ða be-heold martinus þa hæðenan feorran .
and wende þæt hi bæron swa swa heora gewune wæs
heora deofol-gild dwollice ofer heora land .
and worhte þa rode-tacn wiþ þæs folces werd .
and bead him on godes naman þæt hi hit ne bæron na furðor .

the first clause 'sets the scene, and makes a general statement, . . . indicate[s] a continuing situation, . . . while the first *þa* clause narrows the focus, . . . indicates a specific action. . . . This could suggest that there is a closer relationship than merely the juxtaposition of two principal clauses between them, while it may not be as close as that of formal hypotaxis. The "panning in" effect of the *þa* clause, the movement from the more general to the more particular, as well as the sequential relationship, makes this group different from the normal relationship between juxtaposed principal clauses; *þa* is not merely an action marker, either.' She goes on to cite other examples from *ÆLS* 31 (Martin) in which 'there is a similar type of narrowing of the focus from the more general setting to the more particularized incident that is the key point of that particular chapter'.[20] Cf. also *ChronA* 87. 4 (894) above.

7   But the mere reproduction of the punctuation of the manuscripts will not solve all our problems. 'In medieval punctuation', says Harlow, 'grammatical principles will be found to be secondary to rhetorical.'[21] Hence punctuation in OE manuscripts is not necessarily a reliable guide to the grammatical nature or function of individual clauses. Nor is it a complete or reliable rhetorical guide to the method of delivery. 'Many of the Lives', says Skeat, 'are written in a loose sort of alliterative verse; and, as the scribe, in general, has taken pains to mark off the lines by the insertion of points, I have printed them accordingly.'[22] However, examples like *ÆLS* 31. 13

He com of hæðenum magum æþelborenum swaðeah
of wurðfulre mægðe . æfter woruld-þingum .
his fæder wæs ærest cempa . and eft cempena ealdor .
and martinus wæs gewenod to wæpnum fram cild-hade .
and camp-dome fyligde betwux larlicum gefylcum .
ærest under constantine þam æþelan casere .
and eft under iuliane þam arleasan wiðer-sacan .
na swaþeah sylf-willes . forþan þe he fram cild-hade wæs swyðor
onbryrd þurh god to godcundlicum þeow-dome .
þonne to woruldlicum campdome . swa swa he cydde syððan .

---

[20] E. R. Waterhouse *Some Syntactic and Stylistic Features of Ælfric's Lives of the Saints* (Ph.D. thesis, Macquarie University, 1978), pp. 54–62.
[21] *RES* 10 (1959), 18–19.   [22] EETS o.s. 76, pp. vi–vii.

and *ÆLS* 32. 13

EADMUND SE EADIGA EASTENGLA CYNINCG
wæs snotor and wurðfull . and wurðode symble
mid æþelum þeawum þone ælmihtigan god .
He wæs ead-mod . and geþungen . and swá an-ræde þurh-wunode
þæt he nolde abugan to bysmorfullum leahtrum .
ne on naþre healfe he ne ahylde his þeawas .
ac wæs symble gemyndig þære soþan lare .
[gif] þu eart to heafod-men ge-set . ne ahefe þu ðe .
ac beo betwux mannum swa swa an man of him .

suggest that sometimes at any rate it was the sweep of the prose sentence rather than the demands of the alliterative line which dictated the pointing.

As I have already said, each text will present its peculiar problems and may demand its peculiar solution. Sometimes – possibly, for example, in Ælfric – the manuscript punctuation will give the ordinary reader a sufficient and (I believe) better sense of the flow of the OE sentence than modern punctuation. But in others, e.g. the *Chronicle*, the ordinary reader may profit from the kind of help given him by Plummer's compromise:

> A word must be said as to the punctuation. Here, too, I have endeavoured to mark the peculiarities of the MSS. The only stops which occur in the MSS. are as a rule the point either on or above the line (.) (˙), the inverted semicolon (⁏), and the peculiar stops which occur in MS. A., represented in the text approximately by (:) and (:,). All these have been retained; stops not in the MSS. are represented by commas and semicolons. In a few instances, so few that they might I think be counted on the fingers of one hand, the colon and semicolon do occur in the MSS.; here the colon has been retained, the semicolon has been inverted.[23]

The value of this can be demonstrated from one example. Plummer prints *ChronA* 84. 33 (894)

> ne cóm se here oftor eall ute of þæm setum þonne tuwwa. oþre siþe þa hie ærest to londe comon, ær sio fierd ge samnod wære, oþre siþe þa hie of þæm setum faran woldon; þa hie ge fengon micle here hyð, 7 þa woldon ferian norþ weardes ofer Temese in on East Seaxe ongean þa scipu.

Here the semi-colon after *woldon* rightly indicates the absence of manuscript punctuation at this point. Yet both A. H. Smith[24] and D. Whitelock[25] put a full

[23] J. Earle and C. Plummer *Two of the Saxon Chronicles Parallel* (Oxford, 1892), p. ix.
[24] *The Parker Chronicle 832–900* (London, 1951), 3rd edn, p. 44.
[25] *Sweet's Anglo-Saxon Reader in Prose and Verse Revised* (Oxford, 1967), p. 35.

stop between *woldon* and *þa* which, like all editors, they capitalize. I am confirmed by Malcolm Parkes in my belief that *þ* here is not a capital. This, the absence of punctuation, the element order *þa* Subject–Verb–Object, and the sense – '... a second time when they wished to leave the entrenchments because they had taken much plunder and wished to carry it northwards...' – combine to suggest that the *þa* which follows *woldon* introduces a subordinate clause. I cannot understand the reluctance of editors to accept this. But I do assert that Plummer's version gives the vital clue for those readers without access to the manuscript or a facsimile.

8   In *Ex* 9. 10–11 and *ÆLS* 31. 366 (both quoted in II. 6), we see the problem of the ambiguous adverb/conjunction which I discuss below in connexion with the poetry. Other phenomena which occur in the poetry and are discussed in III can also be detected in the prose. The ambiguous demonstrative/relative appears in *Or* 78. 26 *Heora ladteow wæs haten Htesseus; se wæs mid his dædum snelra þonne he mægenes hæfde; se geworhte micelne dom on ðæm gefeohte* (modern punctuation) Latin ... *qui celeritate magis quam virtute fretus* ..., Bede 220. 11 *þa wæs gecoren sexta ærcebiscop Deosdedit to þæm seöle Contwara burge, se wæs of Westseaxna þeode; þane cwom þider to halgianne Itthamar se biscop þære cirican æt Hrofesceastre* (modern punctuation) Latin ... *electus est archiepiscopus cathedrae Doruuernensis sextus Deusdedit de gente Occidentalium Saxonum, quem ordinatus uenit illuc Ithamar* ..., and *ÆCHom* i. 532. 29.

Cwyð nu S̄c̄s Gregorius, þæt sum broðor gecyrde to anum mynstre þe he sylf gestaðelode, and æfter regollicere fándunge munuchád underfeng. Þam filigde sum flæsclic broðor to mynstre, na for gecnyrdnysse góddre drohtnunge, ac for flæsclicere lufe.

S. O. Andrew errs in believing that because the Latin has a relative pronoun, the equivalent form of *se* is necessarily one.[26] The ambiguous principal/ subordinate clause with the element order Verb–Subject but no conjunction can be seen in *ChronE* 133. 27 (1001) *7 þær him ferdon onbuton swa swa hi sylf woldon. 7 him nan þing ne wiðstod. ne him to ne dorste sciphere on sæ. ne landfyrd. ne eodon hi swa feor up* and *ChronE* 220. 15 (1086) *7 nan man ne dorste slean oðerne man. næfde he næfre swa mycel yfel gedon wið þone oðerne* (manuscript punctuation). Two interesting examples of the *apo koinou* construction can be seen in the following passage from MS CCCC 162, pp. 403–4, kindly supplied to me by Joyce Basire:

Ærest on frymðe he geworhte heofonas *and* eorðan. *and* sæ / *and* ealle þa þing þe on him syndon. *and* ealle þa englas þe on heofonum syndon. *and* ealle þa ðe of englum to deoflum forsceapene wurdon; Ealle he hi of him sylfum mid his oroðe ut ableow; and þone þe he foremærestne hæfde

[26] *Syntax and Style in Old English* (Cambridge, 1940), pp. 35–47 (hereafter abbreviated to *SS*).

gesceapene. ofer ealle þa oðre englas. þe lucifer wæs haten. *þæt is on ure geþeode leohtberend gereht*; ac ⟨he⟩ eft þa he hine sylfne his scippende gelic ne don wolde. *and* him þrymsetl on norðdæle heofona rices getimbrian wolde he of þam ricene afeoll *and* ealle þa [ealle þa *altered by later hand to* eallū þā] ðe æt þam ræde mid him wæron. *and* him æfter besawon. ealle hi wurdon of englum to deoflum forsceapene. *and* on helle besceofene. þær hi on ecnysse witu þoliað. forþamðe hi forhogedon heora scippend ælmihtigne god; Syððan. ...

In this 'prose paragraph' the words from *and ealle þa englas* down to *forsceapene wurdon* (ll. 2–3) and from *and ealle þa* down to *æfter besawon* (ll. 7–9) belong both with what precedes and what follows them. *Mutatis mutandis* (including the substitution of *and* for *þa*), the comment by Foster quoted in II. 5 has some relevance here. Whether the devices I suggest in III for marking these phenomena in the poetry could be used for prose texts for ordinary readers must be a matter for discussion. So too must the advisability of adopting some compromise between manuscript and editorial punctuation such as that used in Earle and Plummer's *Chronicle* (discussed in II. 7). But I shall need a lot of convincing before I retreat from my belief that the use of modern punctuation alone is the worst solution. What Henry Sweet, in his memorable Preface to his edition of the *Cura Pastoralis*, called 'the merest tyro'[27] soon learns that it is often impossible to find an exact modern equivalent for an OE word. It would be well if he soon learnt not to accept too easily the equation '*punctus versus* = full stop'.

III. The presentation of verse texts

9   Here I am not certain that the interests of scholars, of ordinary readers, and even of those reading OE poetry for the first time, diverge as much as they do for prose texts. Scholars obviously start with the manuscript punctuation and have also found it profitable to contemplate an unpunctuated text. Ordinary readers and sensitive beginners too have in these ways found poetic insights denied to them by texts presented in modern punctuation. Thus a reading of *The Wanderer* ll. 37–57 with the manuscript punctuation has led some beginners to see for themselves that (to put it in grammatical terms) *secga geseldan* may be used *apo koinou* as both the object of *greteð* and *geondsceawað* and also the subject of *swimmað*.[28] Or (to put it 'poetically') *secga geseldan* can refer to both the wanderer's former companions and to the birds as the grip of *sorg ond slæp* tightens and loosens, and his focus shifts: is he asleep? or awake? In the

[27] EETS o.s. 45, p. ix.
[28] But see *The Wanderer* ed. T. P. Dunning and A. J. Bliss (London, 1969), p. 24. I acknowledge gratefully the profit I have derived from discussion on this and similar points with Joy Jenkyns.

reverie? or out? Which are they? Birds or men or men or birds or both? Any rigid modern punctuation tends to prevent or inhibit or destroy a proper reaction to the poet's triumph in these lines. And this is not an isolated example.

10   We can safely leave the scholar with a sound knowledge of OE syntax to his own devices; Dunning and Bliss's *The Wanderer* demonstrates how much careful and sensitive scholars can derive from the punctuation of the manuscripts of OE poetry. But the ordinary reader and the beginner need more help most of the time than any of the great poetic codices have to offer. In *Beowulf* and in *Judith* the only mark of punctuation is the point, except at the ends of certain of the sectional divisions. Their frequency is unusually low in both poems.[29] In the *Paris Psalter*, the end of lines is marked by a dot or semi-colon and sporadic half-lines are marked off by dots.[30] In the *Meters of Boethius*, there are very infrequent points.[31] In the Junius Manuscript, there is 'a slightly unsystematic but on the whole quite definite metrical punctuation'. Apart from this, the ends of sections 'sometimes have a distinctive mark' and 'there are a few other occurrences of sporadic punctuation'.[32] 'The metrical punctuation in the poems of the Vercelli Book is very irregular, and contrasts sharply with the careful system of metrical points in the Junius Manuscript. A large part of the pointing in the Vercelli Book seems to be syntactical, rather than metrical in purpose.' The ends of sections are usually marked off. But 'the only certain thing about all this punctuation is its extreme irregularity and frequent aimlessness'.[33]

In the Exeter Book, the ends of the poems or of sections of poems are usually marked, a variety of symbols being used to indicate the varying importance of the divisions. For the rest, the only mark of punctuation is the point, which is sporadic and, with comparatively few exceptions, occurs at the end of half-lines. 'But, for the most part, the pointing of the manuscript cannot be said to be either metrical or structural.'[34] However, Dunning and Bliss, after a careful analysis of the use of points in *The Wanderer*, conclude

It is obvious that in the Exeter Book no very elaborate system of punctuation was possible, since the scribe had at his disposal only two marks of punctuation, the point and the point followed by a small capital letter. . . .
   It cannot be claimed that the punctuation is fully systematic; on the other hand, it is far from being random. With a very limited range of symbols at his command, the scribe has chosen to do three things: to

[29] Beowulf *and* Judith ed. E. V. K. Dobbie (ASPR iv, 1953), p. xxx.
[30] *The* Paris Psalter *and the* Meters of Boethius ed. G. P. Krapp (ASPR v, 1933), p. xv.
[31] Paris Psalter *and* Meters of Boethius, p. xli.
[32] *The Junius Manuscript* ed. G. P. Krapp (ASPR i, 1931), pp. xxii–xxiii.
[33] *The Vercelli Book* ed. G. P. Krapp (ASPR ii, 1932), pp. xxviii–xxxii.
[34] *The Exeter Book* ed. G. P. Krapp and E. V. K. Dobbie (ASPR iii, 1936), pp. xxi–xxiv.

mark out sections in the development of the poem; to call attention to sequences of parallel clauses or phrases; and to indicate places where the reader might misconstrue the syntax. (If editors had paid more attention to the punctuation in the manuscript the syntax might have been less often misconstrued.) Even these limited objectives have not been fully achieved....[35]

Craig Williamson tells us that these conclusions 'are also true with regard to the *Riddles*'.[36] His Appendix C to his Introduction – which catalogues all the points in the *Riddles* and analyses their significance – is noteworthy, as are his observations about the difficulty of telling where one poem ends and another begins.[37]

How then ought we to punctuate OE poetry for the ordinary reader and for the undergraduate? Craig Williamson says: 'It is important to understand the medieval scribe's system of pointing in the manuscript in so far as it is possible to do so; it is also important to provide the modern reader with an edited text in which the punctuation facilitates the reading.'[38] The currently almost universal assumption (shared by Dunning and Bliss and by Craig Williamson) is that this can be done by using only the marks available in modern systems of punctuation. This assumption I can no longer accept.

That modern editors do not agree in their punctuation of the same OE poem is notorious. E. G. Stanley has strikingly made the point:

It is obvious that editorial punctuation is not a reliable guide to the sentence structure of *Beowulf*; it tells us only how a modern grammarian, taking German or English as punctuated in his time as his norm, thought it best to punctuate *Beowulf* for modern readers. We can make assumptions about what forms a structural unit regardless of editorial punctuation. We may feel that a structure is interrupted (as at lines 1652–3), or that some dependent clauses are so closely attached to their main clause that Dobbie's English lack of punctuation accords better with what we feel is right than Klaeber's commas; but we have no means of testing the validity of that feeling. When the main clause is expressed by an A3 line the most we can say is that such main clauses give the impression of leading forward to their dependent clauses without interruption. That impression, however, is based on what we should feel in similar cases in Modern English.[39]

[35] Dunning and Bliss, pp. 9 and 11.
[36] *The Old English Riddles of the Exeter Book* ed. Craig Williamson (Chapel Hill, NJ, 1977), pp. 12–19.
[37] *Old English Riddles*, pp. 35–48, and *passim*, especially p. 315, respectively.
[38] *Old English Riddles*, p. 19.
[39] *Old English Studies in Honour of John C. Pope* ed. Robert B. Burlin and Edward B. Irving, Jr (Toronto, 1974), pp. 145–6 (hereafter abbreviated to *Pope Studies*).

I wholeheartedly agree with this and in particular would stress that our 'impression' can only be 'based on what we should *feel* in similar cases in Modern English' and that 'we have no means of testing the validity of that *feeling*' [my italics]. It therefore behoves us to avoid dogmatism.

11   Drawing attention to differences in editorial punctuation does not, of course, imply that there is only one right way of punctuating an OE poem, still less that modern punctuation is a proper tool for the purpose. A. Campbell asked whether *Ða* in *Beo* l. 917

> Ðā wæs morgenlēoht
> scofen ond scynded. Ēode scealc monig
> swīðhicgende tō sele þām hēan
> searowundor sēon; . . .

was to be translated 'Then' or 'When' and replied: 'I think that such passages were open to personal interpretation, and that reciters would indicate their view of the passage by intonation.'[40] This is perceptive and I accept without hesitation the idea that a choice existed. But (as I have said elsewhere) 'I feel – and I use the word deliberately – that Campbell may have presented that choice in starker terms than the actual situation warranted and that there may have been an intermediate stage between "Then" and "When".'[41] Be that as it may, I have come to think that the possibility of different interpretations such as those envisaged by Campbell should be made clear by editorial punctuation. As things stand, the punctuation of OE poetry is prescriptive. It imposes an interpretation of the poem on the reader. T. A. Shippey tells us that 'there is now little doubt that Old English poetic sentences were longer and better organised than early editors thought, and that repeated words such as *forþon*... *forþon* or *þa*... *þa* were used to signal clause-boundaries rather than sentence ones.'[42] A poll among modern editors might support this idea. But I believe that at least sometimes there should be 'doubt' and that failure to recognize this is leading to an acceptance of over-sophisticated syntactical patternings. We are in a sense being forced into unnecessary dogmatism by our use of modern grammatical punctuation, which produces MnE sentences instead of OE verse paragraphs – verse paragraphs which, like those of Milton, sometimes defy strict grammatical analysis.[43] Individual scholars are, of course, entitled to

---

[40] *Philological Essays: Studies in Old and Middle English Language and Literature in Honour of Herbert Dean Meritt* ed. James L. Rosier (Mouton, 1970), p. 95.

[41] *NQ* 223 (1978), 394. [1988. On *Beo* l. 917 see pp. 261–2 and 339 below.]

[42] *Old English Verse* (London, 1972), p. 199, n. 29.

[43] Walter H. Beale 'Rhetoric in the Old English Verse-Paragraph', *NM* 80 (1979), 133–42, discusses the OE verse paragraph and concludes that both native traditions and Latin rhetorical devices go to the creation of successful ones. I have doubts about this; see *RES* 31 (1980), 198–200.

read and to punctuate OE poems in any way they like, whatever I may think or feel, as long as they do not tell me when expounding their own theory that 'such an interpretation seems to present the only rational and comprehensive resolution for the apparent inconsistencies of these two poems.'[44] But that entitlement does not mean that they have a right to impose that reading and that punctuation on others. So I urge the need of a system of punctuation which will draw the reader's attention to the possibility of varying interpretations rather than imposing one particular view. I agree with E. G. Stanley when he writes: 'In many cases, however, what is involved in accommodating Old English verse within modern punctuation is not a matter of right or wrong so much as of evolving a satisfactory consistency. We cannot tell now how the Anglo-Saxons would have proceeded in applying our kind of punctuation to their kind of verse.'[45] But I would argue that 'evolving a satisfactory consistency' would be an easier task if we were to use more marks of punctuation than any modern system has at its disposal.

I distinguish below six contexts where different interpretations were or may have been available to the *scop*. These 'punctuation cruces' should be marked. They are: ambiguous adverb/conjunctions; ambiguous principal/subordinate clauses with initial verb but no conjunction; ambiguous demonstrative/relatives; possible parentheses; *apo koinou* constructions; and examples of what I will for want of a better term call 'enjambment of sense'. Further investigation may reveal more.

12 Full discussion of the ambiguous adverb/conjunction must await my *Old English Syntax*.[45a] But it has already appeared in *Beo* l. 917 (III. 11). S. O. Andrew accepts that the *Ðā wæs* clause in *Beo* l. 917 and that in *Beo* l. 126

> Ðā wæs on ūhtan   mid ǣrdæge
> Grendles gūðcræft   gumum undyrne;
> þā wæs æfter wiste   wōp up āhafen,
> micel morgenswēg

are ambiguous, but adds that many such 'ambiguous *þa wæs* sentence-forms (almost invariably pointed as principal in the traditional text) are better taken as subordinate'.[46] But, hooked as he is on hypotaxis, he does not extend this ambiguity to other sentence forms with initial *þa* in the poetry. He claims that 'sentences of the form *þa com he* (i.e. in which the verb is stressed[47])' are ambiguous in the prose but 'are in *Beowulf*, and most other OE poetry, unambiguously subordinate clauses' and that 'sentences of the form *þa he com* are,

[44] *Anglia* 82 (1964), 290.   [45] *Anglia* 97 (1979), 522.
[45a] [1987. See initially *OES* §§2536–60.]   [46] *SS*, pp. 17–18.
[47] This distinction cannot be accepted. Nor can his claim that in speech, *þa* adv. was always stressed and *þa* conj. always unstressed.

both in prose and verse, always subordinate clauses, and are, therefore, unambiguous'.[48] A long succession of scholars has rightly argued against the wholesale acceptance of these 'rules'. Nils Erik Enkvist, for example, in his article 'Old English Adverbial *þa* – an Action Marker',[49] analyses the use of *þa* in *Beowulf*, rightly argues that 'a sweep over a sample of Old English poetry and prose seems to support rather than contradict the view that one of the functions of adverbial *þa* is to mark actions and sequences of actions', and in his final footnote urges the dangers of rigid application of the rules proposed by Andrew. But we do not have to throw the baby out with the bathwater by completely neglecting Andrew, as many modern editors seem to do. Any reader will have cause for confusion if he asks whether we are intended to take *þa* as 'Then' or 'When' in *Mald* l. 260

> þa hi forð eodon,   feores hi ne rohton;
> ongunnon þa hiredmen   heardlice feohtan,
> grame garberend,   and god bædon
> þæt hi moston gewrecan   hyra winedrihten
> and on hyra feondum   fyl gewyrcan

and will have cause for wonder if he compares *Mald* l. 143

> Ða he oþerne   ofstlice sceat,
> þæt seo byrne tobærst;   he wæs on breostum wund
> þurh ða hringlocan,   him æt heortan stod
> ætterne ord

with *Mald* l. 84

> þa hi þæt ongeaton   and georne gesawon
> þæt hi þær bricgweardas   bitere fundon,
> ongunnon lytegian þa   laðe gystas,
> bædon þæt hi upgang   agan moston,
> ofer þone ford faran,   feþan lædan

and *Mald* l. 89

> Ða se eorl ongan   for his ofermode
> alyfan landes to fela   laþere ðeode.
> Ongan ceallian þa   ofer cald wæter
> Byrhtelmes bearn   (beornas gehlyston)

with *Mald* l. 22

> þa he hæfde þæt folc   fægere getrymmed,
> he lihte þa mid leodon   þær him leofost wæs,
> þær he his heorðwerod   holdost wiste.

[48] All quotations are from *SS*, p. 18.   [49] *NM* 73 (1972), 90–6.

(All these examples are quoted from ASPR. But the other editions I have checked – including those of E. V. Gordon, Dorothy Whitelock, and J. C. Pope – agree in the essential distinctions between principal and subordinate clauses.) Examples could be multiplied to demonstrate that there is in *Maldon*, as in most OE poems, a traditional punctuation which seems to be accepted by successive editors – with a few honourable exceptions, such as Dunning and Bliss in *The Wanderer* – with a blind faith for which I can find no enthusiasm. I am not trying to lay down rules of punctuation. I am merely saying that inconsistencies such as those exemplified above and some of those discussed below are a striking indictment of current editorial attitudes towards punctuation.[50]

13   *Beo* l. 126 (quoted in III. 12) raises the question of what Andrew calls the 'curious superstition' by which, while editors of the poem 'admit the subordination of a temporal clause when it follows the principal sentence, not one of them does so when the clause precedes the principal sentence'.[51] An interesting example is seen in *Beo* l. 320

>   Stræt wæs stānfāh,   stīg wīsode
>   gumum ætgædere.   Gūðbyrne scān
>   heard hondlocen,   hringīren scīr
>   song in searwum,   þā hīe tō sele furðum
>   in hyra gryregeatwum   gangan cwōmon.
>   Setton sǣmēþe   sīde scyldas,
>   rondas regnhearde   wið þæs recedes weal;
>   bugon þā tō bence, –   byrnan hringdon,
>   gūðsearo gumena, ... ,

Where Andrew attaches the *þa* clause to what follows and translates: 'As soon as they had reached the hall [and] set their shields, sea-weary men, by the wall,

[50] Here, I have to confess, I am less charitable than Stanley (*Anglia* 97 (1979), 520).

[51] *Postscript on* Beowulf (Cambridge, 1948), pp. vii–viii, hereafter abbreviated to *Postscript*. Here he speaks of 'all the four modern editions'. But in *SS*, Preface, he says that the editions by 'Grein, Holthausen, Wyatt-Chambers, Sedgefield, Klaeber ... agree, with only slight variations, in the punctuation of the poem'. The edition edited by Gerhard Nickel (Heidelberg, 1976) shows an awareness of the problem. But it fluctuates between the traditional punctuation, e.g. at *Beo* ll. 126 and 917, and a different one, e.g. at *Beo* l. 323, where the note that *cwomon* is to be taken as pluperfect reveals what the punctuation does not, viz. that *þa* is taken as a conjunction; cf. *Mald* l. 260 in iii. 12. In his review, Stanley draws our attention to other departures from the traditional punctuation – not all of them conspicuously successful – but observes that 'it is sad that editors who show lofty awareness of the faults of the *textus receptus* should follow it in its inconsistencies'; see *Anglia* 97 (1979), 521–2. The editions by C. L. Wrenn (1953), by C. L. Wrenn and W. F. Bolton (1973), and by Michael Swanton (1978) – who recognizes that 'loose correlatives allow the poet to develop elaborate paragraphs where a modern writer might consider it proper to use only two or three logically connected clauses' (p. 29) – all follow the traditional punctuation at *Beo* ll. 126 and 917, but attach the *þa* clause in *Beo* l. 323 to what follows.

then bowed they to bench.' I agree with this arrangement, but would prefer to translate 'As soon as they had reached the hall, seaweary they put down their shields by the wall [and] then sat on the bench.'[52] A study of *Mald* ll. 143 and 84 and of *Mald* ll. 89 and 22 (all quoted in III. 12) will show that the editors of that poem are not as consistent in observing 'this curious superstition' as the editors of *Beowulf*. This problem also demands fuller treatment, but it too should in my opinion be taken more seriously than has hitherto always been the case.

Neither the ambiguous adverb/conjunction nor the frequently related 'curious superstition' is restricted to clauses introduced by *þa*; here it is relevant to note Stanley's comment on the ambiguity of 'some of the main bearers of grammatical looking forward or backward' in Old English.[53] Examples in point include (with *þær*) in *Beo* l. 1266

> wæs þæra Grendel sum,
> heorowearh hetelīc,   sē æt Heorote fand
> wæccendne wer   wīges bīdan;
> þǣr him āglǣca   ætgrǣpe wearð

but cf. *Beo* l. 864

> Hwīlum heaþorōfe   hlēapan lēton,
> on geflit faran   fealwe mēaras,
> ðǣr him foldwegas   fægere þūhton,
> cystum cūðe;

(with *þonne*) in *Beo* l. 377

> Ðonne sægdon þæt   sǣlīþende,
> þā ðe gifsceattas   Gēata fyredon
> þyder tō þance,   þæt hē þrītiges
> manna mægencræft   on his mundgripe
> heaþorōf hæbbe.   Hine hālig God
> for ārstafum   ūs onsende,
> tō West-Denum,   þæs ic wēn hæbbe,
> wið Grendles gryre,

which Andrew renders as 'since seafarers ... , God ...';[54] (with *ǣr*) in *Beo* l. 3038

> Ǣr hī þǣr gesēgan   syllīcran wiht,
> wyrm on wonge   wiðerrǣhtes þǣr

[52] Andrew discusses this example at *SS*, p. 76, and *Postscript*, pp. 50 and 90. I quote his translation from *Postscript*, p. 90.

[53] *Medieval Narrative: A Symposium* ed. H. Bekker-Nielsen, P. Foote, A. Haarder, and P. M. Sørensen (Odense, 1979), p. 60 (hereafter abbreviated to *Medieval Narrative*).

[54] *SS*, p. 27, and *Postscript*, p. 18.

> lāðne licgean;   wæs se lēgdraca
> grimlīc gry(refāh)   glēdum beswæled;⁵⁵

(with *oðþæt*) *Beo* l. 1740 and other examples I have discussed elsewhere;⁵⁶ (with *nu*) in *Beo* l. 2799

> Nū ic on māðma hord   mīne bebohte
> frōde feorhlege,   fremmað gēna
> lēoda þearfe;   ne mæg ic hēr leng wesan

but cf. *Beo* l. 939

> Nū scealc hafað
> þurh Drihtnes miht   dǣd gefremede,
> ðē wē ealle   ǣr ne meahton
> snyttrum besyrwan.   Hwæt, þæt secgan mæg
> efne swā hwylc mægþa   swā ðone magan cende
> æfter gumcynnum,   gyf hēo gȳt lyfað,
> þæt hyre Ealdmetod   ēste wære ... ;

(with *siþþan*) *Beo* l. 1232 quoted in III. 17 and *Beo* l. 2069; and (with *forþon*) the notorious examples in *The Wanderer* and *The Seafarer*.⁵⁷ *Sona* too has been added to the list. Thus Andrew sees *sona* as a conjunction in *Beo* l. 1792

> Gēat unigmetes wēl,
> rōfne randwigan   restan lyste;
> sōna him seleþegn   sīðes wērgum,
> feorrancundum   forð wīsade,

where it could be argued that the desire for sleep led Beowulf to summon the chamberlain.⁵⁸ However, in general, I am dubious about *sona* conjunction, my strongest objection being that construing it as such too often inartistically destroys the paratactic sweep of the paragraph, as in *Beo* ll. 739–54, where *sona* appears twice. Here I accept Klaeber's verdict on Schücking's *Britannica* article: 'Die sorgsame Untersuchung endigte mit einem *non liquet*; doch könnte man in dem negativen Urteil sogar noch weiter gehen.'⁵⁹

The use of double commas („) instead of a semi-colon or a full stop would enable editors to indicate and readers to see the possible variations in sequences of sentences introduced by *þa, þonne*, and other words which can be either adverbs or conjunctions.

---

⁵⁵ See *Postscript*, pp. 103 and 152.
⁵⁶ See *NQ* 223 (1978), 390–4. [1987. Item 24 below.]
⁵⁷ See (*inter alia*) Dunning and Bliss, p. 52, and A. D. Horgan *RES* 30 (1979), 43–5.
⁵⁸ *SS*, p. 80.
⁵⁹ *Anglia Beiblatt* 52 (1941), 216. See also Stanley *Anglia* 97 (1979), 521–2.

14 Ambiguous principal/subordinate clauses with initial verb and element order Verb–Subject have already been exemplified in the prose. Examples from the poetry include *Soul* i. 144 *Wære ðu on wædle, sealdest me wilna geniht*, where we may have two statements in asyndetic parataxis (*wære* indicative) or a concessive clause preceding its principal clause (*wære* subjunctive), and *GenB* l. 368

> Wa la, ahte ic minra handa geweald
> and moste ane tid   ute weorðan,
> wesan ane winterstunde,   þonne ic mid þys werode –

where we may have an independent wish followed by an incomplete statement (or boast) or a conditional clause with order Verb–Subject followed by its principal clause. Discussion of the important question raised here concerning the existence or otherwise of concessive and conditional clauses with initial verb must await my *Old English Syntax*.[59a] But the sentences or clauses in examples such as these could also be divided by double commas („).

15 The ambiguous demonstrative/relative too has already been exemplified in the prose. Typical examples from the poetry are *ðæra* and *þone* in *Beo* l. 1345

> Ic þæt londbuend,   leode mine,
> seleræ̃dende   secgan hȳrde,
> þæt hie gesawon   swylce twegen
> micle mearcstapan   moras healdan,
> ellorgæ̃stas.   Ðæra oðer wæs,
> þæs þe hie gewislicost   gewitan meahton,
> idese onlicnes;   oðer earmsceapen
> on weres wæstmum   wræclastas træd,
> næfne he wæs mara   þonne ænig man oðer;
> þone on geardagum   Grendel nemdon
> foldbuende; . . .

Here again double commas („) could be used. A special problem arises in *Wid* l. 142

> lof se gewyrceð,
> hafað under heofonum   heahfæstne dom.

Kock writes: '*Se*, of course, is a demonstrative. Holthausen transforms it into a relative. That is bad for three reasons, and good for none. It involves extraordinary word-order, want of parallelism, and meagre sense.'[60] Holthausen's interpretation is, however, possible. The syntax is supported by other examples

---

[59a] [1987. See *OES* §§3440–50 and 3678–83 respectively.]   [60] *Anglia* 45 (1921), 130.

in which material properly belonging to a subordinate clause precedes the subordinating conjunction, e.g. in *GenB* l. 272

> þohte þurh his anes cræft
> hu he him strenglicran   stol geworhte,
> heahran on heofonum

and in *Jul* l. 32

> Ða wæs sio fæmne   mid hyre fæder willan
> welegum biweddad;   wyrd ne ful cuþe,
> freondrædenne   hu heo from hogde,
> geong on gæste,

where I agree with Campbell – against Kock – in taking *freondrædenne* as dependent on *from hogde* 'despised'.[61] Parallelism is not essential in every sentence in OE poetry. The apparent assumption that *lof* and *dom* are identical is not a certainty; 'he who performs *lof* will win *dom*' seems a possible translation until the lexicographers prove otherwise.

16 Recently, it seems to me, there has been a renewed awareness of the possibility that what are today called 'parentheses' played an important part in the construction of the OE verse paragraph. Some obvious ones are still sometimes overlooked. Thus Miss Whitelock perpetuates the commas adopted by Sweet and Onions when she prints in the latest impression of *Sweet's Anglo-Saxon Reader* (1979) in *Dream* l. 39

> Ongyrede hine þa geong hæleð,   þæt wæs god ælmihtig,
> strang and stiðmod,

whereas the sense and the neuter *þæt* instead of the masculine *se* support the bracketed (*þæt wæs god ælmihtig*) adopted by Dickins and Ross, ASPR, and Swanton. I would myself print – *þæt wæs god ælmihtig!* –, for this is no incidental adjective clause or apologetic aside, but a triumphant affirmation. Dunning and Bliss use parentheses in *Wan* l. 50 and *Wan* l. 55. Bliss's new interpretation of *Beo* ll. 3051–75 involves two parentheses.[62] Stanley suggests a parenthetic punctuation for *Beo* ll. 1131b–38a.[63] E. M. Liggins suggests that a

---

[61] *RES* 15 (1964), 191, n. 4, and *Jubilee Jaunts and Jottings* (Lund, 1918), p. 53. See further *NM* 69 (1968), 58.

[62] See *J. R. R. Tolkien: Scholar and Storyteller. Essays in Memoriam* ed. Mary Salu and Robert T. Farrell (Ithaca, NY, 1979), pp. 41–63. I hope to give elsewhere my reasons for agreeing with him up to the end of *Beo* l. 3073 and for questioning his interpretation of the last two lines. [1987. See item 4 above.]

[63] *Pope Studies*, p. 164, n. 53. In *Medieval Narrative* (pp. 73–4), he agrees with D. K. Fry in taking *Beo* l. 1129b *eard gemunde* as parenthetic.

negated *swa* clause sometimes 'expresses a parenthetical comment rather than a real concession connected with the action of its principal clause'.[64]

In some of the examples already discussed, the scholars concerned have had the courage of their convictions and have firmly marked their parentheses with round brackets or with dashes. In others, it is a matter of possibility rather than certainty. This is true in *Beo* l. 272

>   þū wāst, gif hit is
> swā wē sōþlīce   secgan hȳrdon,
> þæt mid Scyldingum   sceaðona ic nāt hwylc,
> dēogol dǣdhata   deorcum nihtum
> ēaweð þurh egsan   uncūðne nīð,
> hȳnðu ond hrāfyl.

This is Klaeber's punctuation, which does not make it clear whether *gif* introduces a conditional clause (as Klaeber glosses it and the Wrenn–Bolton dashes before *gif* and after *hyrdon* suggest) or a dependent question. Here we could leave the issue open by using broken parentheses (– – ... – –). Other examples where this device might be helpful include *Beo* l. 320 (quoted in III. 13), where – since *Beo* ll. 321b–3a and 327b–8a all refer to the warriors' armour – *Beo* ll. 323b–7a could be parenthetic, and *Beo* l. 1584

>   Hē him þæs lēan forgeald,
> rēþe cempa,   tō ðæs þe hē on ræste geseah
> gūðwērigne   Grendel licgan,
> aldorlēasne,   swā him ǣr gescōd
> hild æt Heorote.   Hrā wīde sprong,
> syþðan hē æfter dēaðe   drepe þrōwade,
> heorosweng heardne,   ond hine þā hēafde becearf,

where the awkward change of subject in the last half-line could be solved by putting *Beo* ll. 1588b–90a in parentheses.[65] A similar solution to a similar problem is possible in *Beo* l. 2296

> hāt ond hrēohmōd   hlǣw oft ymbehwearf
> ealne ūtanweardne;   nē ðǣr ǣnig mon
> on þǣre wēstenne, –   hwæðre *wiges* gefeh,
> bea(du)[we] weorces;   hwīlum on beorh æthwearf,
> sincfæt sōhte,

where, following K. Miyabe, we can take *Beo* ll. 2297b–9a as parenthetical and

---

[64] *Anglia* 88 (1970), 310. See also R. Quirk's comments on *GenA* l. 1565b in *The Concessive Relation in Old English Poetry* (New Haven, Conn., 1954), p. 111 (hereafter cited as Quirk).

[65] I discuss other problems associated with these lines in *ASE* 4 (1973), 22–3.

translate '– yet no man was eager for conflict, for the toil of battle, there in the wasteland –'.[66]

17 I have mentioned in III. 9 the possibility of taking *Wan* 1. 53a *secga geseldan apo koinou*, with the claim that insistence that it must be either the object of the preceding verbs or the subject of the verb which follows destroys the sweep of the verse paragraph. Examples could be multiplied. But, as I return to this point in III. 19 and 20, I mention only a few here. *And* l. 270 and *And* l. 474 I have discussed elsewhere.[67] In *Wan* l. 65

> Wita sceal geþyldig,
> ne sceal no to hatheort   ne to hrædwyrde,
> ne to wac wiga   ne to wanhydig,
> ne to forht ne to fægen,   ne to feohgifre
> ne næfre gielpes to georn,   ær he geare cunne.
> Beorn sceal gebidan,   þonne he beot spriceð,
> oþþæt collenferð   cunne gearwe
> hwider hreþra gehygd   hweorfan wille,

the *scop* could make it clear by his performance whether he expected the audience to take *Wan* l. 69b with *Wan* l. 69a, with *Wan* ll. 70–2, or *apo koinou*.[68] In *Beo* l. 1465

> Hūru ne gemunde   mago Ecglāfes
> eofoþes cræftig,   þæt hē ǣr gespræc
> wīne druncen,   þā hē þæs wæpnes onlāh
> sēlran sweordfrecan;   selfa ne dorste
> under ȳða gewin   aldre genēþan,
> drihtscype drēogan;   þǣr hē dōme forlēas,
> ellenmǣrðum.   Ne wæs þǣm ōðrum swā,
> syðþan hē hine tō gūðe   gegyred hæfde,

Klaeber's punctuation given here links the *þa* clause with what goes before. Carleton Brown puts the semi-colon after *druncen*, thereby changing the emphasis.[69] Andrew takes *onlah* and *dorste* as parallel: 'when he lent ... and did not dare ..., then he lost glory ...'[70] But the *þa* clause could be taken *apo koinou*. The discrepancy noted by Stanley between Klaeber's punctuation of *Beo* l. 1232

---

[66] *Poetica* (Tokyo) 2 (1974), 34–5.
[67] *NM* 70 (1969), 78–81.
[68] Dunning and Bliss, p. 58, n. 1, rightly reject the idea that it could go with *Wan* ll. 66–8. But their note on *Wan* l. 69 (p. 118) seems to envisage the possibility of an *apo koinou* relationship.
[69] *PMLA* 53 (1938), 915.
[70] *SS*, p. 76, and *Postscript*, p. 54.

>   Ēode þā tō setle.   þǣr wæs symbla cyst,
>   druncon wīn weras.   Wyrd ne cūþon,
>   geōsceaft grim*m*e,   swā hit āgangen wearð
>   eorla manegum,   syþðan ǣfen cwōm,
>   ond him Hrōþgār gewāt   tō hofe sīnum,
>   rīce tō ræste.   Reced weardode
>   unrīm eorla,   swā hī oft ǣr dydon.
>   Bencþelu beredon;   hit geondbrǣded wearð
>   beddum ond bolstrum

and that in the Nickel edition, which prints *Syþðan*, could also be resolved by taking the *syþðan* clause *apo koinou*.[71] My tentative suggestion is that such clauses could be marked at the front by an arrow pointing back and at the end by an arrow pointing forward (← ... →). In appropriate circumstances, a single arrow (← or →) could be used; see III. 20 and consider the test case in *GenB* l. 828

>   Gif ic waldendes   willan cūðe,
>   hwæt ic his to hearmsceare   habban sceolde,
>   ne gesawe þu no sniomor,   þeah me on sæ wadan
>   hete heofones god   heonone nu þa,
>   on flod faran,   nǣre he firnum þæs deop,
>   merestream þæs micel,   þæt his o min mod getweode,
>   ac ic to þam grunde genge,   gif ic godes meahte
>   willan gewyrcean.

Here the *þæt* clause is in strict grammar a noun clause object of *gesawe*, as B. J. Timmer explained it.[72] But if we did not have *GenB* l. 830a, we should have to take it as a clause of result dependent on *GenB* ll. 832b–3a, as Th. Braasch,[73] Timmer in another place,[74] and Quirk,[75] explain it. Klaeber tells us that no punctuation can explain this double relationship.[76] But suppose we had

>   ...   ...
>   ne gesawe þu no sniomor ← ...
>   ...   ...
>   merestream þæs micel ← þæt his o min mod getweode ...

---

[71] *Anglia* 97 (1979), 521. Stanley discusses other *siþþan* clauses in *Beowulf*. Some illustrate Andrew's 'curious superstition' (*Postscript*, p. viii). Some can be taken *apo koinou*.
[72] *The Later Genesis* (rev. ed., Oxford, 1954), p. 112.
[73] *Vollständiges Wörterbuch zur sog. Caedmonschen Genesis* (Anglistische Forschungen 76, 1933), p. 128.
[74] Timmer, p. 129.
[75] Quirk, p. 97.
[76] *Anglia* 49 (1925), 368.

The problem raised by R. F. Leslie of how best to punctuate *Sea* ll. 18-22 and *Beo* ll. 1125-31a[77] can also, I suggest, be solved by taking *Sea* l. 19b *hwilum ylfete song* and *Beo* l. 1127a *hamas ond heaburh apo koinou.*

18   One of the ideas behind this paper is that, when one is reading OE poetry with those who must wrestle with the grammar before they can understand the meaning, it is often difficult to help them to appreciate the art of the poet and to feel the magic of the poetry. This difficulty often arises when the poet employs what, for want of a better term, I call 'enjambment of sense'. By this I do not mean the separation of syntactical units by half-line divisions only because of the demands of metre, as in the second line of *Beo* l. 1063

> þær wæs sang ond swēg   samod ætgædere
> fore Healfdenes   hildewīsan,
> gomenwudu grēted,   gid oft wrecen

or the third line of *GuthB* l. 1238

> Symle me onsende   sigedryhten min,
> folca feorhgiefa,   siþþan ic furþum ongon
> on þone æfteran   anseld bugan
> geargemearces,   gæst haligne,

but the sort of separation seen in *Beo* l. 1703

> Blæd is ārǣred
> geond wīdwegas,   wine mīn Bēowulf,
> ðīn ofer þēoda gehwylce

and *And* l. 474

> Ic wille þe,
> eorl unforcuð,   anre nu gena
> bene biddan,   þeah ic þe beaga lyt,
> sincweorðunga,   syllan mihte,
> fætedsinces.   Wolde ic freondscipe,
> þeoden þrymfæst,   þinne, gif ic mehte,
> begitan godne,

where the sequences *Blæd ... ðin* and *freondscipe ... þinne ... godne* give dramatic emphasis – 'Fame ... thy fame' and '... friendship ... thy friendship ... thy gracious friendship'. Perhaps not all will agree with me in what follows, for (it could be argued) speakers of any language which regularly delays a verb to the end of its clause must have a different linguistic expectation and

---

[77] *Old English Poetry: Essays on Style* ed. Daniel G. Calder (Berkeley, Cal., 1979), pp. 117-19 (hereafter abbreviated to *Calder Essays*).

awareness from speakers of Modern English, with its fixed element order. However, I would suggest that, when reading *Mald* 1. 5

> þa þæt Offan mæg   ærest onfunde,
> þæt se eorl nolde   yrhðo geþolian,
> he let him þa of handon   leofne fleogan
> hafoc wið þæs holtes,   and to þære hilde stop;
> be þam man mihte oncnawan   þæt se cniht nolde
> wacian æt þam wige,   þa he to wæpnum feng,

the first-time reader of *Mald* ll. 7–8 will probably have to look up at least two or three of *leofne, fleogan, hafoc,* and *holtes*. He will then have to recognize the unusual dative plural -*on* and to recall or check in his grammar that -*ne* is accusative singular masculine and then to associate it with *hafoc*. By this time some such translation as '... he then let the dear hawk fly from his hands towards the wood' is inevitable. But to the Anglo-Saxon hearer – for whom, I believe, the poetry was recited more slowly than in most modern readings (a point often made verbally by J. R. R. Tolkien) – the effect was probably something more like '... he let from him then from hands the dear one fly – hawk towards the wood'. Here, I would argue, the modern reader misses the excitement of the momentary riddle – 'the dear what?' – which the Anglo-Saxon hearer would have experienced. So, to take two very simple illustrations, there would have been a cumulative effect in *Beo* l. 1197

> Nænigne ic under swegle   sēlran hȳrde
> hordmāðum hæleþa,   syþðan Hāma ætwæg
> tō *þǣ*re byrhtan byrig   Brōsinga mene,
> sigle ond sincfæt,

'None ... none better ... none better hoarded gem of heroes ...' and in *Beo* l. 1484

> Mæg þonne on þǣm golde ongitan   Gēata dryhten,
> gesēon sunu Hrǣdles,   þonne hē on þæt sinc staráð,
> þæt ic gumcystum   gōdne funde
> bēaga bryttan,   brēac þonne mōste

'... in munificence liberal ... a dispenser of rings ...'. In such places, I would suggest the use of a symbol familiar to hymn singers, viz.   , at the end of each half-line or line (except the last) which contains one of these elements. But I recognize that over-use of this symbol would be most undesirable; see IV. 21.

19   The difficulty of striking the proper balance between helpful guidance of, and brutal interference with, a reader's responses means that attempts to mark off poetic variations by special devices are likely to be self-defeating. The class-

room and the tutorial chair are places for explaining the technique of repetition with variation and advance seen in a simple form in *Mald* l. 113

> Wund wearð Wulfmær, wælræste geceas,
> Byrhtnoðes mæg; he mid billum wearð,
> his swuster sunu, swiðe forheawen,

where the first half-line summarizes what follows, the remaining *a*-lines bring Wulfmær closer to Byrhtnoð, and the three *b*-lines expand on *Wund*. This technique once led J. R. R. Tolkien to picture the Anglo-Saxon poet as a man filling in (half-)lines with blocks of different colours: he saw, in the words of *Ex* l. 43, *hleahtorsmiðum handa*. Stanley remarks that

> some sentence structures require marking off by commas in modern practice, especially phrases or clauses thrust into the middle of a structural unit and felt to be separable from it. Vocatives (e.g. 429, 2000), interjected prayers (e.g. 435), interposed explanations (e.g. 706, 967, 2550), or other inclusions (e.g. 731, 1508, 2124, 2855) are punctuated by the editors as they would be in Modern English; and though poetic variation has no commonly occurring counterpart in Modern English, it is near enough to the concept of adjuncts (appositional, or seriate in other ways) to be punctuated similarly, that is, marked off by commas.[78]

Fred C. Robinson makes a similar point in his valuable article 'Two Aspects of Variation in Old English Poetry', which (to reapply his own words) I recommend as 'a helpful guide to understanding the stylistic intentions in a body of poetry for which we have no *ars poetica* and no Skáldskaparmál':[79]

My own definition, which is a respectful modification of that proposed by Walther Paetzel in his treatise *Die Variationen in der altgermanischen Allitterationspoesie* (Berlin 1913), is as follows: 'syntactically parallel words or word-groups which share a common referent and which occur within a single clause (or, in the instance of sentence-variation, within contiguous clauses).' Simply stated, I regard variation as apposition (Sweet's old term), if apposition be extended to include restatements of adjectives, verbs, and phrases as well as of nouns and pronouns.[80]

My aim is similar to that expressed by Robinson – to help modern readers to appreciate the intricacies and charms of a new medium. My suggestions for the punctuation of OE poetry arise, as I have said, from my conviction that by using modern punctuation an editor not only runs the risk of imposing on a poem one particular interpretation but also creates a rigid and alien syntactical structure

[78] *Pope Studies*, p. 146. The line references are to *Beowulf*.
[79] *Calder Essays*, p. 145.
[80] *Calder Essays*, p. 129.

by eliminating options and blurring alternative connexions and associations which were present in the poem created by the poet. Modern punctuation produces modern sentences. In my opinion, the unit of OE poetry was the verse paragraph. There is room for more work here. But my conviction that the poetry moved in paragraphs – which is based on my reading of it – derives some support from Krapp's observation that the small capitals in the Junius Manuscript are 'most frequently . . . logical and mark the beginning of a minor division in the narrative, that is, of a paragraph'.[81]

20   To meet the obvious challenge, I end my consideration of the poetry by presenting two short passages punctuated according to my system. First, *Mald* l. 4

> . . .   and to hige godum.
> þa þæt Offan mæg   ærest onfunde
> þæt se eorl nolde   yrhðo geþolian,,[82]
> he let him þa of handon   leofne fleogan
> hafoc wið þæs holtes   and to þære hilde stop,,
> be þam man mihte oncnawan   þæt se cniht nolde
> wacian æt þam wige   þa he to wæpnum feng.

Then *Mald* l. 161

> . . .   and gerenod swurd.
> þa Byrhtnoð bræd   bill of sceðe
> brad and brunecg   and on þa byrnan sloh,,[83]
> to raþe hine gelette   lidmanna sum
> ← þa he þæs eorles   earm amyrde →
> feoll þa to foldan   fealohilte swurd →[84]
> ne mihte he gehealdan   heardne mece,
> wæpnes wealdan.

---

[81] ASPR i. xx.
[82] In this passage, the first *þa* clause gives both a result of what the poet has just told us and something approaching a cause of what follows. In effect, *þa* means both 'then' and 'when'. Hence the double commas.
[83] Again the *þa* clause gives both a result of what the poet has just told us and something approaching a cause of what follows. In effect, *þa* means both 'then' and 'when'. Hence the double commas.
[84] The arrow → here indicates that *Mald* l. 166 expresses the result of *Mald*. l. 167 as well as the result of *Mald* l. 165. The footnote numbers would not be part of my text except when, as here, the system was being explained.

IV. Conclusion

21 Obviously this paper leaves a lot of loose ends. The double commas („), the broken marks of parenthesis (– – . . . – –), and the *apo koinou* arrows (← . . . →), might find a place in some editions of prose texts and in editions of poems intended for modern readers at all levels. The symbol would, I think, be restricted to verse texts intended for beginners and would be used in perhaps only the first and second poems they were to read and/or in places in which an editor thought it important to draw the reader's attention to a particular example of 'enjambment of sense'. The question of whether any distinction should be made between manuscript and editorial stops and capitals remains to be considered. Those having difficulty in knowing what and what not to put in inverted commas should study the use of italics made by Dunning and Bliss in *The Wanderer*. The extent to which clauses, phrases, appositional groups, vocative expressions, and the like, should be marked off will of course be an editorial decision. But I should be inclined to err on the side of light rather than heavy stopping.

22 I agree that the problems presented by prose and by poetry are different. I agree that each individual manuscript and/or text may demand individual treatment. A criticism which has been levelled against me is that it is an editor's task to make decisions. I agree that it is. But why should we acclaim as responsible a modern editor of an OE text who decides to put a full stop or a comma before an ambiguous adverb/conjunction or demonstrative/relative? He is responsible only for misleading his readers. We would rightly laugh at any scholar who decided that Bede's *Historia* is a television documentary, that *Beowulf* is a film script, or that *Apollonius of Tyre* was intended for radio presentation. Is it any less ridiculous for a modern scholar to pretend that OE texts are suited by modern punctuation? Editorial responsibility? I would argue that it is irresponsible for an editor to pretend that he has the evidence on which to base a decision when he has not. To do so seems to me to dictate and distort in a way which is beyond an editor's duty or right.

Perhaps someone would like to experiment with a new edition, say of *The Battle of Maldon*, incorporating (some of) my suggestions. Perhaps some wealthy institution might think it worth while to sponsor a conference on 'The Punctuation of Old English Texts'. (I should be delighted to suggest desirable venues.) Meanwhile, I conclude with the reminder that this paper is meant to be suggestive rather than prescriptive, exploratory rather than polemic, and with the observation that, while I acknowledge that many are likely to disagree with much of what I have said, none can disagree with the statement that, whatever the *Beowulf* poet meant when he said in Beo 1. 870 *word ōþer fand / sōðe gebunden*, he did not mean that Anglo-Saxon poets, *scops*, or scribes, used modern punctuation.

CODA 1987

To my regret, this paper seems to have sunk without a ripple in the ocean – or pond – of OE literary criticism. I note in particular that it does not appear in the Bibliography of Works Cited in *A New Critical History of Old English Literature* by Stanley B. Greenfield and Daniel G. Calder *With a Survey of the Anglo-Latin Background* by Michael Lapidge (New York and London, 1986). But this is perhaps not surprising in view of the absence of the word 'punctuation' from the Index thereof. Fred C. Robinson and I did not think that the 4th edition of *A Guide to Old English* (Oxford, 1986) was the place to introduce such radical and such untested ideas, although we did include 'A Note on the Punctuation of Old English Poetry' (pp. 281–4). As I said in my Conclusion (IV. 21–2 above), I am sure that I have not solved the problem. But when I think of the conferences that have been held since I wrote in 1980 and the time that has been devoted at them to topics in my opinion of less fundamental significance than the punctuation of OE texts, I can only conclude that I am a prophet preaching in a wilderness of my own imagining.[84a]

[84a] [1988. With the book at press, I add a reference to pp. 339–40 of my Conclusion.]

19
The Syntax of *The Seafarer*, Lines 50-52

1 In Anglo-Saxon Poetic Records iii, these difficult lines read:

> ealle þa gemoniað   modes fusne
> sefan to siþe,   þam þe swa þenceð
> on flodwegas   feor gewitan.

It is obvious that *ealle þa* is the subject of *gemoniað* and that *modes fusne* is its object. It seems necessary to accept the emendation of MS *gewitað* in l. 52 to *gewitan*; the error is easily explained by the sequence of six verb forms in -(i)að and two in -eð in the preceding five lines. The phrase *to siþe* means 'to a journey'. The only syntactical difficulty about the words *swa þenceð/on flodwegas feor gewitan* can be expressed in the question 'What is the subject of *þenceð*?' Possible answers will be offered below.

2 But the remaining words or phrases are more difficult:

   a *sefan* can be accusative singular, parallel to *fusne*, or genitive singular, parallel to *modes*, or dative singular;
   b the relative combination *þam þe*, in which the dative *þam* must in my opinion be taken as singular and *þe* is, of course, indeclinable, can be – in theory –
      (i) an example of the *'seþe* relative, in which both elements have the case required by the adjective clause, as in *Genesis A* l. 138

> Him arn on last,
> þrang þystre genip,   þam þe se þeoden self
> sceop nihte naman;

      (ii) an example of the *seþe* relative, in which the *se* element has the case of the principal clause and *þe* the case of the adjective clause, as in *Genesis A* l. 150

Reprinted from the *Review of English Studies* 36 (1985), 535-7.

> Flod wæs adæled
> under heahrodore   halgum mihtum,
> wæter of wætrum,   þam þe wuniað gyt
> under fæstenne   folca hrofes;

(iii) an example of the *seþe* relative, in which both clauses require the same case, as in *Daniel* l. 33

> þa wearð reðemod   rices ðeoden,
> unhold þeodum þam þe æhte geaf;

(iv) an example of the *þe* relative, with *þam* as antecedent.

3   Let us first consider the role of *sefan*:

a   if it is accusative, *sefan* is parallel to *fusne* and we translate 'all these things urge [the man] eager of spirit, [urge] the mind to a journey . . .';
b   if it is genitive, *sefan* is either
  (i)   parallel to *modes* and we translate 'all these things urge [the man] eager of spirit, of mind, to a journey . . .'; or
  (ii) a genitive of possession 'to a journey of the mind'. I know of no firm parallels for this pattern – see my *Old English Syntax*[1] – and regard it as unlikely;
c   if it is dative, *sefan* can, as far as I can see, be taken only as a dative of interest, shading into possession, dependent on *to siþe* 'to a journey for the mind'; compare the well-attested idiom seen in *Beowulf* l. 1961 *hæleðum to helpe*.

4   In what ways can the relative combination *þam þe* be construed to give grammatical sense in this passage?

a   If its antecedent is the dative *siþe*, it can be the *seþe* relative 'to a journey by which [unexpressed subject] thinks . . .';
b   if its antecedent is *sefan* in the dative, it can be the *seþe* relative 'to a journey for the mind which [nominative] thinks . . .';
c   Gordon[2] takes it as *þam* + the *þe* relative, translating 'All these things urge [the man] eager of spirit, [urge] the heart to the journey, in one who thinks to venture far on the paths of the sea.' I would say that, as Gordon prints it, with a comma after 'journey', this is probably untenable. First, it is not clear whether the man or the heart is to journey – a vital consideration; see 8 below. Second, the accusative *fusne* and the dative *þam* have the same referent and the sequence 'the man . . . in one who' makes no sense. If the two go together, one would expect *þone þe* –

[1] (Oxford, 1985), §1355.   [2] *The Seafarer* (London, 1960), p. 40.

the *seþe* relative agreeing with *fusne* – 'the man who'; it is interesting to note that both Grein and Rieger suggested *þone*.³ With the comma after 'journey' removed, so that the adjective clause has no reference to *fusne*, Gordon's version is syntactically more tolerable and can probably be accepted by those who think that the man is to journey. But I am suspicious about *þam þe* '*in* one who' and would find 'for one who' more in accord with Old English idiom;

d I can think of no way of construing *þam þe* as the *'seþe* relative in this passage, for I can find no possible antecedent in any case other than the dative which would provide sense.

5 Putting all this together, we are left with these possible interpretations of *Seafarer* ll. 50–2:

a that of Gordon discussed and translated in 4(c) above, where the man thinks to journey;
b that discussed in 4(b) above – 'All these things urge [the man] eager of spirit to a journey for the mind which thus thinks to venture far on the paths of the sea' – where the mind thinks to journey;
c that discussed in 4(a) above, where an unexpressed subject thinks to journey. There are two possibilities here, set out in 6 below;
d that discussed in 7 below.

6 For the justification for understanding a subject in a subordinate clause from the governing principal clause, compare *Daniel* l. 33 (2 above) and see my *Old English Syntax* §1510. In this context, the unexpressed subject could be

a *he* = *sefa*, in which event the mind thinks to journey – an explanation already available in 5(b);
b *he* = *modes fus*, in which event the man thinks to journey – an explanation already available in 5(a) but to my mind expressed here in more convincing Old English syntax.

7 The only one of these explanations in which *sefan* is not construed as dative (3(c) above) is 5(a), in which it is taken as accusative (3(a) above). If we take *sefan* as genitive (3(b) above), we seem bound to complete the translation by reading 'to a journey by which he [the man] thinks to venture ...' (3(b)(i)).

8 As far as I can see, this exhausts the syntactical possibilities. We thus have three explanations in which the man thinks to journey – 5(a), 6(b), and 3(b) with 7 – and two in which the mind thinks to journey – 5(b) and 6(a). Whether a

³ Anglo-Saxon Poetic Records iii. 296, note to l. 51.

mind can think or journey cannot be decided on syntactical grounds. But the presence of *swa* does not rule out either the man or the mind as the traveller, for it can refer back to a physical journey (ll. 1–47), which is also mentioned in ll. 55–7, or forward to a journey of the mind (ll. 58–64).[4] Here, acknowledging with gratitude help in conversation and private communications from Christopher Ball and Malcolm Godden, I propose to leave the reader of the poem to choose that interpretation which suits him best.

[4] Bruce Mitchell *NM* 69 (1968), 175–8 [item 12. II above].

20
Reviews

(a) *The Wanderer* ed. R. F. Leslie (Old and Middle English Texts), Manchester: University Press, 1966*

This book is welcome as (almost unbelievably) 'the first separate edition of this favourite anthology piece'. Syntactical points demand first comment:

1. Why does the *þeah þe* clause (l. 2) imply 'fulfilment rather than expectation' in *gebideð* (p. 65)?
2. 'There is no clear evidence that it [*swa*] can point exclusively forward' (p. 3). What of examples like *Panther* l. 69? (But the problem should be formulated differently.)
3. Since the preterite is often used as a perfect, *sceolde* (l. 8) does not certify that 'the wanderer's troubles are over', while, in view of *ana* (l. 8), the adverb *nu* (l. 9) can bear interpretations other than Mr Leslie's (pp. 4–5).
4. Since dependent questions after *gemunan* sometimes have subjunctive verbs, *wenede* does not certify *goldwine* (l. 35) as 'unambiguously singular' (p. 69).
5. *Beowulf* ll. 798 ff. with anticipatory *þæt* supports the suggested construction after *wat* (l. 37) (pp. 72–3). Could *Wanderer* ll. 29–33 be similarly explained?
6. *Swa* (l. 43) gives sense as conjunction 'as' or adverb 'so'; there is neither support nor need for the meaning 'as when' (p. 75), either here or in *Andreas* ll. 926–7.
7. *þonne, beoð,* and *bið*, in ll. 49 ff. also support MS *oft* (l. 53).
8. Can the present subjunctive *gesweorce* (l. 59) bear the meanings suggested by Mr Leslie and Mrs Gordon (p. 79)?
9. In *Wanderer* ll. 58 ff. and *Christ and Satan* ll. 642 ff. *geond þas woruld(e)* could belong to the following noun clause. Is the alliteration on *þas* as significant as Mr Leslie argues (p. 80)?
10. Does *to* (ll. 66 ff.) necessarily imply that 'the value of moderation' is

* Reprinted from the *Review of English Studies* 18 (1967), 104. Most of the points made here are discussed in items 12–14 above.

being stressed (p. 13)? The Wulfstan passages cited (p. 13, n. 1) give dubious support. Could this be meiosis?
11 The punctuation of ll. 37–57 is not final.
12 Mr Leslie's notes on l. 39 and l. 103b suggest that word-order in poetry is syntactically decisive. This seems to me wrong. The order Verb–Subject does not prove that a clause is principal – see *Beowulf* l. 2544b – nor is a clause with final verb necessarily subordinate; see *Wanderer* ll. 1 and 62b–3 (where Mr Leslie's punctuation offends against his own dictum). The initial position of *niþeð* (l. 102) does not prove that its clause is syntactically linked with l. 103b; cf. *Wanderer* ll. 29, 32, 34, 78, 85, 97, and 107.

The Introduction contains much valuable material and some acute observations. Mr Leslie makes a good case for believing that the poem as transmitted is a textual and structural unit. It would be dangerous if this unity were accepted as a proven firm base for all future criticism, but the view that Christian elements are present even in the so-called pagan sections of the poem demands careful consideration. However, one sometimes wonders whether *The Wanderer* was really as complex and ingenious as modern critics suggest; consider Mr Leslie's phrase 'This calculated ambiguity . . .' (p. 14).

It is unfortunate that space permits no more than this catalogue of curtly expressed criticisms, for the book maintains the standard of the series.

(b) *Sweet's Anglo-Saxon Reader in Prose and Verse* (15th edn) revised throughout by Dorothy Whitelock, Oxford: Clarendon Press, 1967*

Admirers of Henry Sweet's *Anglo-Saxon Reader* will find much to praise in the latest revision of 'this classic work'. It is carefully and accurately produced – the few misprints noted include 'its' for 'it' (p. vii, l. 9), xxxiv for xxxv (p. x, l. 2), 'Smetano' for 'Smetana' (p. 249, ll. 22 and 24), and '10/139' for '10/129' (p. 370, l. 2 right). The abandonment in the Glossary of the normalized early West Saxon forms (p. viii) removes one major source of irritation, though some may wish when they see entries such as '*nēosan (ēa)*' that the weak verbs had been marked and the glossing of *ferþ-loca* as simply 'breast' seems inadequate. Some undergraduates have wanted more cross-referencing of variant spellings. One wonders whether Sweet's reasons for not giving them still hold. It can scarcely be maintained today that 'this is not a book for beginners'.

The expansion of the Notes and the abandonment of Dr Onions's immoderate reverence for 'Sweet's views and practice in this matter' will be welcomed.

* Reprinted from the *Review of English Studies* 19 (1968), 415–16. This review gave the Oxford University Press a glimpse of a blueprint of the fourth edition of Bruce Mitchell and Fred C. Robinson *A Guide to Old English*, published by Basil Blackwell in 1986.

It may seem ungracious to complain when such a real advance has been made. Yet there are times when even more comment might have been judicious or helpful. Thus it is twice said that Bede thought that Cædmon had no predecessors in composing religious poetry (p. 45 and p. 242). There is more to it than that, and one might have expected the citation of Professor C. L. Wrenn's article on Cædmon (p. 242) to be followed by references to the comments of objectors. The same is true of the note on piece XXI, l. 89. The observation in the note to piece X, l. 33 that *mē āht singan* is 'the reading in T' may surprise those who have observed the absence of length marks and gaps in the manuscript and may mislead those who have not; cf. p. 46, n. 11. The unhelpful and (I believe) misleading note on piece III E, l. 35 by Onions is reproduced, as is the similar one on piece XX, l. 216 by Sweet; cf. that on piece IV, l. 154 (also by Onions) and AV John 13. 27 'That thou doest, do quickly.' The notes on *hryre* and *ferð* (piece XXVI) could have been more explicit.

Inevitably there is room for comment on points of detail. In piece IV, l. 146, the second *tō þǣm* is taken to mean 'moreover' (so Onions, based on Sweet's note). It seems to me more likely to repeat the first; cf. *swā clǣne gold ne swā rēad* (l. 111 of the old piece XIII). T's reading is accepted in piece X, l. 73. But the weak form *seolfan* is suspicious in this position and the passage in l. 17 cited in the note is not parallel. In piece XX, l. 375, *þǣre* might be expected. But I do not quite see why it 'is required'. On the proposed rendering of the runic version of piece XXV, l. 58a, see now M. Rissanen.[1] The reasons for retaining certain inherited emendations could perhaps have been explained, e.g. piece XXI, l. 47 *ǣttrene*, piece XXII, l. 132 *hafað*, and piece XXVI, l. 23 *heolster* (cf. *Beowulf* l. 470). Some of the new ones may not compel universal acceptance, e.g. piece XXI, l. 190 *þēh*.[2] It is not immediately clear why, in piece XXV, the reading of the Ruthwell Cross is retained in l. 63a *hine* but rejected in l. 58a *tō þām ǣðelinge*.

The fuller textual apparatus is forbidding for the student whose interests are primarily literary. Is it full enough for the student wishing 'to study the transmission of a text'? Can one book serve two masters? What is its aim? Professor Whitelock writes: 'The popularity of Sweet's *Anglo-Saxon Reader* through fourteen editions is evidence that in its general conception it has won approval, and hence the present revision makes few alterations in the choice of texts.' So the ghost of Henry Sweet still stands in the background (I quote from the 7th edition): 'In its present form, therefore, the object of this book is to put before the student who has already mastered the Primer, a series of texts which will give a general knowledge of the language in its chief periods and dialects, without neglecting the interests of literary and antiquarian study....' Do most of its users today really aim to acquire such a knowledge? Can the book serve these ends without neglecting literature? And could the 'popularity' of the book be

[1] *The Uses of* One *in Old and Early Middle English* (Helsinki, 1967), p. 317.
[2] Bruce Mitchell *Neophilologus* 49 (1965), 48.

due more to the absence of many serious rivals at a comparatively low price than to general approval of the choice of texts? The historian and the student of Old English dialects seem to get more consideration than the reader interested in the literature. In these days when the place of Old English in University courses is so much under attack, some may think that there is a good case for more drastic changes in the texts provided or perhaps even for a completely new work designed as a literary anthology. Given Miss Whitelock's aims, the alterations in the chosen texts are unexceptionable. But the inclusion of poems such as *The Battle of Brunanburh*, *The Ruin*, *Deor*, *Wulf*, *The Husband's Message*, and *The Wife's Lament* (either by increasing the size of the book or, if necessary, by omitting the extract from *Beowulf* which is, I should imagine, rarely used), would have suggested that those interested in the literature had been given due consideration.

So in the mind of one user of the book a major doubt remains: was it wise to revise? Is Sweet's *Anglo-Saxon Reader* a vital post to be heroically defended or an ancient fortress better excavated? There can, however, be no doubt that within its own terms of reference the 15th edition of Sweet's *Anglo-Saxon Reader* remains a *cité of noble defens*, worthy to stand proudly beside its predecessors.

(c) *Old English Poetry. Fifteen Essays* ed. Robert P. Creed, Providence: Brown University Press, 1967*

This collection of essays, in the editor's words, 'celebrates two institutions: Brown University on the occasion of its two hundredth birthday and Old English poetry'. Dedicated to the proposition that 'it is the poetry that counts', it illustrates various approaches and sometimes offers differing conclusions – a happy reminder that in many problems of Old English poetry we lack so much vital evidence that there is no excuse for the dogmatism we not infrequently find. Indeed, it may appear to some that, when there is so much important lexicographical and syntactical work to be done, there are certain topics on which speculation or conjectural re-interpretation of agreed basic facts might profitably be banned for a quarter of a century or so.

The essays fall into three divisions: Part One: 'The Harp and Old English Poetry'; Part Two: '*Genesis* and Shorter Old English Poetry'; Part Three: '*Beowulf*'. In Part One, Jess B. Bessinger, Jr's suggestive essay on the Sutton Hoo Harp and Old English Musical Verse makes one envy those who have been fortunate enough to hear his working model of the harp replica. John Nist launches a sharp attack on J. C. Pope's theory of the rhythm of *Beowulf* and offers one of his own (admittedly 'hypothetical at best') – the poem has sixteen

---

* Reprinted from the *Review of English Studies* 21 (1970), 185–6.

basic cadences and its dipodic rhythm depends on the accompaniment of a functional, not a decorative, harp.

Part Two has six essays. Alain Renoir writes helpfully on *Genesis B*, though the remark that the Old Saxon original was 'presumably composed by the author of the *Heliand*' perpetuates the kind of criticism which strives to identify the Hengest of *Beowulf* with the Hengest of the Chronicle entry for 449. In the course of his comparison of the three versions of the Offering of Isaac, Robert P. Creed makes some good points. The significance of his remarks about *Genesis A* l. 2887b should not be overlooked. Although the basic concept of the identification of Dreamer, Cross, and Christ, is not new, Louis H. Leiter's analysis of *The Dream of the Rood* offers some fruitful suggestions and confirms the poem's stature. The question mark in the phrase 'his death being *pearle þenian* "violently extended [?]"' seems more than justified. J. E. Cross of Liverpool offers Brown its sole tribute from the United Kingdom in the shape of his article 'The Conception of the Old English *Phoenix*', in which he argues strongly that the poem is an 'effective medieval homily on the Phoenix' which presents a four-fold interpretation of a real and scriptural bird – historical, tropological, anagogical, and typological. Edward B. Irving, Jr's 'hints and guesses' frequently illuminate the Elegies he discusses. But a few more examples might have been given of the pattern 'so consistently ... carried out' in *The Ruin* and I remain unconvinced that ll. 65–9 of *The Wanderer* contain 'precepts of temperance, self-control, and nothing too much'. George K. Anderson, the present incumbent of the Chair of Anglo-Saxon at Brown, makes some interesting points about the *Leiden Riddle* in an article which concludes Part Two.

The seven articles of Part Three deal with *Beowulf*. Adrien Bonjour argues with authority against F. P. Magoun, Jr's view that *Beowulf* is of composite origin and at the same time further illustrates the artistry of the poem. But the nods of approval from 'the supporters of unity of authorship in *Beowulf*' will no doubt be greeted by counter-arguments from the 'neodisintegrators of the text of the poem'. Larry D. Benson summarizes his main point with another of his idol-toppling titles – 'The Pagan Coloring of *Beowulf*' – in the course of which he opens some important lines of thought. Yet it may seem to some that behind his article lies a rather too easy acceptance of A. G. Brodeur's unserviceable simplification that *Beowulf* was 'composed in an effectively converted England'. Neil D. Isaacs's observations about personification in *Beowulf* do not always convince. His discussions sometimes seem to confuse rather than to clarify textual problems, and sometimes seem a little over-elaborate. Mr Isaacs warns us of 'the pejorative connotations of "merely ... a traditional association"'. However, that over-enthusiasm and over-ingenuity also have their dangers is illustrated by his article and by the next, in which Paul Beekman Taylor has some good points on the use of 'formulae' and 'themes' in *Beowulf*, but sometimes seems too determined to make everything fit, e.g. ll. 1522-4 (Beowulf did not die in this fight) and l. 512 (this is the first use in *Beowulf* of a 'theme' apparently used only there (p. 264). Would the audience have caught all the implications Mr Taylor detects?). Stanley B. Greenfield's analysis of *Beowulf* ll. 702b-36a contains many good things, but naturally does not say everything. Thus, while the statement that ll. 710-19 focus 'exclusively on Grendel's movements and motivations' is in one sense true, it conceals the fact that, if we take the third of the three passages heralded by *com* as extending from ll. 720-38, each of them contains the same four elements in the same order – Grendel, the hall, a comment by the poet, and reference to the fate in store for Grendel. R. E. Kaske seeks to eliminate the Jutes from *Beowulf* and certainly gives one cause 'furiously to think', with his claim that 'my total argument, while it by no means eliminates the possibility of the rendering "Jutes" in these five instances, does seem to me to speak rather for the probability of the rendering "giants"', and with his suggestion that 'this whole arrangement seems to point toward a deliberate manipulation of the word *eoten* by the poet'. Burton Raffel brings the book to a refreshing end with some sensitive observations about problems involved in translating *Beowulf* and some amusing tilts at other translators.

Inevitably the essays differ in value. But each one is worth reading for the stimulus it will offer, whether one agrees, disagrees, or thinks the writer just plain wrong. On behalf of the book the reviewer (who spent a happy year at Brown in 1966-7) may make the claim that the contributors to this pleasantly produced tribute have certainly served Brown University better than its football team did in that bicentennial year.

(d) *The Guest-Hall of Eden. Four Essays on the Design of Old English Poetry* by Alvin A. Lee, New Haven and London: Yale University Press, 1972*

As I read it, this book attempts to carry us further along the road to a pan-allegorical interpretation of Old English poetry (pp. 228ff.). It is only fair to say that I am unsympathetic. It is also fair to say that Mr Lee has discussed some of the objections which follow. But to discuss them is not necessarily to dispose of them.

Mr Lee gets down to the poems.[1] He offers some useful observations about the proper concerns of Old English literary critics (e.g. pp. 74-5), and some sensitive and illuminating criticism, though he sometimes seems inconsistent,

* Reprinted from the *Review of English Studies* 24 (1973), 195-6.

[1] Many readers will doubtless welcome 'the relatively light documentation' (p. 5, n. 3). But this public-spirited decision has its dangers. To take one instance: is the explanation of the last refrain in *Deor* (pp. 166-7) Mr Lee's or Mr Markland's (*MP* 66 (1968-9), 1-4)?

e.g. about Satan (pp. 22, 60, and 119), and sometimes takes disputed ideas for granted, e.g. 'the ingrate Hrothulf' (p. 190). But the literary criticism is in a sense incidental and is made to serve what seems to me a Procrustean purpose, sometimes not without special pleading, e.g. the statement on pp. 193-4 that Part 2 of *Beowulf* is full of 'Cain figures' (was Heardred 'murdered by Onela'?) which enables him to claim that 'human murder is now presented in a narrative context' (p. 215).

Mr Lee's purpose seems to be to establish the proposition that after Cædmon

> a new kind of verse was to take its impetus from religious themes, with the purpose of moving the hearts of many men to despise the world and to aspire toward heavenly things. Each particular song was to be thought of as part of a total pattern already set down in scripture, in what literary critics would now call the Christian mythology (p. 3)

and

> to explore some of the ways in which the Christian mythology outlined by Bede appears to have inspired and shaped a large and central portion of extant Old English poetry – to have provided, in fact, an imaginative context that altered fundamentally the poetic uses of the traditional 'word-hoard' inherited from a Germanic past. (p. 3)

As Mr Lee clearly states, not all Old English poems conform; he does not mention *The Charms* or *The Riddles*, nor does his 'total pattern' embrace *Finnesburh* or *Brunanburh*. But his remark about 'the variety and comprehensiveness of what remains' (p. 7) seems to cloak the assumption that all types of Old English poetry are represented in the extant lines. He postulates a 'relative underemphasis... on the "humanity" of Jesus in Old English poetry' (p. 59) and produces a reason for it (p. 58). But an OE *Heliand* may well have been lost. That '*Beowulf* is unique' (p. 175) is more likely due to accidents of Time than to a once-for-all poetic event. So some at least of the 'fresh insights' afforded by assuming 'a hypothetical principle of unity in our approach to the poetic canon' (p. 6) may be misleading.

Indeed the 'feeling that the unifying and recurrent structural aspects of the group of poems under discussion are being stressed at the expense of differences of detail and texture' (p. 4) is often a strong one; see, e.g. pp. 81 and 15–16 (where he almost admits it himself), pp. 163–4 (where a poet may be unconsciously guided by a model), and p. 221 (could it be that 'the contempt-of-the-world theme' is absent from *Beowulf* rather than 'kept in restraint'?). A pattern seems to be imposed on the poets too – indeed on all the Anglo-Saxons, for 'Anglo-Saxon man thinks of himself as a creature of God with a rational soul ...' (p. 227). Not only 'an effectively converted England', as Brodeur has it; a uniformly converted one too, despite the remarks on p. 6!

Mr Lee speaks of 'an established Old English language of [Christian] mythological symbols' (p. 152). Which came first: the word-hoard or the myth? He gives what is obviously the right answer – the former (pp. 3, 136, and 227). Equally rightly, he points out that many of the images acquired 'symbolic meanings derived from traditional typology' (p. 44). It is not a corollary of this that they lost their original simple meanings. Yet one sometimes gets the impression that Mr Lee thinks this. The imagery, he claims, brings within his 'total pattern' poems like *Wulf, The Wife's Lament, The Husband's Message,* and *Deor* (p. 156), *Fates* (p. 73), *Andreas* (pp. 87ff.), possibly *The Ruin* (p. 153), and *Beowulf* (pp. 171ff.). Hrothgar is Adam, Wealhþeow is Eve, Beowulf is Christ (p. 198). But has the time irrevocably gone when a ruin can be just a ruin (p. 153), Weland just Weland (p. 162), a ship just a ship (p. 199), and a prayer just a prayer (p. 118)? Are we bound to believe that everything in *Beowulf* 'that lacks an exemplary model is meaningless and devoid of reality' (p. 206)? May it not be just as unwise to believe that repeated (half-)lines must carry the same associations as to believe that they must be borrowings (pp. 197, 210, and 215)?[2] Is polarization inevitable – *The Charms, The Riddles, Finnesburh,* and *Brunanburh* on the one side, and all other surviving poems on the other? Is there no room for a rather bumbling *Andreas* poet, as opposed to 'a serious, sometimes almost witty' one (p. 85), or for a rather hesitantly converted Wanderer?

Despite all this and a few minor oddities, such as the reference to 'King Alfred's Late West Saxon version' of Bede (p. 2, n. 2), the book gives some valuable 'fresh insights' (p. 6). I am grateful to Mr Lee, but sadly aware that his sympathizers may hear in this review only the despairing voice of Naivety facing the Dragon of sophisticated criticism; as the *Beowulf* poet puts it:

> Let ða of breostum,   ða he gebolgen wæs,
> Weder-Geata leod   word ut faran,
> stearcheort styrmde.

But I would like to think of that voice *heaðotorht hlynnan under harne stan.*

(e) *The Interpretation of Old English Poems* by Stanley B. Greenfield, Boston and London: Routledge & Kegan Paul, 1972*

Here Mr Greenfield demonstrates anew what has long been known: that he is a sensitive and illuminating critic of Old English literature. Each chapter contains valuable observations on individual passages, and chapter 6, 'Generic

* Reprinted from the *Review of English Studies* 24 (1973), 319–21.

[2] The question of semantic change in Old English under Christian influence is well discussed by D. H. Green (*MLR* 63 (1968), 392–406) in an extended review of E. S. Dick *Ae. dryht und seine Sippe* (Münster, 1965). Mr Lee mentions neither – a strange omission in view of the importance to his argument of the word *dryht*.

Expectations and the Quest for Allegory', gives a much-needed blast against the selectivity, circularity, and rigidity of some allegorical interpretations of Old English poems.[1]

The book, he says (p. ix), is 'an effort to produce a "handbook" for Old English critics and students, to indicate procedures that offer, in my judgment, the best hope for valid insights into the meaning of Old English poems.... The interpretation of Old English *poems* – not *poetry* [his italics].' However, some readers are bound to wonder whether he has chosen the best method. There is much for *critics* (including a lot from other critics), but much that is forbidding to *students* – Mr Greenfield is not sure himself whether he has got very far in chapter 1, 'Towards a Critical Framework' (pp. 27–8), and the argument in chapter 3, 'The Uses of Variation', sometimes seems to topple into the terminological (e.g. pp. 64 and 73–4). Worse – despite the last sentence quoted above – there is a swamping of the *poems*. Mr Greenfield considers excerpts mostly already discussed – note the list of reworked articles on pp. ix–x – and inevitably chosen to demonstrate a particular point. Detailed consideration of a few poems and a concluding summary might have been more effective.

In chapter 2, 'Expectations and Implications in Diction and Formula', Mr Greenfield despairingly doubts 'whether an adequate description of the language as a whole will ultimately be the saving grace in our assessment of the value of a particular poetic usage' (p. 39). Yet he is often willing enough to make use of existing 'descriptions'. But not always. Thus, in his discussion of *Beowulf* ll. 3180–2 (pp. 39–43), he fails to mention three examples of *milde ond monðwære* recorded by Bosworth-Toller. He would probably reply that, being later than *Beowulf*, they are irrelevant (see p. 42). To whose 'meaning'? On p. 133, we are told that we must consider 'both present and historical meaning'. Should this not rather be 'meanings'? As Mr Greenfield – unlike some other writers – recognizes (pp. 9, 37, 154), individual responses differed in an Anglo-Saxon audience, as they do today. And the variety of attitudes possible in an eighth-century audience would differ from that in a tenth-century or modern one. Mr Greenfield further observes (p. 39) that 'such total information as we can obtain may even ... be misleading'. This is no reason against acquiring it, but the danger seems demonstrated at pp. 45–51, where he offends (I believe) against the principles he enunciates on p. 18; is there any reason why the seventh use of the phrase *folces hyrde* must conform in syntax and meaning to the other six, especially when the example in question comes just before *Finnsburh* breaks off? This illustrates one vital principle Mr Greenfield does not express: in our present state of knowledge, arguments that something need not be so can be

---

[1] But I hope to show elsewhere that Mr Greenfield's linguistic reasons for suggesting that Mr Cross was wrong to see a moral or tropological level of allegory in *The Phoenix* are not conclusive. [1987. This discussion forms part of a lecture 'Old English Poetry: Garden or Compost-Heap?', as yet unpublished.]

conclusive (e.g. those against limiting *lofgeornost* to a bad meaning (pp. 39–43)) but arguments that something must be so are rarely conclusive (e.g. is there any reason why a rune-stave should not have been rubbed smooth and re-used (p. 150)?).

Mr Greenfield keeps his promise to return to the question of the value – or rather the dangers? – of 'an adequate description of the language as a whole' (p. 39) in chapter 5, 'Verse Form, Syntax and Meaning'. At the risk of appearing to yield to personal irritation, I must describe what he says at pp. 118–19 as – unhappy. Briefly (1) '... statistically there is very little difference between one example and none'. What about the *Abominable Snowman and the *Loch Ness Monster? (2) Whether *goldwine* in *Wanderer* l. 22 is singular or plural is a matter of choosing between two obvious possibilities. It is quite a different thing from translating *swa* in *Wanderer* l. 43 'as when' in the face of linguistic *facts* (as opposed to 'arguments'). [1987. See item 17 above, pp. 168–70.] (3) So the implication on pp. 13 and 162 that Martin Stevens was guilty of 'special pleading' about *The Wife's Lament* ll. 1–2 can produce only wry amusement; after all, he did have an example to support his case. But on this see my article in *NM* 73 (1972), 222–34 [item 15 above].

Some good points are made in chapter 4, 'The Play of Sound and Sense'. Not all, however, will accept as intended by the poet even those examples of 'an Anglo-Saxon poet's use of ambiguity proper' (p. 90) which Mr Greenfield does approve, viz. *fah* in *Dream of the Rood* l. 13 suggests 'stained' and 'proscribed' (pp. 90–1); MS *wealdes* in *Dream of the Rood* l. 17 should be retained not only as suggesting both 'forest' and 'power', but also as implying the often-accepted emendation *wealdendes* (p. 91) (both these are suggested by Mr Swanton); and in *Beowulf* l. 142 *healðegnes hete* might suggest *helðegnes hete* (p. 94). Can they even be accepted as legitimate 'present meanings'?

How far Mr Greenfield has succeeded in discovering 'whether it is possible ... to develop a critical framework by which we may arrive at more authoritative interpretations and assessments of the Anglo-Saxon poetic achievement' (p. 2) must be a matter of opinion. He does not treat all possible topics (p. 159). However, the validity and value of 'close reading' are convincingly demonstrated throughout the book, though I would be interested to know exactly how this process differs from 'ferreting out'; see p. 118. That there is still much room for close reading can be demonstrated even from the passages he discusses. The reservation I expressed in *RES* 21 (1970), 186 about *Beowulf* ll. 702b–36a (pp. 122–30) still stands, and the use of *scriþan* deserves fuller consideration – in *Beowulf* l. 163 of *helrunan*, in *Beowulf* l. 650 of *scaduhelma gæsceapu*, and in *Beowulf* l. 703 of Grendel, who is both *sceadugenga* and *helruna*. No mention is made at p. 19 of Garmonsway's observations about *wæfre ond wælfus* in *Beowulf* l. 2420; see *Magoun Studies*, pp. 143–4. In my opinion, what emerges most clearly and usefully from the book – by precept and usually by example – is this: that a successful critic must have the necessary knowledge of Old English poetic techniques and possibilities, the application to read closely and accurately, the ability to react sensitively, and the willingness to temper all this with common sense, humility, and restraint. If we all learn this lesson, we shall have reason to be grateful to Mr Greenfield.

Part IV

Old English Language

21
Syntax and Word-order in the *Peterborough Chronicle* 1122–1154

In her edition of the *Peterborough Chronicle*, Miss Clark writes:

> The modernity of this language [i.e. of the Final Continuation] appears also in its syntax. In studying the morphology we have already noted the great simplification of the case-system, in particular the disuse of the dative, and the corresponding adjustments in syntax, including a great increase in the use of analytic constructions. And Rothstein demonstrated how frequently certain constructions typical of Old English, such as inversion of subject and verb after an introductory adverbial phrase, are here abandoned in favour of word-order nearer to that of Modern English.
>
> Indeed, most of the basic developments leading to Modern English are illustrated in this brief text: Toller spoke truly when he described this language as 'almost that of to-day'. These Peterborough annals are not merely one of the earliest Middle-English documents: they are also the earliest authentic example of that East-Midland language which was to be the chief ancestor of our modern Standard English. And this is only a little less true of the First Continuation than of the Final. What from an Old-English point of view seems to be the dissolution of the *Schriftsprache* into unsystematized colloquial dialect appears from the modern point of view as the first step towards a new literary language.[1]

This treatment of the syntax is brief (though brevity about syntax is the rule rather than the exception) and in places misleading. For, as Professor Campbell has observed in his review of the book, 'in some respects the Peterborough language is syntactically very archaic'.[2] This new and independent analysis of syntax, with special reference to word-order, in the First and Second Continuations of the *Peterborough Chronicle* sets out to discover what is 'modern' and what is 'archaic' about it.

Reprinted from *Neuphilologische Mitteilungen* 65 (1964), 113–44.

[1] *The Peterborough Chronicle 1070–1154* ed. Cecily Clark (Oxford, 1958), p. lxvi. The references throughout are to this work, by annal and line. All line references are to the line in which the particular sentence or clause begins.

[2] *MÆ* 28 (1959), 200.

I

Certain Old English constructions which have now disappeared remain in both Continuations.[3] Both show the Old English tendency to split heavy groups of adjectives or nouns, e.g. 1125. 22 *micele gife 7 mære*, 1137. 10 *he milde man was 7 softe 7 god*, and 1137. 55 *Crist slep 7 his halechen*. In 1124. 22 *se king of France 7 ealle þas eorles heolden mid him 7 ealle þa rice men* this pattern and that used today occur side by side, while in 1123. 28 *And se prior 7 se munecas of Cantwarabyrig 7 ealle þa oðre þe ðær wæron munechades men hit wiðcwæðen*, we find only the latter. But it would be misleading to call this 'modern', for it is found in Old English, e.g. *Reader* 10. 9[4] *Đa gestod hine heah weder ond stormsæ* and *Reader* 11. 8 *ðeah him men oððe hundas wið eoden*. Similar fluctuations appear in appositional constructions, e.g. 1125. 25 *Anselm ærcebiscop* and 1140. 36 *Randolf eorl* (a pattern no longer current), but 1127. 8 *Rotbert eorl of Gleucestre* and 1140. 9 *Randolf eorl of Cæstre* (a common arrangement today). Similarly, compare 1125. 30 *se abbot of Sancte Alban Gosfreið* and 1129. 19 *se ærcebiscop Willelm of Cantwarabyrig* with 1140. 53 *Eustace þe kinges sune* and note that 1154. 1 *þe king Stephne*, 1128. 25 *on Urbanes dæi Pape*, and 1137. 76 *on Stephnes kinges time*, would not be used today in similar contexts.[5] This last example and 1140. 23 *Henri þe kinges brother Stephnes* show the Old English system of inflecting both elements of an appositional group. A separated heavy group in the genitive occurs in 1131. 40 *Cristes helpe 7 eall cristenes folces*, where the uninflected *eall* is significant. The pattern seen in 1127. 6 *ðes Caseres wif of Sexlande* and 1140. 54 *þe kinges suster of France* is, of course, a Middle English development.

Failure to express a subject which would be expressed today is not uncommon in Old English and is found in both Continuations, e.g. 1122. 20 *7 weax*, 1123. 11 *7 wearð*, 1131. 20–2, 1135. 6 *sua dide*, and 1140. 15 *7 fuhten*. Similarly, an object is not expressed in 1126. 14–15 and 1140. 17–18. 'Semi-subordination' of the Old English type seen in *Reader* 11. 13 *ond sæt on ðæm muntum ægðer ge dæges ge nihtes, weop ond hearpode* 'sat ... weeping and harping' is also found, e.g. 1125. 15 *beteahte*, 1127. 70 *sæidon*, 1137. 51 *wenden*, and 1138. 2 *wolde*. On the other hand, *he* would not be used today in such sentences as *Stephen* 54. 6 *Seðe his broðor ne lufað, he wunað on deaðe* and 1124. 31 *se man þa hæfde at an market an pund, he ne mihte cysten þærof for nan þing twelfe penegas*. The modern idiom can, however, be seen in *Stephen* 50. 4 *and swa se ðe wæs neoðor on endebyrdnysse, wearð*

---

[3] Many of these, of course, are found in later Middle English. But this is not our present concern.

[4] For convenience of reference, Old English passages for comparison are (where possible) taken from *Sweet's Anglo-Saxon Reader*, revised by C. T. Onions (Oxford, 1950) – abbreviated as *Reader*, references by page and line – and from Ælfric's *Homily on the Passion of St Stephen* – abbreviated as *Stephen*, references by page and line to volume i of B. Thorpe's edition.

[5] Space does not permit a full treatment of this construction, or of many others. A useful collection of Old English appositional constructions will be found in N. Peltola's article in *NM* 61 (1960), 159–203. But I find myself disagreeing with his system of classification. [1987. See *OES* §§1428–63.]

fyrmest on ðrowunge and 1124. 52 *þe nan ne heafde stærf of hungor*. There are, of course, other examples of unnecessary repetition and of clumsy constructions and anacolutha. But these are not the characteristics of any one particular age. Other Old English idioms represented in both Continuations are the *X. wæs gehaten* construction, e.g. 1123. 13 *Rotbert Peccep wæs gehaten* and 1132. 11 *Martin was gehaten*, and the comparative construction seen in 1123. 84–5 and 1140. 10–11. Since the modern forms with 'do' have not yet appeared, the negative is the same as in Old English – the adverb *ne* immediately before the verb – e.g. 1123. 26 *he ne mihte* and 1140. 60 *7 Crist ne wolde*. The 'double negative' still occurs, e.g. 1129. 37 *swa it næfre ær ne wæs* and 1137. 42 *nan ne wæs*. There are variations in the position of a pronoun in the genitive, e.g. 1140. 51 *sume here þankes* but 1140. 37 *her nouþer* and 1125. 4 *here elces riht hand*,[6] of adverbs, e.g. 1123. 18 *Ða hi wæron þær gegaderod*, 1123. 87 *7 swa mycel hearm þær wæs gedon*, 1137. 47 *7 brenden sythen þe cyrce*, and 1140. 28 *þer wæs inne micel hungær*, and of prepositions, e.g. 1123. 41 *togeanes riht* and 1135. 19 *agenes him*, but 1123. 17 *him togeanes* and 1138. 2 *7 Him com togænes Willelm*; in the last two, we have the common Old English 'postposition'. Adverbial genitives occur, e.g. 1122. 16 and 1140. 51–2. Adjective clauses separated from their antecedent further than is normal today can be found in 1123. 61 *Ac þet ofercom Rome þet ofercume ð eall weoruld* and in 1135. 8 for *æuric man sone ræuede oþer þe mihte*; this, too, is common in Old English.

Old English idioms which occur only in Continuation I are the 'inverted' concession in 1128. 15 *wær it tweolf monð oððe mare*, the separable prefix in 1127. 74 *God scawe fore*,[6a] the unexpressed relative in 1123. 53 *7 Gifard wæs þes kinges hird-clerc*, the repetition of *þet* in 1131. 33–5 and 1127. 44 *þa beþohte he him þet gif he mihte ben rotfest on Engleland þet he mihte habben eal his wille* (cf. 1140. 67–71), and the absence of a verb of motion after *mihte* in 1131. 30.[7] The Old English habit of placing an infinitive of purpose or the like after its object appears in 1127. 51, 1129. 21, and (alongside the use which survives today) in 1127. 11 *oc se kyng hit dide for to hauene sibbe of se eorl of Angeow 7 for helpe to hauene togænes his neue Willelm*.[8] In Continuation II the difficulty of combining a noun clause and an adjective clause is resolved in a typically Old English way in 1137. 17 *þa namen hi þa men þe hi wenden ðat ani god hefden*; the modern tendency to use *whom* for *who* in 'Then they took the men who they thought had possessions' or *who* for *whom* in 'Then they took the men whom they thought to have possessions' was not yet a possibility, since the interrogative pronoun had not yet acquired its relative function.

Other important differences are noted below. However, all the constructions mentioned above are disregarded in the discussions on word-order. Thus

---

[6] Note also the use of demonstrative instead of possessive pronoun in 1125. 9 *ælc ðone riht hand*.
[6a] [1987. On this term and the problems involved, see *OES* §§1060–80.]
[7] 1137. 32 need not be so explained.
[8] With the infinitives in 1123. 77, cf. 'a book to sell'.

1140. 60 *7 Crist ne wolde* is treated as if it were *7 Crist wolde* and 'postpositions' are treated as if they were in the position normal today.

II

A new analysis of the syntax of the *Peterborough Chronicle* 1122–54 is necessary because Rothstein's work deals only with word-order and is marred by flaws which render it a dangerous guide.[9] It lumps together the copied annals and Continuation I and gives separate figures for Continuation II only.[10] It fails to make fundamental distinctions in word-order. Thus S.V., e.g. 1140. 58 *He brohte his wif to Engleland*, S. . . . V., e.g. 1137. 45 *ne næure hethen men werse ne diden*, and O.S.V., e.g. 1122. 22 *þæt fir hi seagon*, are all *gerade Stellung*.[11] *Invertierte oder ungerade Stellung* embraces 1124. 50 *Ful heui gær wæs hit*, 1129. 19 *þis bebæd se ærcebiscop*, 1135. 11 *durste nan man misdon wið oðer on his time*, 1140. 66 *7 þoþwæthere fuhtten hi noht*, 1140. 76 *þa was þe king strengere*, and 1137. 74 *7 forþi him luuedon God 7 gode men*.[12] Such indiscriminate classification takes no account of whether it is an adverb, a complement, an object, or a conjunction, which precedes the verb,[13] disregards the influence of initial *ond*, *ac*, and *ne*,[14] and does not appear to care whether the word-order in question is possible or not today – a strange omission in a work so concerned to establish the modernity of Continuation II.

Later writers also fail to take account of the influence of *ond*, *ac*, and *ne*. This weakness invalidates much of Barrett's work[15] and makes it impossible to use his statistics. In a sadly revealing paragraph, he explains that 'after much careful consideration' he decided to include sentences beginning with *ond*, *ac*, and *ne*, 'among the sentences without heads'. It should not have required much consideration to reach the obvious and proper solution – which is to include them among sentences beginning with *ond*, *ac*, and *ne*, respectively.[16] Bacquet similarly overlooks the tendency of *ond* and *ac* to send a verb to the end of the clause, and shows an inability to realize why a verb has final position in other clauses.[17] Thus he groups together a sentence beginning with *ond*, another

---

[9] E. Rothstein *Die Wortstellung in der Peterborough Chronik*, Studien zur englischen Philologie 64 (Halle, 1922). [10] pp. 1–2.

[11] p. 3. S. = subject, V. = verb, O. = object, C. = complement, e.g. 'a fireman' in 'He is a fireman'. [12] pp. 3–5.

[13] Separate figures for these categories are given by Rothstein in the course of the work. But the percentages at pp. 4–5 include all these syntactically dissimilar orders.

[14] It is specifically stated on p. 4 that *ond* and *ac* are not 'heads'. *Ne* is not included among the adverb 'heads' at pp. 7ff.

[15] R. Barrett *Studies in the Word-Order of Ælfric's Catholic Homilies and Lives of the Saints* (Cambridge, 1953). [16] Barrett, p. 2.

[17] e.g. in chapters 3 and 4 of his *La Structure de la Phrase Verbale à l'Époque Alfrédienne* (Paris, 1962) (hereafter cited as Bacquet).

beginning with *ac*, the formulaic *ic nat hwæt*, and the semi-subordinate *hi ne rohton hwær* 'without caring where' (*Parker Chronicle* 891).[18] As a result, he is led to some wrong conclusions.[19] This failure of Barrett and Bacquet is hard to understand in view of Fourquet's clear grasp of the influence of *ond* and *ac*.[20] But it renders the summary which follows less superfluous than it might at first appear.[20a]

In the sentence or clause, Old English prose retained the three ancient Germanic word-orders – S.V. (the only order in Modern English prose except in questions and in a few isolated remnants such as conditions without a conjunction, e.g. 'Had I but plenty of money, I would be lying on a beach in Bermuda'), S. . . . V., and V.S. But word-order in Old English is not as regular as that in Modern German, where S. . . . V. occurs only in subordinate clauses (with the finite verb always in final position[21]) and S.V. is the order of principal clauses except when some element other than the subject begins the sentence, when we have V.S. What are rules in Modern German are certainly tendencies in Old English prose. But (possibly under the influence of verse, where these rules do not apply, and as part of the process which led to the modern fixed word-order) S.V. and sometimes V.S. occur in subordinate clauses, while V.S. with initial verb can occur in principal clauses which are statements, not questions. Pronoun objects and certain adverbs can precede the verb in principal clauses, but the resulting order is a variation of S.V. rather than a type of S. . . . V.[22] However, S. . . . V. does occur in principal clauses with a noun object and is common after *ond* and *ac*.[23] It should be noted that in the order S. . . . V. the verb may be followed by a phrase, e.g. *Stephen* 44. 29 *þæt he tallice word spræce be Moyse and be Gode*, *Stephen* 48. 35 *gif ænig todal beon mæg betwux martyrum*, and

[18] Bacquet, p. 129, paragraph 2(a).
[19] Fuller treatment of this and other points will be found in reviews of Bacquet's work by Professor Campbell and myself which will appear in the *Review of English Studies* and *Medium Ævum* respectively. [1987. See respectively *RES* 15 (1964), 190–3, and item 22 below.]
[20] On this point, see §V. [1987. I qualify my praise of Fourquet in item 22; see p. 245 below.]
[20a] [1987. See *OES* §1731. That some modern writers on OE element order still seem unwilling or unable to grasp this point is suggested by the second paragraph of David Denison's 'On Word Order in Old English', *Dutch Quarterly Review of Anglo-American Letters* 16 (1986), 280, fn. 6.]
[21] Except in such sentences as *Ich glaube, dass die Mutter dem Kind ein Buch wird kaufen können*.
[22] Barrett (op. cit.) fails to make these distinctions. In his chapter I, 'direct order' includes both S.V. and S. . . . V. (p. 1). In chapter II, he distinguishes 'direct order' and 'transposed order' with 'verb medial' and 'verb final'. If *ne* comes between S. and V. we have medial order (p. 63), unless (apparently) coalescence takes place – *and þær nan man næfde nan þing* is direct order (p. 78). This is contradictory and disregards a basic Old English idiom. On p. 78 the order O.S.V. is classified as 'direct order' with a 'head'. The examples of 'verb medial' cited on pp. 64 and 98 show that any of these coming between S. and V. produces 'medial' order – *ne*, *þa* adverb, pronoun O., noun O., preposition, part of the complement, prepositional phrase, infinitive. In addition the influence of initial *ond* and *ac* is again disregarded (p. 64). Such indiscriminate classification means that his percentages are of little significance.
O. Funke in 'Some Remarks on Late O.E. Word-Order' (*EStudies* 37 (1956), 99–104) uses Barrett's statistics.
[23] See further §V. Bacquet's book is a most valuable source of examples on these points.

Matthew 2. 1 *þa se Hælend acenned wæs on Iudeiscre Bethleem, on þæs cyninges dagum Herodes.* Such sentences are included among the examples of S. . . . V. in the tables given below; since neither of these arrangements occurs in Modern English, their relative frequency is irrelevant to our problem.

III

Now let us consider word-order in the First and Second Continuations of the *Peterborough Chronicle*. In simple sentences and principal clauses which do not begin with *ond, ac, ne,* or other conjunctions, or with adverbs or adverb phrases, the subject usually begins the sentence and the word-order is S.V., e.g. 1125. 14 *He com first to þone king on Normandi* and 1137. 42 *Wrecce men sturuen of hungær.* But, as table 1 shows, there are variations and exceptions.

Table 1

Word-order	Number of sentences in Continuation I	Number of sentences in Continuation II
1. S.V.[a]	52	22
2. O.S.V.	4[b]	6[c]
3. C.S.V.	0	2 (1135. 10, 1140. 59)
4. V.S.	1 (1131. 30)[d]	5[e]
5. S.V. . . . past participle	0[f]	1 (1137. 11)
6. S. pronoun O.V.	3 (1127. 69, 1128. 14, 1131. 11[g])[h]	2 (1137. 52, 1154. 19)
7. O.V.S.	2 (1123. 35, 1129. 19)	1 (1140. 71)
8. C.V.S.	1 (1124. 50)	0
9. S.V. expressing a wish	6[i]	0

[a] These figures exclude the *X. wæs gehaten* formula discussed above, since it does not exemplify the order S.V.

The number of examples in these groups cannot always be exact because of examples which conform to two patterns, e.g. 1125. 12 *þet hi ealle abohton* 'which they all paid for' – S.V., but with verb in final position. Again, *Stephen* 44. 30 *þæt folc wearð ða micclum astyred* corresponds exactly to Thorpe's 'The people were then greatly excited'. But it is also the exact equivalent of *Stephen* 56. 27 *Ælc lof bið on ende gesungen* which cannot be rendered 'All praise will be at the end sung'. 'All praise will be finally sung' would not seem to fit the context. However, such examples are not sufficiently numerous to affect the percentages seriously. Other difficulties arise. Thus in 1127. 35–6, *þaræftor,* an adverb clause, and *þa,* all precede the verb. Whose influence produces the order V.S.? Such questions are insoluble and immaterial.

[b] 1122. 22, 1123. 73, 1127. 42, 58. [c] 1135. 12, 1137. 26, 34, 56, 1140. 41, 1154. 2.
[d] 1127. 45 has the verb in first position, but the subject is not expressed.
[e] 1132. 8, 1135. 4, 11, 1137. 44, 1140. 5.
[f] See note a above and 1123. 25 discussed below. [g] 1131. 11 expresses a wish.
[h] 1124. 51 has this order, but the sentence begins with *him,* a dative of 'disadvantage'.
[i] 1127. 74, 1128. 6, 16, 1129. 37, 1130. 20, 1131. 38.

Table 2, showing the figures from *Stephen*, is subjoined for comparison.

Table 2

1. S.V.	39
2. O.S.V.	2 (44. 18, 54. 25)
3. C.S.V.	0[a]
4. V. adverb S.	2 (44. 20, 50. 32)[b]
5. S.V. . . . past participle	4 (44. 30 and 46. 28,[c] 46. 26 and 56. 27)
6. S.O.V.	4 (with pronoun objects 50. 14, 56. 18; with noun objects 50. 17, 30)
7. O.V.S.	3 (48. 29, 50. 7, 56. 10 – all noun objects)[d]
8. C.V.S.	0[e]
9. S.V. expressing a wish	0[f]

[a] But see *Reader* 71. 109.
[b] The verb occurs initially with no expressed subject in 46. 10, 22 and 48. 2. These two arrangements are common in the poetry, e.g. *Beowulf* ll. 1506 and 1425. One example of V.S. in direct question and fourteen with initial imperatives or jussive subjunctives are not included in the table.
[c] Both ambiguous examples; see below.
[d] In 52. 33 a dative pronoun precedes a verb whose subject is unexpressed.
[e] But see *Reader* 13. 11.
[f] But see *Sweet's Anglo-Saxon Primer* rev. N. Davis (9th edn, Oxford, 1953), p. 80, l. 95.

Word-orders 1–3 in tables 1 and 2, which occur in both Old English and Modern English, account for 76 per cent of examples in *Stephen*, 81 per cent in Continuation I, and 77 per cent in Continuation II. The remaining orders 4–9 occur in Old, but not in Modern, English.[24] Such a preponderance of word-orders which are found today certainly helps to create the impression that both Continuations are 'modern' in their word-order. But it does nothing to prove it; that Ælfric would have felt that the English of the *Peterborough Chronicle* 1122–54 differed little in this respect from his own English is suggested by the figures from *Stephen*. If this portion of the *Chronicle* were truly modern, its figures for word-orders 1–3 should be 100 per cent, apart from survivals such as those already noted.

The Old English pattern seen in *Orosius* 270. 17 *He hæfde folc gegaderad* and *Orosius* 32. 3 *hit wearð fram heofonlicum fyre forbærned*,[25] in which the participle in a resolved verb form takes final position, does not appear in Continuation I, except perhaps in 1123. 25 *Ðis wæs eall ear gedon ðurh se biscop of Seresbyrig*,[26] and

[24] It seems to me legitimate to disregard such sentences as 'Came the dawn', 'A prince was he', and 'God save the King'. [1987. Word-order 5 can occur in Modern English with an intervening adverb, e.g. 'He was greatly disturbed.' On this, see note a to table 1 and cf. fn. 26.]
[25] References by page and line to EETS edn.
[26] The possibility of an adverb phrase after the participle has already been noted. Cf. *Stephen* 46. 28.

occurs only once in Continuation II – 1137. 11 *Hi hadden him manred maked 7 athes suoren*. Modern English, of course, has 'He had gathered an army' and 'It was burnt by a fire from heaven', and this pattern occurs six times in Continuation I[27] and once in Continuation II.[28] But it would be a bad mistake to claim this as something new in the Continuations, for the idiom of today already existed in Alfredian English, e.g. *Cura Pastoralis* 417. 19 *We habbað geascod from urum ærestan mæge Adame ðæt* ... and *Cura Pastoralis* 33. 13 *hit is awriten on ðæm godspelle*,[29] and of the seven examples of S.V. ... past participle in *Stephen*, four have the modern idiom,[30] one has an arrangement not possible today in the context – 56. 27 *Ælc lof bið on ende gesungen*[31] – and two are syntactically ambiguous – 46. 28 and 44. 30 *þæt folc wearð ða micclum astyred*. We might expect a similar change in the position of the infinitive after *magan* and the like. But there are no examples in principal clauses in *Stephen* and only two in the *Peterborough Chronicle* 1122–54 – 1131. 25 *Hi scolden nedes*, where the infinitive is not expressed, and 1137. 34 *I ne can ne I ne mai tellen alle þe wunder ne alle þe pines* ..., where we have the modern pattern.

In the *Peterborough Chronicle* 1122–54 a noun object never precedes the verb in simple sentences or principal clauses, as it sometimes does in Old English, e.g. *Stephen* 50. 17 *Ða reðan Iudei wedende þone halgan stændon* and 50. 30 *Stephanus soðlice gebigedum cneowum Drihten bæd*. ... In all the examples of word-order 6 (S.O.V.) cited in the first table, the object is a pronoun, e.g. 1128. 14 *he hit dide* and 1137. 52 *þe biscopes 7 lered men heom cursede æure*. This disappearance of the order S. noun O.V. represents a step towards Modern English. It would be wrong, however, to lay too much stress on the retention of the order S. pronoun O.V., for in Old English *ic hine lufige* is an equivalent of both *ic God lufige* and *ic lufige God*;[32] it is certainly not an unambiguous example of the order S. ... V. Hence such sentences as 1128. 14 *he hit dide* are a survival of an idiomatic variation of the word-order S.V. rather than examples of the so-called subordinate order S. ... V.

To sum up. We have seen that in the type of simple sentence and principal

---

[27] With the verb 'to have' 1124. 21 and 1127. 17; with the verb 'to be' 1125. 10, 1126. 15, 1127. 66, 71.

[28] With 'to be' 1137. 13.

[29] References by page and line to EETS edn.

[30] 44. 15, 48. 20, 50. 9, and 50. 33. See further Bacquet's discussion, chapter IX. [1987. Tadao Kubouchi (private communication) has pointed out that I omitted from my discussion one example from *Stephen* which I included in item 5 in table 2, viz. *Stephen* 46. 26 *Hwæt ða Iudeiscan þa wurdon pearle on heora heortan astyrode*. So there are eight examples in *Stephen* – four with the modern idiom, two – 46. 26 and 56. 27 – unacceptable today, and two syntactically ambiguous.]

[31] On this example, see note a to table 1. In *Stephen* 50. 2 an arrangement impossible today occurs after initial *witodlice*; see §IV.

[32] The order *ic lufige hine* is the exception rather than the rule, but it does occur, e.g. *Orosius* 82. 18. Further on this point, see C. A. Smith in *PMLA* 8 (1893), 220, and Bacquet, pp. 67ff.

clause under discussion, over three-quarters of the sentences in *Stephen* and in both Continuations show a pattern common to Old English and Modern English. All the rest have patterns which occur in Old English, but not in Modern English. There is nothing which is Modern English, but not Old English. Even the modern arrangement of the elements of the resolved moods and tenses occurs in Old English. The greatest claim of the *Peterborough Chronicle* 1122–54 to modernity in these sentences lies in the complete absence of the word-order S. noun O.V.[33]

IV

In simple sentences and principal clauses beginning with an adverb other than *ne* (which is discussed at the end of this section) or with an adverb phrase, the word-order V.S. is the norm in Old English prose. The frequency of exceptions varies with the introductory word or phrase. With initial *þa*, exceptions are rare. In *Orosius* 284. 32–3, the Lauderdale MS reads *þa he gefor*, but the Cotton MS has the expected *þa gefor he*. The exception in *Reader* 33. 36, *þa hie gefengon micle herehyð*..., can be removed by putting a comma after *woldon*, l. 35, and translating ll. 35–7 '... and secondly at the time when they were ready to evacuate these positions when, having seized much plunder, they wished to carry it northwards across the Thames into Essex to the ships'. But even after *þa*, where the tendency to V.S. was perhaps strongest, there are exceptions which cannot be removed unless one assumes the role of a prescriptive grammarian for Old English, e.g. *Cura Pastoralis* 405. 35 *Ða he ðis eal dyde, ða he stod æfter us gewend*....[34]

However, after other adverbs and after phrases we find both S.V. and V.S. Thus in the *Parker Chronicle* we read 832. *Her hæþne men oferhergeadon Sceapige* but 833. *Her gefeaht Ecgbryht cyning wiþ XXXV sciphlæsta æt Carrum*, while Ælfric has *Stephen* 56. 34 *nu todæg hi underfengon Stephanum* and 52. 3 *mid Stephane he bricð Cristes beorhtnysse*, but 48. 30 *Nu andet ure geleafa Cristes setl* and 54. 5 *Be ðan ylcan cwæð se godspellere Iohannes*. The reasons for such variations cannot be discussed here,[35] but their existence must not be forgotten.

[33] [1987. Further on this point, see item 23 below.]

[34] A. Adams in *The Syntax of the Temporal Clause in Old English Prose* (Yale Studies in English 32, 1907) displays a laconic lack of interest in this problem (pp. 158–9). Bacquet (pp. 596 ff.) advances the theory that examples of the pattern S.V. after *þa* are departures for the sake of emphasis. In his view, presumably, the Cotton scribe's alteration in *Orosius* 284. 32–3 above stamps him as a pedant unnecessarily altering a calculated departure from the norm. *Reader* 33. 36 could perhaps be explained as emphatic too. However, it might be argued that Bacquet tends to fall back a little too readily on this explanation; see, e.g. pp. 137–8 and chapter 10. Moreover, some of his alleged exceptions show the influence of *ond* or *ac*, of which he appears to be ignorant, e.g. *Cura Pastoralis* 405. 30–1 (p. 599).

[35] See J. Fourquet *L'Ordre des Éleménts de la Phrase en Germanique Ancien* (Paris, 1938), *passim*, and Bacquet, pp. 647 ff.

Table 3 gives the number of examples of each word-order after an adverb or adverb phrase in *Stephen* and in both Continuations.[36]

Table 3

Word-order	Stephen	Continuation I	Continuation II
V.S.	20	88	43
S.V.	8	4	6
S. ... V.	0	1[a]	0
Adverb O. ... V.	1 (46. 13)	0	0
Dative pronoun V.S.	0	3[b]	0
Totals	29	96	49
Approx. percentage V.S.	70	92	88

[a] This is 1128. 25 *þeah hit litel behelde*, where the context would admit, and the word-order suggests that we may have, a subordinate concessive clause; cf. 1125. 26.
[b] These are 1131. 26, 26, 39.

The number of times the order V.S. occurs can be subdivided as shown in table 4.
The 'others' can be further analysed (table 5).
The examples with S.V. are given in table 6.
Where a resolved mood or tense occurs in the word-order V.S., the Old English pattern seen in *Stephen* 52. 16 *þurh þa soðan lufe wæs þes halga martyr swa gebyld þæt* ... is retained, e.g. 1127. 12–14, 1140. 1–2, 1135. 4 *Wurþen men suiðe ofuundred*, and 1135. 13 ... *durste nan man sei to him naht bute god*, except in 1129. 29 *þa wære þær coren twa papes*. This is scarcely surprising, for the arrangement survives today, e.g. 'Had he not come back, the house would have been burnt down' and 'Had I to do this, I would seek the Professor's help.'
There are also two main clauses in which the verb has first position after a subordinate clause, viz. 1123. 67 and 1135. 13; for S.V. in the same circumstances, see 1124. 32, 1137. 51 and 54. There are no main clauses with the verb first after a subordinate clause in *Stephen*, though they are of course common

[36] The following examples in *Stephen* with initial *witodlice* have been omitted from the table because the variety of Latin words it represents make its exact status dubious: 48. 28, 50. 2, 56. 5 (all with S.V.), 52. 1 (with *næfde* + subject), and 52. 34ff. One S.V. example after *eornostlice* (52. 12) is similarly excluded.

Table 4

V.S. after	Stephen	Continuation I	Continuation II
Prepositional phrase	3	18	8
ealle þis gear, þes ilces geares or variants	0	20	2 (1132. 1, 1137. 1)
þa [a]	6	32	27
þerefter	0	4[b]	4[c]
siðð̆en	0	5[d]	1 (1140. 35)
Others	11	9	1
Totals	20	88	43

[a] Coordinate *þa ... þa* appears respectively 0, 5, and 12, times.
[b] 1122. 10, 18; 1127. 35; 1131. 9.
[c] 1140. 3, 6, 8, 19.
[d] 1127. 20, 33, 37, 40; 1129. 5.

Table 5

V.S. after	Stephen	Continuation I	Continuation II
Genitive phrase	44. 13		
eall[a]		1124. 19	
gyrstandæg	56. 28, 33		
micel[a]			1137. 4
nu	48. 30, 54. 29, 56. 1	1129. 36	
swa		1127. 57, 57	
þær	52. 7	1127. 2, 1130. 3,	
þenon		1127. 42	
þider	52. 6		
þonne	52. 28, 54. 15, 22		
þus		1127. 53, 1128. 28	
Totals	11	9	1

[a] These may not be adverbs.

Table 6

S.V. after	Stephen	Continuation I	Continuation II
Prepositional phrase	50. 21, 52. 3, 56. 5	1130. 17	1137. 69, 77
ðes ilce gæres		1127. 22	
ærost		1124. 49[a]	
eft	54. 7		
nu	52. 3, 56. 30, 34		1137. 76
swiðor	50. 25		
þa			1135. 22[b]
þerefter			1140. 22, 50
þus		1131. 37	
Totals	8	4	6

[a] Pronoun object before verb.
[b] This *could* be explained by Bacquet's rule of 'emphasis' discussed above. But it is rather an isolated departure from the normal V.S.

in Old English; see *Orosius* 244. 20 and 254. 20 but compare *Orosius* 44. 3 and 56. 13.[37]

The adverb *ne* in Old English always immediately precedes the verb. If it begins the sentence, therefore, the word-order will be V.S. When *ne* does not immediately precede the verb, it is a conjunction.[38] Both these uses are found in *Stephen* 56. 21 *Ne beo se rihtwisa gymeleas on his anginne, ne se yfela ortruwige ðurh his unrihtwisnysse*. The few examples in the *Peterborough Chronicle* 1122–54 conform to these rules. In Continuation I the adverb *ne* is immediately followed by the verb in 1127. 60 and 1131. 9, while the conjunction *ne* or *na* is followed by O.V. in 1123. 38 and 1127. 59. In Continuation II we have the conjunction *ne* followed by S. ... V. in 1137. 45, by S.V.O. in 1137. 48, and by infinitives in 1137. 33. In this respect, there can be no claim to modernity.

It is clear from this evidence that, if our only criterion for dating these texts was the frequency of the order V.S. after an adverb or adverb phrase, we should be forced to conclude that Ælfric wrote *Stephen* well after 1154. It is, therefore,

[37] Bacquet, pp. 592–3, has a useful collection of examples of the order V.S. in these circumstances in Old English. It is, of course, still the rule in Modern German. Bacquet is unlikely to be right in his claim that the Old English examples are emphatic. They are rather the norm from which the examples with S.V. deviate as part of the development which led to the modern supremacy of S.V.

[38] Bacquet seems ignorant of this rule; hence his mistaken view that *Ne* + V.S. is an emphatic order (pp. 629ff.).

unfortunate that Miss Clark selected this aspect for special emphasis. Far from being modern here, the Continuations are probably at their most conservative. See further section VII.

V

It is, I think, right to say that all the orders possible today after 'and' or 'but' can be found in Old English and in the *Peterborough Chronicle* 1122–54 after *ond* and *ac*. But these also have word-orders not possible today. The position is set out in tables 7 and 8.

Since the percentage of non-modern word-orders after *ond* and *ac* in *Stephen* (30.6 per cent or 19 out of 62 examples) is one-and-a-half times that in Continuation I (20 per cent or 40 out of 204) and more than twice that in Continuation II (15 per cent or 27 out of 180), the *Peterborough Chronicle* 1122–54 can claim to be more modern here.[39] Participles and infinitives used to form resolved moods

Table 7 Orders which occur today

Word-order	Stephen	Continuation I	Continuation II
ond V.	20	68	89
ond adverb[a] V.	0	9	6
ond S.V.	12	46	38
ond adverb S.V.	2 (50. 21, 52. 4)	25	8
ond S. adverb V.	2 (48. 6, 52. 11)	0	1 (1154. 9)
ond O.S.V.	0	5	0
ond ther was	0	0	2 (1137. 2, 64)
ond adverb þear wearð	0	1 (1128. 5)	0
ac V.	0	2 (1123. 22, 27)	4
ac adverb V.	1 (48. 34)	0	0
ac S.V.	5	8	5
ac O.S.V.	1 (56. 20)	0	0
Totals	43	164	153

[a] 'Adverb' in these tables includes any adverb or adverb phrase.

[39] These figures show the two Continuations in the most favourable light, for in places the actual arrangement of modern word-orders would not be possible now. Thus a subject would have to be expressed today in 1122. 20 and 1135. 14. *Scæ* is misplaced in 1140. 49. A change of subject occurs with no subject expressed in 1123. 11 and 1129. 6. A verb is absent in 1128. 9 and 1129. 24 where it would be expressed today.

Table 8 Orders which do not occur today

Word-order	Stephen	Continuation I	Continuation II
ond S. ... V.	5	1 (1123. 17)[a]	1 (1140. 53)
ond S. pronoun O.V.	4	14[b]	5
ond adverb S. pronoun O.V.	0	2 (1124. 50, 1131. 29)	0
ond ... V.	8	4 (1127. 59, 1128. 19, 1129. 18, 1131. 33)	6
ond O.V.S.	0	1 (1123. 13)	3 (1137. 5, 1138. 2, 1140. 41)
ond adverb O.V.S.	0	0	1 (1137. 74)
ond V.S.	0	1 (1123. 79)	3 (1135. 3, 1137. 84, 1140. 68)
ond adverb V.S.	1 (50. 22)	14	4[c]
ac S. ... V.	0	1 (1123. 30)	1 (1137. 12)
ac S. pronoun O. V.	1 (50. 3)	2 (1123. 43, 1127. 11)	1 (1132. 8)
ac adverb O.S.V.	0	0	1 (1140. 10)
ac V.S.	0	0	1 (1140. 66)
Totals	19	40	27

[a] The intervening element is *swa*, which commonly has the same position in Old English; see Bacquet, p. 69.
[b] Including 1123. 34, 1125. 21, 1128. 21, 1129. 4 and 20, where the pattern is S. indirect pronoun O.V. direct noun O.
[c] They are 1132. 4, 1135. 2, 1140. 66, and 1154. 4. That figures can be only approximate is shown by such examples as 1132. 4 and 1135. 2, in both of which we have *ond* + adverb phrase + clause + *þa* + V.S. These could equally well be included under the heading of *þa* + V.S. Similar difficulties arise throughout. But the percentages are not significantly affected.

and tenses generally conform to modern practice, as they did in main clauses and simple sentences. Thus in 1123. 20 *7 he hem hit wolde typian* and 1140. 21 *7 te lundenissce folc hire wolde tæcen*, we have a modern order except for the pronoun objects.[40] In 1127. 19 *oc hi wæron siððen totweamde for sibreden*, the adverb occupies a position which is still idiomatic.

Here then the *Peterborough Chronicle* 1122–54 has a claim to modernity. In fact it shows us what we should expect – examples of non-modern word-order are much less frequent in Continuation I than in *Stephen*, and are even less frequent in Continuation II.[41] This fits in very tidily with the general development of

[40] See Bacquet, op. cit., chapter 9, for similar examples in Old English, and for a discussion of the Old English usage.
[41] Whether the figures for *Stephen* are typical of Ælfric as a whole remains to be established; Barrett, for the reasons given above, cannot help us.

word-order in English. It fits in too with Fourquet's findings for the earlier parts of the *Chronicle*[42] and with what can be inferred from Bacquet's examples.[43] The figures after *for* are shown in table 9.

Table 9

Word-order	Continuation I	Continuation II
For + S.V.O.	3 (1123. 30, 1125. 5, 1127. 60)	9[a]
For + adverb + S.V.O.	0	1 (1140. 56)
For + adverb + V.S.	0	5
For + S. pronoun O.V.	0	2 (1140. 16, 38)[b]
For + S. . . . V.	0	1 (1137. 13)
Totals	3	18

[a] An adverb comes between S. and V. in 1135. 8. *Ond* precedes *for* in 1137. 3.
[b] *Sithen* also intervenes here.

The only comparable example in *Stephen* is 48. 17 where we have V.S. after *forþi*. The only examples of non-modern word-order in the *Chronicle* are in Continuation II. This must be regarded as the result of chance. The variations here probably reflect the doubt about *for*'s status. Is it an adverb, a co-ordinating conjunction, or (as in 1137. 3) a subordinating conjunction parallel to *forþi ðat* in the preceding line? The real point of interest here, of course, is the full blossoming in Continuation II of what are recognizably modern uses of a word which in Old English had been only a preposition.

VI

Modern word-orders occur in subordinate clauses as shown in table 10.
Word-orders not possible in subordinate clauses today are shown in table 11.
Thus, while *Stephen* has a word-order which is possible today in only 41 per cent of subordinate clauses (49 of 120 examples), Continuation I shows 72 per cent (107 of 147 examples) and Continuation II 80 per cent (71 of 89 examples). This again is what we should expect.

The examples with resolved verb forms call for special comment. *Stephen* regularly shows the Old English pattern in examples which are unambiguously S. . . . V., e.g. 46. 12 *þæt ealle ðeoda on his ofspringe gebletsode wurdon* and 56. 15 *þæt*

[42] Fourquet, pp. 94–100, especially p. 99.
[43] Bacquet (pp. 137–8) speaks of the order *ond* V. noun O. occurring *un certain nombre de fois* in *Orosius*, but the implication of his remarks is that *ond* . . . V. is the commoner order there. His claim that the former is emphatic is, I believe, wrong.

Table 10

Word-order	Stephen	*Continuation I*	*Continuation II*
S.V.	44	69	46
Adverb S.V.	0	1 (1124. 26)	0
S. adverb V.[a]	0	2 (1124. 34, 1129. 23)	1 (1137. 73)
ther V.	0	0[b]	1 (1140. 28)[c]
With resolved verb forms	5	35	23
Totals	49	107	71

[a] Although they follow this pattern, examples such as 1122. 7, 1127. 72, 1132. 6, 1137. 47 and 67, have to be classified as S. . . . V. because they would be impossible today.

[b] 1124. 47 and 1127. 70 are included as examples with resolved forms.

[c] The inclusion of such examples as this among 'modern' word-orders is dubious, for the adverb *inne* is misplaced by modern standards. This and the previous note illustrate the difficulty of producing statistics, and the danger of relying on them too much.

Table 11

Word-order	Stephen	*Continuation I*	*Continuation II*
V.S.	0	1 (1131. 7)	1 (1137. 40)
Adverb V.S.	2 (50. 35,[a] 54. 13)	2 (1123. 26, 1131. 7)	0
O.V.S.	1 (50. 27)	0	1 (1137. 28)
S. . . . V.	53	26	10
S. pronoun O.V.	8	1 (1123. 64)	1 (1137. 59)
Pronoun O.S.V.	1 (46. 4)	0	0
Pronoun O.S. . . . V.	1 (54. 15)	0	0
Other orders	2 (48. 12, 52. 32)	0	0
Resolved verb forms with auxiliary before infinitive or participle[b]	3	10	5
Totals	71	40	18

[a] Here the order of the non-dependent question is retained.

[b] These are discussed in detail below.

þæt se oðer forðyldigan wolde. When such verb forms occur in sentences with S.V., Stephen has the modern arrangement in which the two verbal elements are together, with the auxiliary first and the infinitive or participle after it, in just over half the examples,[44] e.g. 48. 1 *wæs geciged* and 52. 29 *nellað forgyfan*, but 56. 11 *wið þan þæt he moste sumum rican men to bearne geteald beon*. But the Continuations without exception show present-day order of the verbal elements. Usually a completely modern arrangement prevails, as in 1123. 16, 1123. 60, 1132. 2, 1138. 3, and 1129. 12 *þet hi scolden ealle cumen to Lundene*, and, with an adverb between the two elements, 1125. 25, 1127. 70, 1131. 28, and 1128. 12, where *mid alle* would today be replaced by 'completely'.

Most of the departures from a modern arrangement are trifling. An adverb occurs in a position which today would be unidiomatic in 1123. 18, 1137. 32, 1154. 8, and 1140. 60 *ðat he sculde lange rixan*.[45] A pronoun object comes before both elements in 1127. 40 and 1129. 17, and between the two elements in 1129. 16, 1131. 15, and 1131. 37.[46] The remaining six exceptions show more serious departures from the idiom of today, but in all of them the auxiliary precedes the infinitive or participle. There are two examples of S. ... V., viz. 1140. 24 *ðat he neure ma mid te king his brother wolde halden* and 1140. 41 *þat he alle his castles sculde iiuen up*. The other four are 1128. 14–16, 1123. 88 *swa nan man hit cuðe oðer secgen*, 1124. 47 *þet þær wæron manege mid micel unrihte gespilde*, and 1131. 33 *gif he moste Engleland secen*. Here then the victory of the modern pattern is assured in Continuation I and all but complete in Continuation II. Indeed the inclusion in the second rather than in the first table of the examples discussed in this paragraph, while technically right, is in a sense misleading. Here again we see the dangers of undue reliance on statistics.

VII

The word-order of the two Continuations therefore contains much which is common to Old and Modern English, much which cannot occur in Modern English, and nothing which cannot be paralleled in Old English. Any claim to modernity must therefore rest on the relative percentages of the different orders and on the extent to which the constructions which were to survive have ousted the others.

Table 12 sets out these percentages.[47]

---

[44] With participles, 48. 1, 16 and 54. 1 are modern against 56. 11. With infinitives, we have 50. 15 and 52. 29 modern, but 50. 7, 54. 28, and 56. 11. This last example is cited twice.

[45] See Bacquet, pp. 107–9, for similar examples in Old English.

[46] Both these arrangements occur in Old English. Bacquet, pp. 114–15, has an interesting collection of examples.

[47] It has, I hope, been sufficiently emphasized that these statistics cannot be exact. But they are sufficiently reliable to show the general state of word-order in the three texts and to reveal any important developments.

Table 12

Section	Type of clause	Approximate percentages of word-orders which regularly occur today		
		Stephen	Continuation I	Continuation II
III	Main clauses not beginning with an adverb, *ond*, or *ac*, or other conjunctions	76	81	77
IV	Main clauses beginning with an adverb	28	4	12
V	Clauses beginning with *ond* and *ac*	70	80	85
VI	Subordinate clauses	41	72	80

Thus, in simple sentences and principal clauses not beginning with an adverb or a conjunction, both Continuations show roughly the same percentage of archaic word-orders as *Stephen* – some 20 per cent. When introduced by an adverb 70 per cent of them have the order V.S. in *Stephen*, 92 per cent in Continuation I, and 88 per cent in Continuation II; here *Stephen* is much more 'modern' than both Continuations, though (as we should expect) Continuation II is the less 'archaic' of the two. In clauses introduced by *ond* and *ac*, both Continuations show a distinct preference for orders which occur today, while in subordinate clauses the percentage of such orders in the Continuations is almost double that in *Stephen*. Thus the Continuations are more 'modern' in the clauses discussed in sections V and VI, roughly the same in those discussed in section III (only here is Continuation II less 'modern' than Continuation I), and decidedly more 'archaic' than *Stephen* in the clauses of section IV.

Two of the claims Rothstein made in respect of Continuation II are therefore right and can also be made for Continuation I.[48] The first – that there are important developments in the change from synthetic to analytic patterns – has been clearly demonstrated by Miss Clark.[49] The second is that the elements of the 'predicate', especially V.O., show a gradual move to a fixed order. This can be seen in the resolved moods and tenses, in the discarding of the order S. noun O.V. in the principal clauses discussed in section III, and in the changes noted in clauses introduced by *ond* and *ac* (section V) and in subordinate clauses (section VI); in the last, indeed, the change is quite striking. Yet the frequency with which some features of Old English order appear, e.g. pronoun objects

[48] Rothstein, p. 108.
[49] *Passim*, especially p. lviii.

before the verb in what is otherwise S.V.O., suggests that the extent of these developments has sometimes been exaggerated.

But the suspicions entertained in section II about Rothstein's findings are justified in respect of another claim he makes[50] – that inversion is used less frequently in Continuation II. As far as principal clauses beginning with an adverb or adverb phrase or clause are concerned, this gives a totally misleading impression. Rothstein's mathematics may be right; it is his classifications which lead him astray, for (as we have seen) the patterns *ond* V.S., *ac* V.S., O.V.S., C.V.S., and others, are all lumped together with adverb V.S., to produce the 11.2 per cent reduction in the frequency of V.S. in principal clauses *mid Spitze*.[51] One specific example will show the result of this. In section V we find that *ond* is followed by the order adverb V.S. once in *Stephen*, 16 times in Continuation I, and four times in Continuation II. With Rothstein's method of working, the 16 from Continuation I, together with similar examples in the copied annals,[52] would be added to the examples of adverb V.S. in principal clauses to 'prove' that inversion after an adverb is less frequent in Continuation II. But this is an over-simplification. For in clauses beginning with *ond* or *ac* and an adverb two tendencies are conflicting – the increasing tendency to use S.V. after *ond* or *ac* and the old tendency to use V.S. after an adverb. What is surprising is that the latter is strong enough to produce so many examples of V.S. after *ond* in the Continuations; the figures for *ond* adverb S.V. are *Stephen* 2, Continuation I 27,[53] Continuation II 8, as compared with 1, 16, and 5 respectively for *ond* adverb V.S., a proportion of roughly two to one in each case. The strength of the tendency to use adverb V.S. is, of course, more than amply confirmed by the figures given in section IV for principal clauses – 70 per cent in *Stephen*, and 92 per cent and 88 per cent respectively in the Continuations.

Miss Clark therefore seems to exaggerate the modernity of the word-order of the Continuations when she writes:

> Rothstein demonstrated how frequently certain constructions typical of Old English, such as inversion of subject and verb after an introductory adverbial phrase, are here abandoned in favour of word-order nearer to that of Modern English.[54]

Her comment is misleading for two reasons. First, the particular example cited is one in which Rothstein misleads her and us; see section IV for 'proof' that Ælfric was writing after 1154 if the frequency of the order V.S. after adverbial

---

[50] Also on p. 108.
[51] This is discussed in more detail below.
[52] e.g. 1096. 3. Bacquet (pp. 661ff.) cites examples from other texts. But he shows the same failure as Rothstein to distinguish adverb V.S. from *ond* or *ac* adverb V. S.
[53] Including two examples of *ond* adverb S. pronoun O.V.
[54] p. lxvi.

expressions in principal clauses is the sole criterion.[55] Second, she seems to exaggerate Rothstein's claims by the use of the word 'abandoned' and of the expression 'how frequently...', which we tend to take as a dependent exclamation rather than a dependent question.[56]

Thus we see that, while the Continuations in some respects show marked developments in word-order along the way to Modern English, they also show many things which are archaic today. They are 'archaic' too in things other than word-order. Section I contains a list of Old English idioms found in the *Peterborough Chronicle* 1122–54 which have not survived into Modern English. In many other important respects, the syntactical mechanisms are Old English. The indefinite article has not yet developed. Many prepositions are still used in an Old English way, e.g. *at* (1128. 3), *for* (1124. 20), *fram* (1127. 15), *of* (1128. 21), *on* (1124. 18), and *to* (1124. 28). Now-obsolete prepositions still occur, e.g. *mid* (1123. 37) and *toforen* (1125. 1). The interrogatives are not yet used as relatives. The system of relatives in Continuation II is a Middle English development of the Old English system – *þe* for animate antecedents, *þat* for inanimate. This is foreshadowed in Continuation I, but is not modern.[57] Old English conjunctions and adverbs survive, e.g. *ac*, *þeah*, *þeahhwæþere*, and *siðöan*. Adverb clauses are still introduced by their Old English conjunctions – *þær*, *þider*,

---

[55] It is not certain that Rothstein means 'adverbial phrases' when he uses the word *Spitzenbestimmungen* on p. 108; he may have been referring to the figures he gives on pp. 4–5, which are discussed in the next note. The examples for *gerade Stellung* after *eine temporale Bestimmung* on p. 11 include sentences introduced by a prepositional phrase (265. 31 = 1137. 77), by *þerefter* (266. 32 = 1140. 22 and 267. 25 = 1140. 50), and by *ond efsones* (267. 12 = 1140. 39). [Note again the inclusion of examples with *ond* which even today we do not regard as 'principal clauses'.] If we take 'adverbial phrases' to include only prepositional phrases and expressions such as *eall þis gear*, V.S. occurs in 50 per cent of the sentences in *Stephen* (3 out of 6 examples), 95 per cent in Continuation I (38 out of 40), and 83. 3 per cent in Continuation II (10 out of 12). If it had been 11 out of 12 examples in Continuation II, the figure would have been 91. 6 per cent.

[56] After all, Rothstein (pp. 4–5) still found 66⅔ per cent of V.S. in principal sentences *mid Spitze* in Continuation II against 77.8 per cent in the copied annals and Continuation I. 66⅔ per cent does not justify the word 'abandoned'; no prose with such a percentage should be called 'modern'. However, as I have shown above, these figures include sentences beginning with things other than adverbs. If we take some of Rothstein's figures for adverbs, Miss Clark's comment becomes even more exaggerated. Thus the figures Rothstein gives on p. 11 for sentences in which '*die Satzspitze ist eine Temporale Bestimmung*' are, for the copied annals and Continuation I, inversion in 91.3 per cent (65 of 71 examples); for Continuation II 73.7 per cent (14 of 19). We bring this into proportion when we see that, if only 3 more of the 19 examples in Continuation II had been V.S., the figure would have been 89.5 per cent. Four more would have made it 94.7 per cent. The difference in sentences beginning with other phrases is even smaller. His figures for V.S. after temporal adverbs (p. 8) are 87.1 per cent and 81.2 per cent respectively – scarcely a dramatic decline; 14 examples out of 16 instead of 13 would have made the figure for Continuation II 87.5 per cent. [Would this 'prove' that Continuation I was written after Continuation II?] Here again the words 'abandoned' and 'modern' are quite out of place.

[57] See Miss Clark's edition, p. lxiv.

Syntax in the Peterborough Chronicle

þanon, þa, þonne, and so on – and not by the interrogatives. Correlation is still common, and as we have seen the Old English pattern *þa* S. . . . V. or S.V., *þa* V.S. is regularly maintained. Some uses of *swa* are impossible today, e.g. 1127. 54 and 59. The prepositional formulae still occur, e.g. *forþi ðat* (1137. 2), *þurh þæt* (1127. 30), and *fram þet* (1127. 72). The use of asyndetic parataxis, e.g. 1123. 71–4, is frequent.

Certainly many things which belong to English of all periods are present in the Continuations. Lists would be superfluous. The general sentence patterns are frequently those of today. But this is often true in Old English, as has already been pointed out.[58] To claim modernity because of these would be merely playing with words.

There are, as Miss Clark has clearly shown, things which are not Old English. The reduction of inflexions, the loss of the dative in nouns except at times after prepositions, loss of gender, the absence of the genitive after certain verbs and adjectives, and the consequent increase in analytic constructions,[59] are all important developments on the way to Modern English. The use of *til, for,* and *wile*, as conjunctions[60] is certainly modern. But the language of the *Peterborough Chronicle* 1122–54 is Middle, not Modern, English. It is transitional; as Miss Clark happily says 'English is changing from a synthetic language to an analytic one before our eyes'.[61] The struggle can be clearly seen in constructions such as 1137. 18 *be nihtes 7 be dæies* where both the synthetic case ending and the analytic preposition occur; in the resolved moods and tenses which can express some of the modern distinctions but not all, e.g. 1137. 67 *gif he leng moste liuen* 'if he had been spared to live longer'; in the existence alongside the modern resolved passive with the verb 'to be' of forms with *weorðan*, e.g. 1128. 3 and 1135. 4, and of the impersonal *man*, e.g. 1127. 60 and 1137. 5; and perhaps in the higher percentage of sentences beginning with *ond* and *ac* in the two Continuations,[62] though such sentences are common in the earlier parts of the *Chronicle* and may be the result of writing annals. But the transition is not yet completed when uninflected datives occur without prepositions; when the old subjunctives *ware* and *helde* occur alongside the new forms *sculde ben* and *sculde ben* in 1140. 68–70; when the old subjunctive is consistently used in wishes, e.g. 1130. 20, 1131. 38, and 1154. 19; and when the continuous tenses and the periphrastic 'do' forms

[58] See, e.g. *Sweet's Anglo-Saxon Primer* (rev. N. Davis), p. 61.
[59] Clark, pp. xlix ff.   [60] Clark, p. lxv.   [61] Clark, p. lviii.
[62] The figures are (in percentages):

Type of sentence	Stephen	Continuation I	Continuation II
Principal	33.8	31.9	24.3
Subordinate	43.6	28.4	25.7
ond and *ac*	22.6	39.7	50

are completely absent while now-archaic uses of 'do' and 'let' survive, e.g. 1126. 12–15, 1137. 25–6, and 1137. 61.

The language is changing to Modern English, but it has not changed; Miss Clark's brevity in the passage quoted at the beginning of this article produces a misleading impression. The syntax and word-order are still in many important respects Old English. Toller's comment that the language is 'almost that of today'[63] is a singularly unhelpful exaggeration; in syntax and word-order, as well as in pronunciation, spelling, accidence, vocabulary, and punctuation, the two Continuations of the *Peterborough Chronicle* show marked divergences from Modern English.

---

[63] Quoted by Miss Clark, p. lxvi.

22

Paul Bacquet, *La Structure de la Phrase Verbale à l'Époque Alfrédienne* (Publications de la Faculté des Lettres de l'Université de Strasbourg, 145), Paris, 1962[1]

The first words about this book must be of praise, indeed of admiration, for the care and diligence which have gone into its compilation. The author and his printers deserve congratulation on the clearness of its lay-out and on the rarity of misprints. The author further deserves praise for the tremendous industry which must have been involved in classifying the sentences he discusses, and thanks for the mine of examples he has provided. He has certainly saved any future writer on Old English word-order a tremendous amount of sheer drudgery and has made some valuable contributions to our knowledge of word-order in the various types of sentence and clause which occur in Old English. He has also made thought-provoking observations on many topics, e.g. the influence of Latin on Old English word-order (chapter I), the possibility that certain tendencies may have established themselves more firmly in the written than in the spoken language to make up for the absence of intonation in the former (pp. 285–6), and the suggestion that the auxiliary verbs played an important part in breaking down the Old English system of word-order (p. 474). But space does not permit a summary of M. Bacquet's work.

That a summary should be felt necessary suggests that there are weaknesses in the way M. Bacquet presents his findings. This is unfortunately true. First, the book is too long. Very often the author faces problems similar to that discussed on p. 366 and nearly always he makes the same decision:

Il nous a d'abord semblé inutile d'examiner ici dans le détail la relative négative puisqu'on y retrouvait les mêmes faits de position que dans la

Reprinted from *Neuphilologische Mitteilungen* 67 (1966), 86–97.

[1] Where page numbers alone are cited below, the reference is to M. Bacquet's book. His abbreviations for the titles of texts are used. S = subject, V. = verb, nO. = noun object, pO. = pronoun object.

relative affirmative. Si, malgré tout, nous décidons de le faire, c'est dans le seul but d'apporter une nouvelle preuve à l'appui de nos thèses sur la structure de la relative.

Hence findings which, *mutatis mutandis*, apply to more than one type of clause are repeated in chapter after chapter until the mind whirls. Chapters V and VI, which deal with interrogative and imperative sentences respectively, add little new and could have been greatly reduced. The two long chapters on the *ordre de base* in subordinate clauses (chapter VII pp. 274–376 and chapter VIII pp. 377–522) show that M. Bacquet is a slave to a method which inevitably involves wearisome repetition. He is aware of the dangers (p. 727). But he really has not done enough to meet them. And despite its length, the book does not give a complete coverage of the texts of the Alfredian epoch. The six mentioned on p. 64 are sometimes supplemented by the *De Consolatione Philosophiae* of Boethius (pp. 183, 565–6 etc.). But there are omissions, e.g. Bede's *Ecclesiastical History* is taken as post-Alfredian (pp. 748–9). This seems a mistaken decision in the light of Professor Dorothy Whitelock's remarks[2] and a regrettable one in view of the examples the *Bede* contains; M. Bacquet claims for it grammatical independence of the Latin original (p. 48). Two other weaknesses are the absence of an Index, apart from the *Index des Noms d'Auteurs* (which seems of minor importance), and the author's failure to give an adequate and systematic summary of his results. In the event then M. Bacquet's findings are lost in a maze of detail. One way of overcoming this would have been to extend the *Conclusion Générale* (pp. 754–61). Another and better way would have been to reduce the book to some two hundred and fifty pages by ruthless summarizing and by use of appendices. Seven hundred and seventy-five pages on one aspect of syntax in a selection of ninth-century prose texts is just too much; I fear that many will accept the second of Henry Sweet's alternatives: 'If the would-be "junggrammatiker" cannot learn the art of skimming and sifting dissertations and abhandlungs, he had better leave them alone.' This would be a pity. M. Bacquet promises us another book on word-order in post-Alfredian texts (p. 748). I must confess that I view the prospect with bleak enthusiasm if the next work is to be similar to this one in length and treatment. M. Bacquet would be well-advised to ponder the methods adopted by S. O. Andrew in *Syntax and Style in Old English* and *Postscript on Beowulf*, for he is ill-served by his own.

Like several of his predecessors, M. Bacquet seems at times to overlook the tendency of *ond* and *ac* to send a verb to the end of the clause. He is aware that in *ond* and *ac* clauses with no expressed subject the verb tends to have final position (p. 137). But he sometimes suppresses *ond* or *ac* when citing examples where the subject is expressed (e.g. pp. 69, 80, 84) and treats principal clauses beginning with the order S.V. as the same whether or not they begin with *ond* or

[2] *The Old English Bede*, Sir Israel Gollancz Memorial Lecture, 1962, p. 77.

ac (e.g. pp. 68–71 and 78ff.). It now seems to me possible – this qualifies an opinion previously expressed in *NM* 65 (1964), 119 – that this mistake is shared by (and indeed may stem from) M. Fourquet, who, in his *L'Ordre des Éléments de la Phrase en Germanique Ancien*, also suppresses *ond* in some quotations where the subject is expressed (e.g. pp. 39 and 50) and, disregarding the group of eight examples he cites on p. 40, writes 'On dira *se cyning þær nam friþ*, mais, si le sujet n'est pas exprimé: *& þær friþ nam*' (p. 92).[2a] This is particularly significant, for one of the most striking omissions in M. Bacquet's book is his failure to discuss the *ordre de base dans la phrase coordonnée avec sujet* – a failure difficult to understand in view of the fact that the distinction is made when such clauses follow a subordinate clause (pp. 516–22). As a consequence, M. Bacquet finds himself puzzled in chapter X by clauses both positive (pp. 617ff.) and negative (pp. 645ff.) with verbs in final position. Examples of this kind therefore become his third type of *déclarative marquée*. But analysis shows that most of the positive examples he quotes begin with *ond* or *ac* (note the sentence on p. 618 starting 'Que penser de . . .') and that, with the sole exception of *Or.* 114. 5–6, where the sentence has initial *ond*, the negative ones begin with *ne* which, since it is not followed by a verb, is a conjunction – a point M. Bacquet seems not to understand – and therefore shares the tendency to send the verb to the end of the clause. Thus the examples of positive statements with initial subject and final verb are not as numerous as he suggests. It remains to be established that they are *marqué*; they might be explained as part of the 'traces de l'ancien système germanique' of which he speaks on p. 691. But there are other possibilities, as Professor A. Campbell suggested in his Oxford Inaugural Lecture.[2b]

There are other points of Old English syntax which M. Bacquet seems to overlook. (1) In the poetry, the preposition precedes the relative *se* and follows *þe*. The only exceptions to this rule in the examples quoted by M. Bacquet at pp. 346–56 involve the relative *þæt*. But not all these are adjective clauses. In *C.P.* 197. 12–14 and in *Lois* 60. 19 (p. 346), we probably have to do, not with adjective clauses, but with a result and a purpose or result clause (note the subjunctive *ofslea*) respectively. In the first example on p. 347 *æfter* is an adverb or 'separable prefix' rather than a preposition; the five remaining examples – pp. 349, 350, 351, and 352 (2) – can probably be similarly explained, as could *C.P.* 197. 12–14 above. But the relative *þæt* is a frequent offender against most rules.[3] See also p. 346, n. 3. In the first example quoted at p. 347, n. 2 there is no

---

[2a] [1987. See item 21, fn. 20 above.]

[2b] [1987. See A. Campbell 'Verse Influences in Old English Prose', *Philological Essays in Old and Middle English Language and Literature in Honour of Herbert Dean Meritt* ed. J. L. Rosier (The Hague, 1970), pp. 93–8.]

[3] It is the relative in three of the four examples in the poetry in which a preposition seems to follow the relative *se*, viz. *Maxims* I. 135, *Paris Psalm* 88. 3, and *Metres* 28. 80. The fourth is *Riddle* 6. 7 where the relative is *þa*. But all these sentences may contain separable prefixes rather than prepositions; in at least two, the relative is in the wrong case if it is a preposition which follows it.

need to read *þæt* for the second *þe*, for *þurh þe* means 'through thee', as it does in *Christ* 328.[4] (2) It seems strange to me to equate infinitives after *hatan* and *lætan* (where the subject accusative of the infinitive is usually unexpressed) with those after *willan*, *onginnan*, and the like (where the question of a subject accusative cannot arise); see pp. 160–3 and the discussion about *he het ofslean þone syning* (p. 758). (3) Is M. Bacquet aware of the Old English tendency to separate heavy groups? It is clear from some of the examples he cites on pp. 68 and 72 that it is no firm rule. But it seems relevant to discussions on pp. 500, 592, n. 1, and 163 (where the last clauses in the first two examples quoted are arbitrarily cut short: in the text *het* is followed by *7 ahon* and *7 tyhtan* respectively). (4) Why is *hwær* described as one 'des adverbes relatifs' (p. 361)? (5)Is M. Bacquet aware of the use of *scolde* in the sense 'was said to' (pp. 476 and 479)? (6) At p. 758, a comparison between *he hæfde folc gegaderad* and examples like *hie hæfdon þone cyning ofslægenne* might have been relevant. In the latter, *þone cyning ofslægenne* is the object. The order is therefore S.V.O. Hence the opposition noted by M. Bacquet at the top of p. 759 may not exist. (7) The subjunctive *feden* in *C.P.* 137. 17 is unlikely to be as significant as M. Bacquet suggests on p. 381; of the eight *þæt* clauses after *healsian* in the poetry, seven have the subjunctive and one an ambiguous verb form. (8) M. Bacquet might have considered the possibility that the subjunctive mood in direct questions with *hwæþer* S.V. may be significant (pp. 191 ff., 203–4, 211, 215 and n. 1, and 292); the only example with the indicative known to me (apart from those with the ambiguous form *woldest*) is *Matthew* 20. 15. But it should be noted that most of the examples come from the *Boethius*, which has the subjunctive in some questions with *hwy* S.V. as well (e.g. p. 194).

There is some cause for misgiving in the fact that relevant examples which run contrary to M. Bacquet's views are sometimes not quoted. Thus the four examples from *Orosius* cited by Smith[5] in which a pronoun object follows the verb are not, as far as I have observed, mentioned in chapter II (pp. 67ff.), though I would dismiss all except *Or.* 82. 18, since the others begin with *ond* or *ac*. Again, of the nine examples cited by Smith (op. cit., p. 219) in which a pronoun dative follows the verb, at least two (*Or.* 20. 1 and *Or.* 258. 28 – both beginning with *ond*) seem relevant to M. Bacquet's discussion at pp. 95–6. Nor can all his rules be accepted. (1) At pp. 90–2, we are given an unlikely and strangely complicated rule that *þa* temporal and *þonne* causal precede the verb, and *þa* causal and *þonne* temporal follow it. Most of the examples M. Bacquet cites with *þa* before the verb can be taken as causal; note that in *Or.* 114. 1 *þa* represents *igitur*. (2) It is hard to reconcile M. Bacquet's rule for *þeah* (p. 87) with the observations of Professor R. Quirk;[6] this problem needs further

---

[4] Bruce Mitchell *RES* 15 (1964), 137–8.
[5] *PMLA* 8 (1893), 220.
[6] *The Concessive Relation in Old English Poetry* (New Haven, Conn., 1954), p. 21.

investigation. (3) The rule about *þær* in sentences with three or four elements does not seem to rest on any real evidence, for all the examples quoted on pp. 70 and 78 begin with *ond* or *ac*; *Or.* 36. 11 is not quoted in full. It is, moreover, a strangely phrased rule. M. Bacquet restricts it to 'un adverbe de lieu monosyllabique' (p. 69). This is presumably because *þærinne* (see p. 70) is not monosyllabic. But *þider* and *þanon* are not mentioned. Are there no examples? If the difference in position really exists, one might expect the opposition to be between 'simple' adverbs such as *þær*, *þider*, and *þanon*, on the one hand, and 'compound' adverbs such as *þærto* and *þærinne* on the other. (4) The rule that *swiþe* is pre-verbal (p. 75) seems to rest on one example beginning with *ond* (p. 69). (5) There is similar flimsy evidence for the pre-verbal position of *siþþan* (p. 93, n. 1). There are certainly exceptions in post-Alfredian texts, e.g. *Blickling Homilies* 49. 7. (6) On p. 85 *inn* is said to have 'postposition' on the strength of two examples. What is the rule for *ut* (see p. 144)? Can this rule about *inn* be reconciled with Professor A. Campbell's observations in his *Old English Grammar* §§78–80? (7) The misuse of examples introduced by *ond* and *ac* and the failure to cite some relevant examples is also apparent in the discussions in chapter II on the position of *swa* in statements consisting of three or four elements. The one example cited on p. 69 (*Or.* 96. 17) should read *ond he swa gedyde*. Both those on p. 78 have initial *ond*. Of the six examples cited on p. 84, one is quoted with initial *ond*, two (*T.A.* 144. 12 and *Or.* 160. 13) actually have it in the text though M. Bacquet omits it, and one (*Or.* 62. 3–6) is another example of a divided conjunction, to be compared with those cited on p. 277. This leaves two examples of pre-verbal *swa* in a simple statement (*Or.* 54. 23 and *Chr.* an. 853), both of which read *He þa swa dyde*. In opposition to this, there is *Or.* 44. 15 *Hie þæt gelæstan swa* which M. Bacquet does not cite, as far as I can see. (*Or.* 146. 32 with initial *ond* is similar and should have been quoted by M. Bacquet. But it is in my opinion irrelevant.) Are there any more such examples? No doubt M. Bacquet could explain *Or.* 44. 15 as *marqué*. But the misgivings about his treatment of evidence are not stilled by his failure to mention it.

The main theme of M. Bacquet's book is that in each kind of sentence or clause there is an *ordre de base* and an *ordre marqué*; of these he writes (p. 755)

> L'ordre de base coincidera donc souvent avec l'organisation de la phrase parlée ou de la phrase écrite sans préoccupations stylistiques, tandis que l'ordre marqué s'emploiera si l'on veut chanter la phrase ou l'ennoblir pour la hausser au niveau des événements que l'on célèbre.

In the positive statement, the *ordre de base* is S.V.nO. or S.pO.V. (chapter II); certain misgivings about some of the detail in this chapter have been noted above. In chapter III, M. Bacquet tries to establish as the *ordre de base* in the negative statement the pattern *ic hine ne geseo* (p. 134). But here again he includes examples with *ond* and *ac* and suppresses *ond* in quoting others (e.g.

pp. 128 and 129). Worse, he suppresses *forðam* 'because' in *C.P.* 395. 28–9 (p. 132) and includes examples of 'semi-subordination' such as *Or.* 17. 13–15 (p. 129). He is thus left with very few genuine examples. All he quotes except one have pronoun subjects; the exception (significantly) has a coalesced verb form – *C.P.* 27. 25 *ða hierdas næfdon ongit* (p. 129). (This raises a doubt about the rightness of the decision referred to at p. 66, n. 2.) M. Bacquet makes a bold, but hardly successful, attempt at p. 134 to disarm the obvious criticism that he has completely disregarded the relative statistics of the *He hie ne geseah* type against the type *Ne geseah he hine* by taking the latter as *marqué* (pp. 629–45). The table on p. 134 contains more than an element of artificiality and the observation at p. 131, n. 1 that only three examples with impersonal verbs in all M. Bacquet's texts conform to the *ordre de base* is suspicious, to say the least. The rules formulated by S. O. Andrew (*Syntax and Style in Old English*, p. 62) have not been dethroned by M. Bacquet's evidence, and such neat formulae as that on p. 219 cannot be accepted. In chapter IV, the *ordre de base* in coordinate clauses with the subject unexpressed has the verb or the auxiliary in final position (pp. 136 and 162); variations are explained as *marqué* (p. 162 and elsewhere). *Ac* clauses of this type do not seem to be considered. M. Bacquet produces convincing explanations for some of the variations. But it is not always clear why some examples are *marqué* and others are not; there is no obvious reason for treating *Or.* 84. 17–18 and *Or.* 198. 32–3 (p. 142) any differently from *Or.* 126. 11 and *Or.* 192. 3 (p. 141) *if the two latter are considered in context*. And M. Bacquet once again fails to cite some difficult examples. Thus *Or.* 226. 10 and *Or.* 284. 28, both of which have a pronoun object after the verb, are not mentioned at pp. 150–2, and it is not easy to see at first glance how they can be *marqué*. My verdict on this chapter must be that M. Bacquet has been so intent on establishing his theory that he failed to take seriously enough the possibility that analogy was already at work and that some at least of the departures from his *ordre de base* foreshadow the ultimate disappearance of clauses with the verb in final position. Chapters V and VI have already been mentioned. Chapter VII discusses relative clauses. M. Bacquet's examples are almost entirely limited to those beginning with *þe*. By so disregarding clauses introduced by *se*, he fails to treat the big question of whether they are demonstrative or relative clauses; the difficulty is disposed of far too easily at p. 304.[7] We learn that the verb has final position in the *ordre de base* (p. 278) and second position in *ordre marqué* (p. 760). But on p. 304 we learn that 'l'ordre de base n'excluait pas la possibilité de mettre un terme en valeur au moyen de l'intonation'. This is a little bewildering and may seem to some to call into doubt the whole fundamental concept of an *ordre de base* opposed to an *ordre marqué*. At any rate, it is hard to see how M. Bacquet can be so sure that the less frequent order is the

---

[7] On this point, see *Anglia* 81 (1963), 317–19. [1987. See now *OES* §§2109–21.]

ordre de base (p. 326) and yet find that two examples of it on p. 327 possess 'l'accent d'insistance'. Chapter VIII reaches similar findings for other subordinate clauses. Though some interesting points are made, e.g. about the tendency of *man* to take second position after a subordinating conjunction (p. 391 and elsewhere), this long chapter adds little of substance. Contemplation of chapters VII and VIII in retrospect leads to a verdict similar to that expressed above on chapter IV. In chapter IX, M. Bacquet examines the *structures secondaires*, i.e. the infinitive, gerund, participle, and similar, groups. He has some useful things to say, though here again one cannot always accept his interpretation of examples. Thus the arrangement *He wearð fram his agnum monnum ofslagen* seems to me to put more emphasis on the prepositional phrase than the order *He wearð ofslagen fram* . . . (pp. 556–7). Certainly such things are matters of opinion. But it is dangerous to erect rules on a foundation of opinion.

In chapter X, M. Bacquet deals with what he calls 'trois types de déclarative marquée'. The first is the sentence with the initial verb. On p. 591 he writes 'Rien ne s'oppose donc à ce que l'on traite ensemble la phrase précédée de la subordonnée et celle qui ne l'est pas.' This seems to me a mistake in method; theoretical arguments should not take the place of a full treatment of the evidence. Those sentences in which the verb is preceded by nothing else should have been grouped separately from those in which either a subordinate clause or *ond* precedes the verb; these latter types make up the bulk of his material. Sentences beginning with *ne* V. are, of course, much more common than those with initial verb but (as has been pointed out above) the proposition that they are *marqué* can be accepted only if the statistics are disregarded (pp. 629–45). The second type of *déclarative marquée* is that in which initial *þa* or *þonne* is followed by the verb (p. 600). Why this should be regarded as 'une variante de la phrase à verbe initial' (p. 597) is not clear (but cf. Fourquet, op. cit., p. 93). It is, of course, the most common pattern after *þa* and *þonne*, and M. Bacquet does not seem to me to have demolished the view that it is due to a tendency for the verb to have second place. The examples he has found of *þa* S.V. are a valuable addition to our stock. But, while claiming that *þa* V.S. is *marqué*, he regards *þa* S.V. as embodying *le mode emphatique* (p. 599). I am not sure that I understand the difference. The third type – that with verb in final position – has already been discussed. Chapter XI examines other types of *déclarative marquée*. M. Bacquet convincingly confirms the already-known fact that word-order fluctuates after *her* and after adverb clauses, but claims that the sentence is *marqué* when the verb has second place (p. 653). It must be said that *Or*. 198. 5–6 (quoted on p. 655) fits the theory very well. But it is not clear that M. Bacquet cites all the examples in which the subject precedes the verb and the facts he presents do not seem incompatible with the view that the order S.V.O. was beginning to assert itself; thus, for example, the italicized phrase at the bottom of p. 689 has exactly the same order as its Modern English counterpart. Chapter XII continues the discussion of the *ordre de base et marqué* and Appendix I suggests that the word-order in other dialects in the ninth century was the same as in West Saxon. Appendix II will be discussed below. A short *Conclusion Générale*, in which many valuable points of detail are not mentioned, follows at pp. 754–61.

Throughout his work, M. Bacquet rightly lays great stress on the influence of rhetorical and stylistic considerations, the demands of emphasis, and the pedagogic nature of the texts with which he is dealing. But other factors are sometimes a little abruptly dismissed. It is probably true that the presence of an adjective clause does not affect the word-order in *Or.* 54. 7–8 (pp. 98–9). But is the same true of *Or.* 118. 27 and of some of the examples cited on pp. 138–9? The weight of the elements concerned is sometimes admitted as a factor (e.g. p. 659) but at other times not (e.g. p. 283). Could it not have had an influence in determining the position of some prepositional phrases in coordinate and subordinate clauses (e.g. pp. 142, 283, 341, 561, and 562)? M. Bacquet agrees with M. Fourquet in denying that the order of the principal clause has any effect on a clause which is coordinate with it (p. 139), and produces strong evidence at pp. 156–7 to show that such influence does not always operate. Yet one wonders about such sentences as *Or.* 278. 13–15 (cited *in part* at p. 138), where none of the three *ond* clauses has its verb in final position.

M. Bacquet often misses opportunities of comparing Old English patterns with their Modern English equivalents (pp. 87, 96, 242, and 488, but cf. p. 268 and elsewhere). His dismissal of the idea that the pattern adverb V.S. in Old English can have anything to do with similar phenomena in other Germanic languages seems a little brusque (p. 647, and cf. pp. 691 and 747). The striking similarities between word-order in Old English and in Modern German would seem to provide a *prima facie* case for the view that there was some connexion. Has M. Bacquet succeeded in demolishing this, and in explaining why the principles which he thinks govern Old English word-order differ so fundamentally from those at work in Modern German? M. Bacquet opposes the idea that Old English word-order is completely free (e.g. pp. 273, 617, and 728) and makes his case good. Yet his own theories at times seem somewhat elaborate (e.g. p. 695) and it might be claimed that he swings to the other extreme of rigidity in assuming that all departures from his *ordre de base* are necessarily *marqué*. One wonders whether these early writers were always as much in control of their material as he would have us believe; sentences like *C.P.* 4. 1–4 and *C.P.* 6. 6–15 would test his theory.

M. Bacquet's insistence that there is a fundamental difference between *he hie gefliemde* and *7 hie gefliemde* (p. 137) and between *þa he hit geseah* and *he hit geseah* (pp. 275 and 758) may be justified historically. But the fact that the pronoun object occupied the pre-verbal position in all these types, as well as in the pattern *and he hit geseah* (p. 618), must soon have blurred the distinction and contributed to the continuation of this word-order in principal clauses in the *Peterborough Chronicle* 1122–54 after the noun object ceased to have pre-verbal position.[8] But to admit this would be to admit the possibility that analogy was at work and that the language was already evolving towards its modern structure. This explanation often seems relevant. Since *he sæde eac* is regular in statements (p. 119), the appearance of *ond sæde eac* in *Or.* 190. 23 and the like (p. 149) does not seem surprising. Since S.V.nO. is the regular order in statements (p. 70), it is hard to see why the only valid reason for this order in adjective clauses should be the writer's desire to place the noun 'en relief' (p. 279). Again, analogy seems relevant at pp. 136ff. But M. Bacquet will not have this; see p. 435, for example, where he writes: 'Traditionnellement, on a tendance à considérer ce type de variante comme un signe d'évolution de la syntaxe vers une structure moderne. Rien ne saurait être plus inexact . . .' and goes on to explain the variations in different manuscripts of the *Chronicle* as due to different attitudes to the material on the part of the copyists. But these variations could be due to differences in the age and therefore in the language of the copyists; M. Fourquet observes that 'les copistes tendent à généraliser l'ordre verbe – nom' (op. cit., p. 51) and, more tellingly, when speaking of differences between the language of the *Chronicle* up to 891 and that of the *Chronicle* from 892 to 925 (op. cit., p. 99):

> On ne peut donc nier que la langue ait évolué; le résultat statistique brut en donne une idée: l'ordre nom-verbe était deux fois plus fréquent que l'autre dans la première partie; ici c'est l'ordre verbe-nom qui est cinq fois plus fréquent!

This is, of course, in direct contradiction of M. Bacquet's claim in Appendix II (p. 753) that

> la syntaxe de position est donc encore, dans la seconde moitié du XIe siècle, celle que nous avons observée dans les écrits alfrédiens, celle aussi des documenst [*sic*] kentiques ou merciens qui datent de la première moitié du IXe siècle. Une période de deux siècles et plus s'est écoulée sans que la langue évolue en ce domaine, alors que d'autres systèmes tel que le système modal, sont en cours de modification au début du Xe siècle.

The balance of probabilities seems to me on M. Fourquet's side. For M. Bacquet is satisfied that statistics have little, if any, relevance; see pp. 24, 142–4, 161, 267, and 326 (general observations), pp. 154–5 and p. 427 (generalizations based on very few examples), p. 474 (how many *do* conform?), and pp. 177 and

---

[8] See *NM* 65 (1964), 124. [1987. See p. 228 above.]

477, n. 1 (*all* examples of a particular construction are *marqué*). He also seems to have a short way with exceptions; see, e.g. pp. 329–30 and 155–8 (where, as far as I can see, the twenty-two examples mentioned at the bottom of p. 155 do not appear again). One sometimes has the impression that M. Bacquet knew what he was going to find before he started. Be that as it may, he has missed an opportunity of giving us valuable statistics of word-order in Alfredian texts which we could have compared with those in later texts, as far as they are available. How would M. Bacquet account for the changes which have taken place in word-order in the *Peterborough Chronicle*? And when does he think they began?

In conclusion, I feel compelled to take issue once again with those who subscribe (as M. Bacquet seems to do, p. 22) to G. W. Small's dictum that there is now no room for the pure descriptivism of 1910. In the sense in which I understand 'pure descriptivism' (which involves the presentation of statistics), there is room for a lot more of it in the study of Old English syntax; the failure of some recent editors of Old English texts to show that respect for syntax which they show for other linguistic features seems to me to support this view. We may never be able to solve some problems because we are denied the evidence of the spoken language. But until we do know what is there, we are in danger of spending our time on pseudo-problems.[9] Hence we must be grateful to M. Bacquet for this invaluable collection of carefully presented material.

---

[9] For an example see *Neophilologus* 49 (1965), 51–5.

23
The Subject–Noun Object–Verb Pattern in the *Peterborough Chronicle*: A Reply

I am afraid that Mr David L. Shores has misunderstood and misrepresented me in the article with the above title,[1] and I feel compelled to reply. I believe that the middle paragraph on *S*, p. 624, distorts the aims and statements of the article to which Mr Shores objects.[2] He says (*S*, pp. 624–5) that 'he wants to confine himself in this short paper to questioning the significance of the statement that "the greatest claim of the Peterborough Chronicle 1122–1154 to modernity in these sentences [principal clauses] lies in the *complete absence* [emphasis mine] of the word-order S. noun O.V."' This is a clear misrepresentation. The words 'these sentences' in this quotation from *M*, p. 124, do not refer to 'principal clauses', as Mr Shores glosses them. On *M*, p. 120, it is made clear that section III of my article deals with word-order 'in simple sentences and principal clauses which do not begin with *ond*, *ac*, *ne*, or other conjunctions, or with adverbs or adverb phrases'. The last paragraph of this section (*M*, p. 124) reads:

> To sum up. We have seen that in the type of simple sentence and principal clause under discussion, over three-quarters of the sentences in *Stephen* and in both Continuations show a pattern common to Old English and Modern English. All the rest have patterns which occur in Old English, but not in Modern English. There is nothing which is Modern English, but not Old English. Even the modern arrangement of the elements of the resolved moods and tenses occurs in Old English. The greatest claim of the *Peterborough Chronicle* 1122–1154 to modernity in these sentences lies in the complete absence of the word-order S. noun O.V.[3]

Reprinted from *Neuphilologische Mitteilungen* 71 (1970), 611–14.

[1] See *NM* 70 (1969), 623–6 (hereafter abbreviated as *S*).

[2] See *NM* 65 (1964), 113–44 (hereafter abbreviated as *M*) [item 21 above]. It is, of course, true that some of the classifications I used can be further broken down, e.g. S. . . . V.; see *M*, pp. 119–20. Such analysis was irrelevant to the problem to which I addressed myself; see *M*, p. 120. No doubt Mr Shores's promised work (*S*, p. 624, fn. 3) will rectify this.

[3] This paragraph and others throughout the article suggest that, despite Mr Shores (*S*, p. 624), I am not unaware of the idea of continuity.

Here the phrases 'under discussion' and 'in these sentences' make it patently clear that I am talking about the clauses defined on *M*, p. 120, and not about principal clauses in general.

Having thus misread what I said, Mr Shores is in a position to produce two 'exceptions' (*S*, p. 625):

> the chief concern here is about the presence of the SOV pattern with the object filled by a noun. There seems to be at least one occurrence of this pattern, which Mitchell says does not occur, and possibly another. The first is *.ac hi nan treuthe ne heolden.* (263.35) and the second, *.7 hi nan helpe ne haefden of þe kinge.* (267.28). It is possible to consider the first as the special *ac* pattern and the second as a coordinate dependent clause. Both of these, however, can be read as principal clauses. At this point it may be helpful to cite these clauses again, but along with those that occur immediately before them:
>
> Hi hadden him manred maked 7 athes suoren. *ac hi nan treuthe ne heolden.* (263.34–35)
> .7 hi of Normandi wenden alle fra þe king ... *for* he besaet heom til hi a iauen up here castles. *7 hi nan helpe ne* haefden of þe kinge. (267.27–28)

and to explain how I came to 'overlook' them (*S*, p. 626): '[I am assuming that Mitchell did notice these clauses and readily dismissed them as an *ac* pattern and a dependent clause respectively.]' I do not think 'readily dismissed' is quite the phrase. I am certain that no assumption was necessary. If Mr Shores had looked in section V – to which the logic of my article ought to have directed him – he would have found these two examples. They appear in table 8 (*M*, p. 132) under the patterns '*ac* S. ... V.' and '*ond* S. ... V.' respectively. His Earle and Plummer 263. 34–5 is my Clark 1137. 12 and his 267. 27–8 is my 1140. 53.

I agree with Mr Shores that both these can be described as 'principal clauses'; the definition already quoted above from *M*, p. 120, implies this. I deliberately made the distinctions there set out to avoid getting involved in what seems to me the arid terminological problem raised by Mr Shores. We can say whether a clause does or does not begin with *ond* or *ac*. But however carefully we define a 'principal clause', we cannot determine whether a particular clause in the *Peterborough Chronicle* is or is not one when we are unable to recapture the intonation patterns and when (as Mr Shores rightly points out on *S*, p. 625) 'it is difficult to interpret with certainty the punctuation practices in this document'. So it all comes back to the fundamental point that we are not discussing 'principal clauses'; we are discussing the clauses defined on *M*, p. 120. The remarks made in ll. 1–16 of *S*, p. 626, while undisputed, are in my opinion irrelevant to the present problem. Mr Shores, it seems to me, merely blurs the issue by repeating in another form the error made by Rothstein, Barrett, and Bacquet.[4]

I think I have already made out a case for my claim that Mr Shores has misread and misrepresented me. But worse follows and it is difficult to write temperately about his last paragraph (*S*, p. 626):

> It seems then that the presence of these two S.O.V. patterns alone calls into question the accuracy of Mitchell's statement that the S. noun O.V. pattern did not occur at all. Moreover, these two patterns plus the occurrence of the S.O.V. pattern with a pronoun as object in thirty-one other clauses (twenty of which are in independent clauses), the occurrence of the S. noun O.V. pattern in six dependent clauses, and the occurrence of the noun O.V. pattern in several coordinate predicates such as *7 na iustise ne dide* (263.33) should generate some doubt about laying too much stress on Mitchell's statement that the greatest claim to modernity of the latter part of the Peterborough Chronicle is the absence of the S. noun O.V. word-order.

The points must be tabulated:

1 My remark is again distorted. There is no such thing as Mitchell's statement 'that the S. noun O.V. pattern did not occur at all'; the definition on *M*, p. 120, is still relevant.
2 As I point out on *M*, pp. 119 and 124, the pattern S. pronoun O.V. falls into quite a different category from S. noun O.V., because of the different usage in Old English. The two patterns are carefully distinguished throughout my article – S. pronoun O.V. as such and S. noun O.V. under the heading S. .... V.[5]
3 The existence in dependent clauses and co-ordinate 'predicates' of the patterns referred to is admitted and covered by tables 11 and 8 respectively of my article. But these too are irrelevant to the particular problem under discussion here; once again I refer to the definition on *M*, p. 120.
4 The last four lines repeat the basic distortion with an addition. Let me reiterate my position. The remark to which Mr Shores objects was confined to Continuations I and II, not to 'the latter part', of the *Peterborough Chronicle*; it was confined to the types of clause defined on *M*, p. 120. *In these clauses* [my italics], there are still to the best of my knowledge no examples of the pattern S. noun O.V. in either continuation of the *Peterborough Chronicle*.

---

[4] See *M*, p. 118. Mr Shores himself admits the influence of *ac* (*S*, p. 626), but strangely enough not that of *ond*, in sending a verb to the end of a clause.
[5] On this point see again p. 253, fn. 2.

24
Old English *Oð þæt* Adverb?

Various writers in the past have suggested that in Old English poetry *oð þæt* may sometimes be an adverb rather than a conjunction. Here I attempt to bring together all the evidence which bears on this problem – a process just as essential when one is assessing syntactical probability in any one context as it is when assessing semantic probability when that is involved.

These earlier writers include Schücking,[1] Glogauer,[2] Möllmer,[3] Klaeber,[4] and von Schaubert.[5] The last-named scholar, having remarked that *oð þæt* appears at the beginning of a fitt in *Genesis A* l. 1248, *Beowulf* ll. 1740 and 2039 (here there is, however, no numeral), and is written in large capitals at *Genesis A* ll. 715 and 2749 (= *ASPR* l. 2750), goes on to say that 'alle Stellen lassen sich aufs beste als Hauptsatz fassen'. We may not be ready to accept this. But it has to be admitted that, while a clause introduced by *oð þæt* may mark both the termination or temporal limit of the action of the main clause and a transition in the narrative, e.g.

> *Beowulf* l. 99   Swa ða drihtguman   dreamum lifdon,
> eadiglice,   oð ðæt an ongan
> fyrene fremman   feond on helle,

it frequently marks a transition or new development in the narrative without implying that the action of the main clause is completed, e.g.

> *Beowulf* l. 53   Ða wæs on burgum   Beowulf Scyldinga,
> leof leodcyning   longe þrage
> folcum gefræge   – fæder ellor hwearf,
> aldor of earde –   oþ þæt him eft onwoc
> heah Healfdene.

Reprinted from *Notes and Queries* 223 (1978), 390–4.

[1] L. L. Schücking *Die Grundzüge der Satzverknüpfung im Beowulf* (Halle, 1904), pp. 12–15.
[2] E. Glogauer *Die Bedeutungsübergänge der Konjunktionen in der angelsächsischen Dichtersprache* (Leipzig, 1922), pp. 29–31.
[3] H. Möllmer *Konjunktionen und Modus im Temporalsatz des Altenglischen* (Breslau, 1937), pp. 89–91.
[4] Fr. Klaeber *Beowulf* 3rd edn (Boston, 1941), Glossary s.v. *oð*.
[5] In her note on *Beowulf* l. 56.

E. G. Stanley has now given new impetus to the idea that *oð þæt* could function as an adverb by observing in his study on the A3 lines in *Beowulf* that 'as has been remarked before, *oð þæt* can begin a numbered section, and in that position and often elsewhere (where "until" makes unsatisfactory sense) it may be translated as an adverb with some such meaning as "at length".'[6] There is, I believe, syntactical evidence in favour of this suggestion.

First we may note that combinations of a preposition + the appropriate form of the neuter demonstrative *þæt* are often used as adverbs in Old English. Space does not permit full exemplification of the patterns which do occur. But a few illustrations must be given.

Words such as *æfter* and *ær* are adverbs in their own right and it is therefore scarcely surprising that we do not often find them in adverbial combinations such as *ær þon* (*Phoenix* l. 379), *ær þam* (Wulfstan's *Homilies* (ed. Bethurum) XX (*EI*). 81–2 and *Chronicle D* (ed. Earle and Plummer) 176. 21 (1052)) and *æfter þon* (Bede's *History* (ed. Miller) 28. 7 and 40. 24 and *Blickling Homilies* (ed. Morris) 121. 7). It is possible that in the two examples of *ær þam* quoted, *þam* is the result of late confusion between unstressed *-an/-on* and *-am* and is therefore not a true dative. The same may be true of *sip þam* adverb in *Guthlac A* l. 136 and *siððam* conjunction in *Soliloquies* (ed. Endter) 46. 3, for we probably do better to explain *-þan* in *sipþan* as originally instrumental, following Adams:

> This conjunction is, according to Sweet *Student's Dictionary of Anglo-Saxon*, compounded of the preposition *sið* and its object in the dative. Others regard *ðan* as being the instrumental in a phrase of comparison. I incline to the latter view; for *ðæm* does not become *ðan* until the later period of OE, and we have *siððan* in the earliest texts.[7]

However, the proposition that combinations of a preposition + the dative of *þæt* and of a preposition + the instrumental of *þæt* can serve as adverbs is in my opinion established by these examples involving the prepositions *for* and *mid*: *Cura Pastoralis* (ed. Sweet) 5. 16 *forðæm ... forðæmðe* 'for that reason ... because', 259. 23 *forðæm* 'therefore' or 'for that reason' (the word may here be used *apo koinou*), 5. 1 *forðon* 'therefore', 7. 5 *forðy* 'therefore', Boethius's *Consolations* (ed. Sedgfield), 113. 21 *forðæm* 'therefore', *Blickling Homilies* 31. 14 *forþon ... forþon* 'for that reason ... because', Bede's *History* (*B*) 48. 27 *mid þam* 'with that, then', (*Ca*) 48. 27 *mid þy* 'with that, then', *Cura Pastoralis* 55. 11 *mid ðy ðe ... mid ðy* 'when/while ... then', and Ælfric's *Catholic Homilies* (ed. Thorpe) i. 122. 33 *mid þam ðe ... mid þam* 'when ... then'. Here again *þam* may be for *þan*. But the fact that I have not yet found *mid þy/þon/þan* (*þe*) in

[6] E. G. Stanley 'Some Observations on the A3 Lines in *Beowulf*', *Old English Studies in Honour of John C. Pope* ed. Robert B. Burlin and Edward B. Irving, Jr (Toronto, 1974), pp. 139–64. My article has its origin in his observations and has benefited greatly from our discussions of the problem.

[7] A. Adams *The Syntax of the Temporal Clause in Old English Prose* (New Haven, Conn., 1907), p. 100.

any of those works which are generally accepted as being by Ælfric is against this.

That combinations of a preposition + the genitive of *þæt* served as adverbs is in my opinion adequately attested; consider *Daniel* l. 41 *to þæs* 'thither', *Christ and Satan* l. 529 *to ðæs* 'thither', *Andreas* l. 1123 *to þæs* 'to that end', *Beowulf* l. 1616 *to þæs* 'to that extent, so', and Bede's *History* 28. 11 *to þæs... þæt*' and 366. 17 *to ðæs... þæt* 'to that extent, so... that'.

But if we are to make out any real case for the proposition that *oð þæt* can be an adverb, we must produce examples in which a combination of a preposition + the accusative *þæt* serves as an adverb. This can be done. Adverbial *oð þæt* 'till that, till then' and *oð þis* 'till this, till now' do occur, though not at the beginning of their clause; see below. We also find, again not initially, *siðet* glossing *a modo* in Matthew (Rushworth) 26. 29. There are, however, a few late examples of adverbial combinations of a preposition + the accusative *þæt* occurring initially in their clause. They include Genesis 37. 5 *Witodlice hyt gelamp þæt hym mætte 7 he rehte þæt hys gebroðrum; þurh þæt hi hyne hatedon þe swyðor* Latin *Accidit quoque ut uisum somnium referret fratribus suis: quae causa maioris odii seminarium fuit*, where *þurh þæt* certainly cannot mean 'because', and the correlative *þurh þæt þe... þurh þæt* in Wulfstan's *Homilies* XX (*EI*). 152 *And þurh þæt þe man swa deð þæt man eal hyrweð þæt man scolde heregian 7 to forð laðet þæt man scolde lufian, þurh þæt man gebringeð ealles to manege on yfelan geþance 7 and on undæde....*[8]

Second, there is the theoretical point that the adverbial use of *oð þæt* does not surprise those who, like myself, accept Small's proposition that 'it may be laid down as a general principle that in the progress of language parataxis precedes hypotaxis'[9] or, as Mann puts it,

> Wenn wir nach der Entstehung der Konjunktionen forschen, also nach den Hilfsmitteln, die einen Nebensatz dem Hauptsatz unterordnen, müssen wir von der Erkenntnis ausgehen, dass sich die moderne Sprachform der Unterordnung aus der der Beiordnung (Asyndese-verbunde Parataxe-Hypotaxe) entwickelt hat.[10]

We do not have to postulate a long gap in time between these uses. In *A Guide to*

[8] If one of two correlative clause introducers has *þe*, it is safe to assume that it is the conjunction and the other is the adverb. But the presence of *þe* in a clause introducer without a correlative does not necessarily certify that it is a subordinating conjunction. Thus *forþon* in *Blickling Homilies* 25. 22–3 and *forþon þe* in *Blickling Homilies* 25. 20–1 (both quoted below) may be co-ordinating rather than subordinating conjunctions and *þeh þe* in *Orosius* (ed. Sweet), 158. 23 seems to be an adverb. There is room for more work here.

[9] G. W. Small *The Comparison of Inequality* (Baltimore, 1924), p. 125.

[10] G. Mann 'Die Enstehung von nebensatzeinleitenden Konjunktionen im Englischen', *Archiv für das Studium der neueren Sprachen und Literaturen* 180 (1942), 88. See also Möllmer, pp. 2–8 and 113–14.

Old English §169,[11] I suggested that one (if not both) of the stages *for þæm þe* and *for þæm...þe* was essential in the development of the conjunction *for þæm* and *for*. I still believe this to be likely. If the sequence I had in mind were applied to combinations of *oð* + the accusative *þæt*, it would give the series *oð* prep. > *oð þæt* adv. > *oð þæt þe* conj. > *oð þæt* conj. > *oð* conj. (I omit consideration of **oð þæt...þe* because as far as I know at the moment it does not occur.) However, I am doubtful whether *oð þæt þe* was an essential intermediate stage; it could well have appeared after *oð þæt* was used as a conjunction. The rarity of the combinations *þær þe*, *þa þe*, and *þonne þe*, suggests that the stage with *þe* was not essential in the development of *þær*, *þa*, and *þonne*, into conjunctions and the scarcity of *oð þæt þe* and *oð þætte* suggests that the same was true for *oð*. If we follow Adams in viewing *oððe* as *oð* + *ðe* rather than as a weakening of *oð þæt*,[12] we have another argument for not accepting *oð þæt þe* as an essential step. However, I would regard *oð þæt* as an essential step and would therefore omit 'probably' from Adams's statement on this question: 'In origin *oð* is a preposition denoting limit of motion. From this it soon passed into conjunctive use, probably through the dropping out of its object *ðæt* in the more common conjunction *oð þæt*.[13]

I can therefore see no reason why *oð þæt* should not be used adverbially. Just as *for* prefers the dative or the instrumental, so *oð* prefers the accusative. Since *for þæm/þon/þy* can be used as adverbs as well as conjunctions, it seems not illogical to posit the first possibility for *oð þæt* when the second is clearly established. It may be said that Stanley's 'at length' causes no difficulty if it is used to translate *oð þæt* in contexts where it is rightly taken as a conjunction, e.g. Boethius's *Consolations* 14. 26 *Ða geswigode se Wisdom ane lytle hwile oð þæt he ongeat þæs Modes ingeþoncas*, *Apollonius of Tyre* (ed. Goolden) 18. 23 *Æfter þisum wordum he eode on ðone weg þe him getæht wæs oð ðæt he becom to þare ceastre geate*, and

---

[11] Oxford, 1964; 2nd edn 1968.
[12] Adams, pp. 130–1. O. Johnsen in *Anglia* 38 (1914), 92–5, claims that in these combinations '*oð* is an adverb denoting limit in space', '*þæt* is the local-demonstrative adverb', and *þe* is 'originally local-demonstrative particle'.
[13] Adams, p. 131.

I hope to pursue the question of the origin of the Old English conjunctions elsewhere, though not with any expectation of reaching finality. However, it may be said that any treatment of the question will have to distinguish at least four groups of conjunctions: (a) those of demonstrative origin like *þær, þa,* and *þonne*, which are used as adverbs but not as prepositions: (b) prepositional formulae in which the preposition is used alone as an adverb but not as a conjunction (in Old English), e.g. *æfter, to*; (c) prepositional formulae in which the preposition is used alone as a conjunction but not as an adverb, e.g. *butan, for, oð*; (d) prepositional formulae in which the preposition is used as an adverb and a conjunction in Old English, e.g. *ær*. This is far from exhausting the list of non-prepositional conjunctions given in §168 of my *Guide*. The origin of all the words concerned will also have to be considered. [1987. I made a start on this task in item 26 below.]

Christ A l. 306   Wlat þa swa wisfæst   witga geond þeodland
oþþæt he gestarode   þær gestaþelad wæs
æþelic ingong.

So, if *siþþan* could develop from adverb 'after that' to a conjunction *ex quo* and 'after', there seems no reason why *oð þæt* should not have developed from an adverb 'at length' to a conjunction 'until'.

Third, there is the fact that *oð þæt* does occur as an adverb in the works of Ælfric. Examples include Ælfric's *Lives* (ed. Skeat) i. 104–263 *þa het Martianus þa godes menn gefeccan and axode Iulianum hweðer hi aht smeadon ymbe hyre agene þearfe on þære hwile oðþæt* and the passages referred to by Pope in the Glossary to his edition of Ælfric's *Homilies* (s.v. *oþ*), of which the following is typical: *Homily* XXI. 461 *Ælce dæge man sealde ærþan þam leonum twa sceap to bigleofan and twegen leapas oð ðæt*. It must be said that *oð þæt* is not used initially in any of these examples and that in all of them it has its literal meaning 'till that' and can be translated 'till then'. The same is true of the occasional occurrences of *oð þis(um)* 'till now', e.g. Bede's *History* 134. 14, Bede's *History* 150. 12 ... *sum micel gylden Cristes mæl 7 gylden cælic gehalgad to wigbedes þenunge, þa nu gen oð þis mæg mon sceawigan gehealden in Contwara cirican*, *Cura Pastoralis* 173. 14 *Nu ðonne oð ðiss we rehton hwelc se hierde bion sceal*, *Soliloquies* 13. 6 *Wel la, god feder, wel alyse me of ðam gedwolan þe ic on oð þisum dwealde and gyt on dwolige*, and Ælfric's *Homilies* (ed. Pope) II. 223 and II. 241 *Nu smeagað menn foroft hwær hit eal becume þe fram Adame wæs oð ðis gesceapen*. But at least *oð þæt* does occur in positions where it must be an adverb and not a conjunction.

The fourth and last piece of evidence, however, offers stronger support to those who wish to believe that *oð þæt* can be used in the early poetry as a transitional adverb introducing a new sentence. This is the gloss *Eatenus*: *oð ðæt* in the Corpus Gloss.[14] It also appears in the form *Eatenus uel eotenus oð þæt* in Plantin-Moretus Museum (Antwerp) 47 (Salle, iii. 68) + British Museum, Add. 32246[15] and as *Eatenus oþþæt* in Cotton Cleopatra A. III.[16] This is strong evidence for the early occurrence of adverbial *oð þæt*.

What sense or senses could it have borne? According to Plezia's *Lexicon*,[17] *eatenus, ea tenus* adv. has three main uses: I *de modo et mensura* = *eo, usque, tantum*. II *de tempore* = 1. *usque, ad hoc tempus*. 2. *tunc*. III *de causa* = *qua propter, quam obrum, ideo*. Of these, the temporal use seems most promising and most

[14] See W. M. Lindsay *The Corpus Glossary* (Cambridge, 1921), p. 60.
[15] *Anglo-Saxon and Old English Vocabularies* ed. T. Wright and R. P. Wülcker (London, 1884), column 191, no. 14.
[16] *Anglo-Saxon Vocabularies*, column 391, no. 16. In his copy of the work in the English Faculty Library, Oxford, Napier notes that this entry, with others, is taken from the Corpus Gloss.
[17] *Lexicon Mediae et Infimae Latinitatis Polonorum, Słownik Łaciny Średniowiecznej w Polsce* ed. M. Plezia (Academia Scientiarum Polona, 1953).

relevant; such senses as 'and then', 'at that limit', 'in due course', or 'in the end', can reasonably be postulated for adverbial *oð þæt* and come very close to Stanley's attractive rendering 'at length'.

It must however be said that what seems to us a clear-cut distinction was perhaps less obvious to speakers of Old English. Klaeber, after reviewing what had been written on this question up to 1941 and citing parallels from Old English clauses introduced by *ær/ær þon/ær þam þe* and *syþðan* and from Old Norse, Middle English, Modern English, and Modern German, agreed that we are inclined to take the *oð þæt* clauses under discussion and similar clauses as principal sentences. However, he expressed himself as doubtful whether this was justified and decided that, if he had to make a choice, he would prefer to take them as subordinate clauses. 'Es ist schliesslich', he concluded, 'eine Frage des Stils und des Stilgefühls'.[18] Perhaps we should take the hint by concluding that in Old English the relationship between the two clauses was closer than that of two principal clauses and less close than that of a principal and a subordinate clause. Such a relationship could be brought out by using a colon rather than a comma (as did Wrenn) or a full stop (as did von Schaubert) at the end of *Beowulf* l. 1739 – a solution which Klaeber himself suggested in the same article, but did not put into practice in his edition of *Beowulf*, where he had a dash followed by a comma. We should then have

XXV 1740   he þæt wyrse ne con:
oð þæt him on innan   oferhyda dæl
weaxeð ond wridað. . . .

If parataxis preceded and developed into hypotaxis, there was probably – I am inclined to say certainly – an intermediate stage of the sort postulated. There may indeed have been more than one. The fact that in both prose and poetry we cannot always be sure whether words such as *þær*, *þa*, and *þonne*, are adverbs or conjunctions when used initially or whether *se* at the beginning of a clause is demonstrative or relative may be nothing more than the result of our ignorance of Anglo-Saxon intonation patterns. It may, however, be a manifestation of an intermediate stage between parataxis and hypotaxis. A. Campbell, after asking whether *Ða* in

Beowulf l. 917   Ða wæs morgenleohte
scofen ond scynded.   Eode scealc monig
swiðhicgende   to sele þam hean
searowundor seon

was to be translated 'Then' or 'When', observed: 'I think that such passages

---

[18] Fr. Klaeber 'Eine Randbemerkung zur Nebenordnung und Unterordnung im Altenglischen', *Anglia Beiblatt* 52 (1941), 216–19. Cf. G. Rubens *Parataxe und Hypotaxe in dem ältesten Teil der Sachsenchronik* (Halle an der Saale, 1915), pp. 42–3.

were open to personal interpretation, and that reciters would indicate their view of the passage by intonation.'[19] This is perceptive and I accept without hesitation the idea that a choice existed. But I feel – and I use the word deliberately – that Campbell may have presented that choice in starker terms than the actual situation warranted and that there may have been an intermediate stage between 'Then' and 'When'. That such a stage is no figment of the imagination can (I believe) be demonstrated. Writing on Modern English *for*, T. B. Haber observes that 'the only practical conclusion is that the conjunction has two uses, subordinating and co-ordinating, and that punctuation is of no significance in identifying either'.[20] This too may be an over-simplification. In my experience, there are times when even the intonation patterns of an utterance I hear spoken do not enable me to say firmly that *for* is coordinating rather than subordinating or vice versa. That the same difficulty may have existed in Old English is suggested by a comparison of *Blickling Homilies* 25. 22 *Wa eow þe nu hlihaþ, forþon ge eft wepað on ecnesse* with *Blickling Homilies* 25. 20 *Eadige beoþ þa þe nu wepað, forþon þe hi beoþ eft afrefrede*. More convincing examples from Old English are perhaps to be found in two passages from Ælfric's *Catholic Homilies*, where I attempt to reproduce the punctuation of Cambridge University Library MS Gg. 3. 28, using . for *punctus* and ; for *punctus versus*: *ÆCHom* ii. 96. 19 *Hé cwæð þæt hé cuðe Sumne man on romebyrig . his nama wæs Seruulus . ðearfa on æhtum . and welig on geearnungum ; Se læg bedryda fram cildhade . oð his geendunge ; He læg singallice and næfre sittan ne mihte.* and *ÆCHom* ii. 510. 31 *... his hirede . þe ærðan hæðen wæs ; Martinus eac cóm to anes mannes huse his cnapa wæs awed wunderlice ðurh deofol . and árn him togeanes mid gyniendum muðe ; þa bestáng se halga his hand him on múð.*[21] In these two passages, *his* is unlikely to be a relative – though such uses suggest that it may once have been in danger of becoming one – and yet seems unlikely to introduce a new sentence in the modern sense of the word. The appearance of *He* for *Se* in Bodley 343's version

---

[19] A. Campbell 'Verse Influences in Old English Prose', *Philological Essays; Studies in Old and Middle English Language and Literature in Honour of Herbert Dean Meritt* ed. J. L. Rosier (Mouton, 1970), p. 95.

[20] T. B. Haber '"For" as a Coördinating Conjunction', *American Speech* 30 (1955), 151.

[21] I am indebted to Dr M. R. Godden for this punctuation and for the following comments on it: 'In the first passage, all nine manuscripts are in impressive agreement. All have small *h* on *his* but large *S* on *Se* (except for Bodley 343 which has *He* for *Se*). Those which (like Gg. 3. 28) use the *punctus* and *punctus versus* have *punctus* before *his* and *punctus versus* before *Se*, and those which use only the *punctus* have none before *his* but one before *Se*. Large initial *S* appears in odd places in Gg. 3. 28, as on *Sumne* here, but not in the other manuscripts. In the second passage, the other two manuscripts do not use the *punctus versus* and hence have *wæs*. and *muðe*. but no original punctuation after *huse*.' These are not the only such examples. Professor P. A. M. Clemoes has kindly provided me with the punctuation of the Gg. 3. 28 version of *ÆCHom* i. 2. 11 *Ic ælfric munuc 7 mæssepreost swaðeah waccre ponne swilcū hadum gebyrige . wearð asend on æþelredes dæge cyninges fram ælfeage biscope aðelwoldes æft' gengan to sumu mynstre ðe is cernel gehaten þurh æðelmæres bene ðæs þegenes . his gebyrd and goodnys sind gehwær cuðe*; which offers another.

of the second passage and the similarity of punctuation before *Se* and *He* in all other versions of the same passage also warn of the dangers of attempting to draw precise grammatical boundaries in a language for which we have no native informants and no intonation patterns. Here at any rate we had better be *micle mearcstapan.*

25
Old English *Man* 'One': Two Notes

Summary

1. Problems of classification: here I discuss the five senses of indefinite *man* distinguished by Frölich and conclude that, while they can sometimes be made, they must not be pressed too far. 2. *Man* + an active verb form as a periphrasis for the active voice: here I discuss, and dismiss as essentially terminological, objections to the wording used in my heading and suggest that further work in the area is possible.

1. Problems of classification

Man, mann, is frequently used – in the nom. sg. only – as an indefinite. According to Frölich five senses can be distinguished.[1] They are set out here, with one of his examples by way of illustration.

Reprinted from *Language Form and Linguistic Variation: Papers Dedicated to Angus McIntosh* ed. John Anderson, *Amsterdam Studies in The Theory and History of Linguistic Science*, vol. IV *Current Issues in Linguistic Theory* 15 (1982), pp. 277–84.

The abbreviations for the names of texts are those proposed by Christopher Ball, Angus Cameron, and myself in *ASE* 4 (1975), 207–21 and 8 (1979), 331–3.

[1] J. Frölich *Der indefinite Agens im Altenglischen, unter besonderer Berücksichtigung des Wortes Man* (Bern, 1951). He summarizes his findings (which include lists of synonymous constructions) at pp. 111–15.

L. H. Gray, in *Word* 1 (1945), 19–32, distinguishes eleven different uses of indefinite *man* to suit his interest in the origin of the use of *man* = *on*. His criteria are sometimes semantic, sometimes syntactic, sometimes based on the Latin original, and sometimes on other considerations, such as whether *man* appears in a quotation, in a paraphrase, in an addition to the original text, or in a mistranslation. His investigations lead him to reject the idea he had once entertained – 'that *man* = *on* owes its origin to independent renderings of the Vulgate *homo*, this, in turn, being due to the influence of the Hebrew original' (p. 20) – and he concludes:

> In the light of the evidence here assembled, it would appear that the use of a word equivalent to 'man, mankind' as an indefinite pronoun or as a generic term arose independently in various languages; but, for the most part, was employed only sporadically and sparingly. It seems to have enjoyed wide usage solely in Romance and Teutonic, where, so far as the present writer can determine, it evolved independently, the two groups exercising little, if any, influence on each other, though both may conceivably have been affected to

Man 1 denotes 'der Mensch oder ein Mensch', 'mankind or a man' (as opposed to God or other living creatures), e.g. *Matt* (*WSCp*) 12. 12 *Witodlice micle ma mann ys sceape betera* (Fröhlich, pp. 15–17). *Man* 2 means 'ein Mensch, ein Individuum, eine Person, (irgend-) jemand oder (irgend-) einer', 'anyone, whatever individual is chosen', e.g. *Or* 20. 19 *7 þær is mid Estum ðeaw, þonne þær bið man dead, þæt he lið in*... (Frölich, pp. 17–45).

In the remaining senses 3–5 *man* is a 'generell-indefinites Pronomen' (Frölich, pp. 45, 70, and 102). *Man* 3 is 'allgemein' and denotes 'a number of people, everyone [who knows about it, who was there]', e.g. *Or* 10. 28 *On ðæm londe is xxxii þeoda. Nu hæt hit mon eall Parthia* and *Or* 126. 24... *he wolde beladian his modor Nectanebuses þæs drys, þe mon sæde þæt heo hie wið forlege* (Frölich, pp. 45–70). *Man* 4–5 means broadly 'someone'. The distinction seems to depend on the degree to which the 'someone' can be identified and/or on the extent to which the writer was interested in identifying him.

Man 4 is described as 'speziell' in that it denotes a particular agent. Frölich further distinguishes *man* 4(a), where this agent is unknown and cannot be identified, e.g. *Or* 60. 32 ... *æfter þæm ðe mon heora cyning ofslog Sardanopolum*, from *man* 4(b), where the agent can be deduced and *man* replaced by a noun, e.g. *Or* 80. 19 *Ac gesette þa men on ænne truman þe mon hiora mægas ær on ðæm londe slog*, where it is clear that it was the Greeks who slew the relatives of the Persians (Frölich, pp. 70–101). *Man* 5 is 'definierbar'; *mon* refers back to a definite antecedent, as in *Or* 174. 3 *þa com of ðæm wætre an nædre... þa gegaderade Regulus ealle þa scyttan þe on ðæm færelte wæron, þæt hie mon mid flanum ofercome*, where *mon* refers to *ealle þa scyttan* (Frölich, pp. 102–10).

That *man* in these senses 3–5 can refer to more than one person is emphasized by sentences in which there is a change of number in a second verb, e.g. *Or* 88. 11 *7 ælce dæg mon com unarimedlice oft to þæm senatum 7 him sædon* and *Judg* 16. 25 *7 hine man sona gefette mid swiðlicre wafunge 7 heton hine standan betwux twam stænenum swerum*, or in a second parallel subject, e.g. *Or* 226. 17 *Ac þære ilcan niht þe mon on dæg hæfde þa burg mid stacum gemearcod, swa swa hie hie þa wyrcean woldon* ... and *Matt* (*WSCp*) 23. 6–8 *Hig lufigeað þa fyrmystan setl on gebeorscypum 7 þa fyrmystan lareowsetl on gesomnungum 7 ꝥ hig man grete on strætum 7 ꝥ menn hig lareowas nemnon. Ne gyrne ge ꝥ eow man lareowas nemne*, Latin *Amant enim primos recubitos in cenis et primas cathedras in synagogis et salutationes in foro et uocari ab hominibus rabbi. Nos autem nolite uocari rabbi*. In these (as with collective nouns) the sense of different individuals is strong. But the few sentences in which *man* is immediately followed by a plural verb

> some extent by the late Latin (especially Vulgate) use of *homo* in this sense. Even in Romance and Teutonic, it served as a living 'outil grammatical' only in French, Anglo-Saxon, German, and Dutch ... (pp. 31–2)

His evidence seems to support this conclusion.

are to be regarded with suspicion as possible scribal errors. They include *Chron A* 18. 15 (565) *þæt igland þe man Ii nemnað* (a late addition), *CP* 2 (heading) *ðas boc... þe man Pastoralem nemnað*, and *LS* 34. 599 *and man mid witum ofgan willað æt me...* (where Skeat records a variant *ofgan wile*).

As Fröhlich himself recognizes (e.g. p. 112), these five senses inevitably shade into one another. This can easily be seen from his own examples. Thus he classifies *Or* 128. 11 *þa sede man Alexandre þæt Darius hæfde gebunden his agene mægas mid gyldenre racentan* as man 4(a) 'an unknown agent' (p. 71), whereas *Or* 126. 24... *he wolde beladian his modor Nectanebuses þæs drys, þe mon sæde þæt heo hie wið forlege* exemplifies *man* 3 'a number of people, everyone [who knows about it, who was there]' (p. 46). The distinction escapes me. Similarly, it seems just as clear to me that the agents are Romans in *Or* 286. 24 ... *feng Iuninianus to Romana onwalde. Hiene mon geceas on þæm westenne* as that they are Greeks in *Or* 80. 19 *Ac gesette þa men on ænne truman þe mon hiora mægas ær on ðæm londe slog*. Yet the former is classified as *man* 4(a) 'an unknown agent' (p. 72), the latter as *man* 4(b) 'an agent which can be deduced' (p. 80). Again, Fröhlich confidently identifies the agent *mon* in *Or* 196. 9

> þa Romane geacsedan þæt þa consulas on Ispanium ofslagen wæron, þa ne mehton þa senatus nænne consul under him findan þe dorste on Ispanie mid firde gefaran, buton þara consula oþres sunu, Scipia wæs haten, se wæs cniht. Se wæs georne biddende þæt him mon fultum sealde, þæt he moste on Ispanie firde gelædan, 7 he þæt færelt swiþost for þæm þurteah, þe he þohte þæt he his fæder 7 his fæderan gewræce, þeh þe he hit fæste wið þa senatus hæle. Ac Romane wæron þæs færeltes swa geornfulle, þeh þe hie swiðe gebrocode wæren on hiora licgendan feo þe hie gemæne hæfdon, for þæm gewinnum þe hie þa hæfdon on feower healfa, þæt hie eall him gesealdon þæt hie þa hæfdon on þæm færelte to fultume, buton þæt ælc wifmon hæfde ane yndsan goldes, 7 an pund seolfres, 7 ælc wæpnedmon ænne hring, 7 ane hoppan

as the Senate, the subject of the main clause of the preceding sentence. So it is classified as *man* 5 (p. 103). But the fact that the subject of the next main clause is *Romane* casts doubt on both the identification and the procedure; *mon* could just as easily refer to all the Romans who gave the gifts which made the expedition possible.

The Procrustean nature of these distinctions becomes even more apparent when one tries to apply them to one's own examples. Sometimes they work. We can perhaps say that in *ÆCHom* i. 16. 11 *Geweorðe man geworht* and *Met* 31. 16 *Man ana gæð metodes gesceafta / mid his andwlitan up on gerihte* we have *man* 1 'mankind, a man', but in *ÆCHom* ii. 592. 4 *þa heafodleahtras sind, manslitht, cyrcbræce, and þæt man oðres mannes wif hæbbe* and *Beo* 1172 *swa sceal man don* we have *man* 2 'a man, an individual'. But in *ÆCHom* i. 12. 30 *and he wearð þa mann gesceapen on* sawle and on lichaman; and God him sette naman Adam, mann might equally well be placed in either group.² Again, we may agree that we have *man* 3 'everyone' in

Met 8. 49   Se on iglonde
        Sicilia   swefle byrneð,
        þæt mon helle fyr   hateð wide,

man 4(a) 'someone unidentifiable' in *Dream* l. 75 *Bedealf us man on deopan seaþe*, and *man* 4(b) 'someone identifiable' in *Beo* l. 2355 *þær mon Hygelac sloh*, where it is clear from *Beo* l. 2916 that the Hetware slew Hygelac. But even though we know that in *GenB* l. 318 *Worhte man hit him to wite man* means God, it is hard to decide whether we have *man* 4(b) 'an identifiable agent' or *man* 5 referring back to 'a definite antecedent'. This is perhaps the most elusive of the distinctions and Fröhlich might have done well to call 4(a) 4 and to eliminate 4(b).

But even if he had done this there would still be problems. In *ÆCHom* i. 560. 18 *þa sende se casere Traianus gewritu ongean, þæt se halga papa Clemens to hæðengylde gebugan sceolde, oððe hine mann asende ofer sæ on wræcsið*, mann might be taken as *se casere* or as *se hæðena dema* of l. 24 or as some unknown centurion. In *ÆCHom* i. 166. 3 *Ic wolde eow trahtnian þis godspel, ðe mann nu beforan eow rædde*, Ælfric knew who had read the Gospel. We cannot know. At the climax of the story of Ananias and Sapphira, we read *ÆCHom* i. 316. 34 *Heo feoll ðærrihte and gewat, and hi man bebyrigde to hyre were*. Have we here an unknown agent *man* 4(a) or do we turn to the New Testament Acts 5. 9 'Behold, the feet of them which have buried thy husband are at the door, and shall carry thee out'? So, while we can admit that the distinctions can sometimes be made, we must not press them too far; consider, for example, *ÆCHom* ii. 354. 31 *þa betwux ðam oðrum geseah he hwær man bytlode ane gebytlu, eal mid smætum golde, and ða wyrhtan worhton ða gebytlu on ðam Sæternesdæge, and wæs ða fornean geendod*. Let us take refuge in the fact that, if the author did not make clear the identity of the agent, it cannot matter much.

2. Man + an active verb form as a periphrasis for the passive voice

Objections are sometimes made to this way of expressing what seems to be a linguistic fact in Old English. This statement is typical:

---

² The reader will find further examples of this difficulty if he compares *ChronA* 12. 20 (455) *7 his broþur Horsan man ofslog* (*BT* s.v. *man*) and *Laws* (*Th*) i. 78. 2 *Gif hund mon toslite* (*BT* s.v. *mann*); or considers Thorpe's renderings of *Laws* (*Th*) i. 80. 2 *Gif mon swa geradne mon ofslea* 'If a man . . .' and i. 80. 6 *Gif mon twyhynde mon unsynnigne . . . ofslea* 'If anyone . . .' (the last three examples may be found in Liebermann *Laws* 62. 14 (*Af* 23), 66. 9 (*Af* 28), and 64. 6 (*Af* 29)); or examines B. Schrader's claim (*Studien zur Ælfricschen Syntax* (Jena, 1887), §63) that Thorpe and Skeat are wrong to translate the sequence *man . . . he* as 'a man . . . he' in *ÆCHom* ii. 590. 20 ff. and *ÆLS* 1. 237 ff. Since I cannot see a distinction between 'a man' and 'anyone' in the MnE sentences, I am reluctant to import one into OE. It may be noted that Fröhlich (pp. 16 and 28) found examples of *se man*, but not of *an man*, used indefinitely.

Although constructions with *man* are often translated as passives ... they are formally active. It is therefore misleading when Campbell says nominative singular *man* is used frequently giving a periphrasis for the passive voice, e.g. *hine man heng* 'someone hanged him', 'he was hanged', and Fröhlich devotes a whole passage to the 'passive' use of *man* in his study of indefinites.³

This seems to me a debating point in a terminological argument. Campbell's statement (*Old English Grammar* §723) is unlikely to mislead anyone into believing that he thinks that in *hine man heng* the verb *heng* is passive, while Frölich (p. 116) is careful to distinguish indefinite *man* and the indefinite passive (e.g. *Or* 86. 22 ... *wearð micel wundor on heofonum gesewen*) as the two most common OE methods of expressing the indefinite agent. As far as I have observed, he does not speak of 'the "passive" use of *man*'. But he speaks of '*man* mit activer verbform' (p. 7) and distinguishes seven categories of passive periphrases in OE (pp. 10–12).

However we care to put it, it is clear that *man* + active verb form frequently represents a Latin passive in translated texts and is frequently preferred to *wesan*, *weorþan* + second (past) ptc. in original and translated texts. Fröhlich's figures are that in the original portions of *Orosius* the proportion of *man* to the periphrasis is 7:1, in the translated parts 6:1, and in the Gospels (where the reverence for the original is naturally greater) only 3:5 (all figures approximate). However, his figures and discussion support his conclusion that both these constructions are of native origin.⁴ A determination of their relative frequency in other texts must await the full collections which Professor Angus Cameron of Toronto and his *Dictionary of Old English* staff will soon make available.[4a]

---

³ O. E. E. Closs *A Grammar of Alfred's Orosius* (Ph.D. dissertation, University of California, Berkeley, 1964; *DA* 25 (1964), 1899), p. 110.

⁴ See Fröhlich, pp. 116–42, especially pp. 134–42. See further T. F. Mustanoja *A Middle English Syntax* (Helsinki, 1960), p. 219.

[4a] [1987. These collections, now available in *A Microfiche Concordance to Old English* (Toronto, 1980 and 1985), will also help to answer the question whether indefinite *man* 'one' can begin a sentence; see *OES* §3937. Possible examples have been supplied to me in private communications by David Denison (*ÆGenPref* 79. 88) and by Michiko Ogura (EETS 160, 419(3), 419(4), and 420(14), where we find initial *Me* which might be for *Man* 'one', since *me* 'one' occurs within clauses at 419(9), 420(17) twice, and 422(28), but where it might be, as Dr Ogura has suggested, an abbreviation for *Methodius*).]

26
The Origin of Old English Conjunctions: Some Problems

Summary

This paper does not offer a systematic treatment of the origin of Old English conjunctions but is concerned only with certain problems which arise. Its starting point is the assumption that 'it may be laid down as a general principle that in the progress of language parataxis precedes hypotaxis',[1] with the qualification that 'if parataxis preceded and developed into hypotaxis, there was probably – I am inclined to say certainly – an intermediate stage.... There may indeed have been more than one.'[2] It goes on to suggest that the following types of conjunction were used adverbially before they were used conjunctionally:

a one word conjunctions whose demonstrative origin is either agreed, e.g. þæs and þy, or fairly widely accepted, e.g. þær, þa, and þonne;
b combinations which consist of an oblique case of the demonstrative se and a noun, to which may be added þe or þæt, e.g. the ancestor of MnE 'while' which appears as þa hwile... þe (so far recorded only in Or 212. 25), þa hwile þe, þa hwile, (in later texts) þa hwile þæt, and (not until eME) wile;
c combinations which involve a preposition and the appropriate case of a demonstrative, to which may be added þe or þæt, e.g. forþon, forþon ... þe/þæt, and forþon þe/þæt, or which may involve a preposition or be of comparative origin, viz. siþþan and formulae with æfter and ær.

The rest of the paper is primarily concerned with D. Carkeet's article and tries to explain why I disagree with many of his suggestions concerning the origin of

Reprinted from *Trends in Linguistics Studies and Monographs*, vol. 23 *Historical Syntax* ed. Jacek Fisiak (Berlin, New York, Amsterdam, 1984), pp. 271–99. Although I am obviously biased, I have to say that in my opinion this article warrants fairer consideration than it received in *OEN* 19. 1 (1985), 61, at the hands of M.M. and K.D.T. Reasoned disagreement is one thing, contemptuous dismissal another.

[1] G. W. Small *The Comparison of Inequality* (Baltimore, Md, 1924), p. 125.
[2] Bruce Mitchell 'Old English *Oð þæt* Adverb?' *NQ* 223 (1978), 390–4 [item 24 above].

Old English conjunctions and with many of the remarks about the Old English correlative system on which he bases his theory.³

Topics discussed in passing include:

a types of conjunctions not already mentioned here;
b the distinguishing of conjunctions from adverbs of the same spelling by doubling, e.g. *swa swa*, or by the addition of *þe* or *þæt*, e.g. *forþon þe* and *forþon þæt*;
c the function of *þe* and *þæt* in such combinations;
d whether, when two words of the same spelling are used in what appear to be correlative pairs, one of them must be a conjunction;
e some of the conclusions reached by J. Erickson⁴ and S. G. Geoghegan.⁵

1   I begin by stressing that I intend to deal only with certain problems concerning the origin of some Old English conjunctions. I offer no systematic treatment of their origin; of such extensions of meaning as those by which *þonne* 'when' comes to express nuances of cause or concession or condition while still retaining its temporal senses; of the subsequent history of these conjunctions in English; or of the developments of their cognates in other Germanic languages.⁶

2   Looked at as they appear in the language, OE conjunctions can be divided into several groups. First, there are the 'one-word' conjunctions which have their origin in one word or which appear to be one word and are not immediately recognizable as combinations. These include what K. Braunmüller calls 'genuine proto-Germanic conjunctions', 'conjunctions directly derived

---

[3] 'Old English Correlatives: An Exercise in Internal Syntactic Reconstruction', *Glossa* 10 (1976), 44–63.

[4] 'Subordinator Topicalization in Old English', *Archivum Linguisticum* 8 (1978), 99–111.

[5] 'Relative Clauses in Old, Middle, and New English', *Ohio State University Working Papers in Linguistics* 18 (1975), 30–71.

[6] The abbreviations for the names of texts are those proposed by Christopher Ball, Angus Cameron, and myself in *ASE* 4 (1975), 207–21 and 8 (1979), 331–3. The quotations from OE texts are taken from the editions specified there with one exception: *Beowulf* (*Beo*) is quoted from Klaeber's 3rd edn.

For my own writings, I use the following:

D.Phil.: 'Subordinate Clauses in Old English Poetry', unpublished D.Phil. dissertation (Oxford, 1959)

Guide: *A Guide to Old English*, 2nd edn (Oxford and New York, 1968)

OES: *Old English Syntax*, forthcoming.

Some reference to this as an authority for statements which space does not permit me to elaborate here is unavoidable. It is hoped that the two-volume work will appear in 1984. [1987. *Old English Syntax* (Oxford) was published on 24 January 1985, thus missing 1984 by twenty-five days and Australia Day (26 January) by two. I have made the *OES* references in this article specific if they are not easily found from the Contents and/or Indexes.]

from pronouns and other deictic items', and 'conjunctions derived from enclitic particles plus other predications'.[7] His examples include respectively (the equivalents of) OE *and* and *gif*, *þa* and *þæt*, and *þeah*. The demonstrative origin of conjunctions such as *þæs* and *þy* is undoubted. That of *þær, þa, þonne*, and others, is fairly widely accepted; see such authorities as *OED*. A demonstrative origin would be in accordance with the conventional view that words like *þær, þæs, þeah*, and the like, were first used as adverbs and then developed into conjunctions, either alone, in doubled form, or with *þe* or *þæt*; see 4. We do not have to postulate a long period of time between parataxis and hypotaxis. But if, as seems beyond dispute (see *OES* §§1956 and 2109–10), the conjunction *þæt* introducing noun clauses and the relative *se* introducing adjective clauses were originally demonstratives in simple sentences, it seems reasonable to believe that those conjunctions which were originally demonstratives passed through an intermediate stage in which they were adverbs which could introduce or be used within simple sentences.

3   I believe that in OE 'phonological differentiation' existed between demonstrative *þæt* and conjunction *þæt*, despite Braunmüller,[8] between demonstrative *se* and relative *se*, and between adverbs such as *ær, nu, swa, þær, þanon, þider, þa, þeah*, and *þonne*, and conjunctions of the same spelling. But in the absence of intonation patterns and native informants, we are frequently unable to decide which we have. I have discussed the possibility that there may have been an intermediate stage, or intermediate stages, between the two.[9] Failure to recognize the existence of what I call ambiguous adverb/conjunctions and the ambiguous demonstrative/relative *se* in my opinion vitiates much modern work on Old English syntax. Thus, despite S. O. Andrew,[10] there is no reason why the clause introduced by *Ða* in

Beo l. 1600   Ða com non dæges.   Næs ofgeafon
                 hwate Scyldingas

'must be taken as subordinate' and, despite Erickson,[11] it is not certain that '*se* is a relative pronoun' in

Beo l. 369   huru se aldor deah,
         se þæm heaðorincum   hider wisade.[12]

---

[7] 'Remarks on the Formation of Conjunctions in Germanic Languages', *NJL* 1 (1978), 104–5 and 107–9.   [8] p. 112.

[9] Mitchell 'Old English *Oð þæt*', pp. 393–4 [pp. 261–3 above] and 'The Dangers of Disguise: Old English Texts in Modern Punctuation', *RES* 31 (forthcoming), 385–413 [item 18 above].

[10] *Syntax and Style in Old English* (Cambridge, 1940), p. 12 and *Postscript on Beowulf* (Cambridge, 1948), p. 12.   [11] p. 108.

[12] Erickson's paper elsewhere makes what seem to me unwarranted assumptions about OE 'stylistic marking ... the singling out of some sentence element or elements for emphasis'

4 Means of avoiding much, though not all, of this ambiguity arose. Some of these words appear in doubled form in the work of some writers. So, for example, *swa swa* is usually a conjunction. Some appear in combination with *þe*, e.g. *þæt þe* or *þætte*. Some are recorded with both. The forms *þa þa* and *þær þær* are much more common than *þa þe* and *þær þe*. But *þider þe* appears more often than *þider þider* in my collections and I have so far recorded *þanon þe* but not *þanon þanon*. Simple *þonne* is preferred to *þonne þe* and *þonne þonne*, but the latter two do appear. However, the presence of *þe* is not absolute proof that we have the conjunction rather than the adverb; see the comment by Baker quoted in 35, n. 118. The addition of *þæt* sometimes denotes a difference in function; compare *swa*, which is primarily comparative when used as a conjunction, with *swa þæt*, which is primarily final or consecutive. But this is not always so. Thus *oþ* and *oþ þæt* can both be conjunctions and *gyf þæt* appears in *HomU* 44. 284. 9, pre-dating *OED*'s *ʒiff þatt* from *Orrmulum*.

5 It is, of course, a syntactical commonplace that many of these adverb/conjunctions can be used in (what appear to be) correlative pairs. But even such an arrangement does not certify that one of the clauses must be subordinate to the other; consider the conventional, but not necessarily 'correct', punctuation of

> *Beo* l. 126   Ða wæs on uhtan   mid ærdæge
> Grendles guðcræft gumum undyrne;
> þa wæs æfter wiste wop up ahafen,
> micel morgensweg.

(p. 99). He appears to accept a distinction made by Bacquet. But see Mitchell 'P. Bacquet *La Structure de la Phrase Verbale à l'Époque Alfrédienne*', *NM* 67 (1966), pp. 86–97 [item 22 above]. Erickson (pp. 99–100) offers six OE sentences in which he says we have 'stylistic marking' – four from the prose, two from the poetry. Not one of these can be accepted unhesitatingly. The two verse examples *Wan* l. 12 and *Wan* l. 55 are typical of OE, a language in which the pattern 'That he was there is certainly true' has not yet been recorded, and in both of them initial *þæt* may be an unaccented element before the first stress; Kuhn's Law is relevant here. The influence of Kuhn's Law too may account for initial *wæs* in *Or* 34. 25 *Wæs se hunger on þæs cyninges dagum*; see A. Campbell 'Verse Influences in Old English Prose', *Philological Essays: Studies in Old and Middle English Language and Literature in Honour of Herbert Dean Meritt* ed. James L. Rosier (The Hague, 1970), pp. 93–5. But note the Latin *Fuit itaque haec fames magna sub rege Aegyptiorum. Æfter þæm wordum* in *Or* 244. 2 could be resumptive rather than emphatic. Since *ac* as a clause introducer tends to produce the element order S. . . . V., *hit* could occupy an unemphatic position before the stressed subject *God* in *Or* 184. 7. The most plausible example – especially out of context – is *Or* 18. 10 *þa deor hi hataõ hranas*. But it could be read as resumptive in the somewhat clumsy passage in which it occurs. In my opinion, no general principle emerges from *this collection of examples*.

I disagree with what is said by W. O'Neil in 'Clause Adjunction in Old English', *Linguistics* 17 (1977), p. 205, ll. 18–30: *nu* and *þæs* can introduce causal clauses; for equivalents of *þenden* see 6 and 7; and on the functions of *þe*, see 19.

Erickson's statement[13] that in the sequence *forþon* adv. ... *forþon* conj. 'it seems ... suspicious ... that the adverbial should have the same form as the subordinator' is however itself suspect and seems to be contradicted by his later statement that 'in addition to *forðon*, there are other OE main clause adverbials which may co-occur with homophonous subordinators. Among these, Andrew (1940: 31) lists *ær* "before", *nu* "now", *siððan* "after", *swa* "so", *þeah* "though", and *þær* "there/where", and to the list one might also add *þa* "then/when" and *þonne* "then/when".'[14] There was no need, either, for Erickson to add *þa* and *þonne* to Andrew's list. He had already discussed these words at length and the sentence from which Erickson quotes actually contains both of them.

6   The second group of OE conjunctions comprises those which consist of an oblique case of the demonstrative *se* and a noun, to which may be added *þe* or *þæt*. The most interesting of these is the ancestor of the MnE conjunction 'while'. This has its origin in an accusative of duration of time, as in ChronE 129. 16 (994) *7 man gislade þa hwile in to þam scipum*, to which is added a clause introduced by *þe*, e.g. Or 212. 25 *Ic nat eac ... hu nyt ic þa hwile beo þe ic þas word sprece* (the sole example I have recorded in which the two elements are separated) and BlHom 175. 2 *7 þa, þa hwile þa he þær stod, he wearþ færinga geong cniht*. We occasionally find correlative *þa hwile þe ... þa hwile*, e.g. Or 72. 22 and ÆCHom i. 10. 35. The form without *þe* is rarely recorded as a conjunction; examples include Bede (Ca) 188. 4 *þa hwile*, where MS O has *þenden* and MS T *þendæn*. This latter is probably an older word. It is more common in the poetry than in the prose, but disappeared in late OE or early ME times and does not appear in OED.[15] Forms with *þæt* instead of *þe* are late. A. Adams records three examples: Ch 391, dated 'post-Conquest', and ChronE 252. 34 and 253. 1, both in the entry for 1123.[16] The earliest example with the noun alone appears to be *wile* in ChronE 264. 25 (1137). So Braunmüller's statement (1978: 107) that 'ME *the while that* > ModE *while*' cannot be accepted as certain; the development may have been *þa hwile þe* > *þa hwile* > *wile*. The stage without *þe* appears in some later prose texts, e.g. Lch iii. 2. 6 *þa hwile* and Lch iii. 122. 18 *ðe hwyle* and once in the poetry, viz. JDay ii. 83 *þa hwile*, and could well have been common in the spoken language in the eleventh century.

7   The formula *on þære hwile þe*, recorded in Or 130. 9 and 170. 12, is probably no more to be taken as a conjunction than MnE 'during the time that', but it

[13] p. 102.
[14] p. 106.
[15] Bruce Mitchell 'Five Notes on Old English Syntax', NM 70 (1969), 70–84.
[16] *The Syntax of the Temporal Clause in Old English Prose* (New York, 1907), p. 86.

provides a convenient means of transition to the third group of OE conjunctions, viz. combinations involving prepositions. These consist of a preposition followed by the appropriate case of the neuter demonstrative *þæt*, with the possible addition of *þe* or *þæt*, which may immediately follow the demonstrative (grouped formulae) or be separated from it (divided formulae). So we find (with the accusative) *oþ þæt* and *þurh þæt þe*; (with the genitive) *to þæs*, *to þæs þe/þæt*, and *to þæs... þe/þæt*; and (with the dative/instrumental *þæm*, *þam*, *þon*, *þy*, and other spellings) *forþon*, *forþon þe/þæt*, and *forþon... þe/þæt*. Combinations involving *æfter*, e.g. *æfter þæm* (*þe*) and *ær*, e.g. *ær þæm* (*þe*), and the conjunction *siþþan* – *siþþan þe* has not yet been recorded – may belong here. But they may be comparative rather than prepositional formulae; see 26–8 and 30–1.

8   For purposes of this paper, it will suffice to mention a few other types of OE conjunctions. Formulae which certainly involve a comparative include *no ðy ær*, *þon ma þe*, and *þy læs* (*þe*). Formulae with *loc*(*a*), e.g. *loc*(*a*) *hwær* and *loc*(*a*) *hwonne*, and with (*swa...*) *swa*, e.g. *swa hwær swa* and *sona swa*, are also noteworthy. The list is not complete. But it does illustrate the variety of OE conjunctions – a variety which suggests to me that we are unlikely to find one sequence which will explain the origin of all, or even nearly all, of them. Yet the belief that conjunctions such as *þær*, *þa*, *þonne*, and *þeah*, *þa hwile* (*þe*), and *forþon* (*þe*), were originally adverbs introducing simple sentences is satisfying, and will not surprise those who, like me, accept Small's proposition that 'it may be laid down as a general principle that in the progress of language parataxis precedes hypotaxis',[17] or who, like G. Mann, believe that 'wenn wir nach der Entstehung der Konjunktionen forschen, also nach den Hilfsmitteln, die einen Nebensatz dem Hauptsatz unterordnen, müssen wir von der Erkenntnis ausgehen, dass sich die moderne Sprachform der Unterordnung aus der der Beiordnung (Asyndese–verbundene Parataxe–Hypotaxe) entwickelt hat'.[18] However, Carkeet is not content with the simple development set out at the beginning of my last sentence.[19] The rest of this paper is primarily concerned with his attack on what he calls 'a traditional view' of the origin of the OE correlative system, in the course of which he produces a new theory for the development of some OE conjunctions.

9   I begin with the correlative system. Carkeet states that 'correlative adverbs systematically occur in main clauses which follow rather than precede subordinate clauses'.[20] (On p. 52 it is 'almost exclusively'.) This statement requires qualification. It remains to be established for local and temporal clauses in the

[17] Small *Comparison*, p. 125.
[18] 'Die Entstehung von nebensatzeinleitenden Konjunktionen im Englischen', *Archiv* 180 (1942), p. 88.
[19] Carkeet, p. 49.   [20] Carkeet, p. 56.

prose, but seems to me too sweeping; see *OES* §§2514–28 and 2597–9 and consider the table below, which is based on E. M. Liggins's figures for temporal/causal clauses introduced by *þa* (*þa*) with a correlative adverb *þa* and by *þonne* (*þonne*) with a correlative adverb *þonne*.[21]

Conjunction	Principal clause precedes	Principal clause follows
þa	14	270
þa þa	8	116
þonne	50	197
þonne þonne	0	5
Total	72 (11 per cent)	588 (89 per cent)

These figures do not in my opinion justify Carkeet's 'almost exclusively' or indeed his 'systematically'. Those interested can cull further figures from Liggins (*passim*). They will find (*inter alia*) that she lists thirty prose sentences with correlative *nu... nu*.[22] The principal clause precedes the subordinate in seventeen and follows it in thirteen.

10 Carkeet's statement is not valid for clauses of place introduced by *þær* or for clauses of time introduced by *þa* or *þonne* in the poetry if we accept the 'curious superstition' referred to by Andrew which forbids 'the subordination of a temporal clause ... when the clause precedes the principal sentence'.[23] It is broadly true for clauses of concession, though Quirk's figures suggest that the difference is less clear cut in the poetry than, according to Burnham, it is in the prose,[24] and for clauses of condition. It does not hold for clauses of comparison like those in *ÆCHom* i. 4. 14 *þonne cymð se Antecrist, se bið mennisc mann and soð deofol, swa swa ure Hælend is soðlice mann and God on anum hade*; *ÆCHom* i. 94. 1 *And þæt tacn wæs ða swa micel on geleaffullum mannum, swa micel swa nu is þæt halige fulluht*; and *ÆCHom* i. 84. 10 *Ne mihte se manfulla ehtere mid nanre ðenunge þam lytlingum swa micclum fremian, swa micclum swa he him fremode mid ðære reðan ehtnysse hatunge*. It does not hold for the limited number of causal clauses in the prose in which *for* formulae are used as conjunctions with a correlative adverb in the principal clause. For, as a table in *OES* §§3072–80 shows, the principal clause precedes the causal clause in two-thirds (67. 7 per cent) of such examples; the

---

[21] 'The Expression of Causal Relationship in Old English Prose' unpublished Ph.D. dissertation (London, 1955), pp. 223, 228, 230, 252–3, and 259.
[22] Liggins, pp. 296–8 and 303.   [23] Andrew *Postscript*, pp. vii–viii.
[24] See R. Quirk *The Concessive Relation in Old English Poetry* (New Haven, Conn., 1954), pp. 14–19 and J. M. Burnham *Concessive Constructions in Old English Prose* (New York, 1911), p. 28.

usual patterns are those seen in *CP* 363. 4 *Forðæm he cwæð ða word, forðæm ða Saducie antsacodon ðære æriste æfter deaðe 7 ða Farisseos geliefdon ðære æriste* and *CP* 353. 15 *7 forðæm hit is awriten ðæt hiera honda wæren gehalgode Gode, forðæmðe hie ne sparodan ða synfullan ac slogon.*[25] Carkeet, who lists *Cura Pastoralis* among the texts he read,[26] asserts on the basis of John 5. 16, 10. 17, and 12. 18, that such constructions 'are Latin-influenced and atypical of native OE prose'.[27] This enables him to dispose of a construction which runs contrary to his theory. But they seem to me a perfectly natural native development. There is nothing in the Latin of the two examples I quote from *CP* to support Carkeet's assertion. J. Van Dam gives references to more such examples[28] and says that 'the Latin does not appear to have influenced the use of causal conjunctions in the Old English texts under investigation'.[29] In this Liggins concurs; see *OES* §§3007–201 *passim*.[30] All these are in effect exceptions to Carkeet's rule that 'in fact no clause type which consistently follows the main clause, such as purpose and result clauses, can be paired with correlative adverbs occurring in the accompanying main clauses'.[31] There are even exceptions of a sort with clauses of purpose and result, e.g. *Bede* 392. 23 *Wæs mid micle sare getogen, swa ic ær sæde, 7 se earm wæs swa swiðe great 7 aswollen, to ðon þæt he nænge begnisse in þæm elmbogan hæfde*; *Bede* 324. 19–27 (where we also have *swa . . . to ðon þæt*); *ÆCHom* i. 614. 8 *To ðam he wext þæt he fealle; to ðy he sprytt þæt he mid cwyldum fornyme swa hwæt swa he ær sprytte*; and *WHom* 6. 36 *And to ðam hy gesceop God ælmihtig, þæt hy 7 heora ofspring scoldan gefyllan 7 gemænigfyldan þæt on heofonum gewanad wæs*; cf. MnE 'To this end He came from Heaven and dwelt among men, that He might redeem mankind.'

11   Carkeet makes these statements about clause order as reasons for rejecting the proposition that adverbs were the source of conjunctions.[32] But even if they could stand, arguments based on them would in my opinion be irrelevant. It is true that certain subordinate clauses tend to follow their principal clause while others tend to precede it; see *OES* §1925. But there are no firm rules and nothing in the order in which OE clauses are arranged runs contrary to the

---

[25] See the 'Additional comment' on pp. 294–5.
[26] Carkeet, p. 63.   [27] Carkeet, pp. 61–2, n. 9.
[28] *The Causal Clause and Causal Prepositions in Early Old English Prose* (Groningen, 1957), pp. 42–3 and 48.
[29] Van Dam, p. 84.
[30] His attempt to assign a Latin origin here and his failure to note the infrequency of the correlative use of the *for* formula are not the only ways in which Carkeet reveals an unfamiliarity with OE. Despite what he says on p. 46, neither the repetition of a subject nor 'inversion of subjects and verb phrases' nor the splitting of 'conjoined subjects' is 'normally' restricted to sentences containing an adjective clause; see the General Index to *OES*. Carkeet's statements number (1) and (2) at the bottom of p. 49 and the top of p. 52 seem to assume what they help to 'prove'.
[31] Carkeet, p. 55.   [32] Carkeet, pp. 52 and 55–6.

proposition that parataxis preceded hypotaxis. One can readily see that when sequences like the following became complex sentences, the principal clause followed the subordinate clause: 'There/then he waited by the ford. There/then he killed his enemy', 'But/Yet he waited by the ford. But/Yet he did not kill his enemy', 'O were I by the ford! Then I would kill my enemy', 'Who waited by the ford? He killed his enemy', and 'That (one) waited by the ford. That (one) killed his enemy'. But equally one can see that other sequences would produce a principal clause which came first, e.g. 'There/then he killed his enemy. There/then he waited by the ford', 'To that (end) he waited by the ford. Thus he killed/could kill his enemy', 'He was so clever. So clever was his teacher', 'For that he killed the man. For that the man killed his brother', '(But/Yet) he did not kill the man. But/Yet he had waited by the ford', 'I would avenge him. Were I free!', 'He said that. His enemy was dead', and 'That (one) is the man. That (one) is my enemy'. One can also see that correlation is likely to be more frequent in sentences of the first type than in those of the second. So, despite Carkeet,[33] the view that adverbs were 'the historical starting point' *can* 'explain the essential property of the correlative system, which is the very cooccurrence of the conjunctions and adverbs' and *can* account for the fact that correlative adverbs tend to occur in principal clauses which follow the subordinate clause.

12   The transition from two simple sentences to one complex sentence postulated by this view could have come about as the result of changes in stress and intonation affecting particularly the elements where the sentences met. On the possibility of an intermediate stage or stages being represented in extant OE texts, see *OES* §2536. The syntactical (as opposed to phonetic) methods of distinguishing the principal from the subordinate clause – the use of *þe* or *þæt* with the conjunction, the doubling of the word when it was used as a conjunction, and the use of element order to distinguish the two clauses, on which see Campbell[34] and *OES* §3922 – could have arisen simultaneously or subsequently. (I take up these points as they become relevant.)

13   Thus I have yet to be convinced that this 'traditional view', as Carkeet calls it, is wrong.[35] As I have pointed out in 38–40, I believe that it can account for all the phenomena which Carkeet uses as arguments against it. So I turn now to the theory which he evolved to explain the OE correlative system, viz. that most OE conjunctions can be traced back to a group consisting of a preposition + a noun phrase (= demonstrative + noun) in an oblique case [abbreviated by Carkeet to PP, even when there is no preposition[36]] + *þe* or to a similar group without a preposition.[37] Only those which cannot possibly be made to fit this

[33] p. 56.   [34] pp. 93–6.   [35] Carkeet, p. 49.
[36] Carkeet, p. 60, n. 5.   [37] Carkeet, p. 49.

theory are excluded – some specifically, e.g. *gif, nu, swa, swa hwær swa, swa hraþe swa, swa oft swa* and *sona swa*,³⁸ others in almost silent desperation, e.g. *þanon* and *þider*.³⁹ This reinforces my belief that there is no need to assume (as Carkeet does) that all the conjunctions he lists apart from the first seven above must have been developed in the same way and that that method must explain not only the origin of the conjunctions concerned, but also the origin of the correlative system. It is a telling fact against his theory that the more likely it is that a particular conjunction was formed in accordance with his theory, the less likely it is to be used correlatively with itself. The reverse of this statement is also true. As we shall see, there are other arguments against his theory.

14 For prepositional conjunctions, Carkeet visualizes four stages: (1) *æfter þæm timum þe* (which on the evidence of his gloss '*on þam timum þe* "at the time [sic] when"', he takes to mean 'after the time at which/when'): prepositional phrase + relative pronoun;⁴⁰ (2) *æfter þæm þe*: prepositional phrase + relative pronoun; (3) *æfter þæm þe*: conjunction; (4) *æfter þæm*: conjunction.⁴¹ But he adds the comment that 'there are, of course, plausible variations on this suggested chain of development. For example, there might be no stage 3 . . .'⁴² and concludes 'Similar series of rule changes can be set up for the other prepositional conjunctions as well.' So *siþþan* goes back to some such sequence as *sib þæm timum be* [sic].⁴³

15 He then goes on to claim that most non-prepositional conjunctions 'can be historically traced back' to a noun phrase (demonstrative + noun) in the oblique case + *þe*, the development being similar to that for prepositional conjunctions.⁴⁴ Thus *þæs þe* (and presumably *þæs* as a conjunction) are said to derive from *þæs geares þe* or some similar combination, *þa þe, þa,* and *þe,* from *þa hwile þe* or the like, and *þonne þe* and *þonne* from *þone fyrst þe* or the like. The local conjunction *þær*, however, is said to derive from *on þære stowe þe* or the like – a combination involving a preposition.⁴⁵

16 The sequence proposed for prepositional conjunctions may well have some validity. Adams quotes *BlHom* 133. 12 *Mid þon dæge wæs gefylled se dæg þe is nemned Pentecosten..., þa wæron ealle þa apostolas wuniende on anre stowe* as being

---

³⁸ Carkeet, p. 54.   ³⁹ Carkeet, p. 54.
⁴⁰ Carkeet, p. 50.   ⁴¹ Carkeet, pp. 52–3.
⁴² Carkeet, p. 53. Another possible variation in the development proposed by Carkeet is hinted at by Adams (p. 32) when he speaks of the difficulty of deciding whether groups like *on þam dæge þe* introduce 'real temporal' clauses or remain combinations of a prepositional phrase + an adjective clause. He makes the same point about groups like *þæs geares þe* (p. 35). I take up the question whether stage 3 is essential in 33–5.
⁴³ Carkeet, pp. 53–4.   ⁴⁴ Carkeet, pp. 53–4.
⁴⁵ Why not from *on þære hwile þe* as well, since it sometimes means 'when'?

'interesting chiefly for the light it throws on the origin and meaning of the *mid*-formulae in general' and as 'probably another instance in which an earlier syntactical usage has been preserved' in *BlHom*.⁴⁶ This suggests that here Adams had in mind some such sequence as that proposed by Carkeet. He suggests that *on þam þe* 'when, while' – which occurs twice in the late Chronicle viz. *ChronD* 169. 28 (1050) and *ChronD* 179. 16 (1052) – 'probably ... arose from the omission of the substantive in such sentences as' *Or* 180. 21 *On þæm dagum þe Titus Sempronius 7 Gratias Gaius wæron consulas on Rome....*⁴⁷ He also says of *onmang ðam ðe* 'when, while' that 'doubtless the conjunctive use grew out of its employment as a preposition in cases such as this: *ChronE* 241. 14 (1106) *7 onmang þam gewinnan se fæder forðferde*'.⁴⁸ I can, however, find nothing else to justify Carkeet's assertion that 'Adams generally favours the historical derivation of temporal conjunctions from sequences of PP + RELATIVE PRONOUN'.⁴⁹ Adams gives no such hints about sequences involving *æfter*⁵⁰ – here indeed he comes close to suggesting the development which I outlined in *Guide* §169, and which I discuss below – and advances quite different theories, not only for *siþþan* (which, as we have seen above, Carkeet tries to subsume⁵¹)⁵² but also for sequences involving *ær*⁵³ and *oð*.⁵⁴ Indeed, on p. 94, he suggests that *betwux þam þe* 'when, while' may have developed from prepositional phrases like *betwyx þissum*. A comparison of this with his just-quoted comment on *onmang ðam ðe* suggests that here at any rate Adams was reacting to the material he had in front of him rather than formulating any coherent theory about the origin of prepositional conjunctions.

17 Carkeet's claim that Shearin 'offers an explanation along these same lines for OE clauses of purpose introduced by prepositional conjunctions like *to* + dat/inst + *þæt*, *for* + dat/inst + *þæt*, and many others' also seems ill-founded.⁵⁵ What Shearin said on p. 63 was that 'in these formulae, the word immediately following the preposition is almost always in Old English a demonstrative pronominal.... However, rarely a noun may be in the place of the usual pronominal object...', while on p. 64 he observed that 'it will be seen at once that these introductory formulae are merely the phrases already studied ... with the addition of a limiting *ðæt*-clause' – which he defined on p. 63 as 'a substantive clause explanatory of' the demonstrative object of the preposition. Neither here nor elsewhere did Shearin state or imply that the formula with a

---

⁴⁶ Adams, p. 47. On syntactical archaisms in *BlHom* see further A. R. Benham 'The Clause of Result in Old English Prose', *Anglia* 31 (1908), 216, 228, 229, and 230.
⁴⁷ Adams, p. 93.   ⁴⁸ Adams, p. 94.   ⁴⁹ Carkeet, p. 53.
⁵⁰ Adams, pp. 105–6 and 109.   ⁵¹ Carkeet, pp. 53–4.   ⁵² Adams, pp. 100–1.
⁵³ Adams, pp. 115–16 and 119–20.   ⁵⁴ Adams, pp. 127 and 130–1.
⁵⁵ Carkeet, pp. 60–1, n. 6 and H. G. Shearin *The Expression of Purpose in Old English Prose* (New York, 1903), p. 63.

noun was an essential first stage. In view of this and of the fact that he sees the *þæt* clauses as originally noun clauses and not adjective clauses, his explanation is along very different lines from that of Carkeet. Since I am inclined to agree with Shearin, I do not pursue the *to* formulae further. The last element is *þæt*, not *þe* (*OES* §2892), and in terms of the table in 24, they are recorded only in phase 1 *to þam þingum þæt*, phase 2 *to þæm . . . þæt*, and phase 3 *to þæm þæt*; see *OES* §§2889–927.

18   The question naturally arises whether a distinction can be drawn between *þe* and *þæt* in such combinations. It seems to me reasonable to postulate that originally the two were quite distinct and that *þæt* was a conjunction introducing what we would describe as a noun clause in apposition with a preceding object governed by a preposition. This object could be either a demonstrative used independently, as in *Or* 54. 18 *7 mid ungemetlicre pinunge he wæs þæt folc cwielmende, to ðon þæt hie him anbugen*, or a demonstrative + noun, as in *Or* 52. 32 *7 he Cirus Persea cyning hæfde þriddan dæl his firde beæftan him, on þæt gerad, gif ænig wære þe fyr fluge þe on ðæm gefeohte wæs þonne to þæm folce þe þær beæftan wæs, þæt hine mon sloge swa raðe swa mon hiora fiend wolde*. Here I differ from Benham: 'as in the case of purpose phrases, the word following the pronoun is *ðæt*, which, in the original composition of the phrase, was a demonstrative pronoun in relative function introducing an adjective clause'.[56] For I cannot myself see how the *þæt* clauses in the two examples quoted above can be described as 'adjective clauses' in the sense in which I use the term. That the apparent agreement in *on þæt gerad . . . þæt* in *Or* 52. 32 above is illusory is clear from the appearance of formulae like *ÆCHom* ii. 534. 35 *for ðam intingan þæt* and *WHom* 6. 156 *to þam þingum þæt*.

19   The original function of *þe* is even less certain. In my *Guide* (p. 88), I wrote of the formula *for þæm þe* 'because' that 'we can call *þe* (if we wish) a subordinating particle. This is the general function of *þe* and its use as a relative pronoun is probably a special adaptation. . . . We can perhaps get nearest to its original force by translating it as "namely".'[57] Carkeet objects that this 'demands that we assign a brand new property to *þe*, that of "subordinating particle" . . . , whereas the hypothesis proposed in this paper is based on the independently motivated and universally accepted view of *þe* as a relative pronoun'.[58] I do not accept the phrases 'brand new' and 'universally accepted'

---

[56] Benham, pp. 218–19. Shearin (p. 58) also uses the word 'relative': 'Old English *ðæt* . . . [was] originally a pronominal neuter accusative used with relative force as a conjunction.' But, as I note above, he defined the clause introduced by *þæt* as a substantive clause (p. 63).

[57] Small *Comparison*, pp. 148–52; 'The Syntax of *The* with the Comparative', *MLN* 41 (1926), pp. 312–13; 'The Syntax of *The* and OE *þon Ma þe*', *PMLA* 45 (1930), pp. 381–3.

[58] Carkeet, p. 56.

and still hold to my view that the general function of *þe* was that of a subordinating particle.⁵⁹ Even if we accept Carkeet's complicated hypothesis, it can explain only some prepositional formulae with *þe* and the appearance of *þe* 'relative pronoun' in a few non-prepositional formulae such as *þær þe*, *þa þe*, and *þonne þe*, in which *þe* is the exception rather than the rule (see *OES* Indexes) and is therefore more likely to be a later accretion than a fundamental and integral element. It cannot explain the prepositional formulae with *þæt* and cannot explain the appearance of *þe* in *þeah þe*, *þæt þe* conj. – which Benham thinks may be 'the parent form from which *ðæt* [conjunction] is descended'⁶⁰ – (a doubtful proposition⁶¹) – *þætte*, *þy læs þe*, *þon ma þe*, and the like, or how *þe* in these groups can function as a 'relative pronoun'. But the hypothesis that *þe* was a subordinating particle explains these and also its use as a relative. As I suggested in *Guide* §169, it also explains the presence of *þe* in prepositional formulae like *for þæm þe*, where it is hard to see how *þe* could ever have meant 'which' – either with or without a noun before it – but easy to see how it could have meant something like 'namely'. If we accept that the use of *þe* had its origin in formulae like *þa hwile þe* and **æfter þæm timan þe*, we can accept Kivimaa's proposition that it was originally of 'relatival nature' and that its presence in formulae like *þeah þe* and *for þæm þe* was due to analogical use after 'its full values' had 'faded'.⁶² But it seems more plausible to me to argue that in *þa hwile þe*, *for þæm þe*, and *þeah þe*, it was originally a subordinating particle and that in *þa hwile þe* it was subsequently interpreted as a relative '[during] the time in which'; see Mann pp. 91–2 and the quotation from *Guide* (p. 88) with which I began this section.

20   But in either event, the formulae with *þæt* and those with *þe* would be different in origin. This is in fact suggested by Adams as a possible explanation for the solitary example he found of *æfter þæm þæt* conjunction 'after' (*Or* 212. 28):

> The use of *ðæt* in this way is unusual, but may be regarded as one of the early stages in its progress toward its present regular relative use. Beside

---

⁵⁹ The idea that *þe* is a particle which is not used solely in clauses which we think of as adjective clauses did not originate with me. For example, *OED* speaks of '† The, *particle (conj., adv.)*, *relative pron.*'. *OED* and I are not alone; see K. Kivimaa þe *and* þat *as Clause-connectives in Early Middle English with Especial Consideration of the Emergence of the Pleonastic* þat (Helsinki, 1966), p. 160. But other writers, including Kivimaa, have taken the view that *þe* was in origin a relative; see Kivimaa (pp. 160–7), who distinguishes an adverbial relative *þe* from a 'pronominal' one (p. 162).

Geoghegan, who shows some unfamiliarity with Old English, takes a view contrary to that of Carkeet. She speaks of 'the Old English subordinating particle *þe*' (pp. 31 and 50) and says that 'the word *þe* can in no way be considered a pronoun' (p. 43). We can, I believe, safely occupy the middle ground between these two extremes.

⁶⁰ Benham, p. 207.   ⁶¹ Kivimaa, p. 161.
⁶² Kivimaa, pp. 162 and 164–5.

the more common *oð ðæt* we find *oððe*, so that in some connections the demonstrative and the relative were felt to be closely related, even in OE. Or *ðæt* may be regarded as the demonstrative introducing a substantive clause in apposition with *ðæm*.[63]

But Adams's first explanation opens up another possibility, viz. that in all these formulae, *þe* – not *þæt* – was the original and that *þæt* came in only because the originally distinct *þe* and *þæt* became to some extent interchangeable, first perhaps by phonetic weakening of *þæt* to *þe*, as suggested for example by Adams for *oþþæt* and *oþþe*, and then by analogy.

21   This is undoubtedly a plausible and possible chain of events. But I do not accept it. The fact that Adams found so few temporal prepositional formulae with *þæt*[64] means that he was on firm ground when he put forward the idea that they were the result of later confusion. A similar preference for *þe* is apparent in the figures for grouped formulae with *for* in causal clauses in early prose cited by van Dam: 166 with *for þæm/þam/þan þe* but four with *for þæm þæt*(*te*)[65] and 335 with *for þon þe* but three with *for þon þæt*(*te*).[66] The case for believing that in these two constructions the formula with *þe* was the original and the spasmodic examples with *þæt* are intruders is strong. But the reverse is true in clauses of purpose and result. *þæt*, not *þe*, is the norm when formulae with *for* introduce clauses of purpose; see *OES* §§2911–16 for details. Shearin notes only one example of a grouped *to* formula with dative/instrumental + *þe* in purpose clauses against 269 with *þæt* or (rarely) *þætte*.[67] Even this has *þæt* on the testimony of Liebermann: *LawAfEl(EGH)* 13 *aluc ðu hine from minum weofode to þam þæt he deaðe swelte*. In clauses of result, Benham mentions none with *þe* against 202 with *þæt* or (rarely) *þætte*.[68] Neither formula with *to* occurs in the poetry. Here the presumption must be that the formula with *þæt* was the original (*þæt* being an essential element) and that *þe* is the intruder. So the proposition that formulae with *þæt* and formulae with *þe* arose independently but later became confused as a result of phonetic reduction and analogy seems established.[69]

22   We must now ask whether Carkeet's theory is acceptable for prepositional formulae introducing clauses of time. On the evidence supplied by

---

[63] Adams, p. 109.

[64] See his Appendices I and V. Excluding *oþþæt* and its variants, there are only ten examples: two with *æfter*, one with *fram*, three with *mid*, and four with *to*. They are distributed thus: *Alex* (1), *Chron* 1127 (1), *Lch* iii (1), *LS* 10, *Guthlac* (4), and *Or* (3). The solitary *to ð* in *ChronE* 264.13 (1137) is a ME ghost; Clark reads *it ð*[*at*].

[65] Van Dam, pp. 44–5.   [66] Van Dam, pp. 52–3.
[67] Shearin, pp. 63–8 and 78.   [68] Benham, pp. 218 and 228.
[69] Further on the possibility of interchange of function between *þæt* and *þe*, see Kivimaa, pp. 148–67. Her table on p. 161 is of special interest.

Adams,⁷⁰ we can divide the prepositions which appear in these formulae into three groups: first, those which never introduce a formula without a noun, e.g. *binnan*, *geond*, *in*, *of*, and *ymbe*; second, those which never introduce a formula containing a noun, e.g. *æfter* (Carkeet's initial **æfter þæm timum þe* is not recorded), *amang*, *betweoh*, *betwux*, *gemang*, *on*(*ge*)*mang*, and *under*; and third, those which introduce both, e.g. *ær* (only twice with a noun⁷¹ – *Matt(WSCp)* 26. 29 and *HomU* 24. 123. 5), *fram* (without a noun only in *ChronE* 258. 26 (1127)), *framþ*,⁷² *mid* (with a noun only in *BlHom* 133. 12 quoted in 16), *on* (only twice without a noun; see 16), *oð* (see 23), *to* (see 17), and *toforan/foran to* (both with and without a noun only in comparatively late texts⁷³). In general, it can be said of the third group that the less common formula occurs in comparatively late texts. These facts are not inconsistent with Carkeet's theory. In my opinion, however, they are most consistent with the proposition that some of the formulae without a noun developed from those with a noun, that some prepositions never governed a formula with a noun, and that with some prepositions the two formulae evolved independently. In other words, Carkeet's stage 1 was not essential, but was possible.

23   Gender provides us with what seems to me proof of the proposition that Carkeet's stage 1 is not essential. Most of the prepositional formulae involve the demonstrative *se* in the genitive, dative, or instrumental, in all of which the masculine and neuter forms are the same. So it is easy enough to insert masc. *timan* (rather than Carkeet's *timum*) in the formula *æfter þæm þe* and produce **æfter þæm timan þe*. Carkeet ingeniously manages to derive *þær* from *on þære stowe þe* to avoid the difficulty of having to explain how *on þæm stede/staðole þe* became *þær*.⁷⁴ He is able to avoid discussing *oð þæt* (*þe*) because it is not used correlatively. But it is impossible to use Carkeet's stages to derive *oð þæt* (*þe*) from attested formulae such as *ChronD* 99. 29 (915) *oð ðone fyrst þe*, *Bede* 42. 12 *oð ða tide þe*, and similar patterns cited by Adams,⁷⁵ or even from *Bo* 116. 10 *oð ðone first þ*, which I see as the result of the intrusion of *þæt* into what was originally the sphere of *þe*. None of the nouns of time which Adams found in prepositional or non-prepositional formulae – *byre*, *dæg*, *fyrst*, *hwil*, *monaþ*, *niht*, *tid*, *tima* – is neuter except *æfen* (also masculine) and *gear*. We cannot insert these or any other neuter noun of time of which I can think in *oð þæt þe*. Carkeet's attempt to dispose of the problem of gender does not meet this criticism.⁷⁶ Benham suggests that *oð þæt* and *oð þe* 'probably arose from the condensation of a phrase constructed with *oð* [such as *oð þone first ðæt* or *oð ðone first ðe*], while the *ðæt* or *ðe* is the introductory particle to the clause dependent upon the noun constructed with *oð*'.⁷⁷ This is different from Carkeet's proposal, for it

⁷⁰ Adams, pp. 242–5 and *passim*.   ⁷¹ Adams, p. 126.   ⁷² Adams, p. 115.
⁷³ Adams, pp. 126–7.   ⁷⁴ Carkeet, p. 61, n. 8.   ⁷⁵ Adams, p. 139.
⁷⁶ Carkeet, p. 61, n. 8.   ⁷⁷ Benham, p. 217.

involves the dropping of both the demonstrative and the noun. Benham goes on to claim that the likelihood of 'such condensation of phrase ... is proved by the analogous cases of *to*, *wið*, or *embe* + *ðæt*' and refers us to Shearin. But Shearin cites no examples of these prepositions with formulae involving nouns and suggests two possible origins for the formulae cited by Benham:

> First, and far more probably, here we have two *ðæt*'s, the accusative object of the preposition and the *ðæt* introductory of the clause, blended into one.... Second, it is conceivable that the *ðæt*-clause ... is the substantive object of the preceding prepositions ..., which govern it directly without an intervening pronominal. But this is hardly tenable....[78]

It is not clear which of these Adams was embracing when he wrote that 'logically, *ðæt* is the object of the preposition, and the subordinate clause is in apposition with it'.[79] Shearin does cite examples of *on ðæt gerad ðæt* 'on condition that', but *on ðæt (*þe*) is not recorded;[80] the formula is *on ðæm ðæt*,[81] which (if we follow Carkeet) would have to go back to an unrecorded **on þæm gerade þæt*. Similarly, we cannot derive the solitary *fram þ* in *ChronE* 258. 26 (1127) from the attested formulae *fram þam geare*(n)/*dæge*(m)/*timan*(m) *þe*, in all of which *þe* has to be construed as dat./instr.[82] Is it merely chance that while we find *of þære tide þe*, *on þære hwile þe*,[83] and the phrase *for þære wiisan* (*Bede* 70. 21), we do not find *of þære þe, *on þære þe, or *for þære þe? Are we to assume that these actually did once exist and were eliminated by analogy?[84] Or does their non-appearance support the proposition that in *æfter þæm þe*, *þæm* is the dative of the neuter demonstrative *þæt* used independently and that it never qualified a noun? I prefer to believe the latter.

24 So I conclude that Carkeet's stage 1 was not essential. Consideration of the table which follows may allow us to draw further conclusions. I use 'phase' instead of 'stage' to avoid confusion, since I include more patterns than Carkeet. 'No' means 'not recorded'.[85] Whether phases 1a and 1b had any meaningful independent existence is in my opinion doubtful. But see 14 fn. 42. Any form of the dative/instrumental may be represented by *þæm*. 'Prep'

---

[78] Shearin, pp. 76–7.
[80] Shearin, p. 76.
[82] Adams, pp. 114–15.
[79] Adams, p. 127.
[81] Shearin, p. 75.
[83] Adams, pp. 114 and 87.

[84] If Carkeet were to clutch at this straw, he would be in danger of having to eliminate *þa* as a conjunction because, since he derives it from the feminine demonstrative *þa* in *þa hwile þe*, it too could have been eliminated by analogy with *þonne*, which he derives from *þone* + noun of time + relative pronoun *þe*. See Carkeet, p. 53.

[85] Neither Adams's collections nor mine are complete. [1987. For the moment at any rate, I must leave to younger scholars the task of bringing to this problem the collections in *A Microfiche Concordance to Old English*. See *OES* i, pp. lxiii–iv.]

Introductory word	Phase 1a Prep. noun phrase + þe Phase 1b Conjunction	Phase 1c Prep. noun phrase + ... þe	Phase 2 Prep. phrase without noun + ... þe	Phase 3 Prep. phrase + þe > conjunction	Phase 4 Prep. phrase alone = conjunction	Phase 5 One word conjunction
æfter (adv., prep.)	No	No	No	æfter þæm þe	æfter þæm	No
ær (adv., prep.)	ær þæm dæge þe[a]	No	No	ær þæm þe	ær þæm	ær
mid (prep.)	No Mid þon dæge occurs in BlHom 133. 12	No	No	mid þæm þe	mid þæm	No
of (prep.)	of þæm dæge þe[b]	of þæm dæge ... þe[c]	No	No	No	No
on (prep.)	on þæm dagum þe[d]	No	No	on þæm þe	No	No
under (adv., prep.)	No	No	No	under þæm þe	No	No
for (prep.)	for þæm intingan þe[e]	No	for þæm ... þe	for þæm þe	for þæm	for (in late texts)

[a] Adams (p. 126) records this in *Matt (WSCp)* 26. 29, along with *HomU* 24. 123: 5 *ær þam byre þe*. I note *ÆCHom* i. 134. 17 *ær ðam fyrste þe*.
[b] Adams (pp. 113–14 and 214) records five such examples, along with *of þære tide þe*.
[c] Adams (p. 114) records two examples, viz. *ÆLS* 31. 1193 *of þam dæge æfre þe* and *WHom* 18. 78 *of þam timan ærest þe*.
[d] Adams (p. 93) records this in *Or* 180. 21, but implies that there are more. He also notes (p. 87) *on þære hwile þe* in *Or* 130. 9 and *Or* 170. 12.
[e] I find this in *ÆCHom* i. 512. 6. Further on causal conjunctions of this sort see *OES* §3071. They too are rare.

embraces postpositions.[86] I do not regard patterns such as *æfter/on/to þæt* as exemplifying phase 4. On *to* formulae see 17.

25   I have already demonstrated to my own satisfaction that phase 1 was not essential. There is little in the table to support the idea that it even played a part in the development of the prepositional conjunctions; the examples are too few in number and too spasmodic in appearance. Phase 2, in which the adverb phrase is separated from *þe* – as in *Or* 132. 13 *He þa Alexander hit swipost for þæm angann þe he wolde þæt his mærþa wæren maran þonne Ercoles* – is not found in temporal clauses; examples with tmesis occur only with a noun, i.e. in phase 1c – and then (as noted above) only twice.[87] So phase 2 – very common in causal clauses – can be eliminated from the development of the temporal formulae.

26   Where then do we begin? The fact that *ær* appears as a conjunction in the earliest texts, both prose and verse, and that **ær þe* is not recorded means, I think, that adv. *ær* became conj. *ær* without any intermediate steps involving a demonstrative and/or *þe*. But we still have to account for combinations like *ær þam (þe)* and *ær þon (þe)*. Adams writes: 'In itself *ær* is a comparative, and, as such is followed by the dative. Naturally, then, when it came to be used as a preposition, it demanded the dative case. The addition of *ðe* gives this preposition with its object the force of a conjunction.'[88] This would seem to imply that phase 3 was essential in the development of *ær þam* – on this see 27–8 – and that formulae with the instrumental like *ær þon (þe)* were the result of dative/ instrumental syncretism. (They occur too early to be due to phonetic weakening.) It is too exquisite to argue whether conj. *ær þam* ever produced conj. *ær* by shortening if conj. *ær* already existed through the first process described.

27   The fact that 'the simple *ær* seems to be more common in early texts than in later; in general, the use of the relative in prepositional formulae of all kinds increases in later texts' supports the notion of a two-fold development.[89] But it does not prove that *ær þam (þe)* and the like are in origin prepositional formulae. For Behaghel – followed by Möllmer – explains *þon* as a form of the temporal adv. *þonne* and suggests that there were originally two formulae – *er* (OE *ær*), used after a negative principal clause, and *er than* (OE *ær þonne/þon*) used after a positive principal clause.[90] These two usages would spring from two original paratactic constructions which may be illustrated by the MnE

---

[86] See Bruce Mitchell 'Prepositions, Adverbs, Prepositional Adverbs, Postpositions, Separable Prefixes, or Inseparable Prefixes, in Old English?', *NM* 79 (1978), 240–57.
[87] Examples like *Bede* 46. 19 *7 hi wæron sona deade swa hi eorðan gesohtan* are not relevant here.
[88] Adams, p. 119.   [89] Adams, p. 120.
[90] See O. Behaghel *Deutsche Syntax* III (Heidelberg, 1928), §925 and H. Möllmer *Konjunktionen und Modus im Temporalsatz des Altenglischen* (Breslau, 1937), pp. 76–7.

sentences 'I do not go. Sooner he comes' and 'I go before. Then he may come'. This theory does account for the fact that *ær* and *ær þon* are used in the earliest poetry. But if the distinction ever existed, it does not hold in OE poetry, where some 23 per cent (six out of twenty-six) negative principal clauses are followed by *ær þon* against some 22 per cent (fifteen out of sixty-nine) positive principal clauses. Both Behaghel and Möllmer agree that the alleged distinction broke down early. The figures they quote from the *Heliand* demonstrate its breakdown rather than confirm its existence and the fact that Adams found only four examples of *ær ðonne* must cast further doubt on it.[91] Forms such as *ær ðam* (*Dan* l. 587) and *ær þy* (*GenA* l. 2766) would be due to an early feeling that *þon* was instrumental, a feeling which would be quite simply explained by analogy with *æfter þon*, *for þon*, and the like, while the forms with *þe* – according to Möllmer – are due perhaps to the influence of Lat. *antequam/priusquam* or possibly to that of combinations like *æfter þam/þon þe*.[92] The acceptance of Behaghel's theory would mean that *ær þon* is different in nature and origin from combinations like *for þon* and *æfter þon* (if we agree that *æfter þon* is in origin a prepositional formula; see 31). But this in itself is not an argument against the theory.

28   Yet another different origin for *ær þon* is suggested by Small – somewhat overconfidently, it must be said: 'no one, it is believed, will differ with the writer upon the analysis of this subordinate conjunction'.[93] His theory is that in examples like

Phoen l. 377   Forgeaf him se meahta   moncynnes fruma
þæt he swa wrætlice   weorþan sceolde
eft þæt ilce   þæt he ær þon wæs,
feþrum bifongen,   þeah hine fyr nime

ær retains its comparative sense and *þon* is an instrumental of comparison. So we have an adverb phrase meaning 'earlier than that'. To this is added 'the particle, *þe*, to convert the demonstrative phrase into a relative expression'; hence in

Jud l. 250   Hogedon aninga
hyra hlaforde   hilde bodian,
ærðon ðe him se egesa   on ufan sæte,
mægen Ebrea

'the basic meaning underlying the conjunction, *before*, is undoubtedly "*earlier than that, that* the terror was upon them" or, "*earlier than that, namely*, the terror was upon them".' Dative/instrumental syncretism would again account for

---

[91] Adams, p. 220.   [92] Möllmer, pp. 80–1.
[93] Small 'The Syntax of *The* and OE *þon Ma þe*', pp. 389–91.

forms like *ærðæmðe* in *CP* 5. 8–10, which Small quotes. The weakness of this theory is Small's belief that 'the usual forms [of the conjunctional] are *ær þon þe*, and *ær þam þe*' and his assumption that *ær þon þe* is the original one.[94] Behre's probably unknowing modification of Small's theory in part overcomes this weakness by showing how *ærþon* – as opposed to *ærþon þe* – could have become a conjunction, for Behre says that in

Max i. 109
   wuda ond wætres nyttað   þonne him biþ wic alyfed,
   mete bygeþ, gif he maran þearf,   ærþon he to meþe weorþe

'the basic thought is: "he buys meat if he needs more before (or: in preference to) this: he would become too faint (sc. if he did not buy meat)"'.[95] But the early use of *ær* alone as a conjunction remains a difficulty, despite Joly.[96]

29   Not unexpectedly, Johnsen adds yet another theory: to him, both *ær* and *þon* were originally 'local demonstrative adverbs'.[97] I do not propose to adjudicate here. But I will repeat my belief that conj. *ær* arose directly from adv. *ær* and that formulae like *ær þam/þon* (*þe*) arose independently.

30   The possibility of a direct development from adverb to conjunction may arise with *siþ*, which appears as a conjunction once – in *Ch* 1440 *Sið heora tuuege dæg agan sie, þonne agefe mon tuuenti hida....* But, as Adams suggests, it may be a later reduction.[98] Carkeet claims that 'the absence of *þe* in conjunction with *siþþan* in attested Old English does not at all falsify the claim that *siþþan* can be derived historically from some earlier sequence like *siþ þæm timum þe* ...'.[99] If *siþþan* did indeed derive from such a sequence, it would be possible that phase 3 *siþ þæm þe occurred early and is by chance not recorded. But Adams has a telling argument against this idea:

> This conjunction [*siððan*] is, according to Sweet, *Student's Dictionary of Anglo-Saxon*, compounded of the preposition *sið* and its object in the dative. Others regard *ðan* as being the instrumental in a phrase of

[94] My figures for the poetry are *ær* 68, *ærþon/ðon* (written as one word or two) 21, *ærþan* 1, *ær þan* 1, *ærðæm* 1, *ær ðam* 1, *ær þy* 1, and *ærðon ðe* 1. For the prose, Adams (pp. 215–20) lists the following (I give his spellings): *ær* 258, *ær ær* 3, *ær... ær* 37; *ær ðam ðe* 124, *ær ðan ðe* 133 (over 100 of these from Ælfric), *ær ðon ðe* 43 (less than one-third from 'Alfredian' texts); *ær ðam* 14, *ær ðan* 2, *ær ðon* 36; and *ær ðonne* 4.
[95] See F. Behre *The Subjunctive in Old English Poetry* (Göteborg, 1934), p. 169.
[96] A. Joly *Negation and the Comparative Particle in English* (Quebec, 1967), p. 15.
[97] O. Johnsen 'More Notes on Old English Adverbs and Conjunctions of Time', *Anglia* 39 (1916), 117–18.
[98] Adams, p. 105.
[99] See Carkeet, pp. 53–4. As Adams (pp. 104–5) says, the two possible examples of *siþþan... þe* are dubious. *Siþþan þe* has not been recorded.

comparison. I incline to the latter view; for ðæm does not become ðæn until the later period of OE, and we have siððan in the earliest texts.[100]

Small lends his support to Adams:

> There is one other OE subordinate conjunction that is based upon a comparative adverb, and which in form and function exactly parallels the construction that is the subject of this article [viz. þon ma þe], namely, siþ þan þe, 'after', 'since'. The form, siþ, is a comparative meaning 'later', having developed regularly from Com. Gmc. *siþiz (= Go. seiþs). The semantic base of the conjunction, since, is therefore 'later than that, namely, ...' In ME this conjunction survived in the abbreviated form, siþþen, sithen, with later addition of the adverbial -es: sithenes, sins, since.[101]

But in my opinion this particular formulation founders on the absence of *siþþan þe.

31 Since æfter is not used alone as a conjunction in OE, the possibility of a direct development from adverb to conjunction does not arise. So we must postulate at least phase 3 and/or phase 4 if we assume that the formulae with æfter are in origin prepositional. It is interesting however to wonder why Small did not include these formulae along with those introduced by ær and siþ in view of the fact that æfter is in origin a comparative; see OED, s. v. after adv. and prep.

32 As far as I am aware, mid is not used as an adverb except in contexts where it can be taken as a postposition or separable prefix; see OES §2238. Thus the possibility of a direct development is ruled out on two grounds – mid was not an adverb and did not become a conjunction. The direct development must also be ruled out in the case of for, which is not used as an adverb in OE. So phase 3 and/or phase 4 are necessarily involved here. But in view of the many examples with tmesis, phase 2 may also be a necessary step, as van Dam suggests.[102] It is, however, possible that phases 2 and 3 arose independently and that phase 2 is an alternative development rather than an essential one.

33 I must now attempt an answer to the question whether a phase with þe – phase 2 or 3 – is essential. Carkeet says that 'there might be no [such] stage'[103] and I have already given good reasons for believing that it did not occur with siþþan. The rarity of oð þæt þe and oð þætte is suggestive rather than conclusive.[104] Whether forþæm ... þe and/or for þæm þe must have been part of

[100] Adams, p. 100. [101] Small 'The Syntax of The and OE þon Ma þe', p. 389, fn. 21.
[102] Van Dam, pp. 45–6. [103] Carkeet, p. 53. [104] Adams, pp. 129–30.

their particular chain is a more difficult question. Despite Carkeet,[105] it does seem 'plausible' to me to suggest either that *for þæm* prep. phrase developed into *forþæm* (...) *þe* conjunction – in other words, that at least one of phase 2 and phase 3 was essential – and that *þe* was subsequently dropped to give *for þæm* conjunction or that *for þæm* prep. phrase > adverb developed directly into a conjunction, the two being distinguished first by intonation and later by the addition of *þe* to the latter. (On this, cf. 41.) The same sequences – without phase 2 – might be postulated for those temporal conjunctions which are recorded both with and without *þe*, e.g. *æfter/ær/mid þæm* (*þe*).[106] Anyone in doubt about the plausibility of the first development should see Adams,[107] van Dam,[108] and Mann.[109]

34 Geoghegan writes:

Also like *þæt*, *þe* could be deleted, so that *for þæm þe* 'because' on the surface looked like *for þæm* 'therefore'. This did not necessarily pose a problem for the speakers of Old English though because the accompanying change in word order in situations where *for þæm* meant 'because' offers support for the presence of *þe* at some point in the derivation, deleted after it had triggered the change in word order.[110]

I am not sure that element order can be taken as proof that a phase involving *þe* was essential. Even if we concede – as in fact we cannot do – that the prepositional formulae always had the order S.V. when they were adverbs in initial position and S.... V. when they were conjunctions,[111] it is not demonstrable that *þe* had to be present to produce this pattern. The change in intonation postulated in 33 could have been responsible. The same would be true of words like *þær*, *þa*, and *þonne*, where the conjunction regularly has S. (...) V. and the adverb V.S.[112]

35 At the moment, then, while I am unable to demonstrate that a phase with *þe* was essential in the development of any of the prepositional formulae, I believe it to be likely in some, especially in the formulae involving *for*.[113] But, as I have

[105] p. 56.
[106] The fact that both *ær* and *ærþon* appear as conjunctions in the earliest poetry and that *ærðon ðe* occurs only in *Jud* l. 252 may merely be due to the demands of metre, since formulae with *þe* occur in the earliest prose. So the fact that conj. *ærþon* is found in the earliest poetry does not show that it cannot be from *ærþon þe* – despite Möllmer, pp. 81–2. For other theories about the development of these conjunctions see 26–9.
[107] pp. 119–20. [108] pp. xi–xii, 45–6, and 50.
[109] pp. 92–3. [110] Geoghegan, p. 42.
[111] On this see Andrew *Syntax*, §40, Campbell, pp. 93–6, and *OES* §3900.
[112] See Campbell, pp. 93–6 and *OES* §3922.
[113] See P. S. Baker 'The Old English Canon of Byrhtferth of Ramsey', *Speculum* 55 (1980), 25–6 and 33. Baker makes the valid point that conjunctions such as *for þæm* (*þe*) and *þeah* (*þe*) are subject to scribal omission or insertion of *þe* and are therefore not 'very stable'. This makes our task harder.

shown, I also believe that there are some formulae, e.g. *oð þæt* and *siþþan*, in which it is unlikely to have played a part. I do not think that this is surprising. The marked variation in the patterns set out in the table in 24 does not suggest to me that there was any instinct – or whatever you care to call it – which demanded a uniform development.

36 Let us now turn to the non-prepositional conjunctions. Here I find it impossible to accept Carkeet's proposed derivations as in any way plausible. Even if we are willing to agree that *timan* in **æfter þæm timan þe* is a 'semantically empty' noun which 'can easily become an optional item',[114] the same cannot be true of *geares* in *ÆCHom* i. 80. 30 *þæs geares þe*, the only recorded formula with the genitive *þæs* expressing time and one which cannot be fitted into most of the uses of *þæs þe* conjunction 'when, after' – of which Carkeet sees it as the source. Why do we not find **þære þe* from such expressions as *Or* 226. 17 *þære ilcan niht þe* or *þy þe* 'when' from *ChronE* 79. 26 (885) *þy geare þe* or *þæs þe* 'where' from *Bede* 4. 17 *þæs mynstres ðe*? I concede neither the need for, nor the likelihood of, the development postulated by Carkeet.

37 His suggested sequence *þa hwile þe* > *þa þe* > *þa* and > *þe* is even more strange.[115] It seems to me as unlikely as postulating the sequence *se mann þe* > *seþe* > *se* and > *þe*. It is significant that Carkeet is unable to produce any combination of *þone* + noun of time + *þe* to enable him to get to *þonne* and has to fall back on the prepositional formula *on þære stowe þe* to produce *þær*.[116] His statement that 'henceforth we will be calling these oblique case NP's [*þa hwile þe* and the like] "adverbial PP's", even though the preposition may not be present on the surface' seems to me an obvious but unsuccessful attempt to sweep very real difficulties under the carpet.[117] If he is right, why is *þær* not **on þære þe*? What preposition does he imagine once appeared before *þæs geares þe* or before '*þæs dæges* "on that day"'?[118] That confusion between what I regard as the original *þe* and the intruding *þæt* also occurred in non-prepositional temporal formulae is clear from late occurrences of *þa hwile þ* – another pattern which Carkeet's theory cannot explain.[119] Carkeet seems to admit that adverbs like *þær*, *þa*, and *þonne*, and adverb phrases like *ær þæm* and *for þæm* were in existence before his hypothetical developments began.[120] Indeed, this must be so unless he proposes to derive the adverbs *þær*, *þa*, and *þonne*, from the conjunctions which have developed from the demonstratives by his complicated process. He says that 'almost all OE correlative adverbs are of the same root as the conjunctions with which they occur'.[121] In my opinion it is contrary to common sense to claim that at a time when the adverbs were already in existence,

[114] Carkeet, p. 53. [115] Carkeet, p. 53. [116] Carkeet, pp. 53 and 54.
[117] Carkeet, p. 60, n. 5. [118] Carkeet, p. 60, n. 5. [119] See Adams, p. 86.
[120] Carkeet, p. 56. [121] Carkeet, p. 52.

the complicated processes suggested by Carkeet began and ultimately led to the appearance of conjunctions of exactly the same form. It would seem simpler to derive *þa* conjunction direct from *þa* adverb than from *þa hwile þe*. (Whether this necessarily involved an intermediate stage with *þe* is discussed in 41.) *Mutatis mutandis*, this is true of other correlative pairs like *þær* and *þonne* and of at least some of the prepositional formulae. I find it hard to believe that, if dem. *þæt* became conj. *þæt* and dem. *se* became rel. *se*, the adverbs mentioned above could not have developed directly into conjunctions.

38   It also remains a fact that Carkeet cannot really account for conj. *þeah* 'though' by his theory and admits that he cannot explain how *nu* and *swa* became conjunctions.[122] The 'traditional view' can: they too underwent the direct development explained above. The great merit of the 'traditional view' is that it admits the possibility of varying developments within the general thesis that parataxis preceded hypotaxis and is not tied to one particular theory. Some of these variations have just been illustrated. Others are discussed in *OES*; they include *hwonne* and the like, *swa* (...) *þæt*, *þonne* 'than', *þon ma þe* (here I am in basic agreement with Small), and *þy læs* (*þe*).

39   It is impossible to reach certainty in any of these discussions. The same is true when we consider conjunctions like *butan*, *gif*, and *nefne*. *OED* s.v. *but* speaks of the OE adv. and prep. *be-utan*, *butan* functioning 'as a conjunction, with uses arising immediately out of the prepositional sense' – I suppose this means a transition from *butan* (prep. + dat.) as in *ÆCHom* i. 8. 26 *he is ende butan ælcere geendunge* to *butan* (prep. or conj.?) as in *ÆCHom* i. 174. 4 *Hit is awriten on ðære ealdan æ, þæt nan man ne sceal hine gebiddan to nanum deofelgylde, ne to nanum ðinge, buton to Gode anum* to *butan* (conj., since it is followed by the nominative and not by the dative), as in *ÆCHom* i. 174. 6 *forðon ðe nan gesceaft nys wyrðe þæs wurðmyntes, buton se ana seðe Scyppend is ealra ðinga* – and observes s.v. *if* that 'it has not been certainly determined whether the conj. is thus derived from the sb. [represented by OHG *iba* (f), ON *if, ef* (n), and ON *ifi, efi* (m), "doubt"], or the sb. founded on the conj.' But I do not think that anything in their development runs contrary to the general thesis that parataxis preceded hypotaxis.

40   The notion of a direct transition from adverb to conjunction can account not only for the conjunctions discussed above but also for *swilce*, *þanon*, *þenden*, *þider*, *þy*, and so on.[123] In my opinion, this change of function was not

---

[122] Carkeet, p. 54.

[123] Erickson's presumption (p. 111) that '*þy* ... is presumably a variation on *for þy* where the distinctive case marker (instrumental) allows the deletion of the preposition' is unlikely and unnecessary. It is the essence of an inflected language that a case form alone, without a preposition, can mark a distinction. The conjunctional use of *þy* (*þe*) could have arisen from an adverbial use of *þy*

necessarily dependent, as Carkeet (*passim*) seems to imply, on the presence of two adverbs in successive simple sentences which could be taken as correlatives – as in *Or* 14. 26 *Nu hæbbe we scortlice gesæd ymbe Asia londgemæro; nu wille we ymbe Europe londgemære areccean* ... and

Beo l. 126   Ða wæs on uhtan   mid ærdæge
            Grendles guðcræft   gumum undyrne;
            þa wæs æfter wiste   wop up ahafen,
            micel morgensweg –

but could also have taken place when only one adverb was present – as in *Or* 58. 21 *Nu we witan þæt ure Dryhten us gesceop; we witon eac þæt he ure reccend is* and

Beo l. 917   Ða wæs morgenleoht
            scofen ond scynded.   Eode scealc monig
            swiðhicgende   to sele þam hean
            searowundor seon.[124]

41   Was an intermediate stage with *þe* essential in the development of any of the non-prepositional conjunctions discussed above? Some of them, e.g. *nu*, *swa*, *swilce*, and *þenden*, are not recorded with *þe*.[125] So it seems reasonable to suggest that for them the answer is 'No'. *þe* is not common with *þa* or *þonne* (see 4 and *OES*) and I have the feeling that *þe* is a later addition. But Adams is inclined to believe that the forms with *þe* were earlier and essential.[126] *þanon þe* and *þider þe* (both of which are restricted to the prose) are perhaps more common than *þær þe*, which occurs occasionally in early prose and twice in the poetry.[127] But even when full statistics are available, the matter will probably remain one of opinion. Thus the comparative figures for *þeah* (*þe*) in the poetry (necessarily approximate) are *þeah* 135 and *þeah þe* 76.[128] Burnham did not provide figures for the prose, but she observes that 'in view of the adverbial use of *ðeah* ... and in view of the obviously connective character of *ðe*, we may well infer the evolution: *ðeah* adv. > *ðeah ðe* > *ðeah* conj.; though we cannot detect the process'.[129] Here, as with *þa*, *þonne*, *þær*, *þider*, and *þanon*, there are however two possibilities: viz. first, that envisaged by Burnham for *þeah*, in which the stage with *þe* was essential, and second, that in which *þeah* adverb became *þeah* conj. (as I believe happened with *nu* and *swa*) and that *þeah þe* represents 'for that, by that', pointing either forward or back. Similarly, in my opinion, *þæs* (*þe*) 'when, after, since, because, as' is of separate origin from *to þæs* (*þe*) 'to the extent that, so that'. As far as I know, they remain distinct in OE. Erickson speaks of *to þæs* 'when'. Neither Adams nor I record any examples.

[124] See Mitchell 'Old English *Oð þæt*', pp. 393–4 [pp. 261–3 above].
[125] See Kivimaa, pp. 165–6.   [126] Adams, pp. 23–4 and 25–6.
[127] See *OES*.   [128] Mitchell *D.Phil.*, pp. 837–8.
[129] Burnham, p. 14.

a later stage. It is clear that various ways of distinguishing adverbs from conjunctions evolved to supplement or (in writing) replace intonation. Element order has been discussed in 34. Ælfric frequently distinguished *þa* (...) *þa* conj. from *þa* adv. and, according to Burnham, 'shows a very marked preference for *ðeah ðe* – desiring, perhaps, from his strong teaching instinct, to distinguish clearly between the adverb and the conjunction'.[130] It is possible that this exploitation of what I insist on calling 'the subordinating particle *þe*' began in Alfredian times, though it has to be admitted that it was not carried out systematically in the early texts and, in the case of *þy læs*, had not even begun.[131] There is room for more work here.[132] Meanwhile – although it is only fair to say that I have derived stimulus from Carkeet's article – I am content to leave it to the reader to judge whether his theory or the 'traditional view' as expounded above involves the more 'highly improbable' changes.[133]

ADDITIONAL COMMENT [1987. This formed part of the original article.]

Erickson's discussion of causal clauses seems to me to be based on false premisses. He says (pp. 100–1) that *forþon* 'typically appears either in single main clauses, connecting the clause causally with what has preceded' – *forþon* means 'Thus, Therefore' – 'or at the beginning of what is normally classed as a dependent clause, which provides justification for what has been stated in the preceding main clause' – *forþon* (*þe*) means 'for, because'. But for him *BlHom* 3. 10 *forþon heo fæmne cende, forðon heo wæs fæmne geeacnod* exemplifies 'an unusual syntactic construction where a main clause adverbial (*forðon*) appears to anticipate the homophonous subordinator introducing a following subordinate clause'. The exact reference of the word 'unusual', which he repeats at p. 100, is not clear to me. But, for the reasons which follow, I do not find it appropriate.

Causal clauses frequently follow their principal clause in MnE, although correlation is employed less frequently than in OE.[134] It is certainly not 'unusual' for a causal clause to follow its principal clause in OE; see the passage from van Dam referred to by Erickson and his own comment there that 'the normal expectation would be that a causal clause should belong to what precedes rather than to what follows'.[135]

Although Erickson refers to both van Dam and to my *Guide*,[136] he fails to take note of what van Dam and I have to say about correlative *forþon...forþon* (*þe*) 'for that [reason I am about to explain] ... because'. In particular, he overlooks van Dam's comments about correlative causal clauses in early OE prose, which include this: 'In approx. 70% of the cases in which correlated groups

[130] Burnham, p. 13. [131] See *OES* §2929.
[132] See Kivimaa, pp. 166–7. [133] Carkeet, p. 56. [134] See *Guide* §§150–3.
[135] Van Dam, p. 82 and Erickson, p. 111, n. 16. [136] Erickson, p. 111; *Guide* §169.

were noted, the causal clause follows the main clause, which, indeed, is its *usual* position' [my italics].[137] Compare here my '67.7 per cent' (10), which is based on Liggins's figures for OE prose of all periods.

Erickson cites Andrew's comment that 'when the principal sentence comes first, *forðon* (*forði*) shows that stress is laid not so much on the action predicated by the verb as on the reason for it ...' but goes on: 'Andrew's explanation accounts for the stress relationships between the two parts of the sentence, but it fails to give any justification for why the construction has the particular form that it has.'[138] I cannot see the need for more 'justification' than Andrew gives. Since the vast majority of OE causal clauses follow their principal clause, it is scarcely surprising that this is true when the two clauses are linked by correlatives. Erickson's argument that, because we have the sequence subordinate clause principal clause with *Gif*... *þonne* 'If ... then', there is something 'unusual' in the sequence *Forþon*... *forþon* (*þe*) 'For that [reason I am about to explain] ... because', overlooks the fact that in OE 'the normal expectation would be that a causal clause should belong to what precedes rather than to what follows'.[139]

It is true that a table in *OES* §3074 shows that only some 6 per cent of the causal sentences noted by Liggins involve correlation. So the construction described by Erickson as 'unusual' can perhaps be said to be uncommon. But this is not (it seems to me) what he meant. The fact that it is less common does not in my opinion make it less 'typically' Old English than the constructions in which *forþon* (*þe*) appears alone meaning either 'therefore' or 'because'. It merely reflects the fact that, of the three constructions under discussion, it was by its very nature the one most likely to be used least often.

---

[137] Van Dam, pp. 79–80.   [138] Erickson, p. 101; Andrew *Syntax*, pp. 32–3.
[139] Erickson, p. 111, n. 16.

27
Some Lexicographical Problems Posed by Old English Grammar Words

The absence of native informants is felt by all workers in Old English lexicography. The consequent ignorance of intonation patterns is a problem which particularly affects the syntactician/lexicographer concerned with the grammar words. It is one which also particularly concerns literary critics and editors of Old English texts, especially poetry, but they have so far been notably reluctant to involve themselves in it. The two vastly different approaches to the punctuation of Old English poetry represented by Andrew – 'Can anyone believe that such a string of emphatic demonstrative sentences truly represents the genius of Old English poetry?'[1] – and by Tolkien – 'Editors are too shy of breaking Old English verse into short sharp sentences'[2] – pose a question of fundamental importance which as yet has not been taken sufficiently seriously. Editorial handling of Old English verse paragraphs and the punctuation of *þa*

Reprinted from *Problems of Old English Lexicography: Studies in Memory of Angus Cameron* ed. Alfred Bammesberger, *Eichstätter Beiträge Abteilung Sprache und Literatur* 15 (1985), 79–89.

This paper was written in conjunction with Sharon Butler, a member of the staff of the *Dictionary of Old English* project at the University of Toronto, where she was rightly held in warm affection, from 1977 until her untimely death in 1986. I think of her as the author of 'The Cynewulf Question Revived', *Neuphilologische Mitteilungen* 83 (1982), 15–23 – an article which revealed that the findings of Satyendra Kumar Das *Cynewulf and the Cynewulf Canon* (Calcutta, 1942), have been too lightly accepted by generations of scholars. I think of her as 'The Queen of the Stop Words' – a role in which I had a particular interest, as most of the stop words are grammar words, and which culminated in the production with Richard L. Venezky of *A Microfiche Concordance to Old English: The High Frequency Words* (Toronto, 1985); my own copy is inscribed by her with words which include 'For Bruce, one of the few who will really enjoy this Concordance!' I think of her as a valued collaborator in this article. I think of her as a dedicated cook (both practical, as her friends well know, and scholarly, as her publications with Constance Hieatt testify); as a gracious hostess; and as a good friend to my wife and myself.

Requiescat in Pace.

[1] S. O. Andrew *Syntax and Style in Old English* (Cambridge, 1940), p. 97.
[2] J. R. R. Tolkien *The Old English* Exodus: *Text, Translation, and Commentary* ed. Joan Turville-Petre (Oxford, 1981), p. 38, note to l. 41.

clauses in particular give dramatic testimony to this.³ We find ourselves on the whole more in sympathy with Tolkien than with Andrew on this point. But we do not think that such sympathy, or agreement, renders void the notion that the verse paragraph is the basic unit of Old English poetry. For we would argue that, just as different intonations would be required for Subject–Verb–Object sentences and Object–Verb–Subject sentences, there was available to the poet/ reciter an intonation which indicated that a statement was both complete in itself and yet linked to what followed; compare Modern English 'And God said, Let there be light: and there was light.' But we cannot reconstruct these patterns and – as we shall see below – their unavailability creates almost insoluble problems.

2   A second difficulty for the syntactician/lexicographer is that of anticipating the needs of workers in the later periods of the language. Two simple illustrations will suffice here. The first concerns the verb *don*. One of the most striking differences between the verb patterns of Old English and Modern English is the absence from the former of the *do* periphrases and even, as far as is attested at the moment, of any 'embryo' examples of 'I do sing' comparable with the pattern *Ic wille singan* 'I will sing'. It is clear that – despite *OED* s.v. *do* III. 25a, followed by later grammarians – *Or* 48. 8 *7 æfter ðæm hie dydon ægþer ge cyninga ricu settan ge niwu ceastra timbredon* is not one, for *settan*, like *timbredon*, is preterite. Similarly, despite F. Th. Visser,⁴ sentences like Mark (*WSCp*) 10. 7 *hwæt do ic þæt ic ece lif age* is not a prototype of the pattern 'Do I leave this fellow tied like that?', for in the Old English example *do* is a full verb. On this question see *OES* §§665–9.⁵ Any sorting pattern for *don* must ensure that, if there are examples of the type 'I do sing', they do not escape. Similarly, historians of the English language will expect to find in *DOE* any evidence there is for the use, or 'embryo' use, of **sculan* and *willan* as auxiliaries of the future tenses – here the contrast between Bosworth-Toller's blanket gloss for **sculan* and the some dozen main senses it gives for *willan* is notable. The syntactician/lexicographer has here another (almost) insoluble problem, well posed by Visser: 'A good deal of labour has been spent by numerous grammarians on the question when it was that the combination *shall* + infinitive reached the status of a "future tense", without their first saying what a "future tense" really is.'⁶ See further *OES* §§1019–24.

3   No doubt lexicographers would give much for three ten-minute tapes featuring Alfred, Ælfric, and Wulfstan. So too would syntacticians, phonologists, and

---

³ See Bruce Mitchell 'The Dangers of Disguise: Old English Texts in Modern Punctuation', *RES* 31 (1980), 398–402 [item 18 above].
⁴ *An Historical Syntax of the English Language* II (Leiden, 1963–73), p. 731.
⁵ Bruce Mitchell *Old English Syntax* (Oxford, 1985) (hereafter referred to as *OES*).
⁶ Visser III, p. 1582, n. 1.

those interested in many other branches of Old English studies. But alas! the intonation of these three giants *genap under nihthelm, swa heo no wære*. So we must all battle on as best we can – without deluding ourselves that we really are native informants.

The Problems

4 The etymology of grammar words is a task for the specialist and will not be considered here. Indeed, as Gneuss puts it,

> it was decided very early in the planning stage of the new 'Dictionary of Old English' not to treat etymologies in any detail. This seems a sensible and legitimate policy. Etymology has become a highly specialized discipline, and little harm will be done by referring the reader using an Old English dictionary to the *Oxford English Dictionary*, to the etymological dictionaries now available, and to a forthcoming new etymological dictionary of Old English.[7]

5 Problems which concern the lexicographer and the syntactician can be broadly divided into three groups. First, there are those which can be said to be lexicographical rather than syntactical. Some of these will be solved without too much difficulty when all the examples are sorted. These include whether one particular usage of case or preposition after an adjective occurs in prose, poetry, and glosses, or is limited to one or two of these, or to a particular period or dialect (*OES* §218); whether indefinite *hwæþer* is used only independently and with a partitive genitive or whether examples of its dependent use or of its independent use without a partitive genitive do in fact exist (*OES* §435); and whether the personal or 'direct' passive construction occurs with verbs which do not govern the accusative when used actively (*OES* §852). Other problems of this type, however, depend for their solution on personal interpretation of individual examples and so will be more difficult to resolve. These include whether (or perhaps rather how often) indefinite *hwelc* means 'every' or 'each' rather than 'any' (*OES* §422); to what extent, if any, the verbs *aginnan*, *beginnan*, and *onginnan*, have acquired a weakened sense approaching the auxiliary use of their Middle English reflexes (*OES* §§675–8); whether *of* + the dative case ever denotes possession in Old English (*OES* §§1202–3); and whether *oðþæt* ever serves as an adverb.[8]

---

[7] Helmut Gneuss 'Some Problems and Principles of the Lexicography of Old English', *Festschrift für Karl Schneider* ed. Ernst S. Dick and Kurt R. Jankowsky (Amsterdam and Philadelphia), pp. 153–4.

[8] Bruce Mitchell 'Old English *Oð þæt* Adverb?' *NQ* 223 (1978), 390–4 [item 24 above].

6 The second group of problems comprises those which can be said to concern the syntactician rather than the lexicographer. These include whence, how, and why, the non-prepositional and prepositional adverbs and conjunctions developed as they did; the use of the moods in different types of subordinate clauses and the influence thereon of the various governing words and introductory conjunctions; and the expression of subordinate relationships by clauses with an initial verb and no conjunction.

7 Third, and most difficult, are those problems which are of desperate importance to both lexicographer and syntactician. Limitations of space and time permit neither consideration of all these nor a full consideration of those selected. Some of them have already been raised elsewhere, but still require editorial decision. These include the problems of whether to print combination of quasi-prefix and verb as one word (*toteon, togeteon, onahebban*) or as two and the not-unrelated difficulty of how to deal with prepositional formulae such as *for þæm, for þæm þe*, and *for þæm... þe*.[9] Others demand more detailed treatment here.

8 The question 'Is *oð þæt* (§5) or *for þæm* (§7) an adverb or a conjunction?' can be rephrased to read 'Is the clause introduced by *oð þæt* or *for þæm* principal or subordinate?' This difficulty – compounded by the complication that we may be guilty of over-simplifying in so posing the question, because there may have been in Old English an intermediate stage between parataxis and hypotaxis as what were originally 'adverbs' gradually acquired the status of conjunctions[10] – is not restricted to *oð þæt* or *for þæm*. It affects the ambiguous demonstrative/relative *se*,[11] the ambiguous adverb/conjunctions such as *ær, nu, swa, þa, þær*, and *þonne*,[12] and in a sense even words like *hu*, for in

Beo l. 1   Hwæt, we Gardena   in geardagum
             þeodcyninga   þrym gefrunon,
             hu ða æðelingas   ellen fremedon!

it is by no means certain that l. 3 is a dependent rather than a non-dependent exclamation. Nothing more need be said about *hu* except that it and words like

---

[9] See Bruce Mitchell 'Prepositions, Adverbs, Prepositional Adverbs, Post-positions, Separable Prefixes, or Inseparable Prefixes, in Old English', *NM* 79 (1978), pp. 256–7 and Bruce Mitchell and Fred C. Robinson *A Guide to Old English Revised with Texts and Glossary* (Oxford, 1982; repr. 1983), pp. 169–71 (hereafter cited as *Guide*).

[10] See Mitchell 'Old English *Oð þæt*', pp. 393–4 and 'The Dangers of Disguise', pp. 398–9. [1987. See item 24 above, pp. 261–3, and item 18, pp. 186–7.]

[11] Mitchell 'The Dangers of Disguise', pp. 394–5 and 404–5. [1987. See item 18 above, pp. 182–3 and 192–3.]

[12] Mitchell, 'The Dangers of Disguise', pp. 394 and 399–404. [1987. See item 18 above, pp. 182 and 187–92.]

it often pose not only the question 'Dependent or non-dependent?' but also the question 'Question or exclamation?'

9 But *se* and *þa* present additional complications. For *se* we have the homographs *sæ* and *swa*, for *seo*, *seo* 'pupil of (eye)' and *sæ*; the dependent pronominal functions; the independent pronominal functions, including that of subject-changing;[13] and of course the ambiguous demonstrative/relative. For *þa* we have to distinguish the last three uses of *þa* acc. sg. fem. and nom./acc. pl. – being careful not to forget the adv./conj. *þa hwile* (*þe*) – before we tackle the various adverbial and conjunctional ones, including those which are ambiguous. With *swa*, we have a multiplicity of uses to sort out, ranging from *swa hwa swa* through *he dyde swa* to the ambiguous adverb/conjunction. And so on. But enough has been said of the problems. Let us now turn to possible ways of dealing with their sorting. But as we do so, we must take care that we are not so intent on catching the syntactical tide that we miss the lexicographical boat.

The Sorting Systems

10 At the beginning of the filing, the dictionary staff treated the high-frequency words in the same way as any other words – folders were made, and various spellings of the word were filed in the folders. As more and more of the 'stopwords' were printed up, the folders became place-holders in the alphabetical sequence and the words were filed in roomier boxes. But the problem was that we were filing according to traditional (modern) grammatical categories, and that those categories did not always apply clearly to the Old English instances. For example in *þæt hi comon him to* it is not clear whether the *to* is a post-positional preposition, an adverb, or a separable prefix for the verb *tocuman*. Such ambiguous phrases are all too common in Old English and our sorters were spending far too much time per slip trying to decide the best category to use for each instance. It was at this point that the dictionary staff collaborated with Bruce Mitchell in working out a system for sorting the stopwords (and some related words and spellings that had not been stopped). The goal was to provide a system that allowed decisions to be made quickly and reliably, so that all those assigning slips would make the same decision about a particular instance. A second goal was to leave ambiguous cases undecided, so that a single decision could be made at a later time upon reading through all similar slips. We had four categories of treatment for words: (1) words requiring no sorting at this point except for homographs, (2) words where the most useful sorting pattern distinguished between dependent and independent uses, (3) state of being verbs, and (4) prepositions which could also be adverbs, verbal

[13] Bruce Mitchell 'Pronouns in Old English Poetry: Some Syntactical Notes', *RES* 15 (1964), 132–3.

prefixes, or part of compound conjunctions. In addition some words or spellings had special sorting patterns designed to pull together all examples of particular interesting or peculiar phrases. For example, when sorting ær, we had a special category for all instances of no þy ær; for eac, eac swilce; for forþ, heonan forþ and swa forþ; for þa, þa gyt and þa hwile (þe); for þæt, no þæt an (þæt).

11 Some words were not subdivided at this stage. Homographs were filed under their own headwords (that is, ac = 'oak' was filed separately from ac = 'but'), but all instances of each high-frequency word were left filed together. This category included such words as ac, and, eft, gif, he/hit/heo and their inflexions, her, ic, þu, nu, oft, þus. We filed the standard spellings of these words together (and/ond/7, gif/gyf), but kept very odd spellings separate (end for and; æft for eft). A few other words required only the most mechanical sorting, usually sentence initial/non-initial, where a 'sentence' is taken as a non-subordinate clause. This applied to such words as hu, non-demonstrative þa, þær, þeah and siþþan (after the phrases þeah þe and siþþan þe were pulled out). A similar sort was done for ge, with the personal pronoun separated from all other uses, and for ne + verb separated from all other uses. If further sorting were needed, it followed one of the three main patterns described below.

12 The next sorting pattern was designed to be used primarily for pronouns and adjectives/adverbs. Such possessives as min and þin, various inflections of se, and spellings like soþlice, swilce, swiþe, which can be either adjective or adverb, were sorted by this pattern. For these words, there were two categories: (1) dependent use, with noun in agreement, and (2) independent use, without noun in agreement. For most of these words, no sorting was required beyond the homographs and the two basic categories. Min, for example, is overwhelmingly more frequent in its dependent use than its independent use (by approx. 10:1). Phrases like min drihten are found everywhere. But the (possibly) independent use of the possessive must be carefully separated, such as Jul l. 164, Min se swetesta sunnan scima or ÆLS(Thomas) l. 179, Ic wene þæt hit min beo. Similarly, the dependent use of oþer is more frequent than its independent use (by approx. 2:1). Yet the basic categories are very simple: adjectival oþer as in oþre men, oþre naman, oþre bysne alternates only with pronominal usage, such as is found in ÆGram 26. 120, þe oþre maciað præteritum. The inflections of se and the indeclinable fela required a more sophisticated sorting. For most of the inflections of se we added an extra category, one which was very easy to sort. After first removing homographs, we also removed all instances followed by þe so that se þe, þæra þe, þæs þe, etc. were sorted out before dividing the material into dependent/independent categories. þæt, requiring more sorting than usual, had six divisions: (1) with þe, (2) no þæt an (þæt), (3) with verb 'to be', (4) conjunction introducing a clause, (5) dependent use, and (6) independent use.

Fela presented a different kind of problem. Instead of treating the dependent uses of *fela* as a whole, we subdivided them into two: the standard construction of *fela* plus genitive (*fela æhta, fela wundra, fela manna*) and the less usual *fela* plus all other cases (*fela hunig, fela þing, fela bisceopas*). The independent use of *fela*, such as is seen in Ælfric's translation (*ÆCHom* ii (Godden) 5 42. 33) of Matthew 22. 14 *fela sind gecigede, and feawa gecorene*, needed no further refinements.

13 A third kind of sorting pattern was devised for the state-of-being verbs. There were three categories: (1) the verb alone, (2) the verb accompanied by a present participle, and (3) the verb accompanied by a past participle. The participles could be before or after the verb, with or without intervening words. This sorting system was set up for the state-of-being verbs, but will also be applied to *weorþan*.

14 The fourth kind of sorting system was set up for those words which can so often be ambiguous: prepositions, adverbs, verbal prefixes, separable or not, or parts of compound conjunctions. These words, like *ær, be, for, in, of, on, to, wiþ*, were the ones that had given the sorters the most trouble before. The sorting system we devised had three categories after the homographs were removed. The first category held the unambiguous prepositional uses, and was defined as the word plus noun or pronoun in appropriate oblique case for an object, with or without preceding demonstrative or possessive and/or adjective; *for þam geongan cnihte, to ðyssere dæde, wið heofonas*. These will be further sorted by the case of the object. The second category held the compound conjunctions, and was defined as the word plus a demonstrative (often also with *þe* or *þæt*), e. g. *for þam þe*. The third category was a catchall of all other uses. It was invariably smaller than the first, and usually much smaller than the second – but in it are all the most ambiguous uses. When we are ready to write those entries, the third category will be sorted in a detailed way into the following categories: (1) intervening between *ne* and a finite verb, (2) immediately preceding a negated verb, (3) intervening between *ge-* and a finite verb, (4) immediately preceding a verb, (5) used absolutely with no possible object: *he scuton to*, (6) used with what may be an object preceding it, (a) when the object is *þær: þæt þu þær of ne drince*, (b) when the object is the relative *þe*, (c) when the object is a personal pronoun: *hi comon him to*, or (d) with any other object, e.g. a noun, and (7) any remaining slips which do not fit the above categories.

15 The high-frequency grammar words of Old English pose particular problems for both the lexicographer and the syntactician. Only by working closely together can they begin to find answers. A sorting scheme for the verb (*ge*)*don* is appended as an illustration of a possible approach to the analysis of one of

the most complex and important of the grammar words. The sorting scheme incorporates three stages – morphological, syntactic, and finally semantic sorting. Using it the dictionary staff has been moving reasonably rapidly through the approximately 9000 instances of the verb and its *ge-* prefixed form. We expect the sorting scheme for *don*, derived in part from *Old English Syntax* (§§665–9), to be typical of those used for other complex grammar words. If, over the next years, the conclusions of *Old English Syntax* can be tested by and used to structure the raw data of the *High-Frequency Concordance*,[14] then the editors of the Dictionary of Old English may yet reach a safe harbour without foundering on the shoals of the grammar words. We hope others will join us in this task.

APPENDIX: SORTING *(GE)DON*

Stage I Morphological Sort
A Present tense forms
B Preterite tense forms
C Present participles
D Second participles
E Infinitives without *to*
F Infinitives with *to*

Stage II Syntactical Sort
A Present tense forms
  1 used absolutely 'to do, to act', with no expressed object
    a as simple gloss of Latin
    b with object understood from context
    c with dative of interest
    d with adverb: *swa*/others
    e with adverb phrase: *swa*/others
    f with adverb clause: *swa*/others
  2 with objects
    a with single accusative object: alone/with indirect object or dative of interest/with *to*-phrase/others
    b with double accusative object: two nouns alone/with *to*-phrase/others: noun + adjective alone/with *to*-phrase/others
  3 used causatively
    a with noun clause
    b with accusative and infinitive
    c with accusative and *to*-phrase
    d with clause

[14] Richard L. Venezky and Sharon Butler *A Microfiche Concordance to Old English: The High Frequency Words* (Toronto, 1985).

    4 used to avoid repetition of a preceding verb
    5 used with a verb in apposition in same tense and mood
    6 used non-causatively with an infinitive (if any!)
    7 others
  B Preterite tense forms 1–7 as for A
  C Present participles
    1 with *beon/wesan/weorþan* in periphrastic constructions
    2 others
  D Second participles
    1 with *beon/wesan/weorþan* in periphrastic passive
    2 with *habban* in periphrastic perfect
    3 others
  E Infinitives without *to*
    1 dependent on nouns
    2 dependent on adjectives
    3 dependent on verbs
    4 others
  F Infinitives with *to*
    1–4 as for E

Stage III Semantic Sort
A2–A7 B2–B7 on a scheme initially based on and then adapted from BT(S) entries. Remaining patterns can then be integrated.

See *OES* §§665–9. Keep forms of *don* and *gedon* separate.

This is a sorting plan, not an outline of final entry for *don*. Many categories, e.g. those under II E and F, are most unlikely to appear at all in the final entry. But one cannot assume that any particular morphological form or syntactic pattern cannot possibly have a semantic peculiarity.

Stage I Morphological Sort
The ideas behind this were:
  i to establish the variants of the individual forms;
  ii to discover by subsequent sorts whether any particular form had significant peculiarities of sense or usage.

Stage II Syntactical Sort
The ideas behind this were:
  i to establish the various patterns and collocations in which the verb was used;
  ii to establish the senses and frequency of individual patterns so that the editors could decide, for example, whether *don dædbote* 'to repent' or *don betre* 'to prefer' should be recorded or not.

28
Reviews

(a) *A Descriptive Syntax of the* Ormulum by Robert A. Palmatier, Mouton: The Hague and Paris, 1969*

I have tried to be patient with this book. But it has been a difficult task and those who think I have failed must find consolation in the remark made to an author who had been savaged in a review: 'Every lion has fleas.' Yet I believe I have reasons for impatience.

The title is misleading; it should be *A Descriptive Syntax of Part of the* Ormulum. The author says: 'In order to accomplish a syntactic study of such a substantial text within a reasonable length of time, the present investigator has restricted his attention to selected portions of the work' (p. 16). I do not think 'accomplish' the right word here. I do not know what is an unreasonable length of time, but I would have been prepared to wait for a full investigation. It is true that Mr Palmatier says that 'the present study ... does not assume an identical syntactic structure for the entire *Ormulum* or for the portions not selected' (p. 17). That no such identity can be assumed is obvious. So, we may reasonably ask, of what value are his findings for comparison with Old English (p. 18)? Can we be sure as a result of this work that Orm never uses *þe* as a relative (pp. 33-4)? Can we be sure that 'when a clause functions as a subject or direct object in another clause, it *always* [my italics] occurs after the finite verb' (p. 135)? And, despite his denial, Mr Palmatier sometimes comes close to behaving as if such identity did exist. Thus on p. 132 he writes of l. 11990 *Ne þurrh nan manness hellpe* that 'the lack of inflection on *nan*, however, signals that it modifies *hellpe*; for the negative adjective of Order Class F2 is always inflected in *-ess* when it modifies a possessive noun. Therefore, the correct interpretation is "no help of man"'. The use of 'always' and 'correct' is noteworthy. Is Mr Palmatier sure that there is no place in the *Ormulum* where *nan* must be genitive? Is he sure that this is not another example of 'idiomatic forms' used 'for metrical purposes' (p. 20)?[1] To present syntactic studies of

---

* Reprinted from *Medium Ævum* 39 (1970), 370-3.

[1] I must admit that (as far as I know) the gen. sg. of *nan* elsewhere in the *Ormulum* is *naness*, e.g.

individual texts based on selected passages is to put oneself in danger of repeating the classic error of E. E. Ericson, who appeared to believe that 'safe conclusions' could be drawn from 'representative collections'.[2]

Some of the 'basic assumptions' (pp. 18–19) call for comment. Reference might have been expected in the first to R. W. Burchfield's article in the *Trans-*

Dedication l. 274, and ll. 7847, 10692, 12239, and 16137. But in all these places the metre requires a dissyllable.

On p. 117, Mr Palmatier writes: 'All such occasions of "ambi-headedness" as described in the preceding paragraph have been resolved here by the assignment of ambiguous modifiers to the possessive noun head rather than to the non-possessive head of the entire phrase. This decision is based on the fact that only 3 modifiers can be proved to by-pass the possessive noun (*nan*, *alle*, *mikell*) and on the indication. . . .' [I omit the second reason to save space; I do not think it *conclusive.*] What is the evidence? For *nan*, it is (again as far as I know) Mr Palmatier's interpretation of l. 11990. For *alle*, it is examples like l. 410 *alle Godess enngless*; we can agree that in the *Ormulum* this means 'all angels of God' or 'all of the angels of God', not 'the angels of all gods' or 'all angels of gods' (p. 133). For *mikell* it is presumably Preface l. 102 *hu mikell sawle sellþe*, the argument being that the soul is indivisible. So (it would seem) some 'modifiers' do 'bypass the possessive noun'.

But is *nan* one of them? How strong is the evidence for his interpretation of l. 11990? It depends of course on the assumption that *nan* cannot be gen. sg., while the ambiguities of ll. 12210 *all middellardess riche*, 12036 *þe deofless wille*, and 18717 *soþ Godess witt*, arise from the fact that there seems to be no distinctive gen. sg. form for *all*, *þe*, and *soþ*. But if we examine Preface l. 56 *þe Laferrd Cristess karrte* and the three examples just quoted, we will find several uninflected forms which are or may be genitive and are so taken by Mr Palmatier in these or similar examples on p. 117 – *all*, *Laferrd*, *soþ*, and *þe*. Can we then be sure that in l. 11990 *nan* is not an example of lack of inflexion, perhaps arising analogically from phrases like those just quoted and used for the sake of metre? (The possibility still exists, of course, that somewhere in the *Ormulum nan* may be unambiguously genitive.)

The net result of all this may be to strengthen Mr Palmatier's case for believing that, in examples like l. 18720 *soþ Godess Sune ankennedd*, *soþ* goes with *Godess* rather than with *Sune*. But as long as there are exceptions like l. 410 and Preface l. 102 (and there is a reasonable presumption that there are more), it seems wrong to 'resolve' all ambiguous cases; there ought to be room for a third little box labelled 'ambiguous'. The establishment of a 'relative order' (as described, for example, on p. 78) does not mean that the 'relative order' holds in all dubious cases; cf. the last point made in the fourth paragraph of this review.

[2] *Studies in Honor of Hermann Collitz* (Baltimore, Md, 1930), pp. 174–5. Sometimes, of course, it happens that they can. A case in point may be the phrase *off dæþ(e)* which occurs five times in the 'selected corpus', always at the end of a second half-line and always with *-e* (p. 21). This use is very common outside the 'selected corpus', e.g. ll. 4347, 5831, 5981, 9684, 10629, 13405, 13413, 13825, 15509, 15605, 16243, and 16471. But also outside the 'selected corpus' we find *off dæþ* at the end of a first half-line in ll. 4042, 6874, and 19957 (in this last example and in some others, e. g. l. 19961 below, the phrase is dependent on a noun and not on a verb or adverb. But this point is not important here). The form *off dæþe* occurs within the line for metrical reasons in ll. 10297, 10346, and 16487; compare *off dæþ* in the middle of l. 19961, *off dæþe* with elision of *-e* at the beginning of l. 4198, and *off hiss dæþ* (dependent on an adjective) at the beginning of l. 8092. My limited investigations thus confirm Mr Palmatier's deductions and strengthen the case for what he could claim only as a possibility. I suspect that complete investigation of the forms of *dæþ* after prepositions might prove it. But I have not the time to do any more of Mr Palmatier's work for him and do not believe that he will always be so lucky; *sene*, discussed in the fourth paragraph of this review, is perhaps a case in point here. And how are we to know when it is that he has been lucky?

actions of the Philological Society for 1956. (This article, strangely omitted from the Selected Bibliography, might also have been consulted for the *e/eo* question discussed by Mr Palmatier at pp. 16–17.) It is hard to see why the second assumption – 'that the *Ormulum*, though verse, is representative of the spoken English of East Midland circa A.D. 1200' – is either justified or necessary. The phrase 'though verse' would seem to be a not unimportant qualification where syntax is concerned, while ll. 41–4 of the Dedication (quoted in defence of the third assumption) scarcely argue in favour of the proposition that we have to do with idiomatic spoken English. I am not sure that I understand the value of the fourth assumption, which 'prohibits the recognition of a compound predicate'. The difference in word-order between ll. 107 and 103 of the Dedication (pp. 43 and 44) is due to the fact that the former is a principal clause and the latter a subordinate clause introduced by *ʒtatt*; as far as these two examples at least are concerned the remarks at the top of p. 44 make no sense at all. (Is it by definition, chance, or 'rule', that 'if the quotation is indirect, it will be introduced by *þatt*, and *it will consist of a single clause*' (p. 135) [my italics]?)

Mr Palmatier does not always seem to be in command of his material or of his tools. On p. 21 *sene* in l. 18862 is described as 'the only past participle with *-e* in the corpus'. This oddity, along with the fact that in this line *sene* follows and is coordinate with an uninflected adjective, immediately arouses the suspicion that the word may be an adjective (Anglian *gesēne* 'visible'). The same suspicion had occurred to the editors of *OED* (s.v. *sene, isene, a.*) and of Stratmann-Bradley (s.v. *sēne*² adj.). Orm has *seʒhenn* in ll. 3335, 10930, 10959, and 16763, but *sene* in ll. 2173, 2209, 2547, 16880, and 18862 above. A glance at the White–Holt Glossary would have revealed this much. It is Mr Palmatier's job, not mine, to marshal this material and to decide what is what. Does *ʒiff* in l. 12292 really introduce a 'subject clause' (p. 30)? Whether *tu* in *witt tu* (l. 205) is the subject or a nominative of address is probably merely a terminological problem. But why is a verb in the imperative mood 'prohibited from patterning with a syntactic subject' (pp. 48–9; see also pp. 28 and 71)? (See Mustanoja *Middle English Syntax* I, pp. 473 ff.) Is it really true to say that *witt* in this sentence is 'without inflection' (p. 49)? The second paragraph on p. 132 seems muddled: 'Ambiguity can also be resolved.... The ambiguity is resolved.... Therefore the clause *Godd iss Godd* most likely has the following order....' Mr Palmatier has established a possibility. He has resolved nothing.

The work is not always easy to follow. There are minor blemishes, e.g. the use of the same abbreviations with different meanings in different chapters (p. 13), the use of 'idiomatic' where 'metrical' would seem to be required (p. 20, l. 11), and the absence of a comma after 'regardless' (p. 37, l. 13). But the production of a 'structural syntactic analysis' (p. 17) – apparently a finer thing than a traditional treatment (p. 18) – seems to involve Mr Palmatier at any rate in some turgid restatement of the obvious, e.g. 'where there is a change in the form or distribution of words, it can be assumed that there is a change in meaning: grammatical, lexical, or metrical[8]' (p. 17)[3] [footnote 8 is similarly enlightening]; 'Clustering of clauses into macro-clauses, however, is usually signaled by a subordinator – an underived and uninflected word that patterns with the minor (dependent, secondary) clause' (p. 135); and 'Quotation is signaled by the occurrence of one or more clauses as the object of the verb *seggenn*' (p. 135). It also involves him in some jargon of almost incomprehensible and unbelievable complexity, e.g. 'a minor macro-clause is a simple clause that is dependent on the primary clause of a major macro-clause' (pp. 28–9); 'the "pseudo" element in a corpus is a clause or nominal or *to*-infinitive that patterns with a tautological "dative" object, indirect object, direct object, or subject. The tautological element is . . .' [the whole paragraph should be read] (p. 68); the definition of 'the verb-headed phrase' (p. 73); and the observation that 'an exocentric phrase consists of a nominal or verbal (or a nominal phrase or a verbal phrase) to which an underived and uninflected (and uninflectable) "structure" word is pre-posed' (p. 133). I see.

It is only fair to say that there is some useful material and a lot of faithful work in the book, e.g. on word-order (pp. 40–64). But here (as elsewhere) the method of presentation is too complicated for easy absorption of the argument and the summary on p. 64 is too short to be of any real value; the summaries scattered throughout the chapter might have been more useful if assembled here. There is no Index. The wisdom of confining the work completely to 'a synchronic–descriptive basis' (p. 17) is also questionable; consideration of Old English idiom would often have been illuminating, e.g. in the discussion of l. 11990 *nan manness hellpe*. Despite all these strictures, however, I am sure that Mr Palmatier has some important things to say. I sincerely hope that he will face the challenge and produce what is in truth *A Descriptive Syntax of the Ormulum*. If he does, I hope he will also most seriously consider the advisability of dropping the jargon in favour of the old simple terminology – so imprecise, perhaps, but so easy to understand.[4] Books which contain sentences like those quoted above and whose methods result in such remarks as

> (8) The eighth step is to assign symbols to the order classes that will reflect their 'distance' from the head (e.g. F-E-D-C-B-A-H), so that formulas can be used to refer to phrase profiles. The sub-classes may be given contrasting symbols which will follow the order class symbols in

---

[3] Though on reflection I am not sure that this can be assumed. What *is* a change in grammatical meaning?

[4] Not that Mr Palmatier's own terminology is all that unlikely to confuse the reader. Consider some of the examples already quoted, the discussion of coordination (p. 25), of 'major' and 'minor' clauses (pp. 27–9), of the dative (p. 65 and n. 1), and so on.

the formulas: E1-A2-H (quantitative adjective adjacent to noun adjunct adjacent to noun head – *þe Laferrd Crist* 'The Lord Christ') (p. 108) help one to have some dim understanding of what A. E. Housman might have been feeling when he gave vent to some of his less kindly observations.

(b) *A Descriptive Syntax of the Old English Charters* by Charles Carlton, Mouton: The Hague and Paris, 1970*

I began to read this book full of good will and high hopes engendered by its stated purpose (pp. 17-18) and by the sample contained in the author's article 'Word Order of Noun Modifiers in Old English Prose' in *JEGP* 62 (1963), 778-83. I was prepared to accept the method adopted because I thought of the book as in a sense a pioneer work, in that it was attempting to use traditional approaches along with those of modern linguistics but – happily – without the jargon or the diagrams. This and the fact that it said something new were, it seemed to me, the great merits of the article already mentioned. But somehow the high hopes at least gradually evaporated and I was left disappointed with what was actually presented in this carefully prepared and well set-out book – beyond a collection of material. I am in complete agreement with Mr Carlton when he says: 'One can only state and analyze the features of syntax found in these texts; unique, rare, and ambiguous usages will necessarily have to be deferred for full treatment when the complete body of Old English writings has been covered and synthesized' (p. 18). The question is how best to analyse and state results which must inevitably be incomplete for OE as a whole. My own verdict must be that Mr Carlton's is not the way to do it. He has not been fair to himself. The final summary is too general to be of any use. It is more than frustrating to plough through 191 pages of what are largely commonplaces and then to read a paragraph like this:

> Some of the usages for case, mood, and tense found in this corpus differ markedly from those found elsewhere in Old English. This is probably because the corpus is made up of a special body of materials. The syntax used in the prose found in the original Old English charters is not always the same as the syntax used in the Old English prose translations from the classical languages or the syntax used in Old English poetry. The same is true of Modern English which varies greatly in the syntax found in poetry, literary prose, and the prose of special types of writing such as legal documents, scientific reports, and news reports. Therefore, some differences from other types of Old English writing are to be expected. Nevertheless, the syntax found in the charters conforms, in

*Reprinted from *Medium Ævum* 40 (1971), 181-4.

general, to the syntax found in other types of writing in Old English. (pp. 192–3)

Is it unreasonable to ask how Mr Carlton can spot these differences, in the light of his complaints about the failure of previous workers to provide the detailed syntactical analyses of OE texts essential for such comparison (pp. 17–18)? Is it unreasonable to suggest that, if he has spotted them, it might have been kind to the rest of us to spell them out? It was here, I fear, that my good will all but disappeared.

For I must confess that I have not noticed in Mr Carlton's material many 'usages for case, mood, and tense' which 'differ markedly from those found elsewhere in Old English'. Certainly not all phenomena are exemplified and certainly there are situations in which (on Mr Carlton's evidence) the charters use one particular form of a construction which has variants elsewhere, e.g. pp. 52b (position of the possessive pronoun), 75 (the sequence *seo stow . . . heo*), and 102 (8) (the use of *self*). But this merely underlines the fact that a limited corpus, especially one made up of somewhat stereotyped documents like charters, will provide a limited selection of examples.

What I have noticed is a frequent labouring of the obvious, not always with clarity; on this last point see pp. 48 (third sentence), 59 (last sentence in second paragraph), 74 (paragraph beginning 'A noun does not change gender . . .'), and 180 and 195 (the contradiction about the position of adverbs). While I urge the necessity for descriptive studies of OE texts, I have no wish to read any more chapters like Mr Carlton's chapter V on Negation (pp. 67–72), which really tells us nothing the primers do not and fails to make clear the differences in usage between *ne* and *na* which exist in his corpus. Indeed, it is instructive to ask oneself what *is* new in any one of chapters II–VII. Is there not a solemn fatuity about observations like: 'On listing all clauses introduced by *þa*, I found that word order is pertinent to the solution' (p. 33)? Can OE syntacticians not take for granted such things as *ic wit we* etc. (p. 78)? Mr Carlton might have served himself and us better if he had set out briefly and clearly where his corpus consistently used one particular form of a known idiom rather than another and where it departed from those rules which any first year undergraduate knows. This would have left him more room to deal with those things he considered to be of special interest.

Chapter VIII on Word Order demands special treatment, for it involves Mr Carlton's most serious failure of method. I am only too painfully aware of the truth of his observation that 'this listing process is long and tedious, but it is very helpful in making the functional patterns evident by noting comparisons and contrasts' (p. 25). But I cannot go along with him when he decides in his chapter to consider 'only two basic elements at a time in order to avoid unnecessary confusion' (p. 130). Unnecessary confusion is just what he has created; this decision brings us back to the days of blurred distinctions and useless statistics (see *NM* 65 (1964), 117–20 and 67 (1966), 87–8). What is the good of table 3 (pp. 135–6), which gives the respective percentages of sentences with S.V. and V.S., when S.V. includes S.V.O., S. pron. O.V., and S. noun O.V., and when V.S. includes *Ðis is geðinge* ... (see p. 31), ... *þæt hire læfde hire fæder land and boc* ..., *and æfter heora dæge agefe mon* ..., *Æfter þam bæd Ælfsige, Sy hit ælces þinges freoh, ond ðas forecuædenan suæsenda all agefe mon, þonne gebygcge he* ... and so on (all examples cited from pp. 130–5)? Table 4 (pp. 139–40) takes no account of whether the object is a noun, a personal pronoun, or a relative pronoun; the same is true of the examples on p. 141. To claim, as Mr Carlton does, that one particular 'category necessarily overlaps the other categories' (p. 132, fn. 3) is just plain wrong; the reason is bad classification, not necessity. Space forbids further demonstration of the completely unnecessary blurring of vital distinctions which mars the whole of this chapter. Mr Carlton is aware of the existence of at least some of these distinctions (p. 162). But his failure in method here must be linked with the fact that his Selected Bibliography cites works on word order such as those by Dahlstedt (1901) and Funke (1956), but fails to mention those by Fourquet (1938) and Bacquet (1962). If he had consulted the latter work, he would (I think) have seen the folly of his remarks on p. 130. A possible reason for this and other strange omissions from his Bibliography emerges from the following table of dates: publication of the book 1970; date of the preface 1967; date of the Ph.D. dissertation 1958. Because of all this, the whole chapter is of little value except as a collection of materials, and even here its usefulness is lessened by the frequent failure to quote the whole sentence.

Mr Carlton's system of classification is not always happy. First, he sometimes neglects useful traditional distinctions, e.g. statements with the indicative and subjunctive wishes for the future are linked together as 'declarative sentences' (pp. 38–9), *And he hit hæfde VII winter* is called a 'simple sentence' and 'contains one independent clause' (p. 38), dependent statements and dependent questions are not distinguished (p. 60), and clauses beginning with *butan* and *ac* are lumped together (pp. 64–5). Secondly, he sometimes makes new distinctions of dubious value. That between 'initial' and 'sequence' sentences (p. 32) is easily enough made, perhaps, in short documents. But one wonders how many 'initial' sentences there are in (say) the *Cura Pastoralis*. The handling of sentences beginning *þis is* (*sindon*) is peculiar (p. 31). The decision to distinguish class II and class III dependent clauses – a task in which 'there is sometimes difficulty' (p. 59) – rather than the traditional types of adjective and adverb clauses naturally leads to difficulties and needs justification. Thirdly, he sometimes accepts traditional concepts which might be better modified or abandoned, e.g. the classification of genitives (pp. 87–90) and the description of *him* as the subject of *to brucanne* (p. 99). [1987. On the last point see *OES*

[§3786.] Lastly, since the reference numbers in tables 1 and 2 (pp. 19–20 and 29–30) do not coincide, some means of identifying the sentences in the latter would have been helpful.

The rules about *gif* clauses (p. 35) raise a serious issue: Mr Carlton may be too confident about the certainty with which sentences can be separated one from the other; see pp. 33 and 194. Convenient illustrations are *Catholic Homilies* (ed. Thorpe) i. 26. 2–7 and ii. 150. 22–4 (where the proper comparison may be with MnE spoken rather than written prose), *Beowulf* ll. 1713 ff., and *Andreas* ll. 474 ff. (see *NM* 70 (1969), 78–81). I cannot see the superiority of structural over traditional methods here; any modern scholar who claims certainty in places like these has in effect made himself into his own native informant. The possibility exists that OE writers at times at any rate thought in units more analogous to the 'paragraph' than to the 'sentence'. Indeed, Mr Carlton hints at such a possibility (p. 194) and has difficulty in analysing one passage (pp. 39–40).

It is not easy to see why Mr Carlton relies on Birch for documents which have since been re-edited. The famous will of Ealdorman Alfred, his document 12, Birch 558 – said by Mr Carlton to be in a Mercian–West Saxon dialect (p. 19) – is number X in F. E. Harmer's *Select English Historical Documents* and number XXXIV in Sweet's *Anglo-Saxon Reader* (rev. Whitelock). Both these editors and Sweet (*The Oldest English Texts* charter 45) agree in reading a compound noun *wordgecweodu* in the passage which troubled Mr Carlton on p. 114. Similarly, Birch 1306 (Carlton 24) is number XIII in D. Whitelock *Anglo-Saxon Wills* and her translation seems to suggest that *on* in *Her is on sio swutelung hu* ... (Carlton, p. 82) should be taken with *Her* 'Herein ...'. The notion that it could govern the nominative *sio swutelung* is hard to accept and the suggestion that it may be a scribal error had already been anticipated by Kemble and Thorpe.

The book is not without errors, e.g. Birch is wrongly given the credit for the remarkable clause *þa he geendodu* (Birch *geendod*) *wæs* (p. 125). Inevitably there is room for difference of opinion on details. Thus Mr Carlton's idea of a 'distinctive inflection' is peculiar; consider pp. 74–7 and 85 on the ending *-a*. But the over-riding impression is that the method which served Mr Carlton well in his article, where he had something new to say, produces in the book much tedious repetition of the obvious, interlarded with observations which, while they may be true for the selected corpus, are already known not to hold for OE as a whole. It should have been possible to evolve some more economic way of presenting the important results.

(c) *An Analysis of Syntactic Patterns of Old English* by Faith F. Gardner (Janua Linguarum Studia Memoriae Nicolai van Wijk Dedicata, Series Practica, 140), The Hague: Mouton, 1971*

Third time lucky? This has not been my experience with this book, the third I have reviewed from this series ('edenda curat C. H. van Schooneveld Indiana University'); see *MÆ* 39 (1970), 370–3 and *MÆ* 40 (1971), 181–4 [items 28(a) and (b) above]. Despite an initial resolve to be charitable, I am left wondering why it was published. If the author took no advice or ignored negative advice, she was foolish. If she received positive advice, somebody is culpable.

Dr Gardner, upset by detecting in many histories of the English language a tendency to stress the syntactical importance of case-endings in OE and to neglect word order, decided 'to investigate two things: whether word order was important in Old English and whether the trend from a synthetic to an analytic language existed during the Old English period' (p. 17), with special reference to prepositional phrases and subordinate clauses (pp. 18–19). (Do 'synthetic' languages really possess the qualities she assigns them at pp. 25–6 and 79?) Her material is the *Parker Chronicle* to 1070, *Ohthere and Wulfstan*, one Blickling homily, one Ælfric homily, and (for comparison) 192 words from a 1967 review. So her statistics can scarcely be significant.

Generally she is tilting at straw men. She offers some interesting observations about the position of phrases (pp. 32ff.) and clauses (pp. 69ff.), though her method is sometimes faulty; see below. But I hope it will not be out of place for me to say first, that all other points of substance made in her conclusion (pp. 77–82) were made by me in the first edition of *A Guide to Old English* (Oxford, 1965) – see especially §§139–53, 189, and 231–2 – and second, that I was not, and still am not, aware that they were particularly novel.

If Dr Gardner's sole sin were ignorance of my *Guide*, her offence would be slight indeed. But her Bibliography suggests that she is unaware of much relevant work. She mentions only three books on OE syntax – one by 'Samuel Andrew' (a ghost doubtless created by cataloguers who waste everybody's time by dredging up Christian names for authors who used initials), and those by Shannon and Carlton. Why the items by Bale, DeCamp, Einenkel, and Voges, were singled out from scores like them is not clear. Even within these limits she has not always grasped the point; consider her (contradictory?) summaries of Andrew's book (pp. 15 and 41) in relation to her discussion on the position of prepositional phrases within clauses (pp. 32–48), where she jumbles together clauses beginning with subject, verb, adverb (phrase), *ond*, other conjunctions, and relative pronouns. (How many more times will I have to complain about this?) Only when we look at her pitifully perfunctory Bibliography can we

---

* Reprinted from the *Review of English Studies* 23 (1972), 461–3.

relish to the full her concluding sentence (p. 82): 'Future discussions of Old English grammar must go beyond morphology and recognize the importance of syntax.'

So through ignorance or design Dr Gardner has started from first principles. This would be no bad thing if she had good method and a sound knowledge of Old English. Unfortunately neither seems to be the case. There are deficiencies in analysis – there is only one finite verb in *Bl* 67. 16 (p. 19); after consistently failing to recognize 'separable prefixes' (e.g. pp. 28, 33, 39, 67), she catches a belated glimpse of them at p. 75, where she describes *to* in *Lasc* 992. 14 as 'a single adverb which belongs with the verb', though it figures as a preposition on p. 28. There are errors of fact, for example the remarks about *ðeah* (p. 71) and *-um* (p. 77). There are errors in her handling of Old English – *þe heora* in *Bl* 68. 4 (p. 50) and *þæs þe* in *Easc* 855. 13 (p. 52) introduce adjective clauses; on p. 29 she translates *on diaconhade geendebyrdne* 'in arranged deaconship' and *mid wæstmum fægerne* 'with pleasing results'. (No wonder she speaks on p. 77 of 'a superficial study of Old English case endings'.) Such errors may be partly due to her habit of partial quotation; cf. p. 26, where *ær* in *ær Ælfred cyning* is said to be a preposition, though it is perhaps more likely to be a conjunction, since *ær* + accusative is rare. This is symptomatic. Nowhere (as far as I have noticed) does she mention that OE prepositions govern cases; she speaks merely of 'objects'.

This perhaps explains another weakness of the book. Dr Gardner aims to demonstrate that OE was more 'analytic' than (as she thinks) anybody has hitherto realized. So she provides percentages of words used in prepositional phrases against the total number of words in her three groups of texts – eWS 25.7, lWS 29.8, and MnE 31.2 (pp. 21–2). These figures show the tendency we expect. But the method is flawed. She frequently translates OE words or phrases in the genitive by MnE 'of'-phrases and indeed notes that 'the genitive singular *þysre wucan* becomes in Modern English the prepositional phrase "of this week"' (p. 23), apparently without realizing that *þysre wucan* is itself an 'inflexional phrase'. If one wanted to produce statistics, one would also (it seems to me) have to give the relative frequency of phrases with prepositions against those without them. The latter would include OE examples like *þysre wucan* and (from the annals for 755 and 855) *þæs* in *7 hie þæs gefægene wærun, miclum gefeohtum, lytle werode*, and *þy ilcan geare*, and MnE examples like 'all day', 'next year', 'a great deal smaller', 'He went home', and 'He walked miles.'

The book often gives an impression of casualness or banality – consider the analysis of strings of prepositions (pp. 23–4); the remarks about Magoun (p. 17), the syntax of OE poetry (p. 17), and the style of the *Chronicle* (p. 18); and the observation that 'there are more abstractions in the late material' (p. 48). Her small corpus leads her to conclusions known to be false – phrases joined by *ond* are not always grouped together (p. 47); OE prepositions frequently precede relative *se* (p. 62); *ær*-clauses can begin a sentence (pp. 71–2).

It gives me no satisfaction to savage a book. Do editors and publishers not realize that publishing books before they are ready not only damages their own reputation and unnecessarily burdens readers and reviewers, but may also discourage or even silence the author they have wrongly encouraged?

(d) *Imperative Constructions in Old English* by Celia M. Millward (Janua Linguarum Studia Memoriae Nicolai van Wijk Dedicata, Series Practica, 124), The Hague: Mouton, 1971*

The paragraph headed 'Acknowledgments' (p. 5) conceals – for no reason that I can imagine – that 'this study, in its original form', was presented as a Ph.D. thesis in the Department of Linguistics at Brown University, Providence, in 1966. There is no doubt that a lot of care and hard work has gone into it. But in its present form it is still basically a Ph.D. thesis – and one which in my view illustrates all too clearly the dangers of trying to study one particular construction in a language which has a limited corpus and no native informants.

First, such an investigator may have an inadequate knowledge of the language as a whole and of the work previously done on it. Mrs Millward's list of Secondary Sources is not reassuring; it is hard to see, for example, why works like those by Wohlfahrt (1886) and Shearin (1903) appear when numerous similar dissertations do not – in particular K. Suter *Das Pronomen beim Imperativ im Alt- und Mittelenglischen* (Zürich diss., 1955). Although she says (p. 31, n. 3) that 'we assume here that the coordinator *ne* is distinct from the verb negator *ne*', she clearly has not grasped the real distinction (there is no need to assume one). Her examples (110) and (111) are supposed to be exceptions to the 'rule' that after coordinating *ne* the subject precedes the verb (p. 31). But since both clauses have *ne ne* – coordinator + verb negator – the order V.S. is quite normal. Again, like so many of her predecessors (see *NM* 65 (1964), 117–19, and 67 (1966), 87–8), she also seems not to understand the effect of initial *ond* in a clause. Joshua 3. 4 *and nan man ne genealæce neah ðam arce* cannot contravene the rule of word-order which applies in Deuteronomy 24. 5 *ne fare he ut* (p. 28), for it begins with *ond*. To be sure, Mrs Millward does at least quote *ond* here and in example (71) on p. 25, in both cases without realizing its significance. Elsewhere, however, she falls into the age-old trap of omitting it, e.g. in her sentences (5) and (6) on p. 18 and (28) on p. 19. So these examples do not illustrate what she says they do, and there are more exceptions than she admits to her 'rule' about word-order in imperative constructions after *ond* (pp. 30–1). She could have made her chapters 2 and 3 much clearer and much more accurate if she had had a clearer grasp of the well-known rules about OE word-order conveniently formulated in several of the elementary grammars which are rebuked on p. 11 for not calling subjunctive verb forms 'imperative'.

* Reprinted from *English Studies* 55 (1974), 387–9.

Further illustrations of this first danger will be found in the section on *sylf* (pp. 39–40) – it is a pity Mrs Millward did not digest Farr's thesis instead of dismissing it (p. 38, n. 2) – and in the treating of pronoun and noun objects as 'structurally identical' (p. 37).

A second danger is that concentration on one particular construction may lead to a blinkered approach. Here not enough attention is paid to the occasional examples of 2nd pers. sg. subj. forms in *-e* where we might have expected imp. forms in - (p. 19; there are more in Mrs Millward's corpus), especially in view of the parallel use of what appear to be 2nd pers. pl. subj. forms in *-e(n)* alongside 2nd pers. pl. imp. forms in *-aþ* (pp. 19–20). This is symptomatic. I can see that it is not unreasonable to describe examples like *Lives of the Saints* 22. 178 *Cume se blinda to me* and *BlHom* 91. 8 *Uton we ealle wynsumian on Drihten* as 'imperative constructions' (pp. 15 ff.), even though *cume* in the first example is a present subjunctive. But increasing laxity on the part of the author leads to unnecessary confusion of morphologically distinct forms. Thus 'we can identify a syntactically unique first-person plural imperative' (p. 18) – the word 'construction' has already disappeared. At p. 19 we meet the heading 'Imperatives with *-n*' and on p. 20 'Third-person imperatives'. And so we read on until we find on p. 41 that 'in independent clauses with only one finite verb, the distinction between the indicative and the imperative moods is carried primarily by the verbal inflection alone in the first and third persons'. I can see no point in describing unambiguously *subjunctive* forms as *imperative*. It can lead only to confusion in the wider context of OE syntax as a whole.

A third danger is that of deriving 'rigid rules' from (a limited corpus selected from) a limited corpus. The 'blurb' on the inside of the front cover of this work restates another classic error: 'Based on a large *sample* of Old English prose and poetry, it offers *clear evidence* that there are *rigid rules* . . .' (my italics). I have long passed the stage of believing that even a study of everything that survives will reveal 'rigid rules' for Old English. But for Mrs Millward *Beowulf* l. 366 – an example of an idiom well-attested in the poetry – is an exception to two 'rules' (pp. 23 and 24). That such 'rules' can be formulated despite the existence of exceptions which contravene them is now almost an article of faith with investigators of individual constructions or texts in OE. Mrs Millward certainly believes this; see pp. 24, 28, and 39.

I could waste a page or two revealing further faults, but am becoming increasingly reluctant to devote time and energy to such sterile exercises. However, I give a sample. Some texts are not quoted from the standard edition (pp. 69–71). Why are there no examples from Ælfric's *Catholic Homilies*, the *Leechdoms*, or the *Laws* (pp. 12–13)? The useless Appendix A could have been replaced with examples to support the points made at p. 17 (bottom) and p. 24, n. 3. The examples given do not support the conclusion expressed in the first sentence of section 2.2.2.2 (pp. 25–6). Table 2 (p. 17) contradicts the first line of the rule on p. 41. The exceptional John 21. 22 *fylig ðu me* is quoted (p. 19) without the Latin *tu me sequere*; in five minutes I found in the Gospels ten examples of *fylig* (*folga*) *me* without *ðu* and *tu*. Is it surprising that verbs like *gan* and *restan* never appear 'with nonreflexive pronoun objects or other nominal objects' (p. 38)? Diagonal slashes are wrongly used instead of parentheses in the second and last items in table 3 (p. 22). There is a serious error in the ninth line on p. 41, where 'affirmative' should read 'negative'.

In conclusion I can only say that I embarked on this work with high expectations and the hope of writing an enthusiastic review. I am sorry that I cannot do so. But sparing the rod serves no purpose.

(e) *The Language of the* Parker Chronicle, *Volume II: Word-Formation and Syntax* by C. Sprockel, The Hague: Martinus Nijhoff, 1973*

I must in fairness start by saying that I picked this book up in high hopes and put it down in the depths of frustration and indeed despair that so much dedicated labour should have achieved so little. But, as I no longer have the time or patience to restate truisms, I shall content myself with expressing my basic criticisms as briefly and as mildly as possible.

Like volume I, *Phonology and Accidence* – reviewed in these columns by the late C. L. Wrenn (*RES* 17 (1966), 423–5) – this is a careful work. It contains a useful collection of material from the Parker Chronicle which supplements Ann Shannon's limited study, *A Descriptive Syntax of the* Parker Manuscript *of the* Anglo-Saxon Chronicle *from 734 to 891* (The Hague, 1964), but is admittedly not always complete; see pp. 110, 218, and 229. Unlike many writers on Old English, Mr Sprockel is keenly alert to the difficulties caused by our lack of native informants and our ignorance of intonation patterns, and recognizes that certainty is often impossible; see pp. 4–6 and 17–18. Yet he seems overconfident about the status of *se* in some examples on pp. 159–61. He is also more aware than many of the limitations of the Old English inflexional system; see Appendix IV to Volume I and chapter 8 of Volume II. Yet he thinks that preterite verb forms in -*on* are unambiguously indicative (pp. 196–8) and that aspect is a valid category for Old English (pp. 22, 29, and elsewhere).

The work is marred by three basic flaws. The first is the result of Mr Sprockel's summary dismissal (p. 64) of 'studies which confine themselves to one particular problem of OE syntax (and these are quite numerous)' as 'often not very helpful'. Mr Sprockel could have done with the help of Penning (1875), Voges (1883), and Farr (1905) in his discussions of *self* (p. 24 and elsewhere); of Lindemann (1970) in his discussion of *ge*- (pp. 36–9); and of Nickel (1966 and 1967) in his discussions of agent nouns and present participles (p. 42 and

* Reprinted from the *Review of English Studies* 25 (1974), 452–4.

elsewhere). Examples could be multiplied, but one more must suffice: chapter 13 on Word-Order contains the same basic errors which I condemned in *MÆ* 40 (1971), 182–3. It is true that Henry Sweet warned us over eighty years ago that we can 'take the "literature of the subject" – as the Germans, with unintentional irony, call it – much too seriously'. This was not an injunction to neglect or dismiss it.

The second flaw is a tendency to rather ponderous and long-winded terminological discussions. Typical of these is the 'general discussion' about sentences (pp. 67ff.). After reading it, I was not exactly sure what constitutes a 'simple sentence' and was under the impression that a clause beginning with *ond* can be 'called the *independent* or *main clause*' [his italics]. The observations on p. 117 about the clause *7 þa se gerefa þærto rad* confirm this. No doubt the desert is profiting from the sweetness of the late Alistair Campbell's remarks on this point in *RES* 15 (1964), 191, and of mine in *NM* 65 (1964), 117–19; 67 (1966), 87–8; and 71 (1970), 611–14. On p. 3, Mr Sprockel adopts a definition of 'word-formation' which forces him to apologize on p. 49 for discussing the weak verbs. He might have done better if he had more often borne in mind his own dictum: 'A definition would hardly be helpful and very difficult' (p. 81). On the other hand, the term 'pre-particle' (p. 17 and elsewhere) does not seem to be defined and its use alongside 'particle', 'prefix', and 'preposition', does not make for clarity; thus on p. 25 *for þæm* (*þe*) is 'particle + dem. pronoun', but on p. 26 *for þæm þe* is 'preposition + pron. + *þe*'.

The third flaw – an inevitable concomitant of descriptive syntaxes of individual texts undertaken without due regard for what has already been done – is that the work alternates between trivial platitudes, e.g. 'the apposition to a noun in the genitive takes the genitive case' (p. 130), and false generalizations, e.g. the statement on p. 176 that the existence of *on allum þam þe him læstan wolden* can remove the doubt about the status of *þa* 'in examples with "*alle þa þe*"'. Moreover, Mr Sprockel's method leads to much tedious repetition but few positive conclusions. Thus what I call 'the splitting of heavy groups' is exemplified at pp. 88, 89–90, 93–4, and elsewhere, with no real understanding of the idiom, for at pp. 172–4 *7 getimbrede þa burg 7 gestaþolode ær he þonon fore* is said to exemplify 'omission' of the personal pronoun. Again, the reader who conscientiously ploughs through what is said or implied about relative pronouns at pp. 97–8, 112–15, 167–72, 176–7, and 220–1, will achieve little except confusion. Mr Sprockel might have learned something about presentation from those 'not very helpful' works. Thus the material at pp. 90ff. would have been easier to absorb if it had been set out in tabular form, as Carlton did in *JEGP* 62 (1963), 780. (Incidentally, though Carlton and Sprockel contradict one another about the position of *oþer*, both are right!)

Of course, some points do emerge. Chapter IV brings out the greater complexity of style of the annals for 891–924 than of those for the preceding years.

Mr Sprockel rightly rejects Louise Grace Frary's foolish conclusions about *wesan* and *weorþan* in the 'passive periphrases', though in the process he manages to turn her into a man (pp. 210-12). He offers some interesting comments on scribal changes (pp. 125 and 214-15). But his unfamiliarity with much work on Old English syntax and his inability to distinguish the significant from the trivial means that the book is unlikely to repay the time spent reading it.

(f) *Les Propositions Relative en Vieil-Anglais* by Georges Bourcier, Paris: Editions Honoré Champion, 1977[*]

In my opinion, this book has much that a book on the syntax of a dead language should not have. It sets out, according to the publicity sheet, 'pallier l'absence d'une étude globale des relatives en vieil-anglais [a term which, in the best traditions of EEC cooperation, embraces Old and early Middle English]; analyser ces dernières en appliquant les méthodes de la linguistique moderne; fournir, à partir de cette enquête spécifique, des conclusions susceptibles de contribuer à une meilleure compréhension d'un phénomène très général'.

It seems to me that the last aim is unlikely to be achieved by a book which assigns *Blickling Homilies* to the time of Alfred in spite of the date of the MS (pp. 25-6) but *Boethius* and *Soliloquies* to a post-Alfredian period because of the date of the MSS (pp. 80-4) – such decisions (even if necessary) can be made only on the evidence provided by complete descriptive studies of individual texts; which takes no cognisance of variant readings in the different MSS of *Bede* (e.g. p. 526) and (more seriously) of *Dialogues* (e.g. pp. 219 and 533); and which (as I show below) does not cover all relevant texts.

I must question the validity of the second aim. We are still far from having a complete descriptive syntax of OE prose and poetry. Even if we had this, 'les méthodes de la linguistique moderne', requiring as they do a knowledge of the intonation patterns of the language and many other insights which only a native informant can supply, would in my opinion still be inapplicable. Professor Bourcier is aware of the dangers: 'accentuation, intonation, et pauses ne nous sont accessibles, dans l'ensemble, que par l'inférence et la reconstitution' (p. 12). But he seems confident that he can supply what is missing; consider comments like those on p. 1 ('liaison') and pp. 4-5 ('une pause') and diagrams like those on pp. 29, 46, 50, and 62. I do not know whether to blame Professor Bourcier or 'les méthodes de la linguistique moderne' for this observation on the publicity sheet: 'On doit, chaque fois, poser a priori, et jusqu'à preuve du contraire, des règles d'emploi particulières des relatifs....' But this seems to me an unsound procedure for Old English. It results, for example, in a very blurred treatment (p. 65) of the important problem of the case of the *se* element

[*] Reprinted from *Medium Ævum* 48 (1979), 121-2.

when it is used in conjunction with *þe*. I should prefer to see the 'rules' emerge from the examples.

The first aim is entirely laudable. But it has not been achieved. *Parker Chronicle* to 891 receives only partial consideration (pp. 25–6 and 359–60), those homilies of Ælfric edited by Pope receive none (pp. 301–2). Only some of the poems are discussed (pp. 18 and 379–80), and the analysis of those is incomplete: e.g. there are nine, not four, relative pronouns with *se* and/or *þe* in *The Seafarer* (see p. 390). Important phenomena such as indefinite adjective clauses also receive only partial treatment (p. 6).

It is clear that Professor Bourcier has in his files the material for a complete descriptive syntax of adjective clauses in each of his selected texts. I am sorry that he did not choose to present all this material for each text in turn in simple language. Instead, his findings come in a form which makes impossible demands on the reader. Quite apart from the jargon and the diagrams, the book cannot be read within its own covers. Chapter ii. 1 (pp. 81–229) has 822 footnotes (pp. 207–29), many of which demand reference to other works on syntax and 'modern linguistics', to a list of examples cited at pp. 521–609, or to the OE texts themselves. I venture to say that, if Professor Bourcier's real interest had been in the subject which gives the book its title, he would have produced a work of great value to those whose interest is in the syntax of Old English and early Middle English rather than one whose primary appeal must be to those who see Old English and early Middle English as a playground for 'les méthodes de la linguistique moderne'.

(g) *Old English Syntax. A Handbook* by John McLaughlin (Sprachstrukturen, Reihe A: Historische Sprachstrukturen 4), Tübingen: Max Niemeyer Verlag, 1983*

The subtitle *A Handbook* is potentially misleading in that the work is not a systematic study of Old English syntax for the beginner or the working scholar, but rather an introduction to the study of the comparative syntax of Old English and Modern English, with an Appendix on Middle English (pp. 83–105); see pp. ix–x and 78–9. As such, it is perceptive and makes some very good points, e.g. on the voice of infinitives in -(*i*)*an* (pp. 36 and 66); on our ignorance of the intonation patterns of Old English (p. 41); on the absence of *do*-periphrases from Old English (better explained at p. 99 than at p. 52); on nominative/accusative case syncretism (p. 76); and on the refusal of Old English to conform to modern scholarly expectations (p. 26). The discussion on word-order (pp. 66–78), though not without flaws, will repay reading.

The author works within a very limited corpus and often, it would appear,

---

* Reprinted from the *Review of English Studies* 35 (1984), 217–18.

from first principles. There are limitations to his knowledge of the Old English language and of writings thereon. So it is not surprising that his perceptive observations are at times marred by omissions or errors. There are verbs which '*permit either Accusative or Genitive*' (p. 13), e.g. *bidan* and *gemunan*; hence *æfenspræce* could be genitive (pp. 26–7). The '*seþe* and *seþe* relatives are not distinguished (pp. 41–3). Important distinctions between *ne* and *no* are blurred (p. 48). The certainty of Latin influence is too easily admitted (p. 20). The fallacious distinction between *beon/wesan* and *weorþan* in the passive is accepted (pp. 58–61). 'Often' (p. 62, l. 13) is not the right word and seems to depend on the erroneous *Hine* in *Orosius* 62. 6 (p. 62); both Sweet and Bately have the expected *him*, preceded by *7*.

The terminology is often merely different from, not clearer than, the traditional. Thus 'conjoined propositions' (pp. 46–52) seem to be 'coordinate clauses', although the writer is not always scrupulous in distinguishing subordinating conjunctions from coordinating conjunctions or 'sentence adverbs'; compare examples 60 and 61 (p. 46) with examples 30–5, 37, and 38 (p. 50). The term 'covert relatives' (pp. 39–40) does not seem to me an improvement on 'conjunctions introducing adverb clauses'. In theory, it carries unacceptable implications about the origin of Old English conjunctions; in practice, it produces a haphazard collection of adverb clauses of all kinds (pp. 43–6).

Misprints will be found on pp. 13, 17, 20, 23 (two), 26, 36, 44, 50, 68, 74, 75, 78, and elsewhere; perhaps the worst is the unhappy reference to 'Visser's momental work' (p. x). Quite apart from this, the bibliographical element (pp. ix–xii) merits the adjective 'eccentric'. *Beowulf* is rightly (I would say) cited from Klaeber's edition, but for the remaining poems individual editions of widely varying merit are generally preferred to the Anglo-Saxon Poetic Records. Footnote 4 (p. x) cites 'for example' nine monographs from the scores in existence. The selection shows little discrimination, listing as it does without comment works with proven weaknesses and preferring van Dam to Liggins on causal constructions. Footnote 2 (p. ix) claims that Campbell's *Old English Grammar* deals with Old English syntax – a virtue it did not pursue and does not possess. Noting the absence from the same footnote of any reference to Bruce Mitchell, *A Guide to Old English* (Oxford), which devotes sixty pages to Old English syntax, I am inevitably reminded of the remark made by an American woman after she and her husband had checked in at the London Hilton. 'Wilbur', she confided to her friend Mae, 'is quite upset. The manager had never heard of him. Back home in Cedar Rapids, he's world famous.'

Part V
Conclusion

29

1947–1987 Forty Years On

I begin this highly personal account of Old English studies today by saying that the first draft was in manuscript and had been delivered as a lecture in Oxford and Helsinki before the publication of Antonette di Paolo Healey's valuable discussion of 'Old English Language Studies: Present State and Future Prospects'.[1] This deals *inter alia* with five topics which I do not discuss here: the study of etymology, of phonology and morphology, and of glossography, the development of electronic corpora, and the publishing opportunities which exist for authors of new editions and of language studies. The picture she paints is rightly encouraging. Fred C. Robinson had previously discussed some of these points in his 1975 paper 'Anglo-Saxon Studies: Present State and Future Prospects'[2] and had added three which neither Healey nor I mention: the fascinating prospect of new discoveries of Anglo-Saxon manuscripts, syntactical glossing (I have stressed the importance of this in *Old English Syntax*, §3890), and the desirability of an encyclopaedia of Anglo-Saxon culture covering art, archaeology, history, and literature. This last gap is to be filled by a work which is being prepared by R. I. Page, with Catherine Hills, Simon Keynes, and Michael Lapidge, all of Cambridge, and which will bear the same imprint as this book.

There are, of course, some overlaps between these two papers, for which I use the names 'Healey' and 'Robinson' as short titles, and mine. But there are some topics which I alone – *mea culpa*? – raise. Later versions were presented at Sheffield, at Harvard, and at the National Humanities Center, North Carolina, USA. My thanks are due to members of all five audiences for stimulating criticisms which resulted in more than one improvement.

'A life devoted to learning passes quietly away, undiversified by events', remarked Samuel Johnson. This has in essence been my experience since I left the business world in 1947 at the age of 27 – I was managing a firm of process-engravers, stereotypers, and typesetters, valuable experience indeed for an academic – and returned to the University of Melbourne to study for the

---

[1] *OEN* 20.2 (1987), 34–45.
[2] *Mediaevalia* 1 (1975), 63–77.

degree of Master of Arts. Prior to that, I had spent five years as a school teacher, doing a pass Bachelor of Arts degree at night, much of it from country towns without attending lectures, and nearly six years in the Australian Imperial Force.

In 1947, the study of Old English was a compulsory part of the preparation for the Melbourne MA degree. Perhaps my return to Academia in 1947 does qualify as an 'event', because in 1948 Old English was no longer compulsory and I might not have begun to study it at all. But I did. Working part-time as a gardener, a builder's labourer, and a railway porter, in all of which avocations commonsense is useful, I very soon became disenchanted with the books from which I had to learn Old English – I recently came across a pencilled comment I made in 1949 to the effect that most of them were a hindrance rather than a help – and by the fact that the grammars, the glossaries, and the editions of both verse and prose texts, had very little to say about syntax. All the editions of the poems I saw, particularly those in Methuen's Old English Library, seemed to spend pages telling me about the spelling of words and arguing whether they were early Mercian or late West Saxon or whatever, without ever explaining how this affected one's appreciation of the poem. Whereas they frequently said nothing about the syntax, which does affect the meaning of the poem and hence one's appreciation of it. Indeed, we had to wait until 1969 for Dunning and Bliss in their Methuen edition of *The Wanderer* – a book which set a fashion which should be imitated – for editors to give what I consider proper attention to syntax and semantics.

So I became hooked on Old English syntax. In 1948 I wrote a long essay on 'Some Aspects of Sentence Structure in King Alfred's [sic] Orosius'. In 1952 I completed my Master of Arts thesis on 'Adverb Clauses in Old English Prose'. In 1959 I received the degree of Doctor of Philosophy at Oxford University for a thesis on 'Subordinate Clauses in Old English Poetry'. All are still, quite rightly, unpublished. This Rake's Progress culminated in the publication on 24 January 1985 of *Old English Syntax* (2 volumes, Oxford: Clarendon Press). But I am now at work on *Old English Syntax: A Critical Bibliography of Publications to the End of 1984*, to be published by Basil Blackwell.

'Forty Years On'. One remarkable change to be chronicled is the fact that today an academic career would be almost impossible for a person who knew nothing of his subject until he was 27. Today's embryo don of that age – if not already too old – will need a Ph.D., a scattering of articles, and probably a book or two, to stand a chance of even getting on the short list for any advertised job. It was no mere jaundiced asperity that led me to say to a colleague after completing such a list last year: 'With the qualifications we had thirty years ago, you and I would not have put ourselves, let alone one another, on this short list.' Even more remarkable changes are apparent in the field of Old English studies. It is these which are my prime concern.

But I judge it proper first to pay a tribute to those scholars and teachers who have been strong influences in my development. Generations of pupils too have helped me, but individual mention of them would be invidious. It is equally invidious to attempt an honour roll of great scholars of the more distant past. Some are mentioned below, as are some of the great of the last forty years. But – to name but twelve here – I think with gratitude of Thorpe, Grein, Wülker, Sievers, Skeat, Cook, Sweet, Bosworth, Toller, A. G. Kennedy, Krapp, and Dobbie. In Melbourne, I think of Ian Maxwell, Keith Macartney, Vera Jennings, Alec Hope, Tom Dobson, and Dorothy Coldicutt; in Oxford, of Alistair Campbell; elsewhere of Tom Dunning, Simeon Potter, Tauno Mustanoja, Herbert Merrit, Alan Bliss, and Fred Robinson. A fuller list of those who helped me in connexion with my *Old English Syntax* will be found in the Foreword thereto.

Any catalogue of the changes which have revolutionized Old English studies in the last forty years must to some extent at least reflect the bias of the reporter. My impression is that in those days the tradition was still often strongly, doggedly, and crabbedly, 'linguistic' in an old pejorative – as opposed to a modern pejorative – way, little interested in social or literary aspects of the corpus. As Barley put it, 'It is a sad fact that many Anglo-Saxonists tend to study their people not as thinking members of a social community but as generators of scribal errors and manuscript traditions.'[3] There were fewer workers in the field and the pressure to publish was much less desperate. The Greenfield–Robinson Bibliography cites for *The Dream of the Rood* 13 studies from 1844 to 1946, 32 from 1947 to 1972. Corresponding figures for *The Seafarer* and *The Wanderer* are 29/47 and 29/57 respectively. I have not dared to make counts for 1973 to 1987. As I shall suggest later, this plethora of publications is not altogether an unmixed blessing.

But there have been many gains. First, we may note a number of new organizations and projects. The Old English Division of the Modern Languages Association of America sponsors the *Old English Newsletter*, which has appeared twice yearly since 1967. It includes announcements, news, and *The Year's Work in Old English Studies*: a Bibliography of books, articles, and reviews; a list of works in progress; and critical reviews by a panel of experts in various fields – some more expert than others. The *Dictionary of Old English*, now edited by Ashley Crandell Amos and Antonette di Paolo Healey, needs no advertisement from me. But it is a melancholy pleasure to pay tribute to its 'onelie begetter', the Canadian Rhodes Scholar Angus Cameron, who conceived it in Oxford and brought it into being by his enthusiasm. His untimely death in 1983 robbed Old English studies of a towering figure.

Anglo-Saxon England, an annual publication born of cooperation between the

[3] *ASE* 3 (1974), 19.

Old English Division of the Modern Languages Association of America and Peter Clemoes, then Elrington-Bosworth Professor of Anglo-Saxon in the University of Cambridge, has appeared since 1972 bearing the imprint of Cambridge University Press. Clemoes was the chief editor of the first eleven issues, with the assistance of an international panel of scholars. Since the 1983 issue, he has shared that responsibility with Simon Keynes and Michael Lapidge, also of Cambridge. *Anglo-Saxon England* is a periodical aimed at drawing together the many strands that go to make up Anglo-Saxon studies and reflects the increasing realization of scholars in the field that the different disciplines they represent aid each other and are but aspects of a common interest.

The International Society of Anglo-Saxonists was founded in 1981 and holds biennial conferences: 1983 Brussels and Ghent; 1985 Cambridge, England; 1987 Toronto. Most Anglo-Saxonists in the world are members. Some of the papers given at the conferences are published in *Anglo-Saxon England.*

The Sutton Hoo Society was founded in 1984 and hopes to build a replica of the famous ship.

In 1985, an executive committee, headed by Peter Clemoes as Director, was established to create a 'Register of Written Sources Used by Authors in Anglo-Saxon England'. This will work in close cooperation with Helmut Gneuss, who is preparing a 'Bibliographical Hand-List of Extant Manuscripts Written or Owned in England up to 1100', and with a group of North American scholars, headed by Paul Szarmach, which is working to create a successor to J. D. A. Ogilvy's *Books Known to the English, 597–1066.* This committee circulated a questionnaire in the spring 1986 number of the *Old English Newsletter* under the heading *Fontes Anglo-Saxonici.*

The year 1985 also saw the establishment of a Centre for Anglo-Saxon Studies at the University of Manchester, under the direction of Donald Scragg, and the publication of 'North American Research in Medieval Hagiography: A Handlist' compiled by Gordon Whatley.

Work on *The Historical Thesaurus of English* has been proceeding at Glasgow University since 1965, with Jane Roberts of London in charge of the Old English section. The aim is to provide a semantically arranged listing of the English vocabulary from Old English to the modern period. According to *OEN* 13.1 (1979), 10, 'the principal source is the 12-volume *Oxford English Dictionary* together with its supplements.' But, the statement goes on, 'as words which were obsolete by 1150 are generally excluded from the *OED*, newly compiled Old English material is being added to the archive. For this work, Meritt's edition of Clark Hall is being followed for a basic listing, with information on usage drawn from Bosworth–Toller–Campbell.' I have pondered whether the preparation of an Old English thesaurus before the completion of the *Dictionary of Old English* is a case of putting the cart before the horse and am therefore inclined to wonder whether the Old English part of the project is premature.

But Healey (pp. 37–8 and 42) pays tribute to its actual and potential value to the editors of the *Dictionary* and to students of semantics.

Since 1947, there has been an increasing interest in the history of Anglo-Saxon scholarship; see *OEN* 17.1 (1983), 36–40. More attention is also being paid to the important problem of the relationships between the Celts and the Anglo-Saxons. Here the foundation of the Cambridge Mediaeval Celtic Studies in 1981 is to be welcomed. Important work is also being done on Anglo-Latin, a field wide open to potential scholars, as Robinson (pp. 72–3) noted.

Good foundations for dialect studies were laid by the pioneers of Old English studies and the work continues to flourish. Joseph P. Crowley points out that 'the chief factors, then, in shaping the attested Old English dialects seem to have been forces in post-migration England: physiography, military and political history, Christianity and education, and contacts with other languages – in order of descending importance.'[4] He pays particular attention to the linguistic evidence and finds seven criteria, five of which are phonological, one morphological, and the seventh dialect geography. His Bibliography, which spares me the invidious task of singling out particular workers in the field, can be supplemented from Shigeru Ono's article in the Miyabe Studies[5] and from Healey (p. 38). Crowley concludes with an examination of 'the prospects for the studies of Old English dialects'. The possibility of dialectal variants in syntax, mentioned in my Conclusion to *Old English Syntax* (ii, p. 1007), could well have been listed among 'paths worth pursuing' (*OES*, §3976).

The problem of how best to teach Old English has also received much much-needed attention since 1947. Here, I must confess, I can raise no enthusiasm for those methods which involve language laboratories and the like, with their pretence that Old English is a spoken language instead of a realization that what beginners want is a rapid reading knowledge. I might be more enthusiastic if we had the voices of Alfred, Ælfric, and Wulfstan. (I have not had an opportunity to evaluate the computerized exercises prepared by Constance B. Hieatt and O. D. Macrae-Gibson described in *OEN* 20.2 (1987), 26.) I have set out my own views in practical form in what is now Part One of Mitchell and Robinson, *A Guide to Old English*, but would like to supplement them by a passage from my Foreword to the second edition (1968):

> One reviewer observed that the book seemed to be 'written for someone rather slow of understanding'. I am desperately sorry if anyone trying

[4] 'The Study of Old English Dialects', *E.Studies* 67 (1986), 97–112.

[5] Shigeru Ono 'The Old English Equivalents of Latin *cognoscere* and *intelligere* – The Dialectal and Temporal Distribution of Vocabulary', *The History and Structure of the English Language: Presented to Kikuo Miyabe on the Occasion of His Sixtieth Birthday* ed. Yoshio Terasawa, et al. (Tokyo, 1981), pp. 117–45. See also the same author's 'Supplementary Notes on *ongietan*, *undergietan* and *understandan*', *Poetica* (Tokyo) 12 (1981), 94–7.

to learn Old English from it has felt that. I can only say that the *Guide* is (as far as I could make it) the book I should like to have had when I started Old English.

The generous response of the Old English community to the third and fourth editions has led the authors and the publishers to contemplate a fifth edition, in which we hope to rectify one or two of the more obvious omissions such as the absence of an Ælfric homily or saint's life. However, it is impossible to include every text which every teacher regards as essential without making the book prohibitively expensive. So those who, quite understandably, regret the absence of Ohthere and Wulfstan, *Sermo Lupi*, or *The Battle of Brunanburh*, may think it worth while preparing their own classroom version along the lines of the edition of *Wulf and Eadwacer* published by Peter S. Baker in *OEN* 16.2 (1983).

There is another problem: is the prose to be studied for its own sake or is it to be regarded as something which must be got through as quickly as possible so that learners can get to the poetry? The answer, for those at universities at any rate, must to some extent depend on the place of Old English in the syllabus, which is increasingly under pressure. It would, however, seem that for many the real justification for studying Old English lies in the poetry because, as Brian Morton put it in *The Times Higher Education Supplement* on 22 May 1987, 'English poetry begins here.' This argument is, of course, a two-edged sword; it could be argued, for example, that historical writing in English begins with the Anglo-Saxon chronicler's biting comments on cowardice, indecision, and treachery, in the reign of Æthelred and with this laconic observation in the 1052 annal in D – with its special appeal to colonials like myself and, I suppose, to all non-Englishmen:

> But it was hateful to almost all of them to fight against men of their own race, for there was little else that was worth anything apart from Englishmen on either side.

Be that as it may, I confess with some diffidence that I have in mind an attempt to prepare a book under the title *An Invitation to Old English*, which would enable undergraduates and general readers to get to the poetry more quickly than is possible with present methods. But my aim is not to replace the *Guide* but rather to offer an easier way to a more limited knowledge. I firmly believe that some knowledge of Old English is an essential tool for anyone trying to gain an understanding and appreciation of English literature.

The appearance of important reference works over the past forty years must also be noted:

> Dorothy Whitelock *English Historical Documents I c.500–1042* (London, 1955; 2nd edn, 1979)

N. R. Ker *Catalogue of Manuscripts Containing Anglo-Saxon* (Oxford, 1957 and *ASE* 5 (1976), 121–31)

A. Campbell *Old English Grammar* (Oxford, 1959)

J. R. Clark Hall *A Concise Anglo-Saxon Dictionary*, 4th edn, with Supplement by H. D. Meritt (Cambridge, 1960)

J. D. A. Ogilvy *Books Known to the English, 597–1066* (Cambridge, Mass., 1967)

J. B. Bessinger, Jr and Philip H. Smith, Jr *A Concordance to* Beowulf (New York, 1969)

Alistair Campbell *An Anglo-Saxon Dictionary Based on the Manuscript Collections of Joseph Bosworth. Enlarged Addenda and Corrigenda to the Supplement by T. Northcote Toller* (Oxford, 1972)

J. B. Bessinger, Jr and Philip H. Smith, Jr *A Concordance to the Anglo-Saxon Poetic Records* (New York, 1978)

Antonette di Paolo Healey and Richard L. Venezky *A Microfiche Concordance to Old English* (Toronto, 1980)

Stanley B. Greenfield and Fred C. Robinson *A Bibliography of Publications on Old English Literature to the End of 1972* (Toronto, 1980)

David Hill *An Atlas of Anglo-Saxon England 700–1066* (Oxford, 1981)

Angus Cameron, Allison Kingsmill, and Ashley Crandell Amos *Old English Word Studies: A Preliminary Author and Word Index* (Toronto, 1983)

Richard L. Venezky and Sharon Butler *A Microfiche Concordance to Old English: The High-Frequency Words* (Toronto, 1985)

Bruce Mitchell *Old English Syntax* (2 vols, Oxford: Clarendon Press, 1985).

To list all the other important works which have appeared is impossible. Work on archaeology includes Rupert Bruce-Mitford's three volumes on *The Sutton Hoo Ship Burial* (London, 1975–83); the first volume of *The Corpus of Anglo-Saxon Stone Sculpture* under the general editorship of Rosemary Cramp (1984); and David M. Wilson, *Anglo-Saxon Art from the Seventh Century to the Norman Conquest* (London, 1984). Three important reference books have appeared on the sources of the literature:

G. N. Garmonsway and Jacqueline Simpson *Beowulf and Its Analogues* (London, 1968, now available in paperback, New York, 1971)

D. G. Calder and M. J. B. Allen *Sources and Analogues of Old English Poetry: The Major Latin Texts in Translation* (Cambridge and Totowa, 1976)

Daniel G. Calder, Robert E. Bjork, Patrick R. Ford, and Daniel F. Melia *Sources and Analogues of Old English Poetry II. The Major Germanic and Celtic Texts in Translation* (Cambridge and Totowa, 1983).

J. R. R. Tolkien's seminal British Academy Lecture on Beowulf: *The Monsters and the Critics* was delivered in 1936. Kenneth Sisam, *The Structure of* Beowulf

(Oxford, 1965), E. G. Stanley, *The Search for Anglo-Saxon Paganism* (Cambridge, 1975), and Christine Fell, *Women in Anglo-Saxon England* (London, 1984, now available in paperback, Oxford, 1986) deserve mention. Robinson and Healey (both *passim*) discuss other items and comment on their importance for Old English studies, including Hans Schabram's 1965 study on words for *superbia*.

New editions of Old English texts continue to appear. The 1987 reprint of the fourth edition of *A Guide to Old English* notes the appearance since 1972 of seventeen new editions of Old English poems and seven of prose texts. More will appear in the 1988 reprint. The Early English Manuscripts in Facsimile series produced its twenty-first volume in 1983 – that of *An Eleventh-Century Anglo-Saxon Miscellany. British Library Cotton Tiberius B. V. together with Leaves from British Library Cotton Nero D.II.*

Numerous translations of both prose and poetry have appeared – with different aims and of different standards. There is an ever-increasing spate of *Festschriften* of varying merit. As Robinson and Healey (both *passim*) note, there are important works in progress: editions, *A Grammar of Old English* by Richard Hogg, bibliographies, works of reference, revised Microfiche Concordances, and (of course) the *Dictionary of Old English* itself. I am glad to have the opportunity of inserting here an appeal for help from the editors:

> The *Dictionary of Old English* is establishing a remote editor system by which Old English scholars can help produce entries for the *Dictionary*. Those who have particular expertise in the large syntax words of Old English and who are interested in helping are requested to contact the Editors: *Dictionary of Old English*, Room 14285, Robarts Library, University of Toronto, Toronto, Ontario, Canada M5S 1A1.

New desiderata have been defined; they include a comprehensive Bibliography of writings on Old English phonology, morphology, and dialects, a Modern English–Old English dictionary, a Latin–Old English dictionary, a students' dictionary, various vocabulary studies, and editions of Old English prose and poetry with literal facing-page translations into Modern English, on the lines of the Loeb Classical Library (see Robinson, pp. 69–70, and Healey, pp. 41–2). New editions of some prose texts, including Ælfric's *Catholic Homilies* (first series) and the *Blickling Homilies*, are also needed. At the conclusion of this paper, I make a personal addition to this list: a new collective edition of OE poetry.

So in 1987 the heart of Anglo-Saxon studies beats vigorously. But is the body in good health? Is its regimen sound? Or is there need for a change in habits, for medication, or even for surgery?

Some distractions are, no doubt, essential and can be accepted as presumably harmless provided they are not taken too seriously. I do not share the enthusiasm shown by the editors of the *Old English Newsletter* and others for Old

English crosswords and for translations of fairy tales and the like into Old English prose or poetry. I recognize both the value for learners and the long tradition of such translation, fascinatingly described by Michael Murphy.[6] But when I consider the present state of Old English syntax and semantics and the list of desiderata spelt out in my last paragraph, I have to say that I think that the time of mature scholars could be better spent. I also do not share the enthusiasm shown by the editors of the *Old English Newsletter* for abstracts of papers given at conferences or meetings. *OEN* 19.2 (1986) contained seventy-four pages but added an Appendix of such abstracts which filled fifty-four pages. I have not recognized these as publications in my **Old English Syntax: A Critical Bibliography*. It is my own personal opinion that too much time is spent at conferences.

Things such as these can probably be tolerated in the same way as one set of tennis too many or that last beer. But, as I see it, there are more dangerous symptoms. I shall now attempt to describe these and, where possible, to prescribe.

My main area of concern is literature. Much good work is being done and remains to be done. While not of course agreeing with all the details, I applaud the appearance of books like Paul E. Szarmach's collection of essays on earlier Old English prose[7] and Daniel Donoghue's book on Old English poetic style,[8] both of which have added to our knowledge and will provoke or inspire more worthwhile work. But there is, as I see it, a desperate question of academic responsibility. I note in passing the existence of reviews which are so bland and lacking in penetration that they almost qualify for the epithet 'irresponsible', such as those which gave undeserved acceptance to S. K. Das's book on Cynewulf,[9] and I wonder whether one should review a book unless one knows enough about the subject to be capable of saying – when necessary – 'This is a book which should never have been published.' But there is a heavier responsibility: What duty do literary critics working within a closed corpus owe to that corpus?

The remarks which follow mostly concern Old English poetry. As I have said, new editions of some prose texts are needed. But most of the work on the prose seems to me healthy. Those writing generally have their feet on the ground and seem less tempted to excesses, perhaps because there is less opportunity. Critics of Modern English poetry are saved from excessive concentration

---

[6] *OEN* 15.2 (1982), 26–36.

[7] *Studies in Earlier Old English Prose: Sixteen Original Contributions* ed. Paul E. Szarmach (Albany, NY, 1986).

[8] *Style in Old English Poetry: The Test of the Auxiliary* (New Haven and London, 1987).

[9] *Cynewulf and the Cynewulf Canon* (Calcutta, 1942). For a demonstration of the unreliability of Das's evidence, especially statistical, see S. E. Butler 'The Cynewulf Question Revived', *NM* 83 (1982), 15–23.

by a continually expanding corpus. But with a closed corpus like that of Old English poetry there is the danger of complicated exposition and extravagant praise. In 1965 Kenneth Sisam wrote: 'The pressure to find something new is strong, and one of its consequences is a tendency to speculate on the things that are not expressed in *Beowulf.*'[10] This tendency is not restricted to *Beowulf.* Every day, in every way, every poem seems to be getting better and better, more significant, more loaded in every rift with whatever passes for gold in the mind of the critic – the ore may be patristical, liturgical, allegorical, found in other literatures, or purely literary and undistracted by linguistic considerations or by any concern for the strong Germanic element which forms the basis of so many poems.

I shall take up some of these points later. It is not my wish or my intention to condemn every piece of literary criticism on Old English poetry. But I see many of the writings as displaying *over-ingeniousness* begotten by *desperation for publication* out of *shortage of material.* Some of them demonstrate that the feat of making bricks without either straw or clay is well within the compass of their authors. A recent blurb advertising a forthcoming *Festschrift* claimed with apparent pride that the essays it was to contain were 'often daring in speculation'. I dare not offer my own paraphrase of that claim. But consider the various interpretations of *The Wife's Lament.* In 1975 Fred C. Robinson (p. 66) wrote:

> In recent years, for example, five mutually contradictory critical interpretations of *The Wife's Lament* have been argued with approximately equal ingenuity: the poem, we are advised, concerns (1) a woman's passionate confession of her love-sorrow for an absent husband; (2) a man's observations about his comitatus relationship with his lord; (3) the Christian Church yearning, in an allegorical guise, for reunion with Christ; (4) a heathen deity pronouncing a curse on Christ; (5) a female zombie pronouncing from her grave-mound maleficent spells on the erstwhile mate who slew her.

The list can be extended. The poem has been made part of an Anglo-Saxon Odoaker cycle. It has been linked with the genre of erotic women's songs and with that of Germanic death songs. It has been associated with the Orpheus legend as retold by Boethius, and with the Griselda story as told by Boccaccio, Petrarch, and Chaucer. It has been described as a vernacular paraphrase of 'The Song of Songs', as an echo of St Augustine's *Confessions*, and as a reference to Luke 1: 52 *deposuit potentes de sede.* Robinson went on (pp. 66–7):

> Is it enough to shrug off such conflicting readings with 'Quot homines, tot sententiae'? When Whistler's friends tried to settle an argument over art by saying, 'After all, it is a matter of taste', the great painter replied, 'It

---

[10] *The Structure of* Beowulf (Oxford, 1965), p. 27.

is not a matter of taste at all; it is a matter of knowledge.' And so it would seem to be with the interpretation of Old English poems. A knowledge of philology and history would do more than anything else (except perhaps good judgment) to discourage the proliferation of bizarre and arbitrary 'critical readings'.

I find this overproduction of literary articles a strong and dismaying contrast to a not infrequent lack of understanding of texts and sometimes indeed what appears to be a disdain for such understanding. Matthew Marino writes: 'Because contemporary linguistics has begun to encroach on the seemingly well-defined areas of Old English scholarship, there has been an attendant nervousness about what linguists, *sometimes with a limited knowledge of Old English* [my italics], are trying to do.'[11] Quite right too, in my opinion. On the same page he speaks slightingly of 'the particularist arguments that are now the standard fare'. I must say that I find it remarkable that the Anglo-Saxon Poetic Records – the standard edition of the corpus of Old English poetry – punctuates *Maxims* i. 184–5 so that it must be translated: 'The weary man seldom rows against the wind in a broad ship unless it is running under sail.' I find it remarkable that some standard editions of *Beowulf* contain misstatements about the Old English language. I find it remarkable that scholars are willing to let their interpretations of *Beowulf* rely so heavily on unproven and, I believe, untrue statements about expressions like *soðfæstra dom* (see item 4 above). I find it remarkable that in 1985 it was possible and necessary for me to publish an article explaining how *Seafarer* ll. 50–2 can be translated (see item 19 above). What we need is more knowledge of Old English, not the lucubrations of people 'with a limited knowledge of Old English'. I still believe that the techniques of modern linguistics, with their dependence on native informants and intonation patterns denied to students of dead languages, are not relevant to the study of Old English. (This is not to imply that these techniques are out of place for the study of spoken languages.) But I must pursue this point elsewhere.

Now, however, my diagnosis must be made more specific. In an unpublished paper 'Old English Poetry: Garden or Compost-Heap?', I discuss in varying detail the numerological critics, the anti-feminist critics who deny that poems such as *Wulf and Eadwacer* and *The Wife's Lament* could have been put in the mouth of a woman, and that particular brand of oral-formulaist critic which argues that Old English poetry must be judged by standards of criticism peculiar to itself. Some of these receive passing mention below. But I detect other problems.

First, I note the common assumption that all Anglo-Saxon audiences were the same and were homogeneous, sharing the same beliefs and understanding

---

[11] *Mediaevalia* 5 (1979), 1.

each poem in the same way. Witness such titles as *The Audience of* Beowulf (Dorothy Whitelock), 'The Meaning of *The Wanderer* and *The Seafarer*' (G. V. Smithers), and *The Mode and Meaning of* Beowulf (Margaret E. Goldsmith), and the phrase 'the Christian Anglo-Saxon audience' which often seems to me to imply 'the audience, who were all Christian' rather than 'those members of the audience who were Christian'. As Stanley B. Greenfield put it: 'But there must be circularity somewhere in scholars' reconstructions of that silent majority for, bien entendu, their interpretations, however disparate they may be, are exactly what the audience would have expected.'[12]

Second, both poets and audience are credited by many critics with as much theological knowledge and acumen as a Regius Professor of Theology. E. G. Stanley certainly did scholars a great service by revealing the dangers of an over-enthusiastic and undiscriminating search for Anglo-Saxon paganism. But the pendulum has swung too far. Thus R. E. Kaske writes:

> It would be difficult to deny, however, that the great scholars who laid the foundations for our study of this poetry were, in most instances, more interested in Germanic antiquity than in Latin Christianity; and that as a result a disproportionate number of our own major discoveries are likely to come out of the once-neglected *Patrologia Latina*.[13]

But think of the articles which would follow the discovery of a *Patrologia Germanica*! Robinson (p. 66) speaks for me when he observes that some scholars 'feel that the new enthusiasm for emphasizing Christian sources minimizes unjustly the poems' powerful substratum of Germanic myth and culture'. A minor example of this is seen in Alvin A. Lee's insistence that since *heah ond horngeap* is used of the temple of the Lord in Jerusalem in *Andreas* 668, its use of Heorot in *Beowulf* 82 means that 'Heorot is at once a symbol of the individual soul and of God's people who must experience hell's attacks and then be restored but must also, ultimately, be subjected to destroying flames.'[14] A major example is the current prevalence of allegorical or typological interpretations of Old English poems. R. E. Kaske (ibid.) prefaced his article which explains *Riddle 60* and *The Husband's Message* as one allegorical poem to be understood as a continuous address spoken by the Cross with these words:

> To propose a unified religious allegory in what hitherto has been accepted rather generally as two distinct Old English poems, and universally as secular poetry carrying no meaning beyond the literal, is to risk being categorized as a 'pan-allegorist' in literary theory and an evangelist

[12] *The Interpretation of Old English Poems* (London and Boston, 1972) (hereafter cited as *Interpretation*), p. 9.
[13] *Traditio* 23 (1967), 41.
[14] *The Guest-Hall of Eden: Four Essays on the Design of Old English Poetry* (New Haven and London, 1972), p. 210.

in temperament. Let me begin therefore by protesting that if the corpus of OE poetry should ever be unmasked as a series of impeccably Christian allegories, no one will be more astounded or dismayed than I.

But allegory, like alcohol, is potent and addictive stuff. With either, it is dangerous to say 'Just another little one won't do us any harm.' To quote Greenfield again:

> And Alcuin, we might remind ourselves, need never have been concerned about the monks at Lindisfarne listening to tales of Ingeld if the Anglo-Saxon clerical audience had had the single-minded exegetical perspective which modern historical allegorists propose.[15]

But let it not be thought that I am denying the value of the study of Latin sources or originals. Far from it. A recent striking example of its value has personal application. In my *Old English Syntax* §183, I asked whether the phrase *syllicre treow* in *Dream* 4 could be an imitation of a phrase in a Latin hymn now lost. That this is certainly possible – rather than possibly possible – has been shown by Matti Kilpiö's citation of the following lines from Hrabanus' *De Laudibus Sanctae Crucis*:

> O tu, crux speciosa, o pinus pulchrior, omnia
> Quae vicis nemora, ...[16]

The third of the areas needing treatment, as I see it, is a tendency towards over-sentimental identification of superficially similar situations: for example, the not uncommon view that *The Wife's Lament* and *The Husband's Message* are companion pieces involving the same people; or similar identification of persons with the same name: for example, Tolkien's identification of the Hengest of *Beowulf* and of *The Fight at Finnesburg* as 'very probably the Hengest who led the first Germanic invasion of Britain'.[17] Perhaps I am biased by personal experience. Some TV watchers in the United Kingdom at least may recall a show transmitted by the BBC on 24 November 1970 (no. 9 in the second series of *Monty Python's Flying Circus*) in which a new lecturer called Michael is received into the University of Woolamaloo (*sic*) at a faculty meeting around a camp fire, and is renamed Bruce to avoid confusion with all the other lecturers, who are also called Bruce.

What is the relevance of this? If we were talking about something which happened in Anglo-Saxon England or before the Germanic peoples first came to

[15] *Interpretation*, p. 10.
[16] *Neophilologica Fennica, Société Néophilologique 100 ans, Neuphilologischer Verein 100 Jahre, Modern Language Society 100 years*, edenda curavit Leena Kahlas-Tarkka (*Mémoires de la Société Néophilologique de Helsinki publiés sous la direction de Tauno F. Mustanoja*), Tome XLV (Helsinki, 1987), p. 179.
[17] See the dust-jacket of J. R. R. Tolkien *Finn and Hengest: The Fragment and the Episode* ed. Alan Bliss (London, 1982).

England, the evidence for identifying 'Bruce' of *Monty Python* fame with 'Bruce' of St Edmund Hall, Oxford, would be such that many modern scholars of that period would undoubtedly regard the case as proven:

a I, an Australian called Bruce, taught Terry Jones at Oxford 1961–4;
b the same Terry Jones was involved in the *Monty Python* show;
c most people who came into my room in St Edmund Hall were aware of two cards which were certainly there before the *Monty Python* show and, I am confident, were there in his day;
d these cards showed respectively an Australian evening camp fire scene of white men, captioned 'Faculty Meeting Monash University' and a corroboree scene of Australian aboriginals dancing, captioned 'Faculty Meeting Melbourne University'.

The modern identification of (for example) Hengest in *Beowulf* with the Hengest (of Hengest and Horsa) mentioned in the Anglo-Saxon Chronicle entry for 449 AD – accepted by many scholars – rests on evidence far more tenuous than that set out above.

But the tempting identification of 'Bruce' with 'Bruce' is completely wrong. The episode in question was written by two Cambridge graduates neither of whom ever read Old English or had ever heard of me. The 'Bruce' they had in mind was another Australian then and now unknown to me. It is not for me to deny scholars the right to speculate in this way. But we need to remember that we are being given speculation, not history.

Fourth, I turn to the use by editors of modern punctuation for Old English prose and verse texts. This is a complicated and highly technical question. Sandor Rot describes the situation graphically:

> Sentences were not formally indicated in OE manuscripts by capital letters at the beginning and punctuation at the end as they are in MoE. Moreover, at first reading an OE manuscript is likely to give the impression that there is only one long rambling unit composed of many clauses and phrases loosely joined by connectives. This led to controversies in interpreting OE extant texts and discriminating their sentences.[18]

But an editor using modern punctuation is often forced to make arbitrary decisions about whether to use a full stop or a comma in situations where he has no evidence to guide his decision. Simple examples are clauses beginning with *se*, which can be a demonstrative pronoun 'that one, he' or a relative pronoun 'who', and *þa*, which can be an adverb 'then' or a conjunction 'when'. The results of arbitrary decisions on points like these are distorting enough in the prose, especially with editors who cannot even work consistently within their

[18] *Old English* (Budapest, 1982), p. 258, fn. 3.

adopted system: for example, Dorothy Whitelock in her revision of Sweet's *Anglo-Saxon Reader*, p. 3, where she uses '. *Ond*' in the middle of a report of a speech (line 34) and '; *ond*' at the beginning of the next speech (line 35).

In the poetry the problems are compounded by the imposition of rigid metrical rules, including Kuhn's Law. As a result, the fact that, as I believe, the verse paragraph, not the MnE sentence, is the unit of OE poetry is often – perhaps even as a general rule – hidden from the reader and the effects achieved by the artistic use of *apo koinou* constructions, parentheses, and the like, are lost. As with the study of syntax, we are limited by a lack of native informants and an ignorance of intonation patterns. But it is not always sufficiently realized that some at least of the restrictions are the result of the linguistic patterns of the language itself and not of the application of rigid metrical rules. In this connexion it is refreshing to note the frank acceptance by Donoghue throughout his book, *Style in Old English Poetry*, of the fact that the so-called 'rules' admit exceptions and are not inviolable. There is room for continuing critical examination of the validity of present systems of scanning Old English poetry. The debate indeed continues. But I have to say that in my opinion some at least of what is now being written involves circular argument and smacks of taking in one another's washing. The most fruitful developments, I believe, are likely to come from careful investigation of the metrical patterns associated with specific syntactic patterns.

In my *Old English Syntax* (§3947), I called for a critical re-examination of Kuhn's Law. In the first draft of this paper, and in my coda to item 18 above, I said that, to my regret, my article 'The Dangers of Disguise: Old English Texts in Modern Punctuation'[19] seemed to have sunk without a ripple in the ocean – or pond – of OE literary criticism. Hence the applause with which I greet the appearance of the book by Daniel Donoghue to which I have already referred. It has re-examined Kuhn's Law in some syntactical environments and in general has found it sound. But there are difficulties, for example in *Juliana* 133 (p. 192) and *Maldon* 7 (pp. 196–7), and the *apo koinou* constructions which concerned me have not been re-tested. The book has also convinced me that *Ða* in *Beowulf* 917b is an adverb and that the doubts I expressed about this example in *OES* §1686 were unnecessary, and it has helped towards the definition of the Old English verse paragraph which I mentioned above. But the problem of the ambiguous adverb/conjunctions and demonstrative/relative *se* remains to be solved in clauses which have only an independent (or simple) verb form. However, Donoghue has, in the words of the poet of *The Battle of Maldon*, fulfilled his boast: 'I have tried to establish linguistic facts (to paraphrase Bruce Mitchell) that aid our interpretation of Old English poetry' (p. 116).

An excellent case in point is his suggestion (pp. 122–6) that the *Maldon*

---

[19] *RES* 31 (1980), 385–413 [item 18 above].

poet's preference for *weorþan* rather than *beon/wesan* as an auxiliary for the passive – unique in the poetry – reflects a deliberate attempt by a Christian poet to hint at something he could not say outright, viz. that *wyrd* controlled the outcome of the battle. Even more exciting to me was his verdict on *Exodus*: 'It may not be too fanciful to see these features in *Exodus* as a fossilized, literary preservation of a poem originally composed orally and transmitted by word of mouth' (p. 103). This carried me back thirty-five years to a room in the Examination Schools at Oxford where I strained to hear Tolkien, whose lectures were like a badly presented and served Cordon Bleu meal, and scribbled what I could catch about the *Exodus* poet:

> If we have anything left by Cædmon apart from the *Hymn*, it is *Exodus* . . . marvellous word pictures . . . too excitable . . . at the Red Sea he just foams . . . if he'd only stood back, heard it from the top of the hill, he'd have done better . . . great scene . . . he's there . . . what happens? . . . blows up like a bullfrog!

These remarks bear on my fifth problem, which concerns the relationship between linguistic evidence and literary and stylistic considerations, which vary from critic to critic and from generation to generation. Dunning and Bliss, urging the acceptance of the meaning 'as when' for *swa* in *Wanderer* 43 despite my arguments that such a sense is unsupported, say: 'Here, literary considerations must outweigh linguistic arguments.' This seems to me to paraphrase Humpty Dumpty's claim: 'When I use a word, it means just what I choose it to mean – nothing more or less.' My objection was not as they put it, that such a meaning was 'unique', for in *OES* (p. lix) I accept the validity of the proposition: 'There are no examples but this may be one.' My objection was such a usage – a single word conjunction with an indicative verb conveying two concepts (here comparison and time) – is unparalleled and contrary to the whole pattern of the Old English language, and that such a statement constituted what I called a 'linguistic fact'. Commenting on this, R. F. Leslie wrote:

> We should certainly not underestimate these constraints within which we must operate, and my own predilection would assuredly not be to make an editorial decision in deliberate defiance of them. However, incontestable linguistic facts are rare and, as they stand in the manuscript, may appear to be incompatible with each other. An editor may, therefore, be forced to emend on semantic or syntactical grounds.[20]

I accept the necessity for emendation on semantic or syntactical grounds when a passage gives no sense. But I do not agree that 'incontestable linguistic facts are rare', and I still firmly object to emendation when a passage gives good

---

[20] *Old English Poetry: Essays on Style* ed. Daniel G. Calder (Berkeley, 1979), p. 114.

sense because that good sense does not appeal to the editor or does not suit his interpretation of the poem. So I see great dangers in the application of Leslie's next sentence: 'His [the editor's] case for emendation is strengthened, however, if a weak and ambiguous passage becomes a stylistically, as well as linguistically, satisfying one thereby.' To whom? To a modern critic? What about the poet? And what about the Anglo-Saxon hearer or reader?

Sixth, I turn to the use of the computer, the successful harnessing of which to Anglo-Saxon studies has been one of the romance stories of the last twenty years. The *Beowulf* and ASPR Concordances by Bessinger and Smith, the placing of all extant Old English texts in machine readable form, *A Microfiche Concordance* and *A Microfiche Concordance of High-Frequency Words* – these two put every use of every OE word at the disposal of scholars – the generation of slips for *DOE*, and the production of *DOE*: all these form part of that story. The computer has established itself as a means of examining patterns numerically tagged by the researcher – a process which sometimes reveals unexpected or unsuspected similarities or variations. To express reservations about such a benefactor may be (as Eileen Davies said in her retirement speech from the English Faculty Library, Oxford) to behave like a reincarnation of a mediaeval monk-scribe or -illuminator who, having lived through the introduction of printing to England, was confronted in extreme old age by the dissolution of the monasteries. But there is one caveat: the computer cannot think. The editors of *DOE* are well aware of this. But some syntacticians do not seem to be so. As I said in *OES* (§3957),

> Future syntacticians of OE will have to take care that they do not spend happy years programming a computer to produce detailed analyses of OE texts only to find themselves in complete agreement with the computer when it tells them what they have told it. At their present stages of development at any rate, the brain of the scholar is both more speedy and more sensitive for OE syntactical analysis than any computer.

My seventh point concerns the history of the English language. That there were colloquial forms of Old English seems certain. But these are not recorded in our manuscripts, which are concerned on the whole with topics removed from everyday life – charters, wills, learned works of history and theology, sermons, and poems – and are mostly written by linguistically conservative scribes. There is the possibility that, in the words of Lebow, the Anglo-Saxon Chronicle 'was kept by men who wrote as they spoke and who spoke in a manner much more modern than the other writers of the time indicate' (see *OES* i, p. lviii). Some light might also be thrown on colloquial OE usages by working back from more nearly colloquial ME documents (ibid.). But these usages are largely irrecoverable.

The history of English pronunciation is affected by such considerations. As R. W. Burchfield puts it,

> We should, however, allow for the possibility that dissident pronunciations existed among minority groups within the Anglo-Saxon period, and that the historical process was one in which these 'subversive' forms gradually replaced the ones maintained by the conservative scribes in their written texts and by linguistic conservatives in their speech.[21]

But perhaps we should say 'sometimes'.

A point of great interest in the development of English is why a Germanic language very similar to the ancestor of Modern German became an SVO language depending on prepositions and lost the inflexions, the three Germanic element orders, and such things as the strong and weak declensions of the adjectives – features which are all retained in modern German. My own view, shared by others, is that a major factor was the Scandinavian invasions and the consequent establishment of bilingual communities of speakers of English and Scandinavian dialects – all Germanic in origin. As a result, the inflexional endings (which differed from dialect to dialect) were confused and reduced so that they were no longer distinctive. Such reduction was possible only because Old English was already moving towards the SVO order – which replaces the nominative/accusative distinction – and already frequently used prepositions as well as the case-endings which they have almost completely replaced: for example, *of Scyttiscum cynne* and *mid hearpum*. Burchfield (p. 13) argues that 'this view, which supposes a period, however temporary, of creolized and virtually illiterate speech, cannot be sustained.' I personally deprecate the use here of the concept of creole and find it difficult to imagine what 'a period ... of virtually illiterate speech' could mean, since speech is in a sense always illiterate and the Anglo-Saxons were largely so. As Shippey put it in his *TLS* review of 22 March 1985, p. 306, Burchfield's view that the changes were entirely due to the emergence of colloquial or, as he calls it, Vulgar Old English overlooks both the linguistic conservatism of areas not subject to Scandinavian invasion and the intimate nature of the Scandinavian borrowings, which included even the pronouns 'they, them, their'.

My eighth and final point concerns the Anglo-Saxon Poetic Records, that invaluable six-volume set which, in Healey's words (p. 40), gives us 'easy access to almost every poetic text in a format inexpensive enough for a graduate student to own'. Every Old English scholar owes a debt beyond calculation to the editors, George Philip Krapp and Elliott van Kirk Dobbie, and to the publishers, Columbia University Press (New York) and Routledge and Kegan Paul (London). Its accuracy is inhuman; Robinson (p. 76, n. 16) says: 'Throughout

---

[21] *The English Language* (Oxford, 1985), p. 139.

the entire six volumes... I have discovered but a single transcriptional error: *is* for *ic* in *Resignation* 51.' But the work is becoming outdated. Volume i The Junius Manuscript appeared in 1931 and only the 1953 volume iv *Beowulf* and *Judith* appeared after my 1947 entry into the field. Admittedly, even the first volume is not as old as Benjamin Thorpe's 1844 edition of Ælfric's *Catholic Homilies* I. But those reading this paper will not need to be reminded again how much the study of OE poetry has advanced in the last forty years.

A few items which have subsequently been identified or discovered are naturally missing: for example, runic and non-runic alliterative inscriptions, *William the Conqueror*, and *Instructions for Christians*.[22] There are improved techniques for recovering readings. Questions have been asked about the unity of poems, for example, *Resignation*,[23] and indeed of the Exeter Book itself;[24] about whether poems have been incorrectly divided, for example, *The Husband's Message* and *Riddle 60*;[25] about punctuation, as I have already said; about the editorial use of capitals;[26] and about the meaning of compounds.[27]

There are editorial deficiencies. Dobbie himself (volume iv, p. vi) said: 'I now regret the practice adopted in Volumes iii and vi of this series, of not putting such conjectural restorations into the text.' The style of the notes is sometimes Delphic, the content sometimes banal (see *OES* i, p. lvii). There are understandable deficiencies in some syntactical and some semantic comments. Such policies as that of emending -*eþ* to -*aþ* and -*aþ* to -*eþ* conceal important linguistic evidence (see *OES* §20). There is sometimes a lack of consideration for readers, for example, in the failure to put the various versions of Cædmon's *Hymn* and Bede's *Death Song* on facing pages (volume vi, pp. 106-8).

There is also some insensitive criticism. One example must suffice: it passes my comprehension how anyone who had worked as closely on OE poetry as Dobbie could advance as an argument against retaining the manuscript reading *brand* in *Beowulf* l. 1020 the statement that 'bringing a sword into the picture at this point would make *maðþumsweord*, l. 1023, a rather awkward repetition' (volume iv, pp. 167-8). Such repetitions are the very stuff of OE poetry.

So I would plead for a joint venture to produce a new collective edition of Old English poetry. An advantage which I have not yet adduced is the therapeutic value of such an enterprise: it might divert some scholars from the production of more articles entitled 'The Meaning of *X*'.

'And what shall I more say? For the time would fail me to tell....' Perhaps this is just as well; I have probably said more than enough already and so laid

---

[22] See the Greenfield-Robinson *Bibliography* (p. 331 above), pp. 112, 287, and 238 respectively.
[23] Alan Bliss and Allen J. Frantzen *RES* 27 (1976), 385-402.
[24] Patrick W. Conner, ISAS Conference, Cambridge, 1985.
[25] R. E. Kaske *Traditio* 23 (1967), 41-71.
[26] Fred C. Robinson Beowulf *and the Appositive Style* (Knoxville, 1985), pp. 34-5, 40, and 94, n. 41.
[27] Ibid., *passim*.

myself open to the shaft directed by Weber at one of his critics: 'The trouble with that lady is that she cannot hold her ink.' But one must speak as one thinks and feels. So I conclude with the reflection that, in words attributed to Sibelius, no one ever erected a statue to a critic, and with a toast to Old English studies:

Wæs þu hal!

The Published Writings of Bruce Mitchell

1956

Review: *The Concessive Relation in Old English Poetry* by Randolph Quirk (New Haven and London: Yale Studies in English 124, 1954). *Medium Ævum* 25, 36–40.

1958

Review: *The Peterborough Chronicle 1070–1154*, ed. Cecily Clark (Oxford: 1958). *The Oxford Magazine* 77, 48.

1959

['Subordinate Clauses in Old English Poetry' (Oxford University D.Phil. dissertation). Copies will be found in the following libraries: Bodleian, Oxford; Australian National University, Canberra; Dictionary of Old English, Toronto; Centre for Mediaeval English Studies, Tokyo.]

1960

Review: *Syntax und Semantik der modalen Hilfsverben im Altenglischen* von Ewald Standop (Beiträge zur englischen Philologie, 38. Heft, 1957). *Notes and Queries* 205, 273–4.

1962

Review: *The Use of English* by Randolph Quirk (London, 1962). *The Oxford Magazine* 3, 124.
Review: *The Published Writings of Eilert Ekwall: A Bibliography* by Olof von Feilitzen (*Lund Studies in English* 30, 1961). *Medium Ævum* 31, 228.

1963

'The Use of English Paper', The Oxford Magazine 3, 180-3.
'"Until the Dragon Comes...": Some Thoughts on Beowulf', Neophilologus 47, 126-38.
'Old English Syntactical Notes', Notes and Queries 208, 326-8.
'The Couplet System in Havelok the Dane, Notes and Queries 208, 405-6.
'Adjective Clauses in Old English Poetry', Anglia 81, 298-322.

1964

'Pearl, Lines 609-610', Notes and Queries 209, 47.
'Pronouns in Old English Poetry: Some Syntactical Notes', Review of English Studies 15, 129-41.
'Syntax and Word-Order in the Peterborough Chronicle 1122-1154', Neuphilologische Mitteilungen 65, 113-44.
'The Faery World of Sir Orfeo', Neophilologus 48, 155-9.
Review: An Introduction to the Pronunciation of English by A. C. Gimson (London, 1962). Review of English Studies 15, 113-15.
Review: Twelve Beowulf Papers 1940—1960 by Adrien Bonjour (Neuchatel and Geneva, 1962). Review of English Studies 15, 306-7.
Review: An Anthology of Beowulf Criticism ed. Lewis E. Nicholson (Notre Dame, 1963). Review of English Studies 15, 414-15.

1965

A Guide to Old English (Oxford: Basil Blackwell).
The Battle of Maldon and Other Old English Poems trans. Kevin Crossley-Holland, introduced by Bruce Mitchell (London and New York; reprinted 1966, 1974, and in Papermac edition 1967).
'Some Problems of Mood and Tense in Old English', Neophilologus 49, 44-57.
'Bede's Habere = Old English Magan?', Neuphilologische Mitteilungen 66, 107-11.
'The Status of Hwonne in Old English', Neophilologus 49, 157-60.
Review: La Structure de la Phrase Verbale à l'Époque Alfrédienne by Paul Bacquet (Publications de la Faculté des Lettres de l'Université de Strasbourg 145, Paris, 1962). Medium Ævum 34, 244-5.

1966

'Paul Bacquet La Structure de la Phrase Verbale à l'Époque Alfrédienne', Neuphilologische Mitteilungen 67, 86-97.
Review: The Structure of Beowulf by Kenneth Sisam (Oxford, 1965). Review of English Studies 17, 190-1.

1967

'An Old English Syntactical Reverie: *The Wanderer*, Lines 22 and 34-36', *Neuphilologische Mitteilungen* 68, 139-49.
'*Swa* in Cædmon's *Hymn*', *Notes and Queries* 212, 203-4.
'*Vale atque Ave*' (the address before the Graduate School Convocation at the 199th Annual Commencement of Brown University, Providence, Rhode Island, 5 June 1967), *Brown Alumni Monthly* 67 (9), 27-9.
'Old English Prose and the Computer', *Modern Language Association of America Old English Newsletter* 1 (2), 4-5.
Review: *Chicken Inspector No. 23* by S.J. Perelman (New York, 1966). *Brown Alumni Monthly* 67 (4), 26.
Short Notice: *The Wanderer* ed. by R. F. Leslie (Manchester, 1966). *Review of English Studies* 18, 104.

1968

A Guide to Old English, 2nd edn (Oxford: Basil Blackwell; reprinted 1971, 1975, 1978, 1981).
Beowulf trans. Kevin Crossley-Holland, introduced by Bruce Mitchell (London and New York, and in Noonday paperbacks; reprinted 1970, 1972).
'More Musings on Old English Syntax', *Neuphilologische Mitteilungen* 69, 53-63.
'Some Syntactical Problems in *The Wanderer*', *Neuphilologische Mitteilungen* 69, 172-98.
'Two Syntactical Notes on *Beowulf*', *Neophilologus* 52, 292-9.
Review: *Sweet's Anglo-Saxon Reader in Prose and Verse*, 15th edn, revised throughout by Dorothy Whitelock (Oxford, 1967). *Review of English Studies* 19, 415-16.

1969

'Five Notes on Old English Syntax', *Neuphilologische Mitteilungen* 70, 70-84.
'Postscript on Bede's *Mihi Cantare Habes*', *Neuphilologische Mitteilungen* 70, 369-80.
Review: *A Reading of* Beowulf by Edward B. Irving, Jr (New Haven and London, 1968). *Review of English Studies* 20, 202-4.

1970

Introduction to *Beowulf*, in a translation by Kevin Crossley-Holland (Argo Record Company ZPL 1057).
Introduction to The Battle of Maldon *and Other Old English Poems*, in translations by Kevin Crossley-Holland (Argo Record Company ZPL 1058).
'Report from a Meeting in London', *Computers and Old English Concordances* ed. Angus Cameron, Roberta Frank, and John Leyerle (Toronto and Buffalo), pp. 83-7.

'The Subject-Noun Object-Verb Pattern in the *Peterborough Chronicle*: A Reply', *Neuphilologische Mitteilungen* 71, 611-14.
Review: *Old English Poetry: Fifteen Essays* ed. R. P. Creed (Providence, 1967). *Review of English Studies* 21, 185-6.
Review: *A Descriptive Syntax of the* Ormulum by Robert A. Palmatier (The Hague and Paris, 1969). *Medium Ævum* 39, 370-3.

1971

Review: *A Descriptive Syntax of Old English Charters* by Charles Carlton (The Hague and Paris, 1970). *Medium Ævum* 40, 181-4.

1972

'The Narrator of *The Wife's Lament*: Some Syntactical Problems Reconsidered', *Neuphilologische Mitteilungen* 73, 222-34.
Review: *An Analysis of Syntactic Patterns of Old English* by Faith F. Gardner (The Hague and Paris, 1971). *Review of English Studies* 23, 461-3.

1973

Beowulf trans. Kevin Crossley-Holland, introduced by Bruce Mitchell (London).
Review: *The Guest-Hall of Eden: Four Essays on the Design of Old English Poetry* by Alvin A. Lee (New Haven and London, 1972). *Review of English Studies* 24, 195-6.
Review: *The Interpretation of Old English Poems* by Stanley B. Greenfield (Boston and London, 1972). *Review of English Studies* 24, 319-21.

1974

'The *Fuglas Scyne* of *The Phoenix*, Line 591', *Old English Studies in Honour of John C. Pope* ed. Robert B. Burlin and Edward B. Irving, Jr (Toronto), pp. 255-61.
'Bede's Account of the Poet Cædmon: Two Notes', *Iceland and the Mediaeval World: Studies in Honour of Ian Maxwell* ed. Gabriel Turville-Petre and John Stanley Martin (Melbourne), pp. 126-31.
Review: *Imperative Constructions in Old English* by Celia M. Millward (The Hague and Paris, 1971). *English Studies* 55, 387-9.
Review: *The Language of the* Parker Chronicle, *Volume II: Word-Formation and Syntax* by C. Sprockel (The Hague, 1973). *Review of English Studies* 25, 452-4.

1975

'Linguistic Facts and the Interpretation of Old English Poetry', *Anglo-Saxon England* 4, 11–28.
'Short Titles of Old English Texts' (with Christopher Ball and Angus Cameron), *Anglo-Saxon England* 4, 207–21.

1976

'No "House Is Building" in Old English', *English Studies* 57, 385–9.
'The Expression of Extent and Degree in Old English', *Neuphilologische Mitteilungen* 77, 25–31.
'Some Problems Involving Old English Periphrases with *Beon/Wesan* and the Present Participle', *Neuphilologische Mitteilungen* 77, 478–91.

1977

'Old English *Ac* as an Interrogative Particle', *Neuphilologische Mitteilungen* 78, 98–100.
Short Notice: *English – Old English, Old English – English Dictionary* ed. Gregory K. Jember (Boulder, Colorado, 1975). *Review of English Studies* 28, 248.

1978

'Prepositions, Adverbs, Prepositional Adverbs, Postpositions, Separable Prefixes, or Inseparable Prefixes, in Old English?', *Neuphilologische Mitteilungen* 79, 240–57.
'Old English *Oðþæt* Adverb?', *Notes and Queries* 223, 390–4.

1979

'Old English *Self*: Four Syntactical Notes', *Neuphilologische Mitteilungen* 80, 39–45.
'F. Th. Visser, *An Historical Syntax of the English Language*: Some Caveats Concerning Old English', *English Studies* 60, 537–42.
'Short Titles of Old English Texts: Addenda and Corrigenda' (with Christopher Ball and Angus Cameron), *Anglo-Saxon England* 8, 331–3.
'The Language of Shakespeare', *Spicilegio Moderno* 12, 3–17.
Review: The Long Crendon Resurrection Plays from the York Cycle, 1979 performance. *The Crendon Crier*, 6–7 May.
Review: *A Concordance to the Anglo-Saxon Poetic Records* ed. J. B. Bessinger, Jr, programmed by Philip H. Smith, Jr (Ithaca and London, 1978). *Notes and Queries* 224, 347–9.

Review: *Les Propositions Relative en Vieil-Anglais* by Georges Bourcier (Paris, 1977). *Medium Ævum* 48, 121–2.
Short Notice: *AT versus ON, IN, BY: On the Early History of Spatial AT and Certain Primary Ideas Distinguishing AT from ON, IN, BY* by Karl-Gunnar Lindkvist (*Stockholm Studies in English* 49, 1978). *Review of English Studies* 30, 244.

1980

'The Dangers of Disguise: Old English Texts in Modern Punctuation', *Review of English Studies* 31, 385–413.
'Prepositions, Adverbs, Prepositional Adverbs, Postpositions, Separable Prefixes, or Inseparable Prefixes, in Old English? A Supplementary Bibliography' (with Allison Kingsmill), *Neuphilologische Mitteilungen* 81, 313–17.
Review: *Genesis A: A New Edition* ed. A. N. Doane (Madison and London, 1978); *Waldere* ed. Arne Zettersten (Manchester, 1979). *Review of English Studies* 31, 198–200.

1982

A Guide to Old English Revised with Texts and Glossary (with Fred C. Robinson), 3rd edn (Oxford: Basil Blackwell; reprinted 1983, 1984).
'*Beowulf*, Lines 3074–3075: The Damnation of Beowulf?', *Poetica* (Tokyo) 13, 15–26.
'Old English *Man* "One": Two Notes', *Language Form and Linguistic Variation: Papers Dedicated to Angus McIntosh* ed. John M Anderson, *Amsterdam Studies in The Theory and History of Linguistic Science*, vol. IV *Current Issues in Linguistic Theory* 15 (1982), pp. 277–84.

1983

'Bruce Mitchell, *Old English Syntax* (OUP): A Preview', *Mediaeval English Studies Newsletter* (Tokyo) 8, 3–7.
'Bruce Mitchell, *Old English Syntax* (OUP): A Preview', *Revista Canaria de Estudios Ingleses* 7, 155–8 (reprint of previous item).
'A Note on Negative Sentences in *Beowulf*', *Poetica* (Tokyo) 15–16, 9–12.
Review: *Anglo-Saxon Oral Poetry: A Study of the Traditions* by Jeff Opland (New Haven and London, 1980). *Review of English Studies* 34, 200–1.
Review: *A Bibliography of Publications on Old English Literature to the End of 1972* by Stanley B. Greenfield and Fred C. Robinson (Toronto and Buffalo, 1980). *Review of English Studies* 34, 320–1.

1984

'The Origin of Old English Conjunctions: Some Problems', in *Trends in Linguistics Studies and Monographs 23 Historical Syntax* ed. Jacek Fisiak (Berlin, New York, Amsterdam), pp. 271–99.

Review: *Old English Syntax: A Handbook* by John McLaughlin (Tübingen, 1983). *Review of English Studies* 35, 217-18.

1985

Old English Syntax, 2 vols (Oxford: Clarendon Press; reprinted 1985, 1987).
'Approaches to Life' (An address at Jiju-Gakuen School, Tokyo, 20 November 1984), *Gakuen Shinbun* (Papers of the Jiju-Gakuen) 356, 4, and 357, 4.
'Cædmon's *Hymn*, Line 1: What is the Subject of *Scylun* or its Variants?', *Sources and Relations: Studies in Honour of J. E. Cross*, *Leeds Studies in English* 16, 190-7.
'Some Lexicographical Problems Posed by Old English Grammar Words' (with Sharon Butler), *Problems of Old English Lexicography: Studies in Memory of Angus Cameron* ed. Alfred Bammesberger, *Eichstätter Beiträge Abteilung Sprache und Literatur* 15, 79-89.
'The Syntax of *The Seafarer*, Lines 50-52', *Review of English Studies* 36, 535-7.

1986

A Guide to Old English Revised with Prose and Verse Texts and Glossary (with Fred C. Robinson), 4th edn (Oxford: Basil Blackwell; reprinted 1987, 1988).
Short Notice: *Learning and Literature in Anglo-Saxon England: Studies Presented to Peter Clemoes on the Occasion of His Sixty-Fifth Birthday* ed. Michael Lapidge and Helmut Gneuss (Cambridge, 1985). *Review of English Studies* 37, 550-1.
Short Notice: *The Old English Catalogue Poems* by Nicholas Howe (Anglistica 23) (Copenhagen, 1985). *Review of English Studies* 37, 624.

1987

'*Old English Syntax*: Happy Second Birthday?', *Old English Newsletter* 20, 2, A30-1.
Short Notice: *Studies in Earlier Old English Prose: Sixteen Original Contributions* ed. Paul E. Szarmach (Albany, NY, 1986). *Review of English Studies* 38, 291.

In press

On Old English: Selected Papers (Oxford: Basil Blackwell).
'Relative and Personal Pronouns in *Beowulf*: Eight Notes', *Philologia Anglica: Essays Presented to Professor Yoshio Terasawa on the Occasion of His 60th Birthday*.
'*Beowulf*: Six Notes Mainly Syntactical', *Leeds Studies in English*.

In preparation

Old English Syntax: A Critical Bibliography of Publications to the End of 1984 (Oxford: Basil Blackwell).
'Literary Lapses: Some Notes on *Beowulf* and its Critics'.
'Bruce Mitchell, *Old English Syntax* (Oxford: Clarendon Press, 1985; reprinted 1985, 1987): A Review of the Reviews'.
A Guide to Old English (5th Edition) with Prose and Verse Texts and Glossary (with Fred C. Robinson) (Oxford: Basil Blackwell).
An Invitation to Old English (Oxford: Basil Blackwell).

ABBR# Index

Figures in roman refer to page numbers; figures in **bold** refer to (page and) line numbers. Unnumbered footnotes are referred to simply as fn. This index does not include references to what are merely passing mentions of persons, poems or prose texts, places, or things. Names of scholars are normally included only when there is some discussion of their work; mere quotation does not necessarily qualify.

The letter æ follows a, þ/ð follows t. The prefix ge- is ignored in alphabetization, so that gebidan appears under b.

In combinations like æfter (...) (þæm) (þæt/þe), the brackets indicate optional features and the solidus alternatives. Spellings such as þæm, þon, or ðy, cover all possible forms of the dative and instrumental of se.

ac 224–5, 233–5, 244–5, 246, 247, 248, 254, 255 fn.4
accusative and infinitive 246
Adams, A. 229 fn.34, 278–9, 281–2, 284 & fn.95, 286, 287, 288–9
Adams, Revd Dunstan, OSB 48
adverb/conjunction, the ambiguous 182, 186–92, 201, 256–63, 269–95 passim, 299, 338, 339; see also clauses, principal or subordinate
adverbial use of cases 23
adverbs, prepositional 256–63 passim, 275–95 passim; source of conjunctions 271, 276–7
agan 73–81
agent, expression of 264–8 passim
Alexander's Letter to Aristotle **14.1** 141–2
allegory 9 fn.32, 13–14, 26, 28, 56, 145 fn.53, 146–51, 211, 212–14, 214–15, 336–7
alliteration 24 fn.1, 110 fn.53
Alternative Service Book, The 51–2
amang, gemang, on(ge)mang 279, 283

ambiguity 156, 208, 216; see also adverb/conjunction, the ambiguous; amphiboly; demonstrative/relative, the ambiguous
amphiboly 45–6, 54; see also ambiguity
ana, ane 135–6 & fnn.11 & 11a
Anderson, George K. 211
Andreas 214; **257–8** 17; **474–80** 105 fn.26; **668** 336; **926–7** 207
Andrew, S. O. 119 fn.5, 158 fn.21, 173, 182, 187–91, 196 fn.71, 244, 248, 271, 275, 295, 296–7; see also 'curious superstition'
Anglo-Saxon culture, encyclopaedia of 325
Anglo-Saxon England 327–8
Anglo-Saxon Poetic Records 335, 342–3
apo koinou 38 fn.13, 103, 105 fn.26, 147 fn.4, 182–3, 183–4, 187, 195–7, 201, 257, 339
apposed meanings see meanings, apposed
apposition 92, 132, 144, 199, 201, 222 & fn.5, 284

archaisms, syntactical 279 fn.46
arguments and methods, dubious and fallacious, use of in OE studies (*see Old English Syntax*, i, pp. lviii–ix) 22, 23, 33, 34, 35–6, 43–4, 59, 61, 78, 86 fn.23, 92, 94, 100–1, 123–4, 132–3, 135, 136 fn.15, 137, 142–4, 153–71 *passim*, 162 & fn.32, 215–16, 224–5, 237 & fn.47, 239–42, 243–52 *passim*, 253–5, 266–7, 268, 305–21 *passim*, 327, 328, 333–41 *passim*; *see also* interpretations, arbitrary; parallels, literary, as evidence; 'proof' in OE studies
aspect 100, 158–9, 317
arrow(s), use of in punctuation 196, 201
audience, Anglo-Saxon 3, 5, 6–7, 12–15, 32, 41–2, 85–6, 92–5, 103, 156, 212, 215, 335–6, 337; *see also Beowulf*, audience of
authors, OE, control of material by 147–51, 208, 250

æfter (...) *(þæm) (þæt/þe)* 274, 278, 279, 281, 283, 284, 285, 287, 289, 290
æfter þæt 286
Ælfric 161, 164, 173, 176–81, 257–8, 260, 294; *Catholic Homilies: First Series*, new edition needed 177, 332, 343; *Homily on ... St Stephen* 222 fn.4; *Lives of the Saints*, printed as verse or prose 176, 180–1
ær (...) *(þam) (þe)* 190–1, 257, 261, 273–4, 279, 283, 285, 286–91, 314
ær ðonne 287

Bacquet, Paul 224–5, 229 fn.34, 232 fnn.37 & 38, 235 fn.43, 243–52, 255
Baker, P(eter) S. 290 fn.113, 330
Ball, Christopher 91, 206
Bambas, R. C. 142
Barrett, R. 224–5, 234 fn.41, 255
Basire, Joyce 182
Battle of Maldon, The see Maldon, The Battle of
Baum, P. F. 6
Beale, Walter H. 186 fn.43

Bede 11, 25–6, 52–3, 65–95, 209; OE version (ed. Miller) **342.29** 65–8, 73–81; **346.1** 82–7, 95; **480.21** 141–2
Behaghel, O. 286–7
Behre, F. 121, 288
Benham, A. R. 279 fn.46, 280, 281, 284
Benson, Larry D. 86 fn.23, 211
beon/wesan 319, 321, 340
Beowulf, damnation of 8–10, 30–40, 42–54
Beowulf: **67–70** 21, 170; **82** 336; **86–98** 44–5; **92** 45–6; **126–9** 187, 189 & fn.51; **170–88** 44–5, 46; **272–7a** 104–5; **320–8** 189–90, 194; **702b–38** 212, 216; **884b–9** 59, 165; **917b–20a** (*see initially entry on 339*) 186, 187, 189 fn.51, 261–2, 339; **1020–4a** 343; **1125–31a** 197; **1129b** 193 fn.63; **1138–41** 16–22; **1232–40a** 195–6; **1331b–3a** 5 fn.9a, 166; **1465–72** 195; **1495b** 158 fn.21; **1509b–12** 158–9; **1584b–90** 165, 194; **1792b–5** 191; **1925–62** 5 fn.11a; **2035** 22–3; **2147** 140; **2296–300a** 194–5; **2329–32** 9 fn.30(6); **2819–20** 32, 34–5, 50, 52; **2852b–4** 158–9; **3038–41** 37 fn.11, 39; **3074–5** 30–40; **3077–8** 8; **3107–9** 50, 52; **3180–2** 8, 10, 27–8, 153, 170–1, 215 (*see also lofgeornost*)
~ : articles and reviews 3–62, 210–12; audience of, homogeneous? 41–2, 156, 336; 'Cain figures' in 213; composition of 85–6, 212; consistency of, internal or literal 4–5, 56, 58, 159 & fn.21a, *see also [Beowulf]*, effect of the moment, poet's concern with; date of 24 & fn., 47–8; effect of the moment, poet's concern with 4–5, 33 fn.8, 45, 159 fn.21a, *see also [Beowulf]*, consistency of, internal or literal; *habban*, periphrases with 163–5; 'intentions' of poet 5, 6–15 *passim*, 26–9, 31, 46, 51–4, 58–60; Jutes in 212; 'meaning' 3–15, 24–9 *passim*, 30–40, 41–54, 56, 59, 117 fn.74, 214; new edition of threatened xii; punctuation of 189 fn.51, *see also* 'curious superstition';

punctuation; speculation on 334, 335, 337, 338; structure of 3–15 *passim*, 26–7, 56, 58–60, 211
Bessinger, Jess B., Jr 210
betweoh, betwux (þam þe) 279, 283
Bible, Authorized Version of 52
gebidan 99–101
binnan 283
Blake, N. F. 146–7 & fn.3
Blickling Homilies, new edition of needed 332
Bliss, A(lan) J. 30–40, 107 fn.34, 112, 136 fn.15, 152–3, 154–5, 157, 167–9, 184, 189, 195 fn.68, 201, 326, 340
Bonjour, Adrien 5, 55–7, 211
Book of Common Prayer, The 51–2
Bourcier, Georges 319–20
Braunmüller, K. 270–1, 273
Brodeur, A. G. 5, 22–3, 44, 211, 213
Brooks, K. R. 105 fn.26, 108 fn.42
Brown University 210–12, 315
Burchfield, R. W. 342
butan 292
Butler, Sharon (co-author of item 27) 296 fn., 333 fn.9
Byrhtnoth 9, 117, 166

Calder, Daniel G. 202
Callaway, Morgan, Jr 76 fn.21, 77–8
Cameron, Angus 327
Campbell, A. 139–40, 186, 193, 221, 225 fn.19, 245, 247, 261–2, 268, 318, 321
capitalization 45, 201, 343
Carkeet, D. 269–70, 274–94 *passim*
Carlton, Charles 309–12
cases: function of 18–19, 23, 34–5, 203–5; syncretism in 257, 287, 288–9, 320
cataloguers, library 313
Cavanaugh, Denise 20 fn.21a, 22 fn.28a
Cædmon 65–95, 209, 213; *Hymn* 1 88–95; 3 69–72
Cedar Rapids 321
Celtic, relationships with Anglo-Saxon studies 329
Chadwick, N. K. 5

Chambers, R. W. 3, 41
charters, OE 309–12
Chase, Colin 24 fn.1
Christ and Satan **642-3** 207; **723-5a** 119
Christianity 7–11 *passim*, 12–15, 25, 26, 27–8, 30–40 *passim*, 44–54, 56, 59, 117, 166, 208, 211, 213–14, 336; *see also* ethos, heroic; paganism
ChronA **84.33(894)** 181–2, 229 & fn.34 (=*Reader* **33.36**)
Chronicle, Anglo-Saxon 177, 179, 181–2, 183, 251, 317–19, 330, 341
Chronicle, Peterborough (1122–54) 221–42, 251–2, 253–5, 282 fn.64
Clark, Cecily 221–42
clause order 119 fn.5, 189–91, 196 fn.71, 274–7, 294–5, 313
clauses: adjective 223, 245–6, *see also* pronouns, relative; of cause 275, 282, 286, 294–5; of comparison 275; of concession 275; of condition 275; of place 275; of purpose 276, 279, 282; of result 276, 282; of time 282–3, 286; principal, positive and negative, influence of 286–7; principal or subordinate 177–82, 186–93, 299, *see also* adverb/conjunction, the ambiguous; demonstrative/relative, the ambiguous; subordinate, material from precedes subordinating conjunction 192–3, 207; with initial verb 187, 192
Clemoes, P(eter) A. M. 152 fn.3, 177, 262 fn.21, 328
Closs, O. E. E. 268 & fn.1
comitatus see ethos, heroic
commas, double 191, 192, 201
comparative, absolute 36–9 & fn.11, 337
compounds, meaning of 46, 343
computers, use of 329, 341
concord 35 fn.9, 134–45 *passim*, 147–51, 158, 265–6
conferences 201, 202, 333
conjunctions: adverbs source of 271, 276–7; consisting of an oblique case of demonstrative + noun (+ þæt/þe)

269, 273–4, 277, 278–81, 283–5, 288, 291; 'derived from enclitic particles plus other predications' 271; 'directly derived from pronouns and other deictic items' 259 fn.13, 269, 270–3; divided, defined 274; doubled 270, 272, 277, 294; 'genuine proto-Germanic' 270; grouped, defined 274; involving a comparative 274, 286–9; involving *swa* 274, 278, *see also sona swa; swa; swa (. . .) þæt*; non-prepositional 259 & fn.13, 278, 281, 291–4; origin of 259 & fn.13, 269–95; prepositional 256–63 *passim*, 269, 274, 275–95 *passim*; with *þe*, instability of 290 fn.113; variety of 274; *see also* adverb/conjunction, the ambiguous
considerations, literary 152, 167–70, 340–1
consonants: doubling of 138; simplification of 138, 143
constructions, OE, in Peterborough Chronicle (1122–54) 222–4
conventions, OE poetic, our ignorance of 12–13, 14–15, 26, 56
Cook, A. S. 123
corpora, electronic 325
correlation 258 fn.8, 270, 274–8, 291–5
Creed, R(obert) P. 156, 210–12
critics: attitudes and responsibilities of 296, 333–41 *passim*; desirable characteristics in 216–17; *see also* arguments and methods; interpretations, arbitrary; parallels, literary, as evidence; 'proof' in OE studies
Cross, J. E. 147–51, 157, 211
Crowley, Joseph P. 329
Crowne, D. K. 5
cruces, punctuation 187–201; *see also* punctuation
'curious superstition', described by S. O. Andrew (*Postscript on* Beowulf, pp. viii, 21) 119 fn.5, 189–91, 196 fn.71, 275
cweþan 157
Cynewulf 85 fn.22, 333

Daniel: **130–3** 121; **392** 138 fn.24
Das, S. K. 333
demonstrative/relative, the ambiguous 182, 187, 192–3, 201, 248, 261–2, 271, 292, 299, 338, 339
Denison, David 225 fn.20a, 268 fn.4a
descriptivism, place in syntactical studies 252
desiderata 177, 210, 325, 332, 333, 342–3
dialect studies 329
dialogue 99, 103 fn.18
Dictionary of Old English 298, 300–4, 327, 332, 341
Dobbie, E. V. K. 18–19, 21, 165, 342–3
dom 193
don, embryo, essentials for 326
(ge)don 297, 302–4, 320
Donahue, Charles 35 fn.9
Donoghue, Daniel 333, 339–40
Dream of the Rood, The 211, 216; **4** 37 fn.11, 337; **33–4** 17; **39–40** 193; **52a** 211; **58a** 167; **103–9** 17
Dunning, T. P. 112, 152–3, 157, 167–9, 184, 189, 195 fn.68, 201, 326, 340

Early English Text Society 176
eatenus 260–1
editors, problems and responsibilities of 100, 124–5, 136–7, 172–202 *passim*, 208–10, 212 fn.1, 296–7, 326, 340–1
element order 110–12, 153, 155–6, 179 fn.18, 182, 187, 192, 197–8, 208, 221–42, 243, 244–52, 253–5, 276 fn.30, 277, 290, 297, 310–11, 313, 315, 318, 320, 342
Elene: **56–61** 18; **172–80** 18
ellipsis 22
embe ðæt 284
emendation 340–1
English language, changes in 341–2: *see also* Middle English, beginning of; verbs, auxiliary
'enjambment of sense' 187, 197–8, 201
Enkvist, Nils Erik 188
eoten 212

Erickson, J. 270, 271 fn.12, 273, 292 fn.123, 294–5
-*est* 119 fn.7
ethos, heroic 6–7, 8–9, 10–11, 13, 25, 26, 41–54 *passim*, 117
etymology 298, 325
evidence, linguistic, suppression of 173, 343
'excitement of momentary riddle' 198
exclamation, dependent *see* question and exclamation, dependent
Exeter Book 343
Exodus 340

facts, linguistic 34–5, 152–71, 267, 339, 340–1
fægen 116–17
Finnesburgh, the fight at 5, 337
'for' 262
for 235, 257, 275–6, 279, 284, 285, 289
foran to 283
formulae 5, 25, 56, 211–12
forþon (. . .) *(þe)* 186, 191, 235, 248, 273–6, 280–2, 287, 289–92, 294–5
Fourquet, J. 225, 245, 251–2
fram (þ) 283, 284
Frary, Grace Louise 319
Frölich, J. 264–8
Funke, O. 225 fn.22
future tense 297
future-in-the-past 21, 119–22
future perfect 161 fn.29

g and *ġ*, alliteration of 24 fn.1
Gang, T. M. 7, 13
Gardner, Faith F. 313–15
Gardner, Dame Helen 167
Garmonsway, G. N. 106 fn.29, 125 fn.18
ge- 99–100, 149
gender 283
Genesis, book of 51
Genesis A: **1565b** 194 fn.64; **2887b** 156, 211
Genesis B 211; **368–70** 192; **828–35a** 196
Geoghegan, S. G. 270, 281 fn.59, 290

geond 283
gielp 117 fn.74
gif 278, 292, 295; *see also gyf þæt*
glossing, syntactical 325
glossography 325
Gneuss, Helmut 328
Godden, M(alcolm) R. 173, 176–8, 206, 262 fn.21
Goldsmith, M. E. 6, 7, 8
Gordon, I. L. 204–5, 207
Gorrell, J. H. 104 fn.25
Gradon, Pamela 18
Gray, L. H. 264 fn.1
Greenfield, S(tanley) B. 100–1, 102 & fn.14, 152–3, 167, 168–9, 202, 212, 214–17
groups, splitting of 222, 246, 276 fn.30, 318
gyf þæt 272

habban, used as auxiliary 163–5
habere 65–8, 75
half-lines, repeated 214
hapax usages, syntactical 109, 167, 168–70
harp 210–11
Harvey, L. P. 174–5
Healey, Antonette di Paolo 325–44 *passim*
Hengest 211, 337–8
her 229, 249
Herbison, Ivan 30 fn.1
heroic ethos *see* ethos, heroic
Hieatt, Constance B. 296 fn., 329
Hill, Thomas D. 48
Hills, Catherine 325
Hilton Hotel, London 321
his 177–8, 262
hlagol 113 fn.61
Hoad, T. F. 32 & fn.4, 154 fn.7
Hogg, Richard 332
Housman, A. E. 38, 153, 309
Hroþulf, a traitor? 59–60, 61–2, 213
hu 103–4, 106, 299–300
Husband's Message, The 336, 337, 343
hwær 246
hwæþer 246
hwonne 292

hypotaxis *see under* clauses, principal; parataxis

identification, sentimental 211, 337–8
imagery 214
in 283
infinitives 223, 246, 320
inflexions 45, 84 fn.13, 118, 135 & fn.6, 137 fn.20, 138–45 *passim*, 146–51 *passim*, 156–8, 312, 314, 317, 342
informants, native, lack of 103, 124, 156, 163, 178, 261, 263, 271, 296, 298, 312, 315, 317, 319
inn 247
inne 16–22
'intentions' of poets 156; *see also Beowulf*, 'intentions' of poet
interpretations, arbitrary 33, 168, 172–3, 185–6, 187, 199–200, 201, 210, 212–14, 333–41 *passim*; *see also* arguments and methods; parallels, literary, as evidence; 'proof' in OE studies
intonation 75 fn.16, 91, 103, 124, 156, 163, 178–9, 243–52 *passim*, 254, 261–3, 271, 277, 290, 294, 296–7, 298, 312, 317, 319, 320; *see also* stress
invasions, Scandinavian, linguistic influence of 342
irony 59, 61
Irving, E. B., Jr 25, 60–2, 211
Isaacs, Neil D. 211

Jenkyns, Joy 183 fn.28
Johnsen, O. 259 fn.12, 288
Johnson, Samuel 5, 54, 95, 152 fn.3, 153 fn.3a, 325
Juliana: **133** 339

Kaske, R. E. 212, 336–7
Kemp Malone, *see* Malone, Kemp
kennings 25
Ker, W. P. 3
Kershaw, N. 157
Keynes, Simon 325, 328
Kilpiö Matti 337

Kivimaa, K. 281 fn.59, 282 fn.69
Klaeber, Fr. 5, 13, 20, 41, 75–6, 79 fn.40, 80, 158, 191, 261
Kock, A. E. 192–3
Krapp, G. P. 342
Kubouchi, Tadao 228 fn.30
Kuhn's Law 271 fn.12, 339

Lapidge, Michael 325, 328
Latin, influence of 141–2, 157, 164, 178, 182, 243, 244, 268, 276 & fn.30, 321
Latin sources, importance of 337
Lee, A. A. 151, 212–14, 336
Lee, D. W. 56
Leiden Riddle 211
Leiter, Louis H. 211
Leslie, R. F. 21, 99–130 *passim*, 207–8, 340–1
lexicography 153, 296–304
Leyerle, J(ohn) G. 33 fn.8, 103, 117 fn.74
Liggins, E. M. 275, 276, 295, 321
'linguistic', meaning of 152 fn.3, 327
linguistic evidence, suppression of *see* evidence, linguistic, suppression of
linguistic facts *see* facts, linguistic
linguistics, modern 152 fn.3, 309, 319–20, 335
literary considerations *see* considerations, literary
loc(a) hwær/hwonne 274
lof 117 fn.74, 193
lofgeornost 8, 10, 27–8, 43, 46–50, 51, 117 fn.74, 153 & fn.3a, 216
Lucas, Angela M. 134, 135 fn.8, 136 fn.15, 137, 138, 142, 143

McBryde, John M. 73, 80
Mackie, W. S. 102–3
McIntosh, Angus 174, 264 fn.
McLaughlin, John 320–1
McNamee, M. B. 13, 56
Macrae-Gibson, O. D. 329
magan 65–8, 73–81
Magoun, F. P., Jr 85, 86 & fn.23, 94, 211
Maldon, The Battle of 9, 117, 166, 201;

5-10 198, 200, 339; 89-90 117, 188-9,
  190, 201, 339-40
Malone, Kemp 4-5, 119 fn.5
man 249, 264-8
manuscripts, Anglo-Saxon: facsimiles of
  332; Hand-List of 328; new discoveries
  of 325, 343
Marino, Matthew 152 fn.3, 269 fn.1, 335
marking, stylistic 271 fn.12
'marqué' (term used by Bacquet) 243-52
  passim
Maxims i **184-5** 335
'meaning' of poems see poems, 'meaning'
meanings, apposed 45, 49
meiosis see understatement
methods, dubious and fallacious see
  arguments and methods, dubious and
  fallacious
metre 32 fn.4, 136-7 & fn.15, 143, 154-5 &
  fn.7, 163, 170, 210-11, 339
mid (þæm) (þe) 257, 283, 285, 289
Middle English, beginning of 221-42,
  243-52 passim, 253-5
milde ond monðwære 153, 170-1, 215
Millward, Celia M. 315-17
Miyabe, K. 194-5
Moehring, H. R. 71 fn.8
Möllmer, H. 286-7, 290 fn.106
Monty Python's Flying Circus 337-8
mood: imperative 315-17; indicative 39,
  118-25, 161 fn.29, 246; subjunctive 21 &
  fn.23, 39, 118-25, 127-8, 245, 246
morphology 325
Mossé, F. 123
gemunan 119-20
Mustanoja, Tauno F. 67 fn.15, 134
Mynors, Sir Roger 74, 79 fn.41

ne 136-7, 223, 224-5, 232-3, 245, 248, 249,
  310, 315, 321
nefne 292
negation see ne
Nicholson, Lewis E. 57-8
Nist, John 210-11

no ðy ær 274
nu 130-3, 191, 273, 275, 278, 293

of 283, 284, 285
Ogura, Michiko 268 fn.4a
Old English: closed corpus, critics'
  responsibilities to 315, 333-41 passim;
  colloquial 341; teaching of 326, 329-30;
  see also Old English studies
Old English, A Guide to xv, 313, 321, 329-30
Old English, *An Invitation to 330
Old English Newsletter 327, 332-3
'Old English Poetry: Garden or
  Compost-Heap?' 215 fn.1, 335
Old English Poetry see Old English
  studies; poems; poetry; 'proof' in OE
  studies
Old English studies: attitudes to 327;
  contemporary 325-44; distractions
  from 332-3; encyclopaedia of Anglo-
  Saxon culture 325; history of 329, 333;
  new organizations and projects 327-9,
  332; place in university syllabuses 210,
  330; 'proof' in see 'proof' in OE
  studies; recent new editions of texts
  332; reference books 330-2; toast to
  344; see also arguments and methods;
  critics; interpretations, arbitrary;
  parallels, literary, as evidence
Old English Syntax 270 fn.6, 303, 326
*Old English Syntax: A Critical Bibliography
  of Publications to the End of 1984 326
on (þæm þæt/þe) 279, 283, 284, 285
on þære hwile þe 273-4, 278 fn.45, 285 fn.d
on þæt 286
ond 179, 224-5, 233-5, 244-5, 246, 247-8,
  249, 254, 255 fn.4, 315, 318
O'Neil, W. 271 fn.12
Onions, C. T. 83, 105 fn. 28, 106, 208-9
Ono, Shigeru 76, 78, 81 fn.47
oral formulae see formulae
Ormulum 305-9
Orosius **48.8** 297
oð 272, 279, 283

oð ða tide þe 283
oðþæt (þe), oð þætte 191, 256–63, 272, 282–3, 289–91
oððe 282, 283
oð þis(um) 260
oð ðone fyrst þ/þe 283
Oxford University Press 208 fn.

Paetzel, Walther 199
paganism 10, 13, 27–8, 44–6, 47, 49–54, 208, 211, 336; *see also* Christianity; ethos, heroic
Page, R. I. 325
Palmatier, Robert A. 305–9
paragraph: prose 178–80, 183, 312; verse 186, 189 fn.51, 193, 195, 200, 296–7, 312, 339
parallels, literary, as evidence 4–5, 32–3 & fn.8, 37, 166–70; *see also Beowulf*, consistency of, internal or literal; *Beowulf*, effect of the moment, poet's concern with
parataxis: distinction, from hypotaxis, difficult *see under* clauses, principal or subordinate; ~, too rigid because of intermediate stage 179–80, 186–8, 261–3, 269, 271, 299, *see also* clauses, principal or subordinate; precedes hypotaxis 258, 261, 271, 274, 277, 286–7, 290
parenthesis: broken marks of 194, 201; in poetry 187, 193–5, 199, 339
Parkes, Malcolm 179, 182
*Patrologia Germanica 336
Patrologia Latina 336
Peltola, Niilo 222 fn.5
perfect, preterite as *see under* preterite
personification 211
Phoenix, The 146–51, 211; **583–98a** 146–51
phonology 325
pluperfect, preterite as *see under* preterite
poems, OE: integrity of traditional divisions 13, 26, 86 fn.23, 185, 208, 211, 343;

'meaning' 154, 156, 166, 168, 212–14, 214–17, *see also Beowulf*, 'meaning'
poetry, OE: composition 85–7, 212; conventions *see* conventions, OE poetic; critical attitudes to *see* critics, attitudes and responsibilities of; new collective edition needed 332, 342–3; paragraph *see* paragraph, verse; performance 33 fn.8, 85–7, 93–5, 103, 180, 195, 198, 262; shaped by Christian mythology 213–14; study by beginners 330; transmission of *see* transmission, of poetry; *see also* 'Old English Poetry: Garden or Compost-Heap?'
poets, OE, control of material by *see* authors, OE, control of material by; 'intentions' of 134, 144–5, 146–7, 150–1, 165, 199; *see also* allegory; *Beowulf*, 'intentions' of poet
Pope, J. C. 99, 102, 103 fn.18, 117, 130, 131, 132–3, 140 fn.34, 176–7, 210
positura 179
postpositions 233, 247, 286, 289
prefixes, separable 19–20, 223, 245 & fn.3, 289, 314, 318; *see also* postpositions
prepositional adverbs *see* adverbs, prepositional
prepositions: adjective clauses governed by 245–6; cases governed by 18–19; (non-)repetition of 141, 144; *see also* adverbs, prepositional; conjunctions, prepositional
pressure to publish or speculate 144–5, 210, 327–34
preterite: as perfect 100, 160–1, 164–5, 207; as pluperfect 33 fn.8, 159–66, 189 fn.51
problems, terminological 17 fn.3, 131 & fn.23, 135, 139 & fn.29, 140 fn.33
pronouns: demonstrative 269, 271, 280, *see also* demonstrative/relative, the ambiguous; *þæt*, demonstrative; relative 203–5, 223, 245–6, 248–9, 271, 279, 280–1, 318, 319–20, 321, *see also* clauses, adjective; demonstrative/relative, the

ambiguous; *se*; *þæt*, relative pronoun; *þe*
pronunciation 341–2
'proof' in OE studies 101, 103, 120–1, 128 fn.11, 135–6, 166–70; *see also* arguments and methods; parallels, literary, as evidence; interpretations, arbitrary prose, OE: critical attitudes to 333; paragraph *see* paragraph, prose; present studies in 333; study by beginners 330
Psalter, Paris: **Ps.57.4** 17; **Ps.61.12** 17–18
publication: opportunities for 325; pressure for 327, 334
punctuation 38 fn.13, 45, 103, 105 fn.28, 109–12, 119 fn.5, 148, 172–202, 208, 254, 261, 262–3, 296–7, 338–9, 343
punctus 177–8
punctus versus 177–8, 183
puns 35 fn.9; *see also* ambiguity; amphiboly

question or exclamation, dependent 118–22, 127–8

Raffel, Burton 212
readers, consideration for 41, 343
Renoir, Alain 211
'repetition with variation and advance' 199
Resignation 343
responsibilities: of critics *see* critics, attitudes and responsibilities of; of editors *see* problems and responsibilities of; of reviewers *see* reviewers, responsibilities of
Riddle 60 336, 343
reviewers, responsibilities of 305, 315, 317, 333
Rissanen, Matti 135 fn.11, 142 fn.42, 143, 167
Roberts, Jane 328
Robinson, Fred C. 12 fn.34a, 21, 43, 45–50, 54, 153, 158 fn.21, 199, 202, 325–44 *passim*

Rothstein, E. 221, 224, 238–42, 255
Ruin, The 211

Scandinavian invasions *see* invasions, Scandinavian, linguistic influence of
Schaar, C. 105 fn.26
Schabram, Hans 332
Schaubert, E. von 256
Schrader, B. 267 fn.2
Schücking, L. L. 52
scops, performances by *see* poetry, performance
Scragg, Donald 328
scribes, attitude of 251, 319, 341
scriþan 216
*sculan 297
se 271, 292, 300, 317, 319–20
Seafarer, The 10, 12, 13, 27–8, 47, 320; **18–22** 197; **33–5** 130–3; **50–2** 203–6, 335; **61** 144 fn.52; **72–80** 117 fn.74.
self 82–4, 134, 138–45
semantics 124–5, 143, 158–9, 214 fn.2, 328–9; *see also individual words listed in Index*; vocabulary
sentences, OE, definition of 176–7, 179
Shakespeare, modern interpretations of 42
Shearin, H. G. 279–80, 280 fn.56, 284
Shippey, T. A. 186, 342
Shores, David L. 253–5
Short, Douglas D. 160–6
Sibelius 344
Sigemund 59, 165
Sigurðr-Sigfrit 165
Sisam, Kenneth *dedication*, 4, 5, 27, 58–60, 61
sið 288–9
siþþam 257
siþþan 191, 247, 257, 260, 273, 274, 278, 279, 288–91
siþþan (. . .) þe 274, 288–9
Skeat, W. W. 176
Small, G. W. 287–9
Smith, A. H. 89–91
Smithers, G. V. 5, 12–14

sona 191
sona swa 278
sorting systems 300–4
soðfæst 34–5
Soul i: **144** 192
sources 328, 337
sparrow, Bede's 11, 25–6, 52–3
speculation: pressure for 144–5, 210; *see also* identification, sentimental
'speech, represented' 147 fn.4
Sprockel, C. 317–19
Stanley, E. G. 36, 39–40, 43, 46–52, 152 fn.3, 185–6, 187, 189 fnn. 50 & 51, 190, 195–6, 199, 257 & fn.6, 259, 261, 336
Stevens, Martin 134–45, 216
stopwords 297 & fn., 300–4
stress mark ͜ 198, 201
stress, OE 20 fn.21a, 174, 187, 277, 295; *see also* intonation
subject, grammatical: change of 108; repetition of 276 fn.30; unexpressed 38–9, 88–95, 205, 222–3
Sutton Hoo 210
swa 69–72, 101–3, 106–9, 152, 167–9, 179, 194, 206, 247, 272–4, 278, 292, 300
swa (...) þæt 272, 292
Sweet, Henry *dedication*, 183, 208–10, 244, 318
Sweet's Anglo-Saxon Reader: ed. Onions 222 fn.4; ed. Whitelock, emendations discussed 209; ~ , notes discussed 209; ~ , readings discussed 209; reviewed 208–10
swilce 292, 293
syntax, points of interest xi, 5 fn.9a, 16–23, 34–5, 36–8 & fn.13, 38–9, 45, 65–8, 69–72, 73–81, 82–4, 89–91, 99–117, 118–25, 130–3, 134–45, 159–68, 172–201, 203–6, 207–8, 221–42, 243–52, 253–5, 256–63, 264–7, 268–95, 296–304 *passim*, 305–21, 326, 329, 332, 333, 338–40
Szarmach, Paul E. 328, 333

Taylor, Paul Beekman 211
tenses 159–66; *see also* future tense;
future-in-the-past; future perfect; preterite
themes 211–12
thesaurus, OE 328–9
Tironian sign 179
to 112–17, 207–8, 274, 279–80, 283
toforan 283
to ð, a ME ghost 282 fn.64
to þæm (...) þæt 280, 282
to þæs (þe) 165, 292 fn.123
to þæt 284, 286
Tolkien, J. R. R. 3 & fn., 4–5, 7–9, 12, 14, 34, 53–4, 117 fn.74, 198, 199, 296–7, 340
translations: from OE 212, 332; into OE 333
transmission: oral tradition independent of Bede 65, 67, 78, 81, 85, 93–5; of poetry 85–7, 92–5
T[urner], K[athleen] D. 269 fn.1

þa 178, 179 fn.18, 180, 186–91, 200 fnn.82 & 83, 246, 269–95 *passim*, 296–7, 300, 310
þa hwile (þæt/þe) 273, 274, 281, 284 fn.84, 291–2
þa þe 278, 281, 291
þanon 272, 278, 292, 293
þær (þe) 179, 190, 247, 272–5, 278, 281, 283, 290–3
þæs (þe) 278, 291, 292 fn.123
þæt: 'because, in as much as' 16–18, 132; classification 301; conjunction 38, 104–5, 130–3, 173, 271, 279–80, 292; demonstrative 207, 292; relative pronoun 18–21, 245; use with conjunctions 269–95 *passim*
þætte, þæt þe 281
þe: in *The Seafarer* 320; use with conjunctions 256–63 *passim*, 269–95 *passim*
þeah (þe) 246–7, 273, 274, 281, 292, 293–4
þenden 273, 292, 293
þider 272, 278, 292, 293
þon ma þe 274, 281, 292
þonne: 'than' 292; 'then, when' 190, 191,

246, 270, 272–5, 278, 284 fn.84, 286, 290–5
þonne þe 281
þurh 274
þy (þe) 291, 292 & fn.123
þy læs (þe) 274, 281, 292, 294

under (þæm þe) 283, 285
understatement 61, 112–17, 167, 207–8
Ushigaki, Hiroto 42–5
ut 247

Vainglory **77–80** 103–5
van Dam, J. 276, 294, 321
variation 199
verbs: auxiliary, and the breakdown of OE system of element order 243; impersonal 248
Visser, F. Th. 297, 321
vocabulary: flexibility of meaning of 46, 153–4, 183; heroic, Christian senses of 47, 213–14; *see also individual words listed in Index*; semantics
voice 267–8, 319, 320, 321, 339–40

wac 116 fn.69
wæfre 125 fn.18, 216
wælfus 216
Wanderer, The 12, 13, 99–130, 207–8, 214, 216, 326; **1–5** 99–102; **6** 101–3, 147 fn.4; **7b** 156–8; **8–11** 126–7; **22–4** 118–25, 157, 170; **25–7** 21; **29b–33** 103–6; **34–6** 118–25; **37–44** 103–6; **37–57** 109–12, 183–4; **43** 106–9, 152, 167–9, 340; **51** 155; **53** 127, 195; **58–9** 127–30; **65b–72** 112–17, 195, 211; **102** 157; **111** 102, 147 fn.4
Waterhouse, Ruth 179–80
weamod 115 fn.65
Weber 344
weccan 158–9
Wentersdorf, Karl P. 44
weorþan 319, 321, 340
Whatley, Gordon 328
Whitelock, Dorothy 48, 73, 78, 83 fn.12, 193, 208–10, 338–9
Widsith **142b–3** 192–3
Wife's Lament, The 134–45, 216; **1–2a** 134–45, 216, 334, 335, 337; **11a** 159–66; **15a** 159–66; **18** 136–7, 143, 170
willan 17, 297
Williamson, Craig 185
Wilson, Edward 73 fn.5
witodlice 230 fn.36
wið ðæt 284
word order *see* element order
Wrenn, C. L. 16, 65, 67, 78, 85, 95, 209
Wulf and Eadwacer 142, 335
Wulfstan 113–16, 174
wyrd 339–40

ymbe 283